WHEN STATES KILL

Of all the forms of murder, none is more monstrous than that committed by a state against its own citizens. And of all murder victims, those of the state are the most helpless and vulnerable since the very entity to which they have entrusted their lives and safety becomes their killer. When the state murders, the crime is planned by powerful men. They use the same cold rationality and administrative efficiency that they might bring to the decision to wage a campaign to eradicate a particularly obnoxious agricultural pest.

—CLYDE SNOW
quoted in *Witnesses from the Grave: The Stories Bones Tell,*
by Christopher Joyce and Eric Stover

WHEN
STATES
KILL

Latin America,
the U.S., and
Technologies
of Terror

Edited by

Cecilia Menjívar and Néstor Rodríguez

UNIVERSITY OF TEXAS PRESS, AUSTIN

Printed in the United States of America
First edition, 2005

Requests for permission to reproduce material
from this work should be sent to Permissions,
University of Texas Press, P.O. Box 7819, Austin,
TX 78713-7819.

♾ The paper used in this book meets the minimum
requirements of ANSI/NISO Z39.48-1992 (R1997)
(Permanence of Paper).

Library of Congress Cataloging-in-Publication Data

When states kill : Latin America, the U.S., and tech-
nologies of terror / edited by Cecilia Menjívar and
Néstor Rodríguez. — 1st ed.
    p.   cm.
  Includes bibliographical references and index.
  ISBN 0-292-70647-2 (cl. : alk. paper) —
ISBN 0-292-70679-0 (pbk. : alk. paper)
   1. State-sponsored terrorism—Latin America.
I. Menjívar, Cecilia. II. Rodríguez, Néstor.
HV6433.I3W46 2005
303.6'25'098—dc22

                          2004019668

For the victims of state terror in Latin America—
with hope for justice.

Contents

List of Illustrations

Tables

Figure

Acknowledgments

WE WOULD LIKE to acknowledge several people who have assisted us in bringing this project to fruition; if we inadvertently have left anyone out, we apologize.

We would like to thank Theresa May, editor-in-chief at the University of Texas Press, for readily supporting our project. We also would like to express our gratitude to two reviewers for their excellent comments and suggestions, although we did not always heed their advice. In addition, we are thankful to Sandra Coliver and Charles Munnell for taking time to read and comment on the chapters.

Our special thanks to Gabriela Torres for helping us with the cover, and to Mary Fran Draisker, from the Publication Assistance Center at Arizona State University, for once again doing a first-rate job in preparing the different versions of this manuscript. We would also like to thank the College of Arts and Sciences at the University of Houston for generous assistance and to thank Mary Duncan and Lonnie Anderson in the Department of Sociology.

Finally, we would like to thank our friends and colleagues at Arizona State University, at the University of Houston, and in other environments, who supported the idea for this book over the years that it took to become a reality.

Cecilia Menjívar
Néstor Rodríguez

All royalties from the sales of this book will be donated to the Center for Justice and Accountability (www.cja.org).

PART ONE

◆

INTRODUCTION

State Terror in the U.S.–Latin American Interstate Regime

CECILIA MENJÍVAR AND NÉSTOR RODRÍGUEZ

Introduction

What causes the state-directed political violence that has characterized political culture in much of the Latin American region since the mid-twentieth century? What motivated the campaigns of terror that "disappeared" thousands throughout the region? That practiced genocide of whole villages in Guatemala and El Salvador? That continued to repress indigenous peasants in Mexico? Is the source of this violence found in the Latin American psyche? Is it in Latin American culture?

Some observers view Latin American political violence as part of the heritage of the brutal European conquest of the region. Rosenberg (1991, 17), for example, answers the question of what underlies the growth of Latin American political violence as follows: "If I had to give just one answer, it would be: history. Most of Latin America was conquered and colonized through violence, setting up political and economic relationships based on power, not law. These relationships still exist today—indeed, in some countries they are stronger than ever." From this perspective, Latin American political violence represents an atavism that harkens back to the origins of countries that today are ruled by law.

Most of the chapters in this book take an opposite perspective: that is, that state-directed political violence developed as a product of a regional political structure in which U.S. political interests have weighed heavily. According to this view, contemporary Latin American states have practiced different forms of terror, including torture and physical punishment, not in a primitive or "traditional" manner, but in a politically rational, calculated, modern fashion.[1]

The use of terror by modern Latin American states in a Weberian, bureaucratized manner therefore is not a remnant of a past colonial experience. As Rejali (1994) observes, state-sponsored terror is part of a modern political system based on the same rationality that characterizes modern, bureaucratic societies.

The perspective that sees Latin American state terror as a derivative of a U.S.-dominated regional system is not meant to reduce all explanations of Latin American political violence to a one-dimensional causality of U.S. involvement, nor is it meant to claim that systemic causes underlie all cases of political violence in Latin America. As Smith (1986) reminds us, not everything that developing countries do or can do should be attributed solely to the international system or to the powerful core countries that dominate it. Some cases of politically related violence have been instances of local violence perpetuated within a larger arena of national violence to settle land disputes or old family scores. Members of Guatemalan civil defense patrols, for example, sometimes used their new paramilitary capacity during the civil war of the 1980s and 1990s to attack families with whom they had land disputes or grudges. While larger geopolitical developments led to the creation of the civil defense patrols, it would be farfetched to attribute conflict over land plots among villagers in remote corners of the Guatemalan highlands to the workings of a world system.

In addition, cases of political violence have had varied causes in the geographically large and socially diverse Latin American region. Some groups who oppose the states in power also have been protagonists of political violence in their own countries or regions. In Peru, for example, Sendero Luminoso (Shining Path), led by Chairman Gonzalo (Abimael Guzmán), was a prime example of such groups, as the movement used violence against all sectors of Peruvian society in an attempt to bring down the state (Poole and Rénique, 1992). Rather than focusing on the actions of leftist or rightist political actors who have engaged in destructive violence to overthrow established power structures, this volume deals primarily with the regime of terror organized by those who are already in control of institutions of power but who, rather than relying only on formal authority, rules, laws, and legitimate means, resort to systematic violence, coercion, fear, and technologies of terror to exert control in the larger regional political system.

The case studies of state terror presented in this book indicate a clear and persistent pattern of U.S. influence over the political violence conducted by

Latin American states. In some cases, Latin American governments enthusi-astically received U.S. support for their campaigns of terror, and in other cases U.S. state agencies pressured "weaker" states to undertake such campaigns. Cardoso and Faletto (1969) argue that developed or powerful states could im-plement certain policies in weaker states only when a local elite with similar interests could support them. Thus, the United States did not unilaterally im-plement a system of terror across the continent but was able to do so with the cooperation and, to a large extent, due to a coincidence of interests and objec-tives with the local military, and with political and economic elites.

Taken by themselves in their national contexts, the cases of political vio-lence affected by U.S. influence may appear unique and fashioned only for particular situations, but when examined together across national boundaries they constitute a regional pattern—one integrated within the geopolitical con-tours of larger U.S. political interests in Latin America. As the chapters dem-onstrate, in some cases U.S. involvement was indirect and conveyed by third-party allies; in other cases involvement was direct, as in the case of Nicaragua, where the U.S. military organized la Guardia (the national guard), which from its beginning used violence against political opponents and at times against the population in general. A U.S. institution that figures prominently in the involvement of the United States with military bodies in Latin America is the U.S. Army School of the Americas (SOA). As we describe below, this institu-tion provided training for many Latin American military officers associated with major cases of violence and human rights abuses.

A number of works have described U.S. involvement in state-sponsored terror in Latin America in past decades (see, for example, Burbach and Flynn, 1984; Lernoux, 1980; Klare and Arnson, 1979). So why is it important to com-pile a book on the topic in the early twenty-first century? The answer to this question is at least threefold. First, U.S. support for state tactics of terror in Latin America continues, and thus the issue remains relevant. Indeed, if any-thing, with the availability of huge computer databases and high-tech track-ing and surveillance systems, support for state terror has become much more sophisticated than during the era of gunboat diplomacy in the opening de-cades of the twentieth century. Second, the rise of global theories in the social sciences enables greater theoretical comprehension of the U.S. systemic in-volvement with state methods of coercion in Latin America. Third, the use of terror and violence by political actors has increased, not lessened, in the early twenty-first century (see Dugas, this volume). Indeed, as we discuss in the concluding chapter, a feature of the new age of political violence is that its practice has become greatly dispersed among new regions and political groups, and the capacity for political violence among new political actors outside the state is greatly enhanced as they obtain access to more efficient and effective means of terror, as developments since the beginning of the twenty-first century have demonstrated.

Geopolitical Systemic Context

We see the occurrences of state terror described in the following chapters as outcomes of a common policy affected by a larger system of interstate relations concerned with maintaining and reproducing a particular political and economic framework that governs the Latin American region. Many analysts have described how U.S. and Latin American state interests have joined to promote social conditions favorable to capitalistic development and an accompanying supportive political order (see, for example, Green, 1995; Rosen and McFadyen, 1995; Frank, 1969). Instead of taking a single-country perspective, we focus on the regime of terror in the region, uncovering powerful supranational links and ideologies that are crucial to understanding state terror in the region but that would have eluded single-country analyses. As Walter (1969) observed, to study regimes of terror is to study power in extremis, and when extreme situations are examined in depth, the inquiry can shed new light and reveal features that are ordinarily invisible under less extreme conditions.

As theorists have commented concerning the larger world-systems framework, the international system of states is a fundamental structural feature of the world economy (Lunday, 1981). It is within the interstate system that states are defined (as, for example, "strong" or "weak") and limitations are made on their modes of political behavior (Wallerstein, 1985). That is to say, states do not operate as independent, sovereign equals but as members of a system in which relations among the states affect the limits and definitions of state functions. At first this may be readily evident in the international dealings of a state, but it eventually also becomes clear in its domestic affairs as well, such as in the interstate pressure for a state to initiate economic austerity programs (see, Green, 1995; Rosen and McFadyen, 1995). Moreover, when a state declares itself outside the interstate system or unwilling to abide by its rules and expectations, a crisis emerges in the political world order.

During three periods in the development of the capitalist world economy a single state has enjoyed unrivaled dominance in the interstate system and the world economy. These are periods of hegemony, in which the dominant power "imposes its rules and its wishes" in the economic, political, cultural, and military arenas of the world system (Wallerstein, 1985, 38). The most recent hegemonic period, marked by domination by the United States, occurred in the period from the end of World War II to the intensification of the Vietnam War, which the United States failed to win militarily. While world-system theorists have done much to explain how hegemony functions globally, they have done less to explain how it functions regionally, a problem, no doubt, that is a consequence of their taking the entire world system as the unit of analysis. The end of hegemony by a state in the world system, moreover, may not necessarily mean the end of its dominance in a regional interstate system.

The geopolitical history of the global system in the latter half of the twentieth century indicates that regional international systems serve as basic blocs or regimes that configure the larger global system. The Soviet bloc and the NATO alliance are prime examples of such groupings, but other regional interstate regimes exist, even as they may be identified less definitively in political or ideological terms. Some regional interstate regimes may be formally organized but have little political potency, such as the Association of South East Asian Nations (ASEAN), which primarily seeks economic integration, while other regional interstate regimes may depend less on formal organization and more on a tradition of patronage, such as in U.S.–Latin American state relations, to implement a zone of strong political influence.

Ultimately, the strength of a regional interstate regime depends less on formal organization and more on established practices of influence in an identifiable political space. The geopolitical framework of regional interstate regimes helps to explain in part why the United States takes a harsh view of Communist-led Cuba, while it takes a cooperative view of the Communist-led states of Vietnam and China. The former is found inside the U.S.-dominated sociospatial regime, while the latter two are not. In the early twenty-first century, the actions of militant Muslim groups to unite Muslim populations against Western intervention in the Middle East indicates that regional political regimes need not be initiated necessarily by state apparatuses alone, as ethnic movements acting with religious authority also can attempt to develop political suprastructures.

Broadly speaking, various structural conditions can set in motion actions of terror in a regional international system. Social inequality, conflict of interest, and systemic imperatives have been central catalysts in this regard. The role of social inequality in stimulating state terror as a response goes beyond the demand for a redistribution of wealth. Social inequality contains ideological foundations, which the state supports but which are invariably challenged by dissidents to one degree or another. Operating within the context of a global system, regional state regimes have to negotiate their interests with other powers and interests. At times this negotiation occurs by means of conflict with domestic groups perceived to be allied with foreign interests.

Formation of the U.S.–Latin American Interstate Regime

The cases of state violence described in this volume occurred during a particular moment of the political development of Latin America. It was a moment of political trial and crisis for the U.S.-led regional interstate regime in the area. Whether the political developments indeed were as threatening to the regime as they were perceived to be is an academic question, since perception carried the political day and motivated the political responses of those in power. W. I. Thomas's maxim that things perceived as real are real in their consequences had no truer moment. It is important to review briefly U.S. political involvement in Latin America in order to understand better the nature of the state-sponsored political repression that visited the Latin American region in the late twentieth century. The history of this involvement created the relations that later promoted the establishment of the regional political regime.

The United States intervened militarily in Latin America frequently from the presidency of Theodore Roosevelt in the opening decade of the twentieth century to the mid-century presidency of Franklin Delano Roosevelt, especially in the Caribbean region (Barton, 1997). Theodore Roosevelt's ambition to build the United States into a major world power had special designs for Latin America under the Roosevelt Corollary to the Monroe Doctrine. In 1903 he helped Panama separate from Colombia, and in 1905 he forcibly installed an American "economic advisor" in the Dominican Republic. As Grossman points out (this volume), the U.S. Marines first landed in Nicaragua in 1909 to support the Conservative revolt against the Liberal presidency of José Santos Zelaya. The Marines returned in 1912 and maintained a presence in the country until 1927, helping to establish the Nicaraguan national guard.

Franklin Roosevelt's Good Neighbor Policy, initiated in 1933, brought a welcome change for Latin American countries, as it formalized the U.S. transition from "big stick" interventionism in the presidencies of Teddy Roosevelt, William Howard Taft, and Woodrow Wilson to one of persuasion through diplomacy combined with various aid programs (Grieb, 1976). But this policy change had started with the presidency of Warren G. Harding in the early 1920s. Harding strove for amicable solutions to conflicts in Latin America as a means to enhance trade relations and, no doubt, to lessen the cost to U.S. taxpayers of interventionist practices (Gellman, 1979). While the Good Neighbor Policy emphasized mutual agreements and goodwill in U.S.–Latin American relations, no one doubted that the United States represented the senior partner in the Western Hemisphere.

In 1940, after the outbreak of war in Europe, the U.S. government launched its first comprehensive intelligence gathering and training effort in Latin America. The endeavor was organized through the development of the Special Intelligence Service (sis), which was authorized by President Roosevelt to gather information on Axis agents and sympathizers from Japan, Germany, and Italy who were active outside of their home countries. Responsibility for sis nonmilitary intelligence work in the Western Hemisphere was assigned to the U.S. Federal Bureau of Investigation (fbi) under Director J. Edgar Hoover (Whitehead, 1956).

Working undercover as salesmen, stockbrokers, reporters, as well as in other occupations, and as "legal attachés" to U.S. embassies, fbi agents tracked down Nazi and other Axis agents in Latin America and compiled a blacklist (given the cover name, "The Proclaimed List of Certain Blocked Nationals") of Latin American business firms and individuals who were thought to support the Axis powers. At times the covert fbi agents worked with national or local police agencies in Central and South American countries and provided training to these agencies on countering espionage and sabotage. Argentina refused to cooperate with the undercover fbi program until 1944 when it severed relations with the Axis powers. Prior to 1944, Argentine agents trailed suspected fbi agents and arrested fbi informants, supplementing their interrogations with use of the *picana eléctrica*, a device that caused much pain when placed in sensitive parts of the body (Whitehead, 1956).

A second wartime measure that formally brought together the United States and several Latin American countries on issues of regional security was the formation in January 1942 of the Emergency Advisory Committee for

Political Defense. This body, which developed a permanent office in Montevideo, consisted of representatives from the United States, Argentina, Brazil, Chile, Mexico, Uruguay, and Venezuela, developing programs that targeted Axis nationals (Report of the Commission on Wartime Relocation and Internment of Civilians, 1997). Acting under policies established by the advisory committee or in response to U.S. security requests, sixteen Latin American countries interned at least 8,500 Axis nationals during World War II, and twelve Latin American countries—Bolivia, Colombia, Costa Rica, the Dominican Republic, Ecuador, El Salvador, Guatemala, Haiti, Honduras, Nicaragua, Panama, and Peru—sent about 3,000 Axis nationals in total (mainly Japanese nationals and their families) to the United States (Report of the Commission on Wartime Relocation and Internment of Civilians, 1997).

The sis program in Latin America represented a significant new development in interstate relations for the Western Hemisphere; it was the first U.S.-led program for the comprehensive monitoring and neutralizing of suspects across Latin America through bureaucratic coordination with national and local police forces. Although U.S. agents likely trailed Communist agents in Latin America (such as Leon Trotsky in Mexico) soon after the 1917 Bolshevik Revolution in Russia, there are no records to indicate that these earlier activities were as comprehensive as was the wartime sis program.

Indeed, in a 1946 letter to FBI Director J. Edgar Hoover concerning the sis program, Assistant Secretary of State Adolf A. Berle stated, "Told or not, it is the story of a great piece of work. I do not think a similar operation has ever been carried on; and I can personally attest to the brilliance of the results" (Whitehead, 1956, 210). The bureaucratic aspect of the sis program itself represents a noteworthy modernization of surveillance and coercive social control within the U.S.–Latin American interstate regime. The sis program put in place a new science and technology of surveillance and social control, a bureaucratic method of following "suspects," gathering information from "informants" or "interrogations," keeping "files," constructing "lists," and centralizing "data" at high administrative levels to develop counteraction strategies for lower-level agency personnel to carry out. Writing in the early twentieth century, Max Weber described bureaucracy as being the most highly developed and efficient form of organization, one that can create great power in the hands of its controllers, who seek superiority by keeping secret their knowledge and intentions. According to Weber, as highly rationalized structures, bureaucracies have no personal regard in their objectives—they conduct tasks based solely on official rules and duty (see Weber, 1978).

Crisis in the U.S.–Latin American Interstate Regime

U.S. hegemony after World War II did not go unchallenged, as Communist movements gained major ground across different world areas. The Soviet Union expanded to cover the eastern half of Europe and the northern third of Asia, and in East Asia the Chinese Communist Party and the People's Liberation Army took control of the Chinese mainland. Throughout Europe, Asia, and Latin America, a number of Communist political parties also surfaced or strengthened.

In addition, a large number of social movements worldwide challenged both the capitalist world order as well as established Communist parties in the 1960s and 1970s. In the United States, such movements included those promoting civil rights, black power, Chicano power, Native American power, women's rights, and welfare rights, and those engaging in activities against the war in Vietnam. The U.S. movements were not simple matters of emerging social identities; in several cases, police and military units were used to put down urban revolts with lethal force (Feagin and Hahn, 1973).

In Europe, workers, immigrant workers, students, women, and peasants prompted significant episodes of social unrest, in France bringing the country to the verge of social revolution or a military takeover in May 1968. In France and Italy in the 1960s and 1970s autonomous worker struggles and student movements confronted the Communist Party and the Communist-dominated trade unions in order to escape their control (Cleaver, 1979). On the periphery of the world system, as in Vietnam, Mozambique, and Algeria, national liberation movements struggled to oust Western colonizers. Even the Communist states of the Soviet Union and the People's Republic of China experienced social outbreaks by national or ethnic groups in the 1960s and 1970s (Banister, 1987; Cleaver, 1979).

In Latin America, opposition to the established social order of the U.S.–Latin American interstate regime expanded rapidly. The use of a common language in most of Latin America facilitated circulation of the ideas that served as the foundations for shared social struggles. *Concientización* of social injustices and the need for social action resonated throughout the region's Spanish-speaking populations as well as in Brazil. In the late 1960s, a common Catholic heritage among many Latin Americans also enabled a liberation theology to spread widely, promoting concepts of religion-based collective action directed against structures of violence and injustice (Lernoux, 1980).

What was seen by U.S. and Latin American officials as a monolithic threat of Communist world domination was in fact a collection of diverse popular movements. Some of these movements were aligned with Communist interests abroad, such as with the Cuban Communist government (Castañeda, 1993), but many were local autonomous struggles waged without external support. According to Jorge G. Castañeda, the diverse movements represented a "grass roots explosion" and were the result of new poverty in Latin America. The struggles of church groups, urban residents, women, students, and human rights activists were "organized and mobilized along lines of issues, not class" (Castañeda, 1993, 205). In the 1950s and 1960s, many social movements were concerned with land reform, since the majority of Latin America's population was concentrated in rural areas, and the region had notoriously unequal land tenure systems (which it continues to have today).

In the 1970s, and continuing into the twenty-first century, social movements and protests also surfaced to oppose increases in the costs of living and state austerity programs (Gilbert, 1998), particularly those identified with the International Monetary Fund (IMF)(Walton and Seddon, 1994). Such movements included aggressive but usually nonviolent collective actions by poor populations seeking survival in conditions of misery, such as land takeovers by poor peasants seeking land to farm, and land invasions on urban fringes by poor workers wanting to build shanty housing (Kowarick, 1994). The 1970s also saw an increasing expansion of social movements into armed struggle (see Eckstein, 2001).

Some of these movements sought a reordering of society through the appropriation of private wealth by the state, land redistribution, and greater roles for urban workers and peasants in the administration of state institutions. In Peru, starting in the Ayacucho region in the early 1970s, the guerrilla movement Shining Path violently attacked all sectors of society, including leftist groups, in an effort to bring down the state and rebuild society through the principles of "Gonzalo Thought" (Poole and Rénique, 1992).

Latin American armed struggle did not always occur in areas far from the United States. The Cuban Revolution of the late 1950s was one case in point, but perhaps equally significant to U.S. state security agencies was the emergence in 1965 of armed struggle in areas of Mexico near the U.S.–Mexico border and adjacent to the growing Chicano movement in the southwestern United States. On September 23, 1965, an armed group of young professors and students attacked a military installation in the northern Mexican state of Chihuahua (Poniatowska, 1980). The suicidal attack failed, but it motivated the formation of the September 23 Communist League and numerous other revolutionary groups that began to operate in urban areas near the U.S.–Mexico border.

Fighting the Cold War in Latin America

In the Cold War, marked by political posturing, perceived threats, and localized conflicts, the security of the United States and maintenance of the U.S.–Latin American interstate regime was a high priority (Hendrickson, 1988; Whitehead, 1956). A secret report prepared for President Dwight Eisenhower in 1954 expressed the concern of the Central Intelligence Agency (CIA) regarding the perceived Communist threat and advised the president to respond with a no-holds-barred approach:

> It is clear that we are facing an implacable enemy whose avowed objective is world domination by whatever means and at whatever cost. There are no rules in such a game . . . long-standing American concepts of "fair play" must be reconsidered. We must develop effective espionage and counterespionage services and must learn to subvert, sabotage, and destroy our enemies by more clever, more sophisticated, and more effective methods than those used against us. It may become necessary that the American people be made acquainted with, understand and support this fundamentally repugnant philosophy. (Quoted in Olmsted, 1996, 13)

The tense days of the Cuban missile crisis in October 1962 dramatically showed how far the U.S. state was willing to go to oust a foreign Communist power from its Latin American zone of influence.

In September 1947, at the beginning of the Cold War, the United States and Latin American countries signed the Rio Pact to ensure mutual protection against a Soviet attack, and in 1951 the U.S. Congress passed the Mutual Security Act to work toward the modernization of the military forces of Latin America. By the time of the Kennedy presidency in the early 1960s, however, the military strategy had changed from preparing for an external attack to organizing for counterinsurgency against internal movements, primarily those movements considered to be communist inspired and supported (Klare and Arnson, 1979). Additionally, U.S. state planners gave greater attention to conditions of poverty and underdevelopment as causes of insurgency.

In 1961, President John F. Kennedy launched the Alliance for Progress to improve Latin American economic conditions and spread a pro-U.S. ideology in the region. The Alliance for Progress had a parallel program of military assistance to promote the internal security needed for stable economic development. Money from the Military Assistance Program (MAP) paid for equipment and training for Latin American militaries to enable them to conduct counterinsurgency activities. In addition, the Office of Public Safety (OPS) within the Agency for International Development provided funds to enhance the intelligence, communication, and mobility capacities of Latin American police forces to wage counterinsurgency work, primarily in the cities (Klare and Arnson, 1979). A systematic process was developed in which Latin American military and police personnel trained in a variety of counterinsurgency methods, including interrogation, assassination, and torture, at U.S. installations or in their own countries.

From their beginnings, U.S.-led efforts in counterinsurgency planning for Latin America involved high-level officials in a number of U.S. federal agencies. In the early 1960s, U.S. counterinsurgency planning involved an interagency committee, under the direction of a high-ranking army general and including the director of the CIA, the chairman of the Joint Chiefs of Staff, the deputy secretaries of state and defense, the foreign aid administrator, and the director of the U.S. Information Agency (Klare and Arnson, 1979). By the 1970s and 1980s, counterinsurgency techniques taught to Latin American militaries and police forces were informed by the United States's experience in the Vietnam War. Some of the U.S. advisers, for example, who helped set up the Salvadoran intelligence apparatus that operated death squads in the 1970s and 1980s had backgrounds in U.S. covert political work in Vietnam, such as in the Phoenix Program, which systematically targeted Vietnamese civilians for interrogation, torture, and assassination (Valentine, 1990). But the U.S.-trained Latin American forces did not always operate with the pinpoint precision of covert operations. On December 11, 1981, the U.S.-trained Atlacatl Battalion of the Salvadoran Army killed hundreds of men, women, and children in one blow in the village of El Mozote in El Salvador (Danner, 1993). The soldiers of the elite Atlacatl Battalion decapitated villagers, raped young girls before killing them, and massacred men, women, and small children in separate groups with their U.S.-supplied M-16 weapons.

To be sure, Latin American military leaders generally needed little or no encouragement from the United States to participate in the Cold War in their own countries. Some Latin American military leaders, especially those with authoritarian or fascist orientations, became vigorous planners and practitioners in the anticommunist crusade, and some even criticized the United States government for not doing more in the political struggle (Rockefeller, 1969). In Argentina, Brazil, Chile, and other Latin American countries, some of the military leaders who seized power through coups d'état described their actions as a frontline fight to preserve Western civilization and Christianity in the Western Hemisphere (Feitlowitz, 1998; Constable and Valenzuela, 1991). In Argentina, even before a military junta seized power in 1976 and carried out a "dirty war" against leftists and other suspects, the Peronist government had organized the Triple-A (Argentine Anti-Communist Alliance) death squads to rout the Montoneros and other leftist groups who had killed several hundred police agents, military members, and industrialists (Feitlowitz, 1998). Indeed, given their desire to preserve what were wholly oligarchical social structures, Latin American officials likely felt a greater urgency to respond to political threats than did U.S. officials in Washington.

Thus, in the view of Latin American governments and military officials communist subversion included any activity that opposed them politically or that did not meet with their approval. It included the actions of nonpartisan or even nonpolitical social movements and individuals, as well as the dissidence of fellow government and military leaders. Additionally, the criteria for identifying targets for elimination were broad; the governor of the province of Buenos Aires demonstrated this during the Argentine dirty war against leftists with the following statement:

> First we will kill all the subversives, then we will kill their collaborators, then . . . their sympathizers, then . . . those who remain indifferent; and finally we will kill the timid. (Quoted in Feitlowitz, 1998, 32; emphasis in original)

As McSherry describes in the following chapter, in 1975 anticommunist military leaders from six South American countries established Operation Condor, a highly coordinated transnational network of military repression used to kidnap, transport, torture, and kill persons viewed as politically suspect or undesirable. A large part of what is known about Operation Condor comes from the discovery in Paraguay in 1992 and 1993 of the so-called Archives of Terror, a collection of materials that contained thousands of files, personal documents, photographs, and recordings of kidnapped and disappeared persons from several Latin American countries.

It is noteworthy that Paraguay under the dictatorship of General Alfredo Stroessner (in power 1954–1989) became a center of political repression even before Condor. Stroessner is considered to have been one of Latin America's most corrupt leaders, representative of a classic nineteenth-century dictatorship (Fitzgibbon, 1971). No method was too vile for Stroessner to manage his political functionaries or to punish his enemies. Receiving U.S. support for his anticommunism (he often boasted of having turned Paraguay into the most anticommunist nation in the world) and Brazilian training in counterinsurgency for his military officers and police agents, Stroessner wiped out political opposition including, in 1975 and 1976, a peasant network of Christian communities that had been supported by the country's Catholic bishops (Lernoux, 1980). With Stroessner's strong-arm control, Paraguay became an ideal center for transnational operations to detain, torture, and eliminate political targets.

Terror as Social Policy

What is the purpose of the most brutal tortures? Are they intended only to establish a generalized climate of fear? Are they meant to keep in place a docile workforce with low wages to benefit the wealthy and multinational corporations? Are they to eliminate the opposition? To extract a confession? To set an example? One of the most common answers to the question of why officials resort to torture is that they must obtain a confession, information, or answers to a particular set of questions. Crelinsten (1995) points out, however, that torture is not merely about making people talk, obtaining information, or eliminating suspects; it is also about demonstrating power.

Amnesty International notes that in Guatemala newspapers have been allowed to publish pictures of dead torture victims, but the articles must follow the government line (Amnesty International, 1976). In such cases terror does not cease with the victim's death, because it is only after the death that the acts accomplish their purpose—to show others that this could happen to them as well. Indeed, Lauria-Santiago and Torres (this volume) observe that in El Salvador and Guatemala unidentifiable victims of torture were meant to send a message to the living that the victim could have been anyone, since the identity of a disfigured body remained unknown. Many victims of terror are "disappeared" from their normal existence, thus making the disappearance itself a powerful message of what awaits others who sympathize with the opposition.

Some have argued that the doctrine of national security in Latin America leads to the use of terror because such doctrine is predicated on the assumption that all social conflict is intrinsically negative (Comisión para la Defensa de la Salud, de la Ética Profesional y los Derechos del Pueblo [hereafter: CODESEDH]), 1987). From this perspective, any opponent to the established social order is considered an enemy of the state, which is the protector of society, and so must be eliminated because of the threat he or she poses to social stability. As enemies of the state, opponents are outside the bounds of state protection and thus vulnerable to arbitrary treatment, such as torture, and ultimately extermination.

According to Hannah Arendt (1966), state terrorism serves as an instrument to frighten a large population. Terrorism not only kills political opponents but also terrorizes more broadly in the population, so that even *potential* collaborators are eliminated. The people the state seeks to affect through generalized terror are usually different from its political targets, which gives terror a somewhat random, unpredictable quality. Fear is engendered by the unpredictability and yet regularity of terror. In the atmosphere of terror, everyone knows that they are at risk of becoming victims because everyday life has become uncertain. This is precisely what state terror is supposed to accomplish, to engender fear in everything people do so that the opposition does not gain sympathizers. In this environment people fear and mistrust many things in their everyday lives, such as a knock on the door, a neighbor's questions or gossip, a child's indiscretion, an unknown person's gaze, even a wrong number on the telephone.

Everyone is made to feel vulnerable, and even the innocent can be prime targets for terror. "Kill today and find out if the person is guilty tomorrow," people used to say to refer to this tactic in Guatemala and El Salvador. In Kafkaesque fashion, people were accused not because they were guilty; they were guilty because they were accused. Thus, generalized fear serves the state to eradicate opponents and purge *potential* sympathizers. In the process, as torture, disappearances, and other techniques of terror become commonplace, a profound insensibility toward human life emerges (Martín-Baró, 1990).

States use various forms of terror, such as disappearances, death squads, prolonged detentions, psychological trauma, massacres, and extreme physical torture.[2] The Brazilian project *Nunca Mais* identified 283 different types of torture used by the Brazilian state (Weschler, 1990). Latin American states also have included in their repertoire of terror the total control of the media, including bans on the publication, distribution, and sale of any printed material considered to threaten national security. Those same states, however, also use all forms of the media to inform, and often misinform, the public.

The different terror tactics have in common their institutionalization. They are regulated through norms, tasks, statutes, hierarchies, knowledge, and procedures of operation. Tactics involve defining objectives, selecting techniques, training staff, and finding locales to practice. Those in charge of carrying out terror campaigns are usually state personnel or subcontracted agents,[3] which means they have occupations and salaries that are regularized by statutes and training. Terror campaigns thus are conducted by individuals doing professional work "within the state's internal security framework and . . . dedicated to the service and protection of the state" (Kelman, 1995, 28).

Training for Terrorist Work

"Violence workers" must be trained to prepare for their roles in the technology of terror (Huggins, Haritos-Fatouros, and Zimbardo, 2002). As with practitioners in other fields, violence workers must meet admission requirements for training, take courses, attend seminars, and even "graduate," ready to use their new skills and knowledge. In some cases, their work is meticulously documented as a bureaucratic procedure, leaving records such as the Paraguayan Archives of Terror. Lauria-Santiago (this volume) attributes such careful record-keeping in the Salvadoran case to the intentions on the part of the United States to create in that country a political regime different from the traditional military and elite sectors.

The U.S. Army School of the Americas (S O A) is perhaps the best-known facility for training in counterinsurgency work in Latin America. According to its official website, s o A has trained more than 61,000 officers and soldiers, who "have helped foster a spirit of cooperation and interoperability among militaries throughout the hemisphere . . . and also helped avoid interstate conflict in the hemisphere" (Western Hemisphere Institute for Security Cooperation, 2003). The Latin American Training Center-Ground Division was first established in Panama in 1946, and it trained more than 8,000 U.S. military personnel, with Latin Americans training alongside them. Four years later, the Latin American Training Center expanded and became the U.S. Army Caribbean School, with the additional mission to help modernize Latin American and Caribbean militaries. In 1963, under President Kennedy's Alliance for Progress, the training center was expanded again and renamed the U.S. Army School of the Americas. In 1984, as the Panama Canal treaties expired, the school was relocated to Fort Benning, Georgia.

s o a graduates have been among Latin America's worst human rights abusers, including the most notorious dictators of the region. The s o a curriculum for senior and junior officers taught a variety of subjects, including sniper training, commando and psychological warfare, military intelligence, and interrogation tactics (Western Hemisphere Institute for Security Cooperation, 2003).[4] All the instruction was conducted in Spanish. The s o a generated manuals and used c i a publications, such as *Nicaragua Manual: Psychological Operations in Guerrilla Warfare*, in its training. The s o a instructional materials detailed techniques that included "wheedling," used for obtaining the greatest amount of information and useful intelligence, how to record details such as the color of the list under which a particular targeted individual should be placed, and how to locate and neutralize a target (School of the Americas Watch, 2003).

A Salvadoran death squad member who described his training at s o a explained how the U.S. instructor in one course emphasized "psychological techniques" and demonstrated new and more effective ways of using electric shocks during interrogations. On the final day of the course, students practiced techniques on real prisoners. "They were peasants," the death squad member recalled, "no one noteworthy" (quoted in Crelinsten, 1995, 50). After the practice exercise, the U.S. instructor evaluated the class on what they had done right or wrong.

Having fulfilled its Cold War–era mission, s o a closed in December 2000. But in January 2001 it reopened under the name of the Western Hemisphere Institute for Security Cooperation (w h i n s e c), an institution explicitly designed to meet new, twenty-first-century challenges. In contrast to s o a's explicit military mission, w h i n s e c's goals also include the strengthening of democracy, instilling a respect for the rule of law, and honoring human rights. It trains students (in Spanish, with plans to offer courses in Portuguese) to solve border conflicts, fight terrorism, counter drug traffic and organized crime, and support peacekeeping efforts. Although w h i n s e c has a new mission, according to the School of the Americas Watch, nothing much has actually changed.

The United States also trained Latin American police in counterinsurgency. Huggins (1998) describes how, with support from the Office of Public Safety, the U.S. Agency for International Development (u s a i d) assumed responsibility for police training by the International Police Academy (i p a) in Washington, D.C. The academy provided cover for c i a operations not only in Latin America but also in different regions of the world (Marchetti and Marks, 1974); its activities were less easily traceable to the c i a because they were regularly written into economic development plans initiated by u s a i d, among whose stated intentions was the creation of democratic institutions. Hidden behind this u s a i d cover, according to Huggins (1998, 108–09), "the c i a could focus on recruiting informants and establishing relations with political police."

Training under the auspices of the i p a for midlevel police officers took place at the c i a's Panama Canal station, where selected officials took courses on intelligence gathering, interrogation procedures, methods of riot, and crowd control (Huggins, 1998). i p a training was meant to promote police coordination with the military, so as to confront the opposition from multiple angles and link national security objectives with internal policing and narcotics control.

Many Latin American violence workers became experts in particular techniques and trained other Latin Americans in terrorist work. For instance, Argentine instructors trained others in Central America and Bolivia, including anti-Sandinista forces based in Honduras (see Armony, this volume). Central Americans trained Colombians, and Brazilians opened "torture schools" in Brazil attended by Latin Americans from different countries. This international collaboration, Kelman (1995) notes, is part of the professionalization of torture, as torturers from different countries meet and exchange information about their work.

Variations in Terror

Kelman (1995, 26) notes that states make use of repression when the opposition represents a challenge to the legitimacy of those in power, and thus present "a fundamental threat to their continued ability to maintain power."

In this conceptualization, a wide range of states—from dictatorships to democratic regimes—can turn to terror if they perceive their ability to stay in power threatened. This threat has made the state turn to terror techniques in countries with political histories as different as Mexico, Guatemala, Chile, Argentina, Nicaragua, El Salvador, Brazil, and Uruguay.

Internal constellations of political, economic, historical, and military factors in the different countries have produced different modalities of state terror, however, and as a result local manifestations of state terror have varied significantly. For instance, although disappearances became the most widely practiced form of terror throughout the region, the disappearances of children, pregnant women, and the elderly were signature tactics of the dictatorship in Argentina (CODESEDH, 1987), while in Uruguay the use of torture, prolonged detentions, and a high number of political prisoners and exiles were more common (see Ryan, this volume). In El Salvador and Guatemala, massacres and scorched-earth campaigns were more frequent, as was the leaving of cadavers with signs of torture by roadsides or ravines (see Torres, this volume).

Terror techniques also have varied over time in the same Latin American country. For instance, in El Salvador between 1980 and 1983 the state relied mostly on massive violations of human rights and nocturnal disappearances, but from 1983 on victims were targeted more selectively and detained for longer periods of time through legal means (Code 50) that granted captors wider powers over their victims (CODESEDH, 1987). While U.S. policies and training have fundamentally shaped polices of social control in the Latin American region, individual states have modified practices of terror as their priorities and political needs have changed.

States do not always act as monolithic structures in their involvement in campaigns of terror. Contradictions can exist between different state agencies (see, for example, Giraldo, 1999; Dugas, this volume). While some state agencies terrorize citizens through disappearances, massacres, and torture, for instance, other agencies of the same state apparatus may be genuinely working on improving human rights conditions, on locating disappeared persons, and on advocating for the release of prisoners.

Contradictions also occur at the interstate level. U.S. representatives, including ambassadors and other diplomats, may criticize the deplorable human rights record of specific countries at the same time that the United States is providing arms, military aid, and training on terror techniques to the militaries and police forces of the same countries. Indeed, these contradictions have an ironic twist: often the granting of military aid is conditioned on respect for human rights. In her study of U.S. training of police in Brazil, Huggins (1998) notes that U.S. programs used to assist foreign police to supposedly promote public safety can have opposite effects. Cases of contradiction demonstrate the complex relations within and between bureaucratic structures and between state agencies and the societies within which they operate.

Case Studies of State Terror in the Americas

The chapters that follow demonstrate many of the aspects of state terror that have been addressed in this introductory chapter. In Chapter 2, Patrice Mc-Sherry continues our discussion of systemic links by concentrating on Operation Condor, the interstate network of terror that operated in several South American countries in the 1970s to kidnap, detain, torture, and kill political opponents and suspects.

Parts Two and Three contain country-centered case studies, which together bring to the foreground the breadth and depth of state terror in the region, including outlines of its historical development, analyses of human rights violations, and examples of cases involving indigenous groups and women. Part Two focuses on Mexico and the countries of Central America and Part Three on South America.

Part Two begins with historical examinations by Grossman and Lauria-Santiago. In Chapter 3, Richard Grossman analyzes the formation of the Nicaraguan Guardia under the direction of the U.S. military and observes how this institution had from its very beginning little regard for human safety or dignity in its mission of social control. In Chapter 4, Aldo Lauria-Santiago examines state terror and repression in El Salvador from the perspective of the local context. Lauria-Santiago's "deep" examination of the Salvadoran repression focuses on local ideological, cultural, and iconographic elements.

In Chapter 5, Kristin Norget analyzes state repression and the terror campaign against Zapotec subsistence farmers in the Loxicha region in the Mexican state of Oaxaca, arguing that the recent political opening in Mexico has meant only a military democracy to the subsistence farmers in Loxicha. In Chapter 6, Gabriela Torres introduces what is almost a symbolic interactionist perspective to the study of state terror in Latin America by analyzing the symbolic functions of cadavers left behind by death squads and other perpetuators of terror in Guatemala. As Torres describes, the display of cadavers became a system of communicating intimidating messages to the general population about its vulnerability to terror during the conflict.

In Chapter 7, Joan Kruckewitt examines the rise of U.S.-supported death squads in Honduras during the 1980s, focusing on how U.S. support for militarization helped Honduran military leaders rise to political dominance at a cost to the many Hondurans who fell victim to the country's military and paramilitary groups. Chapter 8, by Annamarie Oliverio and Pat Lauderdale, describes how the United States pressured the relatively tranquil setting of Costa Rica to take on a military character during the Central American political conflicts of the 1980s. As Oliverio and Lauderdale explain, Costa Rica walked a tightrope as it attempted to maintain both a neutral posture in the region and cooperative relations with the political leadership in Washington.

Chapter 9, by John Dugas, focuses on the large array of political violence committed by different groups in Colombia. As Dugas explains, in Colombia the state has a fragmented and incoherent relationship to political violence, and other actors, such as paramilitaries and guerrilla movements, play an increasingly major role in the country's political terror. In Chapter 10, Abderrahman Beggar examines the expansion of Peru's state terror across various government administrations. Beggar describes a dynamic political scene in which all sectors of society are at risk of political violence and in which the U.S. military's support in the drug war helped to strengthen military institutions known to be major abusers of human rights.

In Chapter 11, Jeff Ryan analyzes the conversion of the Uruguayan military from an institution subject to civilian rule to a force of state terror as brutal as any other military institution in South America. Ryan examines the role of the United States and other external political military actors in helping to promote this transition. In Chapter 12, Ariel Armony presents a model of Argentine state terror to analyze the linkages between actors and contextual conditions that undergirded the rise of terror during the dirty war against leftists and other suspects by the military. As Armory describes, the Argentine military played a significant role in training military forces in other countries of Latin America, which highlights the regional interstate cooperation that is the focus of this volume. Finally, in Chapter 13 we conclude with a review of prospects for state terror in the U.S.–Latin American interstate regime for the coming years of the twenty-first century.

NOTES

1. Rejali (1994, 185) notes that the decrease in corporal punishment as societies modernize might not necessarily result because they have become enlightened but, rather, because individuals learn to regulate themselves according to their consciences, also a byproduct of the rationalization of the economy.

2. Crelinsten (1995, 41) observes that there are "myriad, perverse and ingenious ways that have been and are to this day being used to torture victims; suffice it to say that the least of them is terrible beyond words for the sufferer."

3. Sometimes the state employees (officers, torturers, physicians) do not directly carry out these campaigns but contract other groups, usually the so-called paramilitaries, to do so. This subcontracting is another characteristic of modern states, normally associated with new economic modes of production.

4. At the time of this writing, the U.S. government has admitted to the use of questionable practices in extracting information from suspected terrorists captured in Iraq, Afghanistan, and elsewhere, essentially arguing that the information they may provide justifies the means expended to obtain it.

BIBLIOGRAPHY

Amnesty International. 1976. *Debriefing, Guatemala*. London: Amnesty International Publications.
Arendt, Hannah. 1966. *The Origins of Totalitarianism*. New York: Harcourt, Brace & World.

Banister, Judith. 1987. *China's Changing Population*. Stanford: Stanford University Press.
Barton, Jonathan R. 1997. *A Political Geography of Latin America*. New York: Routledge.
Burbach, Roger, and Patricia Flynn, eds. 1984. *The Politics of Intervention: The United States in Central America*. New York: Monthly Review Press.

Cardoso, Fernando Henrique, and Enzo Faletto. 1969. *Dependencia y Desarrollo en América Latina: Ensayo de Interpretación Sociológica*. Mexico: Siglo XXI.
Castañeda, Jorge G. 1993. *Utopia Unarmed: The Latin American Left after the Cold War*. New York: Vintage Books.
Cleaver, Harry. 1979. *Reading Capital Politically*. Austin: University of Texas Press.
Comisión para la Defensa de la Salud, de la Ética Profesional y los Derechos del Pueblo (CODESEDH). 1987. *La Tortura en América Latina*. Buenos Aires: Comisión para la Defensa de la Salud, de la Ética Profesional y los Derechos del Pueblo.

Constable, Pamela, and Arturo Valenzuela. 1991. *A Nation of Enemies: Chile under Pinochet.* New York: W. W. Norton & Co.

Crelinsten, Ronald D. 1995. "In Their Own Words: The World of the Torturer." Pp. 35–64 in *The Politics of Pain: Torturers and their Master,* eds. Ronald D. Crelinsten and Alex P. Schmid. Boulder: Westview Press.

Danner, Mark. 1993. *The Massacre at El Mozote.* New York: Vintage Books.

Eckstein, Susan, ed. 2001. *Power and Popular Protest: Latin American Political Movements.* Berkeley: University of California Press.

Feagin, Joe R., and Harlan Hahn. 1973. *Ghetto Revolts: The Politics of Violence in American Cities.* New York: Macmillan Publishing.

Feitlowitz, Marguerite. 1998. *A Lexicon of Terror: Argentina and the Legacies of Torture.* Oxford: Oxford University Press.

Fitzgibbon, Russell H. 1971. *Latin America: A Panorama of Contemporary Politics.* New York: Meredith Corp.

Frank, Andre Gunder. 1969. *Latin America: Underdevelopment or Revolution.* New York: Monthly Review Press.

Gellman, Irwin F. 1979. *Good Neighbor Diplomacy: United States Policies in Latin America, 1933–1945.* Baltimore: The Johns Hopkins University Press.

Gilbert, Alan. 1998. *The Latin American City.* 2nd ed. London: Latin American Bureau.

Giraldo, Javier, S. J. 1999. "Corrupted Justice and the Schizophrenic State in Colombia." *Social Justice* 26 (4): 31–54.

Green, Duncan. 1995. *Silent Revolution: The Rise of Market Economics in Latin America.* London: Latin American Bureau.

Grieb, Kenneth J. 1976. *The Latin American Policy of Warren G. Harding.* Fort Worth: Texas Christian University Press.

Hendrickson, Mark. 1988. "US Security Concerns Are Real." Pp. 118–24 in *Latin America and U.S. Foreign Policy: Opposing Viewpoints,* ed. Bonnie Szumski. St. Paul: Greenhaven Press.

Huggins, Martha K. 1998. *Political Policing: The United States and Latin America.* Durham: Duke University Press.

Huggins, Martha K., Mika Haritos-Fatouros, and Philip G. Zimbardo. 2002. *Violence Workers: Police Torturers and Murderers Reconstruct Brazilian Atrocities.* Berkeley: University of California Press.

Kelman, Herbert C. 1995. "The Social Context of Torture: Policy Process and Authority Structure." Pp. 19–34 in *The Politics of Pain: Torturers and their Masters,* eds. Ronald D. Crelinsten and Alex P. Schmid. Boulder: Westview Press.

Klare, Michael T., and Cynthia Arnson. 1979. "Exporting Repression: U.S. Support for Authoritarianism in Latin America." Pp. 138–68 in *Capitalism and the State in*

U.S.–Latin American Relations, ed. Richard R. Fagen. Stanford: Stanford University Press.

Kowarick, Lucio. 1994. *Social Struggles and the City: The Case of Sao Paulo*. New York: Monthly Review Press.

Lernoux, Penny. 1980. *Cry of the People: United States Involvement in the Rise of Fascism, Torture, and Murder and the Persecution of the Catholic Church in Latin America.* Garden City: Doubleday & Co.

Lunday, James E. 1981. "Political Regionalism and Struggles for State Hegemony." Pp. 123–38 in *Dynamics of World Development*, ed. Richard Rubinson. Beverly Hills: Sage Publications.

Marchetti, Victor, and John D. Marks. 1974. *The CIA and the Cult of Intelligence*. New York: Knopf.

Martín-Baró, Ignacio. 1990. "Political Violence and War as Causes of Psychosocial Trauma in El Salvador." *International Journal of Mental Health* 18 (1): 3–20.

Olmsted, Kathryn S. 1996. *Challenging the Secret Government: The Post-Watergate Investigations of the CIA and FBI*. Chapel Hill: University of North Carolina Press.

Poniatowska, Elena. 1980. *Fuerte es el Silencio*. Mexico: Ediciones Era.

Poole, Deborah, and Gerardo Rénique. 1992. *Peru: Time of Fear*. London: Latin American Bureau.

Rejali, Darius M. 1994. *Torture & Modernity: Self, Society, and State in Modern Iran*. Boulder: Westview Press.

Report of the Commission on Wartime Relocation and Internment of Civilians. 1997. *Personal Justice Denied*. Seattle: University of Washington Press.

Rockefeller, Nelson A. 1969. *The Rockefeller Report on the Americas: The Official Report of a United States Presidential Mission for the Western Hemisphere: The New York Times Edition*. Chicago: Quadrangle Books.

Rosen, Fred, and Deidre McFadyen. 1995. *Free Trade and Economic Restructuring in Latin America*. New York: Monthly Review Press.

Rosenberg, Tina. 1991. *Children of Cain: Violence and the Violent in Latin America*. New York: Penguin Books.

School of the Americas Watch. 2003. *Counter Insurgency* [online]. Fort Benning, Ga.: School of the Americas Watch [cited 6 March 2003]. Available from http:// www.soaw.org/new/article.php?id=67.

Smith, Tony. 1986. "The Underdevelopment of Development Literature: The Case of Dependency Theory." Pp. 25–66 in *The State and Development in the Third World*, ed. Atul Kohli. Princeton: Princeton University Press.

Valentine, Douglas. 1990. *The Phoenix Program*. New York: Avon Books.

Wallerstein, Immanuel. 1985. *The Politics of the World Economy: The States, the Movements and the Civilizations.* Cambridge: Cambridge University Press.

Walter, Eugene Victor. 1969. *Terror and Resistance: A Study of Political Violence, with Case Studies of Some Primitive African Communities.* New York: Oxford University Press.

Walton, John, and David Seddon 1994. *Free Markets and Food Riots: The Politics of Global Adjustment.* Oxford: Blackwell.

Weber, Max. 1978. *Economy and Society,* vol. 2. Berkeley: University of California Press.

Weschler, Lawrence. 1990. *A Miracle, a Universe: Settling Accounts with Torturers.* New York: Pantheon Books.

Western Hemisphere Institute for Security Cooperation. 2003. "What Is the Western Hemisphere Institute for Security Cooperation?" [online]. Fort Benning, Ga.: Western Hemisphere Institute for Security Cooperation [cited 6 March 2003]. Available from http://www.benning.army.mil/whinsec/about.asp?id=37.

Whitehead, Don. 1956. The *FBI Story: A Report to the People.* New York: Random House.

CHAPTER 2

Operation Condor as a Hemispheric "Counterterror" Organization

J. PATRICE MCSHERRY

Introduction

This chapter shows that Operation Condor, the Latin American military intelligence network of the 1970s, functioned within, or parallel to, the structures of the larger inter-American military system led by the United States. Condor, a covert inter-American program of political repression, was a top-secret component of the hemispheric strategy designed to prevent and reverse emerging movements in Latin America that were advocating political and structural change. The Condor militaries (originally in the key countries of Argentina, Chile, Uruguay, Paraguay, Bolivia, Brazil, and later joined by Ecuador and Peru in less central roles) carried out combined, illegal, extraterritorial operations using disappearance, torture, and extrajudicial execution to eliminate political enemies.

Did the U.S. government have a behind-the-scenes role in creating or controlling Condor? The totality of the U.S. relationship with Condor remains unknown, but it was undoubtedly more substantial than has been publicly acknowledged thus far. The Pentagon, the Central Intelligence Agency (CIA), and other U.S. security agencies have declined to declassify more than a few heavily censored documents. Overall, the selectively declassified and fragmentary U.S. official record presents an incomplete and, therefore, misleading picture. Recently declassified materials must be integrated with existing scholarship and evidence from other, largely Latin American, sources.[1] U.S. documents do indicate, nevertheless, that U.S. national security officials considered Condor a legitimate and valuable counterinsurgency or counterterror organization, and U.S. agencies collaborated with some Condor operations.[2]

Certainly there is abundant scholarship detailing the decisive (and often covert) role that U.S. military and intelligence forces played in creating new Latin American intelligence bodies focused on countering "internal subversion," and their role in converting militaries from conventional forces into lethal counterinsurgency organizations that adopted "internal defense" as their primary mission (for a revealing case study, see Rempe, 1995).

Especially after the 1959 Cuban Revolution, the U.S. security establishment dramatically reoriented, reshaped, expanded, and mobilized the existing hemispheric security system to combat the threat of communist-inspired subversion (Child, 1980, chaps. 3 and 4). A new security doctrine encouraged the hemisphere's military–security forces to view domestic social conflicts through the prism of the East–West struggle, effectively internationalizing them, and to adopt unconventional warfare strategies. Under U.S. guidance and tutelage, the region's military mission was redefined to combat "internal enemies" as the primary threat, and militaries were reorganized and trained to undertake aggressive counterinsurgency operations within their own societies. U.S. strategists also urged Latin America's previously adversarial armed forces to carry out combined countersubversion actions and coordinated intelligence efforts, and worked to integrate the militaries within a dense network of continental defense organizations.

The inter-American security system consisted of interlinking components: a set of hemispheric military structures and networks (such as the Inter-American Defense Board and the Conference of American Armies); a Cold War security doctrine with heavily ideological overtones; a complex of professional training centers (including the U.S. Army School of the Americas [SOA]); a system of military attachés; linked hemispheric communications networks; systematized resource disbursement and training grants (through programs such as the U.S. Military Assistance Program [MAP] and International Military Education and Training [IMET] program); and standardization of equipment and technologies of violence (especially U.S.-provided weapons designed for counterinsurgency). The U.S. Southern Command (SOUTHCOM) and Special Action Forces were "unilateral components" of the system, to ensure U.S. dominance and control (Child, 1980, 167).

The CIA worked in tandem with SOUTHCOM and U.S. military intelligence structures to assist in creating military intelligence units in Latin America to centralize countersubversive efforts and to train the armed forces in psychological warfare, counterguerrilla tactics, interrogation, and other "special warfare" techniques for vastly expanded internal security programs. U.S. military training courses drew on the French experience during anti-colonial struggles in Algeria and Vietnam, and encouraged the use of counter-terror tactics and closely controlled irregular or paramilitary networks. U.S. Mobile Training Teams, specializing in counterinsurgency warfare, advocated unconventional tactics (such as subversion, sabotage, and terrorist activities) against insurgents. U.S. training, doctrine, organizational models, technology transfers, weapons sales, and ideological attitudes profoundly shaped security forces in the region.

As the Latin American militaries reorganized to fight internal enemies, they—in conjunction with U.S. advisors—also created elite units modeled on U.S. Special Forces teams (experts in covert operations, direct offensive action, and political and psychological operations). Counterterror doctrine—which was, and still is, largely classified—advocated forming covert "special action" squadrons to use methods of terror, such as abduction and assassination (McClintock, 1985, 24; 1991; 1992, chap. 10; McSherry, 2000, 2001). These forms of organization and tactics characterized Operation Condor. A 1976 Defense Intelligence Agency (DIA) report stated, for example, that one Condor unit was "structured much like a U.S. Special Forces Team," and described Condor's "joint counterinsurgency operations" to "eliminate Marxist terrorist activities" (DIA, 1976). Several Uruguayan survivors of Condor abductions testified that twelve- to fifteen-man squadrons of Argentines and Uruguayans seized, tortured, and imprisoned them in secret detention centers (McSherry, 1999, 157–59). Condor's cross-border disappearance–torture–execution operations against exiles, like the other campaigns of state terror carried out by Latin American national security states during the Cold War, cannot be seen in isolation from the inter-American counterinsurgency regime.

U.S. Counterrevolutionary Strategy

Populist, nationalist, and anti-imperialist sentiment arose throughout Latin America in the 1960s and 1970s, challenging local political elites and oligarchies as well as U.S. corporate interests. The wave of social protest was linked to the rise of third-world nationalism and the growing demand for self-determination and development by peoples in the third world (see, for example, Sigmund, 1980; Yachir, 1988, chap. 4). In Latin America, too, many people began to perceive foreign control of national resources as an intolerable symbol of foreign domination and as a cause of their own poverty.

Moreover, as in the United States and Europe, the generation of the 1960s in the more economically developed Latin American countries, such as Uruguay, Argentina, Brazil, and Chile, was critical of the exclusionary and ossified nature of power relations and the social injustice in their societies. In the poorer areas of Latin America with large indigenous populations (as in Central America and most of the Andean region), sharp class divisions were linked to racial and ethnic hierarchies, fuelling social discontent. Workers' movements and peasant struggles arose with their own grievances. Throughout Latin America newly politicized sectors—workers, peasants, students, intellectuals, and religious activists—were demanding new rights and social justice. The Cuban Revolution ignited a series of radical struggles, including several new guerrilla movements, as well as conservative reactions throughout the region. Latin American elites, as well as U.S. officials, were increasingly alarmed by social mobilization in Latin America.

During the Cold War, Washington's overarching security paradigm shaped its foreign policy and military-to-military relations throughout the world. The U.S.-Soviet confrontation was considered the defining factor in the strategic environment, and smaller internal conflicts and insurgencies worldwide were viewed as manifestations of the East–West struggle (Metz, 1995, 31–41). Underlying Washington's strategic paradigm were military, economic, and political interests: containment and defeat of communism, access to raw materials and markets in the developing world (see Child, 1980, 111, 121), and maintenance of stable, pro-U.S. governments in areas of interest. A secret U.S. State Department document of September 1962, "United States Overseas Internal Defense Policy," made these interests clear, and called for the creation of counterinsurgency forces *even if there were no insurgents*:

> Where subversive insurgency is virtually nonexistent or incipient (PHASE I), the objective is to support the development of an adequate counter-insurgency capability in indigenous military forces through the Military Assistance Program, and to complement the nation-building programs of AID [Agency for International Development] with military civic action. The same means, in collaboration with AID and CIA, will be employed to develop a similar capability in indigenous para-military forces. (U.S. State Department, 1962, 28)

This document clearly shows the U.S. strategy to build up military–security and paramilitary forces in the developing world, even in the absence of an insurgent threat, to control populations and prevent outcomes seen as inimical to U.S. interests.

In the aftermath of the Cuban Revolution, the Kennedy administration (determined to "prevent another Cuba") introduced a new mission for the armed forces: counterinsurgency. A new U.S. security doctrine, termed Internal Defense and Development (IDAD), encouraged the region's militaries to carry out intense counterinsurgency campaigns to root out "subversion," while coupling those activities with expanded civic action projects and capitalist development to alleviate poverty and diminish the attraction of socialism (Child, 1980, 143–52, 190–95; Johnson, 1998, 126–28). The new security doctrine visualized the militaries as the key line of defense against internal subversion. Washington dedicated vast resources to create and fortify counterinsurgency forces and intelligence organs in Latin America and elsewhere to monitor restive populations and neutralize "internal enemies" (Johnson, 1998, 61–68; Loveman and Davies, 1997a, 3–37; McClintock, 1991, 1992; McSherry, 1997). The U.S. security establishment also sponsored a major reorganization of the hemispheric defense system to counter new revolutionary and popular movements in the Americas.

Many Latin American militaries had long held dominant roles in their societies, to the point of staging coups and presiding over military regimes. The new continental doctrine, however, legitimized a central role for the militaries in all aspects of national life and justified domestic repression and the use of extralegal methods in the name of national security. In Chile and Uruguay, long-standing democracies, the militaries had been constitutionalist and respectful of civilian authority until the 1970s. Over time, however, large sectors of the armed forces across Latin America began to view themselves as holy warriors in an apocalyptic East–West conflict.

U.S. military study plans and manuals from the 1960s were suffused with suspicion of popular movements, demonstrations, and public gatherings, assuming a shared communist origin (Latin American Working Group, 1999; McSherry, 2001). Moreover, U.S. military and CIA training manuals, declassified in the mid-1990s, provide documented evidence that U.S. Army and CIA instructors taught methods such as the use of electric shocks, the use of drugs and hypnosis to induce psychological regression, the sequential use of sensory deprivation, pain, and other means in interrogations, as well as assassination methods and the use of threats against and abduction of family members to break down prisoner resistance (see the manuals at U.S. Central Intelligence Agency, 1963; School of the Americas Watch, n.d.; see also McPherson, 1999, 621–32; McSherry, 2000, 2001; Priest, 1996, 1997; Weiner, 1997).

The Conference of American Armies was first organized by SOUTHCOM in 1960 in Panama. Early meetings focused on discussions of the continental doctrine to fight "communist aggression," interchange of intelligence about subversive groups and international communism, establishment of a permanent inter-American intelligence committee (located in the Canal Zone), organization of intelligence schools in each country, creation of a system of encoded telecommunications among the region's militaries, and development of training programs for all the armies in strategies of countersubversion, counterrevolution, and internal security (Nevares, 1985).[3] The U.S. government trained tens of thousands of Latin American officers in inter-American training centers, provided technological support for counterinsurgency warfare, and offered intelligence, advice, financing, and other forms of sustenance for Latin American counterinsurgency campaigns.

U.S. policy was intended to facilitate indigenous counterinsurgency efforts by providing indirect support. Overt U.S. intervention was a last resort, considered too costly both economically and politically, and the CIA remained in the shadows. As one expert noted:

> Encouragement of foreign military coups is deliberately indirect and ambiguous. The CIA does not like to leave a paper trail. Its officers speak and write in circumlocutions. This leaves room for doubt and dispute over whether a coup is, in fact, American-inspired. (Holt, 1995, 149)

A history of the U.S. Marine Corps from this era similarly suggests this in-the-background strategy:

> The US Army Special Forces (the "Green Berets") are military personnel with training in basic and specialized military skills, organized into small multipurpose detachments, *whose mission is to train, organize, supply, direct, and control indigenous forces* in guerrilla warfare and counterinsurgency operations and to conduct unconventional warfare operations. (Donovan, 1967, 138 [emphasis added]; see also U.S. Army Special Forces, n.d.)

In essence, the U.S. government, the hegemonic power in the hemisphere and throughout the noncommunist world, internationalized its anticommunist and counterrevolutionary security agenda through the imposition of a continental security doctrine and establishment of the machinery of the inter-American security system (see, for example, Huggins, 1998). While some military sectors in Latin America resisted U.S. influence, over time military institutions throughout the region adopted the counterinsurgency mission. Each military adapted the doctrine and strategy to its own national conditions, and political repression took different forms in different countries. But the counterinsurgents shared key goals: to permanently remake their states and societies, eliminate actual and potential "internal enemies," and consolidate military power at the center of their nation's political life.

Impact of the Security Doctrine in Latin America

The continental doctrine and mission had fateful consequences in Latin America. Governments and leaders who challenged the anticommunist hemispheric regime or U.S. orientations were destabilized or overthrown by military–security forces usually backed by Washington (to see the militaries' own justifications, see Loveman and Davies, 1997b, 157–218). A series of coups swept the region in the 1960s and 1970s, leaving nearly all of Latin America under military dictatorship. Military institutions in many countries imposed a new form of rule, the national security state, based on the tenets of the new security doctrine (McSherry, 1997, 5–7, 49–55). The national security state combined systematic repression and use of state terror with transformative politico-economic projects designed to permanently end "subversion" (broadly defined). Under military rule, little distinction was made among peaceful dissent, political opposition, subversion, and communism. Operating under the tenets of the national security state, security forces in the region classified and targeted persons based on their political ideas rather than on any presumed illegal acts. The regimes hunted down dissidents and leftists, union and peasant leaders, priests and nuns, intellectuals, students, and teachers, as well as guerrillas (who were also entitled to due process). The militaries dismantled democratic and populist structures and expanded organizations for surveillance, intelligence, and repression; several opened their economies to world market forces and foreign (mainly U.S.) investment. The national security states of Latin America targeted as internal enemies tens of thousands of persons, who then were secretly "disappeared," tortured, and killed.

Latin Americans had previously experienced regimes that abused human rights. The region's national security states, however, greatly expanded the scope and intensity of repression. They institutionalized, modernized, and made more efficient the subjugation of whole populations and their brutalization through torture. National security doctrine legitimated "counterterror" methods as dirty, but effective, means to an exalted end. New military counterinsurgency structures and operations in the region—of which Condor formed a part—were thus tightly linked to the interstatal security regime fostered by Washington.

The U.S. government played a key role in creating the intelligence organizations in several Latin American dictatorships that went on to form the nucleus of Operation Condor. (Elsewhere in the world in the same period, the CIA also helped set up Mossad in Israel, SAVAK in the Shah's Iran, and the KCIA in South Korea [Holt, 1995, 71]). After the 1973 Chilean coup, U.S. personnel helped to organize, and worked closely with, Dirección de Inteligencia National (Directorate of National Intelligence, DINA), which became the main instrument of state terror under the regime of General Augusto Pinochet. DINA commander Colonel Manuel Contreras stated in 2000 that shortly after the coup, Pinochet instructed him to ask the CIA for assistance in organizing DINA. Contreras said he met with General Vernon Walters, deputy director of the CIA and, in March 1974, the CIA sent eight officers to Chile to help set up the intelligence organization. According to Contreras, the CIA officers tried to assume permanent leadership positions within DINA, but Pinochet blocked the move (La Tercera, 21 September 2000; Franklin, 2000; Jornal do Brasil, 22 September 2000). The CIA later stated that Contreras himself had been a CIA asset between 1974 and 1977 and that he had received an unspecified payment for his services (CIA, 2000, 17). During these years, Contreras was a leading organizer and proponent of Operation Condor.

In Paraguay, the Technical Department for the Repression of Communism (la Técnica), the nerve center of dictator General Alfredo Stroessner's repressive apparatus, was originally organized with U.S. support. The Paraguayan police archives—known as the Archives of Terror—contain official requests to track suspects, sent to and from the U.S. embassy, the Federal Bureau of Investigation (FBI), the CIA, and their Paraguayan counterparts. The CIA provided lists of suspects and other intelligence information to Paraguayan intelligence as well as to other military states.

In Brazil, the fearsome Serviço Nacional de Informações (National Information Service, SNI) was established in 1964, two months after the military coup in that country. The c i a and the U.S. Office of Public Safety were key influences on that intelligence organization. A U.S. public safety adviser pre- pared a draft organizational chart for the Brazilians and provided a list of "qualified personnel"—persons who had attended c i a training courses in the Canal Zone at the Inter-American Police Academy—for incorporation in the nascent s n i. The s n i became the most powerful political intelligence or- ganization in the country and retained its close contacts with the c i a (Hug- gins, 1998, 126–27).

At minimum, U.S. national security policy provided a permissive or sup- portive environment for Operation Condor. Newly uncovered evidence, how- ever, suggests a more direct role: that top U.S. officials approved of Operation Condor and condoned Condor dirty-war methods, while U.S. agencies pro- vided intelligence and logistical support for those operations.

Operation Condor: Offensive Weapon against "Subversion"

The military forces taking part in Condor activities engaged in terrorist prac- tices to destroy the "subversive threat" in their own societies and in neigh- boring countries as well, a radically new development in the region. Operation Condor targeted political exiles and refugees considered to be enemies of the state. Its larger targets were rebellious sectors of society and popular move- ments demanding democratic or social change. Condor disappearances and assassinations demonstrated that opponents of the national security states were unsafe anywhere in the world. Traditions of political sanctuary were violated with impunity and rendered irrelevant.

According to declassified U.S. documents, the Condor system consisted of three levels (see Federal Bureau of Investigation, 1976). The first was based on mutual cooperation among military intelligence services, in- cluding coordination of the political surveillance of targeted persons and exchange of intelligence information. The second called for covert action: organized cross-border operations to detain and disappear dissidents, carried out by multinational squadrons. The third, and most secret, was termed "Phase III": it called for the formation of special teams of assassins from member countries to travel worldwide to eliminate "subversive enemies." Phase III was aimed at political leaders who were especially feared for their potential to mobilize world opinion or organize broad opposition to the military states.

Victims of Phase III operations included constitutionalist Chilean General Carlos Prats and his wife Sofía Cuthbert, assassinated in Buenos Aires (1974); leader of the Chilean Christian Democrats Bernardo Leighton and his wife Ana, severely wounded in Rome (1975); Chilean Orlando Letelier—foreign minister under deposed president Salvador Allende Gossens and a fierce foe of the Pinochet regime—and his U.S. colleague Ronni Moffitt, killed in Washington, D.C. (1976); nationalist former president of Bolivia Juan José Torres, assassinated in Buenos Aires (1976); and two Uruguayan legislators and opponents of the Uruguayan military regime, Zelmar Michelini and Héctor Gutiérrez Ruíz, killed also in Buenos Aires (1976). In the Leighton and Letelier–Moffitt cases, respectively, agents of DINA "contracted" neofascist organizations in Italy and right-wing Cuban exiles in the United States to collaborate in carrying out the crimes. Michael Townley, a U.S. expatriate and DINA assassin often linked to the CIA, admitted his operational role in three of these terrorist acts.[4]

Operation Condor was not a rogue or ad hoc operation but a well-organized, sophisticated, and well-equipped network with systematized planning and training, operations and communications centers, and a chain of command in each country. Condor operatives utilized dedicated communications networks and received specialized instruction. Several clandestine detention and torture centers were established in Buenos Aires explicitly for Condor's foreign prisoners. The most notorious was Orletti Motors, an abandoned garage equipped with torture devices and staffed by Uruguayan and Argentine military officers and former torturers of the Triple-A death squads sponsored by the previous Peronist government. Hundreds of Uruguayans, Bolivians, and Chileans were held in Orletti Motors; survivors have said that military personnel of Argentina, Bolivia, Chile, Paraguay, and Uruguay conducted combined operations there (*Dignidad*, 1985).[5]

Condor was established officially in November 1975 during the first Inter-American Working Meeting of Intelligence, held in Santiago, Chile. A letter found in the Paraguayan archives, dated October 1975 and signed by DINA commander Contreras (M. Contreras, 1975), establishes that the system of transnational coordination was to be institutionalized in a November meeting. Contreras's letter invited General Francisco Brites (or Britez), commander of the Paraguayan police, to "a Working Meeting of National Intelligence" to be held in Santiago under "strict secrecy." Several months earlier, in August 1975, Contreras had visited the CIA deputy director Vernon Walters in

Washington, D.C., and then traveled with a D I N A team to Argentina, Bolivia, Uruguay, Paraguay, Brazil, and Venezuela—to advocate regional collaboration in counterinsurgency operations (Dinges and Landau, 1980, 155–57; Brandt, 1998). A Venezuelan officer later testified that Contreras had urged his Venezuelan counterparts to collaborate with D I N A by keeping Chilean exiles under surveillance and reporting back to D I N A on their activities.

In his letter to Brites, Contreras wrote that the purpose of the planned November 1975 meeting was to establish "an excellent coordination and improved action to benefit National Security." The proposal for the meeting included a plan of action and an organizational structure, as well as a security system with three elements: an Office of Coordination and Security that would include a computerized central data bank of suspect individuals and organizations, "something similar to Interpol, but dedicated to Subversion"; an information center with special communication channels, a cryptography capability, telephones with scrambling mechanisms, and message systems; and permanent working meetings. The Chileans offered Santiago as the headquarters of the system, specifying that the participating countries would be equally represented in the "technical personnel" of the system. These technical personnel would have diplomatic immunity, and the Chileans proposed that they be from intelligence services. The term itself—technical personnel—reflected the routinization and bureaucratization of terror represented by Condor.

Officers representing Argentina, Bolivia, Chile, Paraguay, and Uruguay signed the closing act of this meeting on November 28, 1975 (*Posdata*, 1999, 19–20). (Brazil became a full member soon afterward.) The original proposals were adopted and the participants agreed to initiate "rapid and immediate contact when an individual was expelled from a country or when a suspect traveled in order to alert the Intelligence Services" of Condor countries. They decided to "establish a complete directory with the names and addresses of those persons who work in Intelligence so that they can directly solicit the antecedents of persons and organizations connected *directly or indirectly* with Marxism" [emphasis added]. Item 5g of the agreement recommended installing intelligence operatives in each country's embassies, where they would be fully accredited and, thus, have cover stories and identities. (In many cases, Condor officers were named as military attachés in member countries.)

The officers scheduled their next meeting for one week before the upcoming meeting of the Conference of American Armies in Santiago in

June 1976. At the suggestion of the Uruguayan delegation, they named the system Condor in honor of the host country, which used the condor as a national symbol. Colonel Contreras, "Condor One," signed the act, as did Colonel Benito Guanes Serrano of Paraguay, Captain José Casas of Argentina, Major Carlos Mena of Bolivia, and Colonel José A. Fons of Uruguay.

A declassified U.S. document demonstrates the systematized, bureaucratic nature of Condor as the program extended through the South American military and intelligence forces. In 1978, a CIA memo reported that Ecuador had agreed to participate in Condor. Outlining the Condor chain of command, the memo continued: "The overall responsibility for Ecuador's participation and activities in Condor lie with the Ecuadorian Joint Command of the Armed Forces; however, the Joint Command has assigned various individual responsibilities to the army, navy, and air force. . . . [T]he National Intelligence Directorate (DNI) of Ecuador was incorporated into the Condor organization with the name of Condor 7" (CIA, 1978). At that time, an Argentine officer was in Quito supervising the installation of the special telecommunications system, Condortel, in the defense ministry, while Chile was offering training grants for Ecuadorian intelligence personnel.

Operation Condor within the Inter-American System

Although Condor's formal founding occurred in November 1975, the system was operating earlier by means of secret and unwritten arrangements. A September 2000 CIA report to the U.S. Congress stated:

> Within a year after the [September 1973 Chilean] coup, the CIA and other US government agencies were aware of bilateral cooperation among regional intelligence services to track the activities of and, in at least a few cases, kill political opponents. This was the precursor to Operation Condor, an intelligence-sharing arrangement among Chile, Argentina, Brazil, Paraguay, and Uruguay established in 1975. (CIA, 2000)

That is, the Condor prototype was already functioning some two years before the official founding meeting, as coordinated operations by combined security forces in one another's territory—the essence of Condor—were already occurring in 1973 and 1974. Other declassified U.S. documents confirm the earlier time frame. One top-secret CIA *National Intelligence Daily*, for example, reads: "In early 1974, security officials from Argentina, Chile, Uruguay,

Paraguay, and Bolivia met in Buenos Aires to prepare coordinated actions against subversive targets" (CIA, 1976a).

In 1976 the Condor system was upgraded with a computerized intelligence database and the telecommunications system, Condortel. Condortel linked the Condor countries together and enabled them to coordinate transnational intelligence and operations more efficiently. In fact, an Argentine military source told a U.S. embassy contact, in 1976, that the CIA had played a key role in setting up the computerized links among the intelligence and operations units of the six Condor states (Landau, 1988, 119; 1999). Indeed, no country in Latin America had the technological capacity to set up such a system. Other new evidence points to deep U.S. military and inter-American military system involvement in providing operations support for Condor counterterror coordination.

In a recently declassified 1978 cable, ambassador to Paraguay Robert White reported to Secretary of State Cyrus Vance on a meeting requested by General Alejandro Fretes Dávalos, the commander of Paraguay's armed forces. Fretes had informed White that a U.S. facility in the Panama Canal Zone was the site of a secret telecommunications center for Condor intelligence coordination throughout Latin America (White, 1978; Schemo, 2001). According to the Paraguayan general, intelligence chiefs from Brazil, Argentina, Chile, Bolivia, Paraguay, and Uruguay used "an encrypted system within the U.S. telecommunications net[work]," which covered all of Latin America, to "coordinate intelligence information." In the cable, White drew the connection to Operation Condor and advised the Carter administration to reconsider whether this linkage was in the U.S. interest. He told the *New York Times* in 2001 that he never received a response.

The significance of this connection can hardly be overstated. Essentially, U.S. military and/or intelligence forces put their official channels of inter-American communication at the disposal of Operation Condor. Clearly, such technological and operations support was a crucial foundation for coordinating Condor intelligence and covert operations, reflecting a significant collaboration by U.S. forces. The sophisticated communications network allowed Condor intelligence commanders to communicate with their operations centers and to track the movements of persons among countries. According to White (2003b), such telecommunications systems were generally established for allied militaries so that U.S. personnel could monitor their communications and alert their superiors of planned operations. In other words, U.S. forces had complete knowledge of Condor operations coordinated through the U.S. network.

Other communications systems had been set up earlier within the Permanent Commission of Inter-American Military Communications (COPECOMI), including a network control station in the Canal Zone and subsidiary stations in participating countries. As Child (1980, 163–64) notes, "It is hard to avoid the impression that these communications nets came under U.S. aegis since their net control stations functioned as adjuncts to U.S. military communications facilities in the Canal Zone." The U.S. military also provided such systems to the Central American and Indonesian militaries in the context of counterinsurgency collaboration (McClintock, 1985, 67–70, 204; Kadane, 1990, 1997). According to McClintock, the U.S. military, under cover of the U.S. Public Safety Program, established in 1964 the Central American and Panama Telecommunications Security Network, which linked the intelligence agencies of each country with SOUTHCOM in Panama, where the parent station was located. In 1966 the commander of SOUTHCOM explained the operational importance of such systems for counterinsurgency:

> Essential to the success of regional organizations are regional communications systems and joint operations centers . . . [A regional communications system] is the initial step toward the goal of developing effective national and regional military command and control systems for support of counterinsurgency operations. (Child, 1980, 164)

White subsequently underlined the importance of the Condor link to the Panama base, saying that his interchange with Fretes had convinced him that the U.S. government was intimately involved in Operation Condor. Recalling the conversation, White said in 2001 that Fretes essentially told him that Condor operations "were run out of the School of the Americas" (White, 2001; see also White, 2003a). White believed that Fretes meant that the operation was run out of the Panama base, which included the SOA, the headquarters of SOUTHCOM, a large CIA station, and the headquarters of the Special Forces and other military branches. The Panama base was certainly the center of the hemispheric counterinsurgency effort. According to one military graduate of the SOA, "the school was always a front for other special operations, covert operations" (Nelson-Pallmeyer, 1997, 31; see also Fischer, 1997, 189). Despite a vague denial by the former DIA commander,[6] it is inconceivable that any foreign officer or military group could make use of the secure

U.S. telecommunications system without the deep knowledge, collaboration, and engagement of U.S. military and intelligence services.

There are other indications that Condor operated within the structures of the inter-American system. A declassified document suggests that Condor officers used the Inter-American Defense Board as a vehicle for Condor coordination (U.S. Embassy, Santiago, 1976). In 1976, Ambassador David Popper in Chile reported information obtained from military sources by a U.S. journalist, Frank Manitzas: Colonel Mario Jahn, former deputy director of DINA, had been assigned to the defense board in Washington, D.C., and might be trying "to drum up support with his Southern Cone colleagues for joint intelligence and security operations." Since Condor was already well established, however, sponsoring multiple combined operations by this time (including Phase III assassinations), it is quite likely that more advanced coordination was occurring within the structures of the defense board. In fact, the ambassador reported the information in the context of the Letelier–Moffitt assassinations, which had recently occurred. He urged his superiors in the Department of State to consider the "implications for the investigation of Letelier's death," of Jahn's presence in Washington, and the "question of the role of the Inter-American Defense Board with respect to activities of Southern Cone governments." Popper seemed to be hinting that Condor officers were utilizing the board to advance Condor's extralegal agenda, including Phase III assassinations.

These examples suggest that Condor officers operated within inter-American security organizations and infrastructures to coordinate and expand the program's counterterror and countersubversion campaigns. The inter-American system, already geared toward the anticommunist crusade, essentially harbored a transnational state terror apparatus.

Top-Level U.S. Knowledge of Condor

Recent evidence indicates that top U.S. officials were closely informed of Condor and supportive of Condor's counterterror operations. In 1999, for example, a high-ranking Argentine military source—familiar with Argentine junta secrets from 1976—said that during a meeting on June 10, 1976, at the Organization of American States (OAS) conference in Santiago, Secretary of State Henry Kissinger had assured the Chilean and Argentine juntas of the Ford administration's support and cooperation for counterinsurgency operations—and for Operation Condor (Amato, 1999).[7] In fact, many of Condor's victims, and several judges in Latin America and Europe, suspect that Kissinger was more deeply involved in Condor. Judges in France, Chile, and Argentina have officially requested his testimony in cases related to Condor crimes and, in 2002, human rights lawyers in Chile filed a criminal complaint against Kissinger, accusing him of having a role in organizing the Condor network (Rohter, 2002).

A cable dated July 20, 1976, released by the State Department in August 2002, shows that Kissinger was well informed on Condor. The cable, signed by Kissinger and sent to all U.S. diplomatic missions in Latin America (and some in Europe), confirmed the February 1974 meeting of Condor officers:

> Over two years ago, security officials from all the Southern Cone countries except Brazil met in Buenos Aires and reportedly formalized arrangements to facilitate information exchanges and the movement of security officials on government business. (Kissinger, 1976, 4)

This sanitized Condor description contrasts with a passage—excised from the version of the cable earlier made public—which states:

> [A] reliable Brazilian source has described a Brazil-Argentina agreement under which *the two countries hunt and eliminate terrorists* attempting to flee Argentina for Brazil. Brazilian and Argentine military units reportedly have operated jointly and inside each other's border when necessary. (Kissinger, 1976, 4; emphasis added)

Here the cable clearly describes Condor cross-border "hunter-killer" operations. The cable also states that Brazil became a full-fledged member of Condor in June 1976.

Although Kissinger's memorandum provides an account of Condor operations, it understates the violent and extralegal nature of Condor and appears intended to downplay evidence of a systematic intergovernmental conspiracy. Rather, the cable posits that a "uniquely Argentine set of factors" explains the recent wave of Condor disappearances and assassinations in that country. Two months earlier, in May 1976, the two Uruguayan legislators Michelini and Gutiérrez Ruiz had been abducted and murdered. In June, Bolivian ex-president Torres had been abducted and found dead. Also in June a team of armed men had ransacked the office of the Catholic Commission on

Immigration in Buenos Aires, stealing the records of thousands of refugees. Two days later, twenty-four Chilean and Uruguayan refugees whose names had been in the files (all of whom were under United Nations protection) had been kidnapped, tortured, and released, with warnings to leave the country. Several had reported that their interrogators included Chilean and Uruguayan officers. The CIA was aware that the armed men were multinational Condor teams coordinating operations against targets in Argentina (CIA, 1976b; see also U.S. Embassy, Buenos Aires, 1976). Moreover, other Phase III assassinations had occurred before 1976: that of Prats and his wife in 1974, and Leighton and his wife in Rome in 1975. In September 1976, shortly after Kissinger sent the cable, Condor assassin Townley acted again as a key member of a Condor death squad. This time Orlando Letelier and Ronni Moffitt were murdered in a car bombing in Washington, D.C.

Kissinger sent another memo, dated August 23, 1976, to the U.S. embassies in the six Condor countries. In it, he ordered his ambassadors to convey the U.S. government's concern to the military regimes regarding "rumors" of assassination plans through Operation Condor (U.S. Secretary of State, 1976). While intelligence exchanges and countersubversive coordination among the national security states were useful, according to the memo, assassinations could not be countenanced. None of the documents released indicate that the ambassadors acted on these instructions (Dinges and Kornbluh, 2002; Schemo, 2002). Failure to act would be a curious response to a directive by the Secretary of State, however, and, according to former ambassador Robert White, an inconceivable one. Based on his experience, White said the ambassadors would have immediately approached the CIA station chief, or possibly the DIA, within a day or two, to have them determine the best way to communicate the message to the military regimes (White, 2003b). Indeed, the next day (August 24), Ambassador Popper in Santiago replied to the memo, telling the Secretary of State that Pinochet might be offended by a direct approach. Furthermore, he wrote, "[C]ooperation among Southern Cone national intelligence agencies is handled by the DINA." Popper's reply continued:

> ONE LINE DELETED purpose of instruction will be best achieved if he conveys the message to ONE LINE DELETED. He can do it in the context of having heard a rumor which he cannot believe... PHRASE DELETED believe this would be the most effective way of getting the message across without undesirable complications. (U.S. Embassy, Santiago, 1976)

This fragment seems to confirm White's analysis that Popper went to the C I A or D I A immediately for consultations.

In another twist, on September 20, 1976—the day before the Letelier–Moffitt murders—the State Department *rescinded* the instructions to express concern about assassinations to the Condor regimes, purportedly because there was no evidence of Condor activity (Dinges and Kornbluh, 2002). Former ambassador White surmised that the original cable had generated so much angry opposition from the Latin American intelligence organizations—and, perhaps, from the C I A and D I A—that the State Department decided to withdraw it (White, 2003b). The retraction of the instructions again highlighted Washington's reluctance to deter the dictatorships, their dirty war methods—and Operation Condor. Yet in 2002, the Bush administration specifically mentioned the original demarche as proof that Washington—and Kissinger—opposed the activities of Condor.[8]

The Argentine junta had the strong support of top-ranking officials of the Nixon and Ford administrations, as well as the Pentagon and the C I A, for its dirty war (National Security Archive, 2003a, 2003b), despite the human rights concerns of lower-ranking State Department officials and members of Congress. In the case of Chile, minutes of a private conversation between Kissinger and Pinochet on the day before the June 1976 O A S meeting show that Kissinger essentially told the general to disregard his upcoming speech on human rights since the U.S. government supported Pinochet's dictatorship (Kornbluh, 1999). It appears that Kissinger, in effect, assumed one attitude toward Condor "for the record" and another in secret.

U.S. Reporting on Condor

In a section titled, "Southern Cone Counterterrorism Plans," a C I A report provides further evidence of C I A knowledge (and implicit approval) of Condor assassination operations:

> Security officials of Chile, Argentina, and Uruguay are reportedly expanding their cooperative anti-subversive activities to include assassination of top-level terrorists in exile in Europe. . . . The Chilean, Argentinian, and Uruguayan services now plan to train teams in Buenos Aires for the missions in Western Europe. The plans and targets of the teams will be withheld from at least some government leaders. (C I A, 1976c)

A key point here is that U.S. intelligence officers were fully aware of Condor's assassination program and its global reach. Other declassified documents indicate that even after the double assassination of Letelier and Moffitt on the streets of Washington, top U.S.-government officials still did not try to stop Condor. Produced a month later, a section called "Condor Activities Continue" in a heavily censored State Department report states:

> PHRASE DELETED reports that Uruguayan authorities have decided TWO LINES DELETED to limit the countersubversive organization's assassinations to known terrorists. A Condor training course now being conducted in Buenos Aires will conclude in early December when at least two Uruguayan operatives will be sent to Paris to perform unspecified duties. (U.S. State Department, 1976)

This document suggests that U.S. officials, as well as their Latin American counterparts, were aware that political opponents (not "terrorists") had previously been the targets of Condor assassination operations.

Another declassified document—a March 1977 "Memorandum for the Record" of an ARA/CIA weekly meeting (ARA signified the American Republic Affairs section, later known as Inter-American Affairs, within the State Department)—gives a glimpse of the thinking of Carter administration officials:

> Mr. [William H.] Luers said that Ambassador [to Uruguay Ernest V.] Siracusa has asked for our current views on Condor. PHRASE DELETED said that it really exists, and that the CIA has PHRASE DELETED reporting on it. Mr. Luers said that it would be helpful to have an update on the subject of Condor, what we know about it, and how we should deal with the knowledge that we have. We might want to think again about whether we should raise the subject with the governments involved. *We haven't seen anything lately about Condor planning executions. Our attitude would be different if only exchanges of intelligence are involved.* PARAGRAPH DELETED. [Emphasis added] ([Signed], Francis De Tarr, INR/DDC/OP)

However, Condor continued to target and disappear lesser-known activists in extraterritorial actions throughout this period, as was documented by the

Argentine organization Centro de Estudios Legales y Sociales, among others (Centro de Estudios Legales y Sociales [C E L S], 1984). Although these actions were not Phase III assassinations, they routinely resulted in torture and extrajudicial execution.

U.S. Cooperation with Condor

A key case that illustrates U.S. involvement with Condor countersubversive operations is that of Jorge Isaac Fuentes Alarcón, a Chilean sociologist accused of being a courier for a Chilean revolutionary group. Paraguayan police seized Fuentes as he crossed the border from Argentina to Paraguay in May 1975. Chile's Truth and Reconciliation Commission later learned that the capture of Fuentes was a collaborative effort by Argentine intelligence services, personnel of the U.S. embassy in Buenos Aires, and Paraguayan police. Fuentes was transferred extralegally to the Chilean police, who brought him to Villa Grimaldi, a notorious D I N A detention center in Santiago. He was last seen there, savagely tortured (Comisión Nacional de Verdad y Reconciliación de Chile, 1991, 595–96; Committee for the Promotion and Defense of the Rights of the People [CODEPU], 1996, 78–83).

The legal attaché in the U.S. embassy in Buenos Aires informed the Chilean military, in writing, of the capture and interrogation of Fuentes. Also listed were names and addresses of three individuals living in the United States whose names had been in Fuentes's possession. The memo stated that the F B I was conducting investigations of the three in the United States (National Security Archive, n.d.). This letter, among others, confirmed that U.S. officials and agencies were cooperating with the military dictatorships and acting as a link in the Condor chain. Perhaps most striking was that this coordination was routine (if secret) standard operating procedure within U.S. policy.

Other cases also suggest that some U.S. security officers were regularly briefed on Condor operations and privy to highly classified Condor intelligence reports, including planned summary executions. Reports by a regional security officer (R S O), declassified in 2002, show that he and his superiors had prior knowledge of the planned "permanent disappearance" of Argentine Noemí Gianetti de Molfino and three other persons in 1980. The four were detained/disappeared in Lima, Peru, on June 14, 1980, by a combined Condor team of Argentine and Peruvian intelligence officers. In a June 19 report to the U.S. ambassador (Blystone, 1980b; see also J. Contreras, 2002), the R S O cited a meeting with an Argentine military intelligence officer— obviously from the Argentine army's notorious Battalion 601, the cerebrum of the clandestine disappearance-torture-killing apparatus. The Argentine informed him that the four disappeared persons "will be held in Peru and then expelled to Bolivia where they will be expelled to Argentina. Once in Argentina they will be interrogated and then permanently disappeared. Source stated that 601 had had a good record on apprehending terrorists who had fled the country and were preparing to reenter." Clearly, the R S O had been briefed on a top secret Condor operation involving the intelligence services of three separate countries.

According to 1998 Argentine press reports, Gianetti de Molfino was a Mother of the Plaza de Mayo (a mother of the disappeared). She had denounced the 1979 disappearances of her daughter and son-in-law before the United Nations and was working with human rights groups in Peru. Gianetti de Molfino's body was discovered on July 21 in Madrid. Spanish judge Baltasar Garzón (known for his extradition request for Pinochet) reopened the case in 1996 at the request of Gustavo Molfino, the slain woman's son. In December 1999, Gustavo was awarded an indemnity from the Argentine government for the death of his mother. It was the first time the Argentine state had officially recognized its responsibility in the death of an Argentine citizen in a Condor operation (McSherry, 2001).

In another memo, dated April 7, 1980, the same R S O reported that he had "jokingly" asked his Argentine intelligence contact what had happened to two Montoneros (members of an Argentine guerrilla group) who had disappeared during a trip from Mexico to Rio de Janeiro. The Argentine again told the R S O top-secret information: that they had previously captured a Montonero who, under interrogation, had revealed the time and place of a meeting in Rio. The report continued:

The Argentine military intelligence (601) contacted their Brazilian military intelligence counterparts for permission to conduct an operation in Rio to capture two Montoneros arriving from Mexico. Brazilians granted their permission and a special team of Argentines were [sic] flown under the operational command of Lt. Col. Roman, to Rio aboard an Argentine air force C130. Both of the Montoneros from Mexico were captured alive and returned to Argentina aboard the C130. . . . These two Montoneros are presently being held at the army's secret jail, Campo de Mayo. (Blystone, 1980a)

The R S O's report fails to acknowledge that barbaric torture was routine during interrogations at secret detention centers such as Campo de Mayo. These two persons were never seen again. In 2000, the Brazilian government granted an indemnity to their families (and to the family of one other Argentine disappeared in Brazil). In 2002, an Argentine judge opened a criminal case regarding the disappearances of some twenty Montoneros in late 1979 and early 1980, including these two, and indicted thirty-two Argentine officers.

These declassified reports are rare in that they document a U.S. official's advance knowledge of top secret and extralegal Condor operations. They also reflect implicit acceptance or approval of dirty-war tactics. Clearly, this U.S. official was accepted within the highest levels of the Argentine Condor structure. Such officials tacitly, or explicitly, provided a green light for Operation Condor's human rights crimes.

Conclusion

Operation Condor was a top-secret inter-American intelligence and operations system that functioned within the larger hemispheric security architecture. Various data indicate that Condor officers utilized inter-American military and intelligence structures—including the official U.S. telecommunications network, the Conference of American Armies, the U.S. Army School of the Americas, the regional system of military attachés, and the Inter-American Defense Board—to conduct Condor planning and operations.

Documentary evidence shows that at least one secretary of state (Henry Kissinger) approved of cross-border counterinsurgency operations by the military dictatorships within the framework of Condor. Washington's strategy to remain in the background, combined with the doctrine of plausible deniability and security agencies' refusal to clarify their role, has meant that the U.S. government's full relationship with Condor is difficult to document. Weighty evidence, however, indicates that U.S. national security officials gave a virtual carte blanche to the Condor militaries and their savage counterinsurgency campaigns (see National Security Archive, 2003a, 2003b) and condoned or endorsed Operation Condor, and that U.S. personnel directly assisted at least some cross-border Condor operations. Certainly U.S. military and intelligence agencies worked closely with the intelligence organizations that carried out Condor operations, despite the opposition and concerns of some U.S. officials and many members of Congress.

Condor operations conformed to U.S. counterterror doctrine—the use of "terror to fight terror"—and took place within the larger context of counter-subversive "hemispheric defense" (supranational counterinsurgency operations). Condor was a professionalized and rationalized system of terror, with advanced communications and infrastructure. It had access to considerable national and international resources and operated with formal command structures, specialized training courses, and operations centers in each country. Condor thus substantiates the analysis given in Chapter 1: it was a modern bureaucratic system that applied scientific concepts and advanced technology to make repressive operations more lethal and social control more effective. Condor manifested the region's common countersubversive doctrine as well as the covert warfare strategy of counterterror, which were diffused throughout the region via inter-American structures and military-to-military exchanges. Essentially, Operation Condor represented the internationalization of state terror.

NOTES

AUTHOR'S NOTE: J. Patrice McSherry is grateful to Brian Loveman, Michael McClintock, and Raúl Molina Mejía for their incisive comments on earlier versions of this chapter. Of course, any errors of fact or analysis are the author's responsibility. She is indebted to Long Island University and to the International Relations Programme of the World Council of Churches for support of her research on Operation Condor.

1. The author's work draws on archives, interviews, and published materials gathered during research in five of the six Condor countries. Sources include the Paraguayan Archives of Terror, Centro de Estudios Legales y Sociales (CELS, Argentina), Arquivo Ana Lagôa (Universidade Federal de São Carlos, Brazil), Servicio Paz y Justicia (SERPAJ, Uruguay), and reports from Comisión Nacional sobre la Desaparición de Personas (CONADEP, Argentina) and Comisión Nacional de Verdad y Reconciliación de Chile (the Rettig Commission of Chile). Other useful sources are the National Security Archive (n.d.) at George Washington University and the Equipo Nizkor (n.d.) web site.

2. Some U.S. officials in the embassies and in Washington were deeply concerned about Condor's human rights abuses and extralegal methods, but security interests

usually superseded human rights concerns during the Cold War (see, for example, National Security Archive 2003a, 2003b).

3. The author is grateful to French journalist Pierre Abramovici for sharing this document with her.

4. Townley admitted his role in the Letelier assassination as part of a plea bargain in a U.S. court in the late 1970s. He received a minimal sentence and went into a witness protection program. Prison letters he wrote in the late 1970s, intercepted by the FBI, showed his knowledge of the Prats and Leighton assassination operations. In 1995 Townley testified in an Italian court to his role in organizing the Leighton attack. In 1997 that court condemned him, in absentia, for attempted murder. Townley confessed his role in the Prats assassination to an Argentine judge investigating that case in 1999.

5. *Dignidad* reproduces the testimony of an Uruguayan survivor of Orletti, Enrique Rodríguez Larreta.

6. He said that "if such an arrangement existed on an institutional basis, I would have known about it, and I did not then and do not now," but added, "that such an arrangement could have been made locally on an ad hoc basis is not beyond the realm of probability." Schemo, 2001.

7. Analysts already knew that Kissinger had given a "green light" to the repressive campaigns of the Chilean and Argentine juntas. See Andersen (1987a, 1987b) and McSherry (1997, 81).

8. In late November 2002, the same week in which George W. Bush offered Henry Kissinger the chairmanship of the committee to investigate the September 11, 2001, attacks, the Argentine minister of justice received a communication from the U.S. government stating that Kissinger would not appear to give testimony in a criminal case involving Operation Condor. That same week, Chilean judge Juan Guzmán, who was investigating the death of Charles Horman (a U.S. national executed in Chile after the 1973 coup) received a similar official message from Washington. In a response to legal letters rogatory from the Chilean judge, Washington replied that Kissinger could remember no details concerning the case. The response to Argentina mentioned the Kissinger document cited here to show that the U.S. government was not complicit with Condor. The Argentine and Chilean media reported these events, but the U.S. Justice Department office in question refused to comment when contacted by this author on December 4, 2002.

BIBLIOGRAPHY

Amato, Alberto. 1999. "Anatomía de una Dictadura." *Clarín*, 21 March, Argentina, Zona sec.
Andersen, Martin Edwin. 1987a. "Argentina 1976." Montevideo, Uruguay: *Brecha*, 23 October, n.p.

———. 1987b. "Kissinger and the 'Dirty War.'" *The Nation*, 31 October: 477–80.

Blystone, James J. 1980a. "RSO Conversation with Argentine Intelligence Source, to Ambassador via Chaplin." Washington, DC: Department of State, April 7.
———. 1980b. "Meeting with Argentine Intelligence Service." June 19.
Brandt, Daniel. 1998. "Operation Condor: Ask the D E A" [online]. San Antonio, Texas: Public Information Research, Inc., 10 December [updated 2002; cited 16 May 2003]. Available from http://www.namebase.org/condor.html.

Central Intelligence Agency. 1976a. *National Intelligence Daily*. No. 168. Washington, DC: Central Intelligence Agency, June 23.
———. 1976b. *Weekly Summary*. No. 1398 [secret]. Washington, DC: Central Intelligence Agency, July 2.
———. 1976c. "Latin American Trends: Staff Notes. Counterterrorism Plans." Washington, DC: Central Intelligence Agency, August 11.
———. 1978. Report [title blacked out][secret]. Washington, DC: Central Intelligence Agency, February 14.
———. 2000. "C I A Activities in Chile." Report to Congress [online]. Washington, DC: Central Intelligence Agency, 18 September [updated 14 May 2003; cited 16 May 2003]. Available from http://www.cia.gov/cia/publications/chile/ index.html.
Centro de Estudios Legales y Sociales (C E L S). 1984. "Uruguay/Argentina: Coordinación Represiva." Buenos Aires, Argentina: Centro de Estudios Legales y Sociales.
Child, John. 1980. *Unequal Alliance: The Inter-American Military System, 1938–1978*. Boulder: Westview Press.
Comisión Nacional de Verdad y Reconciliación de Chile. 1991. *Informe Rettig*, 2 vols. Santiago: Chilean Government and Ediciones del Ornitorrinco.
Committee for the Promotion and Defense of the Rights of the People (C O D E P U), Equipo DIT-T. 1996. *Más Allá de las Fronteras: Estudios sobre las Personas Ejecutadas o Desaparecidas Fuera de Chile 1973–1990*. Santiago: LOM Ediciones.
Contreras, Joseph. 2002. "Latin America: Knowing Too Much." *Newsweek*, Periscope, International Editions, 27 October, p. 6.
Contreras, Manuel. 1975. Letter, in Paraguayan Archives, item 151.

Defense Intelligence Agency (D I A). 1976. "Special Operations Forces." Washington, DC: U.S. Army, 1 October.
Dignidad (Argentina). 1985. "El Juicio Público a los Dictadores," 25 June.
Dinges, John, and Saul Landau. 1980. *Assassination on Embassy Row*. New York: Pantheon Books.
Dinges, John, and Peter Kornbluh. 2002. "An Assassination, A Failure to Act, A Painful Parallel." *Washington Post*, 22 September, p. B1.
Donovan, James A. 1967. *The U.S. Marine Corps*. New York: Praeger.

Equipo Nizkor. n.d. Human Rights Links [online]. Madrid: Equipo Nizkor [cited 16 May 2003]. Available from http://www.derechos.org/nizkor/eng.html.

Federal Bureau of Investigation. 1976. "Foreign Political Matters, Argentina, Chile." Washington, DC: Federal Bureau of Investigation, 28 September.

Fischer, Mary A. 1997. "Teaching Torture." *Gentlemen's Quarterly* (June): 182–89, 237–40.

Franklin, Jonathan. 2000. "Ex-spy Chief Says CIA Helped Him Set up Pinochet's Secret Police." *Guardian,* 23 September, Foreign Pages, p. 17.

Holt, Pat M. 1995. *Secret Intelligence and Public Policy: A Dilemma of Democracy.* Washington, DC: CQ Press, Congressional Quarterly, Inc.

Huggins, Martha K. 1998. *Political Policing: The United States and Latin America.* Durham: Duke University Press.

Johnson, Kermit D. 1998. *Ethics and Counterrevolution: American Involvement in Internal Wars.* Lanham, MD: University Press of America.

Jornal do Brasil, 22 September 2000.

Kadane, Kathy. 1990. "Ex-agents Say CIA Compiled Death Lists for Indonesians" [online]. Washington, DC: States News Service [cited 16 May 2003]. Available from http://www.namebase.org/kadane.html.

———. 1997. Letter to the Editor. *New York Review of Books* [online]. New York: The New York Review of Books, 10 April [cited 16 May 2003). Available from http://www.namebase.org/kadane.html.

Kissinger, Henry. 1976. "South America: Southern Cone Security Practices" [online]. Washington, DC: Department of State, 23 July [cited 16 May 2003). Available from http://www.gwu.edu/~ nsarchiv/NSAEBB/NSAEBB73/ index3. htm #docs.

Kornbluh, Peter. 1999. "Kissinger and Pinochet" [online]. *The Nation,* 29 March [cited 14 May 2003). Available from http://www.thirdworldtraveler.com/Kissinger/ KissingerPinochet_Nation.html.

La Tercera, 21 September 2000.

Landau, Saul. 1988. *The Dangerous Doctrine: National Security and U.S. Foreign Policy.* Boulder: Westview Press.

———. 1999. Personal communication with author. February 13.

Latin American Working Group. 1997. *Inspector General's Report on Army Manuals a Feeble Response: What the Recently Declassified Manuals Contain.* Washington, DC: Latin American Working Group.

Loveman, Brian, and Thomas M. Davies, eds. 1997a. *Che Guevara and Guerrilla Movements,* 3rd ed. Wilmington, DE: Scholarly Resources.

———. 1997b. *The Politics of Antipolitics,* 3rd ed. Wilmington, DE: Scholarly Resources.

McClintock, Michael. 1985. *The American Connection*, vol. I: *State Terror and Popular Resistance in El Salvador*. London: Zed Books, Ltd.

———. 1991. "American Doctrine and Counterinsurgent State Terror." Pp. 121–47 in *Western State Terrorism*, ed. Alexander George. New York: Routledge.

———. 1992. *Instruments of Statecraft: U.S. Guerrilla Warfare, Counterinsurgency, Counterterrorism, 1940–1990*. New York: Pantheon Books.

McPherson, Sandra B. 1999. "The Misuse of Psychological Techniques under U.S. Government Auspices: Interrogation and Terrorism Manuals." Pp. 621–32 in *Collective Violence: Effective Strategies for Assessing and Intervening in Fatal Group and Institutional Aggression*, eds. Harold V. Hall and Leighton C. Whitaker. New York: CRC Press.

McSherry, J. Patrice. 1997. *Incomplete Transition: Military Power and Democracy in Argentina*. New York: St. Martin's Press.

———. 1999. "Operation Condor: Clandestine Inter-American System." *Social Justice* 26 (Winter): 144–74.

———. 2000. "Analyzing Operation Condor: A Covert Inter-American Structure." Paper prepared for the twenty-second International Congress of the Latin American Studies Association (LASA), Miami, 16–18 March.

———. 2001. "Hidden Cold War History: Operation Condor's Structures and Operations." Paper prepared for twenty-third International Congress of Latin American Studies Association (LASA), Washington, DC, 6–8 September.

Metz, Steven. 1995. "A Flame Kept Burning: Counterinsurgency Support After the Cold War." *Parameters* (Autumn): 31–41.

National Security Archive. n.d. U.S. Embassy Letter. Chile document 30–01 [online]. Washington, DC: National Security Archive, 6 June 1975 [cited 16 May 2003]. Available from http://www.gwu.edu/~ nsarchiv/NSAEBB/NSAEBB8/ch30-01.htm.

———. 2003a. "The Pentagon and the CIA Sent Mixed Message to the Argentine Military" [online]. Washington, DC: National Security Archive, 28 March [cited 16 May 2003]. Available from http://www.gwu.edu/~ nsarchiv/NSAEBB/NSAEBB85/.

———. 2003b. "Argentine Military Believed U.S. Gave Go-ahead for Dirty War" [online]. Electronic Briefing Book No. 73, Part II, ed. Carlos Osorio. Washington, DC: National Security Archive, 28 March [cited 16 May 2003]. Available from http://www.gwu.edu/~ nsarchiv/NSAEBB/NSAEBB73/index3.htm.

———. n.d. The Digital National Security Archive [online]. Washington, DC: George Washington University [cited 16 May 2003]. Available from http://www.gwu.edu/~ nsarchiv/.

Nelson-Pallmeyer, Jack. 1997. *School of Assassins*. New York: Orbis Books.

Nevares, Henry (Lt. Col.). 1985. "Antecedentes sobre las Conferencias de Ejércitos Americanos: Trabajo y Presentación Efectuado por el Delegado del Ejército de los EEUU." Santiago: Secretaría Permanente, XVI Conferencia de Ejércitos Americanos.

Posdata (Uruguay). 1999. "Acta Fundacional del Plan Cóndor: Uruguay Propusó el Nombre en Homenaje a los Anfitriones Chilenos." *Posdata* (Uruguay), 18 June, pp. 19–20.

Priest, Dana. 1996. "U.S. Instructed Latins on Executions, Torture." *Washington Post*, 21 September, sec. A, p. 1.

———. 1997. "Army's Project X Had Wider Audience." *Washington Post*, March, final ed., sec. A, p. 1.

Rempe, Dennis M. 1995. "Guerrillas, Bandits, and Independent Republics: US Counter-insurgency Efforts in Colombia 1959–1965." *Small Wars and Insurgencies* 6 (3): 304–27 [online]. Available from www.derechos.net/paulwolf/colombia/smallwars.htm.

Rohter, Larry. 2002. "As Door Opens for Legal Actions in Chilean Coup, Kissinger Is Numbered among the Hunted." *New York Times*, 28 March, late ed., final ed., sec. A, p. 13.

Schemo, Diana Jean. 2001. "New Files Tie U.S. to Deaths of Latin Leftists in 1970s." *New York Times*, 6 March, late ed., final ed., sec. A, p. 7.

———. 2002. "Latin Death Squads and the U.S.: A New Disclosure." *New York Times*, 23 October, late ed., final ed., sec. A, p. 6.

School of the Americas Watch. n.d. *Manuals* [online]. Washington, DC: School of the Americas Watch [cited 16 May 2003]. Available from http://www.soaw.org/new/article.php?id=98.

Sigmund, Paul E. 1980. *Multinationals in Latin America: The Politics of Nationalization*. Madison: University of Wisconsin Press.

U.S. Army Special Forces. n.d. "De Oppresso Liber" [online]. Washington, DC: Special Forces.net [cited 16 May 2003]. Available from http://www.specialforces.net/army/sf/.

U.S. Central Intelligence Agency. 1963. *KUBARK Counterintelligence Interrogation* [online]. Mind Control Forums, July [cited 16 May 2003]. Available from http://mindcontrolforums.com/kubark.htm.

U.S. Embassy, Buenos Aires. 1976. "Aftermath of Kidnapping of Refugees." Buenos Aires: U.S. Embassy, Buenos Aires, 15 June.

U.S. Embassy, Santiago. 1976. "Chile: Report re Ex-DINA Official in Washington." Santiago: U.S. Embassy, Buenos Aires, 27 September.

U.S. Secretary of State. 1976. "Operation Condor." Washington, DC: Government Printing Office, 16 August.

U.S. State Department. 1962. "United States Overseas Internal Defense Policy" (Secret). Washington, DC: Government Printing Office, September.

———. 1976. "INR Afternoon Summary." Washington, DC: Government Printing Office, 23 November.

Weiner, Tim. 1997. "The Spy Agency's Many Mean Ways to Loosen Cold-War Tongues." *New York Times*, 9 February, late ed., final ed., sec. 4, p. 7.

White, Robert. 1978. Cable to Secretary of State [online]. Washington, DC: U.S. Embassy [cited 16 May 2003]. Available from http://foia.state.gov/documents/StateChile3/000058FD.pdf.

———. 2001. Lecture at John Carroll University [online]. Cleveland, Ohio: John Carroll University, 21 March [cited 16 May 2003]. Available from http://www.jcu.edu/pubaff/eyeonjcu/white_audio.htm.

———. 2003a. Personal communications with author. January.

———. 2003b. Interview with author conducted by telephone. 8 April.

Yachir, Faysal. 1988. *Mining in Africa Today*. New York: United Nations University.

PART TWO

◆

CENTRAL AMERICA AND MEXICO

CHAPTER 3

"The Blood of the People"

The Guardia Nacional's Fifty-year War against the People of Nicaragua, 1927–1979

RICHARD GROSSMAN

> *Who Are We?*
> *We Are Tigers!*
> *What Do Tigers Eat?*
> *Blood!*
> *Whose Blood?*
> *The Blood of the People!*
>
> —Guardia Nacional training chant, 1970s[1]

Introduction

In an interview in 1978, Father Fernando Cardenal, SJ, noted, "Nicaragua is a country invaded by its own army" (Black, 1981, 46). As Father Cardenal spoke, an insurrection was seeking to overthrow Latin America's longest running family dictatorship, the Somozas of Nicaragua. The response of the Somoza regime to the uprising was to unleash its military, the Guardia Nacional de Nicaragua, against the population. When the fighting ended in July 1979, the dictator Anastasio Somoza Debayle had fled Nicaragua, but the triumph had been costly: at least 40,000 people killed, 1.5 percent of the 1979 population of less than 3 million (Wheaton and Dilling, 1980, 76).

While the Guardia Nacional had finally been defeated, its war against the Nicaraguan people had lasted for fifty years, from the time when the Guardia itself had been created. A number of Latin American militaries had become repressive institutions over the course of their development; in contrast, the

Guardia Nacional de Nicaragua had been formed as an institution for re-pression. Unlike other militaries in the region, the Guardia was wholly a cre-ation of the United States. It was created as an occupation army, and it func-tioned like one for its entire fifty-two-year history.

By the dawn of the twentieth century, the United States had begun the con-struction of its own "empire" in the Caribbean region. In relation to that ef-fort, Nicaragua was a country of particular concern for the United States. At the beginning of 1927, Assistant Secretary of State Robert Olds wrote a confidential and telling memo describing the official U.S. view of Nicaragua. He noted:

> This Government indisputably has what may be designated a Carib-bean policy. . . . The Central American area down to and including the Isthmus of Panama constitutes a legitimate sphere of influence for the United States. . . . The Panama Canal is a vital asset, and the effec-tive control of the only other potential water route . . . through the Re-public of Nicaragua, is equally vital to our national interests. (National Archives and Records Administration [hereafter NARA], 1927, mi-crofilm 817.00/5854)

Beginning as early as the nineteenth century, military occupation, usually by the Marine Corps, was one facet of the assertion of U.S. hegemony over the region. Among the activities undertaken by these occupations was the creation by the United States of a native constabulary, whose purpose was to institute a new armed force that would help establish political stability within the country and alleviate the need, and expense, for continued direct U.S. military intervention (LaFeber, 1984; A. Millett, 1980). These constabularies were not developments from within a country that reflected the internal dy-namics of that particular society. Instead, these constabularies were created by the United States to replace U.S. soldiers and marines—who had occu-pied certain countries—and to achieve overall U.S. policy objectives.

Nicaragua was one of the places where a U.S. military intervention led to the creation of a national constabulary, the Guardia Nacional de Nicaragua. U.S. Marines landed in Nicaragua in 1909 and returned in 1912, with a lega-tion guard remaining in the country until 1925. When the last U.S. Marine was withdrawn from Nicaragua in that year, U.S. officials insisted on the for-mation of a constabulary. Nicaragua then entered another period of civil war

between the Liberal and Conservative factions and this original Guardia col-
lapsed. The Guardia Nacional was reformed in 1927 as the civil war was ended
by the return of the U.S. Marines and a diplomatic effort led by Henry L.
Stimson. Robert Olds, in the memorandum quoted previously, described
why U.S. troops were needed in Nicaragua:

> Until now Central America has always understood that governments
> that we recognize and support stay in power, while those which we do
> not recognize and support fall. Nicaragua has become a test case. It is
> difficult to see how we can afford to be defeated. (NARA, 1927, mi-
> crofilm 817.00/5854)

As thousands of U.S. Marines occupied Nicaragua, Stimson was able to convince the leaders of the warring factions to accept U.S. peace proposals and
disarm. A central U.S. proposal called for the re-creation of the Guardia, and
the process of re-establishment was almost immediately launched (R. Millett,
1977).

In 1927, one of the Liberal leaders, Augusto C. Sandino, rejected the U.S.
brokered peace and began a guerrilla war that would last for almost six years
(Grossman, 1996; Macaulay, 1985). Sandino was an ardent nationalist. The
name of his army itself emphasized his nationalist aims: the Ejército Defen-
sor de la Soberanía Nacional de Nicaragua (Army in Defense of the National
Sovereignty of Nicaragua, EDSNN). The EDSNN was organized by Sandino
to fight the U.S. Marines and the U.S.-formed Guardia Nacional. By 1932
the United States had decided again to withdraw the last of its forces from
Nicaragua. When the last of the Marines had again departed, Sandino agreed
to peace negotiations, leading in February 1933 to a cease-fire agreement between Sandino's forces and the Nicaraguan government. With this resolution, Sandino was not defeated but was at the height of his military and political strength. The war, however, had exhausted the people and consumed
the resources of Nicaragua, and Sandino had achieved many of his stated
goals (such as the withdrawal of the Marines). Sandino had decided to switch
to the political arena to accomplish his remaining objectives, most importantly the abolition of the Guardia.

Upon the withdrawal of the Marines from Nicaragua in 1933, the command of the Guardia was turned over to Anastasio Somoza García. The new
Jefe Director, militarily inexperienced but politically ambitious, took over the

institution and transformed it into a personal army (R. Millett, 1977; Walter, 1993). Somoza's objective was to seize power in Nicaragua for himself, but first he had to eliminate Sandino. In February 1934, after another negotiating session that ended with a dinner with the Nicaraguan president, Sandino was detained by Guardia members and murdered. Somoza and the Guardia leadership clearly had ordered the assassination. While there is no evidence that the United States was directly involved in the plot, the U.S. likely approved of the action.

Somoza's next step was to fire any Guardia officer not demonstrating complete loyalty to him. Having consolidated power over the Guardia, Somoza overthrew the elected president and took control of Nicaragua, ruling the country for twenty years before being assassinated in 1956. Despite Somoza's assassination, however, the regime continued. Eldest son Luis became the next president, and Anastasio Somoza Debayle (a graduate of the United States Military Academy at West Point) became the new Jefe Director of the Guardia. In 1967 Luis died of a heart attack and Anastasio, whom some Nicaraguans called the Last Marine, once again combined the positions of president and Jefe Director of the Guardia.

During the long Somoza family dictatorship, there was always some opposition to the regime. Anastasio Somoza García was a wily politician who tried to co-opt opponents whenever possible, but even he faced outbreaks of armed resistance, culminating in his assassination. The late 1950s and early 1960s were a period of widespread discontent in Nicaragua. In 1961, inspired both by the Cuban Revolution and the model of Augusto Sandino, the Frente Sandinista de Liberación Nacional (FSLN) was formed. The FSLN would lead a guerrilla movement that finally climaxed with the general insurrection that overthrew Anastasio Somoza Debayle in July 1979 (Black, 1981; Zimmermann, 2000).

Using the Guardia, in the early 1930s Somoza García created a new personalist regime that dominated Nicaraguan political life for the next forty-five years. The only legal armed force, combining both military and police functions, the Guardia Nacional became the dominant political and military force within Nicaragua. While the Somozas, at times, allowed surrogates to be named president, they never relinquished direct control of the Guardia. Throughout its existence, the Guardia Nacional remained an army of occupation, at war against the Nicaraguan people. The repressive tactics learned in the war against Sandino were refined and expanded. Over the years, thousands would be killed, tortured, and imprisoned without trial. The Somoza regime was always based on coercive force, and the Guardia was their instrument of state terror.

In 1981, after the Somoza regime had been overthrown, the Geneva-based International Commission of Jurists issued a report on human rights in Nicaragua that summarized the human rights record of the deposed regime. The report noted:

> The Somoza policies resulted in a persistent and systematic denial of the civil, political, economic and cultural rights of Nicaraguans. . . . These human rights violations were not the result of excesses by the National Guard beyond the government's control. On the contrary, they were part of conscious policies originating at the highest levels of power. (Fragoso and Artucio, 1981, 53)

The repressive nature of the Somoza regime was clear from its origins, even to the United States. For example, in July 1937, just six months after Somoza García had seized control of the government, the U.S. ambassador in Managua sent the following cable to the secretary of state:

> There is now no *open* opposition to the President or open criticism of his acts or policies. This condition is a consequence of factors . . . and above all there is the efficacy of the Guardia Nacional as a threat of repression. (NARA, 1937, microfilm 817.00/8657, 3, 5; emphasis in original)

Despite a lack of democracy and ongoing repression in Nicaragua, the U.S. government continued to support the Somoza regime for nearly five decades. While there was never much direct U.S. investment in the country, in a troubled world Nicaragua was seen as a secure and loyal ally. Time and again the Somozas demonstrated their loyalty and usefulness to the United States. By allowing its territory to be used as a staging area, Nicaragua actively supported the coup that overthrew the Guatemalan president Jacobo Arbenz in 1954 and the Bay of Pigs invasion of Cuba in 1961. In 1965, Guardia Nacional troops accompanied U.S. forces in the occupation of the Dominican Republic. In the 1960s, Nicaragua even offered to send Guardia members to fight alongside U.S. forces in Vietnam.

With the 1976 election of Jimmy Carter to the U.S. presidency, the United States–Nicaragua relationship became strained. The Carter administration emphasized human rights as one focus of U.S. foreign policy, a concern

clearly lacking in Nicaragua. While the new administration tried to push Somoza Debayle toward reforms, it also continued both military and economic
aid. Finally, in 1979, after the anti-Somoza insurrection had begun, Carter
cut off direct U.S. aid to Nicaragua. While such funding was eliminated, however, the U.S. continued to support a $66 million loan granted by the Inter-
national Monetary Fund in May 1979. U.S. intentions at the time were to
convince Somoza to leave Nicaragua but to keep the Somoza system, especially the Guardia Nacional, intact. As thousands were being murdered, the
White House declared that the Guardia was still needed to "preserve order"
in Nicaragua (LaFeber, 1984, 233).

The Guardia and the United States

At the time of the Nicaraguan constabulary's re-establishment in 1927, the
U.S. Marines formed, organized, and commanded the Guardia Nacional de
Nicaragua. The ideology, organizational style, military strategies, and tactics
of the American officers commanding the Guardia reflected those of the U.S.
Marine Corps. The Guardia was, in fact, intended to be almost a mirror image of the Marines. Guardia training, being led by members of the Marines,
tried to establish an esprit de corps for the force that emphasized the Guardia
as a distinct organization. It also separated the Guardia from Nicaraguan
civil society and politics: Guardia members, for example, did not shout "Viva
Nicaragua," which was a Sandinista slogan, but "Viva la Guardia" (Long live
the Guardia).

Unlike its earlier occupations of Haiti and the Dominican Republic, the
United States did not form an occupation government in Nicaragua; instead,
the civilian Nicaraguan government remained in place and officially governed the country. However, Nicaragua's military forces were under the direct control of the United States, and the Marines commanding the Guardia
reported to the U.S. secretary of the navy. The Guardia was, in effect, a hybrid
organization: officially, it was Nicaraguan, but the officer corps was comprised of North Americans who reported to their superiors in Washington
and only incidentally to the Nicaraguan government (Buell, 1930, 333).

From its origins the Guardia saw itself as distinct from Nicaraguan civilian control. In 1930, for example, the Guardia arrested Charles Thomson, the
Latin American secretary of the U.S. pacifist organization Fellowship of Reconciliation, while he was on a fact-finding tour of Nicaragua. When Thomson

complained that the arrest was in violation of the Nicaraguan constitution, a North American Guardia officer was quoted as replying, "In practice, the National Guard is the Constitution of this country" (Buell, 1930, 332). With the withdrawal of the Marines the command of the Guardia was turned over to Anastasio Somoza García, and the continuing tensions between the government and the Guardia were resolved when Somoza seized political power in 1936. However, tensions between the Guardia and Nicaraguan civil society persisted, and the ongoing relationship between the United States and the Guardia would remain complex. While nominally an independent force, for the rest of its existence the Guardia was dependent upon the United States for equipment, training, and ideology.

When the U.S. Marines left the country in 1933, at the height of the Great Depression, there was not much aid of any form offered to Nicaragua. However, with the start of World War II the United States saw the necessity for continued political stability in the region, and U.S. military aid started to flow. Beginning in 1941, the United States promised Nicaragua under the Lend-Lease Act $1.3 million worth of equipment at a reduced cost. After World War II ended, the United States developed a number of new military aid programs, including grants, loans, and the free transfer of surplus military equipment, and Nicaragua continued to be a recipient of substantial U.S. assistance. In total, between 1946 and 1978, Nicaragua received about $350 million in direct U.S. government assistance, including both economic and military aid. While the vast majority of this amount was economic aid, some of this money had military applications.[2] For example, in 1974 the U.S. Agency for International Development gave a $14 million loan to the Nicaraguan Instituto de Bienestar Campesino (Institute of Peasant Welfare). The stated goal of this grant was the promotion of "rural development," but it was in reality to be used to support part of the government's pacification program in an area marked by guerrilla activity (Jonas, 1976, 24).

Over the course of the postwar era, the United States did give the Nicaraguan government millions of dollars in direct military aid. In 1954, Nicaragua was the first Central American country to sign a mutual defense assistance pact with the United States; with this agreement it became eligible for direct assistance through the Military Assistance Program (Johnson, 1985, 79). Between fiscal year 1946 and fiscal year 1971, U.S. military aid to Nicaragua totaled $14.1 million; from 1971 until 1978 this aid increased to nearly $30.6 million.[3] While the annual amount of U.S. military aid might appear insignificant, it comprised a considerable portion of the Nicaraguan defense budget.

As important as weapons and money was continued U.S. training of the Guardia. Beginning immediately after the United States opened a training facility in the Panama Canal Zone in 1947 (the institution that would later become the U.S. Army School of the Americas), the entire class of the Nicaraguan military academy would spend their senior year there, a practice that continued until 1979 (R. Millett, 1977, 200). Beyond the cadets, many Guardia officers and enlisted were sent to the School of the Americas (SOA) for more specialized training. Between 1947 and 1979, 4,318 Nicaraguans attended the SOA, more than from any other country.[4]

The importance of SOA training cannot be underestimated. Father Fernando Cardenal, SJ, in 1976 testimony to the Subcommittee on International Organizations of the U.S. House of Representatives' Committee on International Relations, accused twenty-six specific Guardia officers of human rights violations. All of the accused had received training from the United States, twenty-five at the School of the Americas (U.S. Congress, 1976b, 30–31, 231–34). In August 1978, the Guardia announced a reorganization of its general command. Of those officers named by Father Cardenal, twelve were in top command positions. For example, Colonel Gonzalo Evertsz had been the Guardia commander in Rio Blanco, the area where most of the human rights violations were occurring in 1976. Evertsz himself had been denounced as participating in these violations. By 1978 he was promoted to major general. Evertsz had taken seven classes at the SOA and had attended both military intelligence orientation and police executive training classes in the United States.

Listed in this 1978 reorganization were all the command positions, including the members of the general staff, and the military commanders of each province, the air corps, hospital corps, immigration, engineers, police, and traffic. Ninety-one officers were named; of these, seventy-nine were SOA graduates. Of the seventeen province commanders, sixteen had graduated from the School of the Americas. Moreover, each of the graduates had attended several different courses. For example, the commander of Estelí province, Gonzalo Martínez, had attended eight different courses. The first was in 1951 and the last, the command and general staff class, was in 1977. He took cadet courses and then returned as a lieutenant, captain, lieutenant colonel, and finally colonel. Those who did not attend the SOA included Anastasio Somoza Portocarrero (son of Somoza Debayle), who trained in the

United States at the U.S. Army Command and General Staff College at Fort Leavenworth, Kansas, and air force and medical officers, who probably attended other programs.[5]

While the SOA was the best-known facility, the United States had many other training programs available to Nicaraguan soldiers. Between 1943 and 1972, 592 Nicaraguans attended the Inter-American Air Forces Academy (IAAFA; like the School of the Americas, located at the time in the Panama Canal Zone).[6] According to a 1976 U.S. congressional report, 164 separate programs existed within the United States for training foreign military personnel (U.S. Congress, 1976a). Between 1950 and 1972, 693 Nicaraguans were trained at U.S.-based facilities. Among the programs they attended were the U.S. Army Infantry and Ranger School, the Command and General Staff College, and the International Police Academy (U.S. Congress, 1976a, 222–25). Of the twenty-six officers accused of human rights violations by Father Cardenal, twelve had attended programs in the United States, but the United States also had military training programs based in Nicaragua. Between 1950 and 1975 over 4,000 Guardia were trained by U.S. military personnel within the country (Black, 1981, 48). The United States maintained in Nicaragua a permanent military advisor group, which was based at the Guardia's headquarters, as well as a small number of military attachés at the U.S. embassy. The number of advisors varied somewhat from 23 in the early 1960s to 17 in 1976 (Johnson, 1985, 111).

Other U.S. advisors, operating as part of what were called mobile training teams, were rotated in and out of Nicaragua. By the 1960s there were regular training programs conducted on the ground by U.S. Army Special Forces. According to one former Green Beret, his team of twelve had three separate training assignments within Nicaragua from mid-1967 until early 1968. The object of these missions, which together lasted for more than six months, was the "training of the Guardia Nacional in counter insurgency tactics." He also suggested that the programs continued until the late 1970s and that "the training and support we provided seemed to work well."[7] In a report written in 1967 by the U.S. defense attaché to Nicaragua, one of the reasons for this success was described as Somoza's "orders to GN [Guardia Nacional] commanders to capture and eliminate without publicity anyone suspected of insurgency or terrorism" (Johnson, 1985, 117).

Looking at the numbers of soldiers involved in these programs it is important to note that for most of its history the size of the Guardia was never more than several thousand, only growing to more than 7,000 in the late

1970s.[8] Thus, almost every officer and soldier of the Guardia received some direct training from U.S. sources. This training went beyond the mere use of weapons and tactics. While the Guardia was committed to protecting the Somoza regime and maintaining political stability, U.S. training also included a more formal ideology: anticommunism. Particularly after the Cuban Revolution, U.S. policymakers saw Latin America as an arena of Cold War confrontations. The United States increased its military aid and training programs with an increase in the focus on anticommunism. In the early 1960s, the School of the Americas, as described in an article in *Adelante*, the institution's official magazine, reorganized its courses:

> The traditional courses were organized into two departments—Tactics and Logistics; but a third one, the Internal Security Department, was added in 1961. This department offered courses in counterinsurgency, military police and military intelligence. . . . This signified a shift to the hemispheric acknowledgement of Latin America as a regional Cold War player and recognition of a genuine threat—Fidel Castro's revolutionary exportation machine. (Ramsey, 1996)

The SOA's wide range of courses met the needs both of the United States and of the Latin American militaries training there. Courses ranged from radio repair, auto mechanics, and cooking to counterinsurgency, jungle warfare, urban warfare, and military intelligence interrogation. By the 1960s most of the courses, whatever their focus, had some class time devoted to discussing the threat of communism. For example, according to the 1969 catalog, the course for "basic medical technician" had a section on "intelligence and security" which included discussion of the "nature of the Communist world threat" and "countering the insurgency threat" (Wolpin, 1972, 78). Three Nicaraguans attended that course in 1969.

It is significant that U.S. training was not intended to prepare the Guardia to defend Nicaragua from foreign attacks. Instead, the Guardia was taught to defend Nicaragua from internal threats. Thus, while the formal ideology was anticommunism, in reality this meant resistance to any challenges to the Somoza regime. As one expert noted, the U.S. training effort

> to politically indoctrinate Central American . . . soldiers about the "evils" of communism has probably helped increase their fear of political

groups that advocate reform. . . . The . . . training . . . also seems to have augmented the tendency of the Central American military officers to justify the use of military repression under the pretext of retarding communism. (U.S. Congress, 1976c, 127)

Over time, anticommunism became the doctrine to rationalize any and every act. Colonel Armando Parajón was one of the highest-ranking Guardia officers captured after the overthrow of the Somoza regime. He had been a member of the Guardia for almost twenty years and had attended seven classes at the s o a. In an interview after his capture, he acknowledged the importance of U.S. aid and training. Colonel Parajón stated he was a professional soldier and an "anticommunist." Communism, he said, was "destruction, death . . . misery, hunger . . . nothing more." Colonel Parajón was tried for various crimes including torture and murder. In just one accusation, witnesses claimed that Parajón personally took a bayonet and castrated and then killed one victim (Reiman and Rivas Sanchez, 1988, 163, 166–67, 184–85).

Guardia Terror in the War against Sandino

Under the command of U.S. Marines, in the late 1920s and early 1930s the Guardia participated in counterinsurgency activities against the guerrilla forces of Augusto Sandino. While Sandino unquestionably organized a nationalist resistance force, U.S. policymakers defined Sandino and his soldiers as bandits (Grossman, 1996). This decision helped define the military tactics that were to be used. Since the United States was not fighting a legitimate military foe, it was argued, the rules of war (such as they were) did not apply. The Marines and Guardia saw little distinction between the Sandinistas and the civilian population; not only combatants but also civilians were targeted. As Marine General Dion Williams noted, "a large portion of the inhabitants of the mountain regions of the north were *potential* bandits" (Williams, 1930, 21; emphasis added). Thus, almost the entire civilian population was considered a justifiable target. Tens of thousands would be affected by this use of state terror.

Indeed, murder was a powerful tool and executions did take place. Some 130 executions and civilian murders can be documented from Marine and Guardia archives (Grossman, 1996, 309). The documents show that these incidents continued and grew through the six years of Sandino's resistance

(1927–1933). These were not combat deaths; indeed, patrols opened fire on civilian houses with casualties including men, women, and children. In one example, a patrol reported seeing people around a "suspicious" house. The patrol opened fire with heavy automatic weapons (there was no return fire). Two men of about fifty years old were captured and "a woman apparently sixty or seventy years of age was found dead." The report continued, "It is quite possible these people were not bandits, though very probable that they were aiding and abetting them." The commander of the patrol noted in his summary that the shooting was "quite justified" (NARA, 1928, R G 127, E 204, Box 3, Folder: 56.0, 20 June).[9] Marine officers openly discussed the need for executions in their reports and letters. One Captain L. B. Reagan wrote, "I think a few executions in the case of proven bandits will do a world of good" (NARA, 1928, R G 127, E 206, Box 3, Folder: Northern Area).

All the evidence demonstrates that the Marines and Guardia shot first, many times fairly indiscriminately. This appears to have been the unofficial policy. While there were no written orders, the Marines' officers did discuss it among themselves. In a personal letter, Major Harold Utley wrote to Captain Edson to give him this praise and advice: "You are making history. . . . Shoot 'em first and then stumble if you must" (United States Marine Corps Historical Center, 1928, letter found in the personal papers of Harold Utley, Box 3, Folder August 1928–May 29, 14 August). In many areas every man was considered a potential bandit, every house a bandit camp, and hence all tactics, and all casualties, were justified. There are documented cases of the Guardia decapitating Sandinistas. The most famous involved a picture of Guardia Lieutenant O. E. Pennington posing with the severed head of one Silvino Herrera. Herrera was a local Sandinista leader who was killed in combat in June 1930. According to Macaulay, "Pennington admitted that the photograph was genuine but denied personally beheading the guerrilla" (Macaulay, 1985, 229).

Other reports suggest that torture or excessive force was used. In February 1931, one Francisco Pérez (who was unarmed) was shot and wounded by a Guardia patrol. The report noted that Pérez "refused to divulge name of jefe nor could we get more information from him. He was left where he fell, seriously wounded, jaw broken, right arm broken also shot through back" (NARA, 1932, R G 127, E 202, Folder: 53.0). The report does not say how his jaw and arm were broken; one can only speculate. But not all of the uses of excessive force were described in the official reports. Nicaraguan survivors of the war give many other examples. A number of the people interviewed mentioned beatings. They also described being kicked or "stomped." One described the process: "If they [the Marines or Guardia] grabbed someone alive . . . they tortured him, they kicked him."[10] Several also stated that the Guardia committed rapes. For example, another said a Marine grabbed two young women, "'one for me,' he said [the Marine], 'the other for the sergeant.' . . . They raped them. Then after they were raped, he grabbed them and bang! bang! He killed them as well" (Instituto de Estudio de Sandinismo, 1980s, 055–1–2, 11).

From the beginning of the war in 1927 until the end in 1933, the Marines and Guardia also carried out a "semi-scorched-earth" policy. Houses, food, animals, and whatever other types of supplies that might be used by the "bandits" were to be destroyed. The commander of the Marines in northern Nicaragua, Colonel R. H. Dunlap stated, "When bandits are found in a house, make sure it is their house before destroying it" (NARA, 1928, R G 127, E 220, 23 May). In another memo he stated, "I therefore recommend that the houses of positively identified Guardia Civica [Sandino's militia], as well as bandit couriers [sic] and agents be burned. Of course, every precaution must be taken to insure that no innocent person is made to suffer" (NARA, 1928, 1928, R G 127, E 206, Box 2, Folder: Bandit Leaders and Descriptions, Memorandum, 20 December).

While these instructions might appear to promote limited destruction, their effects were just the opposite. Since the Marines and Guardia assumed that the entire population of the region supported Sandino, everyone was the enemy. Almost every house that was burned down was listed as a house of a "known bandit." One Guardia report stated that twelve "bandit" houses had been burned, and then added, "Not all houses were burnt on the account of my shortage of matches" (NARA, 1932, R G 127, E 202, Folder: Patrol Reports, 9 January). The Guardia adopted the concept of (to use a more modern term) "collective guilt" and, therefore, "collective punishment." There were no trials or hearings before the destruction of these houses. Once identified as a "bandit," and no matter how this identification was made, you were one, and hence were guilty. And the destruction of the civilian structures came from the air as well as the ground. For example, in only four months (February to May 1928) there were thirty-seven documented unprovoked air attacks against civilian targets (Grossman, 1996, 304). Marine airplanes attacked anything that looked "suspicious." What made something "suspicious"? One report noted:

The area surrounding Remongón is very suspicious. Every indication of inhabitants in the area, such as smoke from the houses, washing out to dry and extensively cultivated cornfields, yet no people were observed in the area. (NARA, 1928, R G 127, E 220, Box 2, Folder: 816 [5], Air Service Reports, 21 November)

The Marines would bomb or machine-gun anything they felt was suspicious, but they considered an area to be suspicious if they could not see the people—who were obviously hiding, since the planes attacked anything suspicious, including daily activities such as the washing of laundry. Of course, all Nicaraguans were also "potential" bandits, and therefore their actions were all "suspicious."

The air service reports describe the bombings and attacks but not the effects on the civilian population, however on occasion ground patrols reported on the aftermath of the air attacks. One patrol visited a house that had been bombed. There they

> found that three persons had been wounded by the bomb fragments. . . . The wounded in this shack were Lorenzo Mendoza, his wife and a small child. . . . The old man was slightly scratched on the back. The old woman had a couple of small chunks of flesh torn from her left leg near the knee. The child, which in my opinion was the worse wounded of the three, had a piece of shrapnel in her right arm. (NARA, 1931, R G 127, E 202, Folder: 57.0, Patrol Reports, 14 December)

A policy that affected many more people than the executions was founded on mass arrests and relocations. Many people were arrested simply on "suspicion" of supporting or aiding the "bandits." The Marines, and then the Guardia, also tried a policy of "concentration," where whole areas were supposed to be cleared of civilians, forcibly if necessary, and the areas turned into what were later called "free fire zones." Thousands of Nicaraguans were arrested or forcibly moved by the Marines and Guardia. At times there was confusion among the Marine officers over the extent of their powers. As the detentions were taking place, one wrote a request to his superior officer asking for clarification on the arrest policy. The response from his superiors: "It has *never* been necessary to obtain the authority of the Nicaraguan Government to arrest & detain any bandit or agent or suspicioned of being such. Arrest them on suspicion & hold them" (NARA, 1929, R G 127, E 206, Folder Misc. 29, 19 April memo; emphasis in original). Thus, a large number of people were arrested on "suspicion," a vague term broad enough that anyone could be arrested. Many were not tried and were imprisoned for long periods. One report dated 19 August 1929, for example, listed thirty-seven prisoners being held in the northern city of Ocotal. Four of the prisoners had been held since September 1928 and five from October 1928. There is no indication that trials were held for any of these prisoners (NARA, 1929, R G 127, E 200, Box 1, Folder A, 19 August memo).

In addition to individual arrests, the Marines and Guardia did, at times, try a mass round-up or concentration policy. In one example, in June 1929, about 1,500 people were forcibly relocated from surrounding areas into the town of Yali (the 1920 census gave a figure of 3,360 as the total rural population for the municipality of Yali). Despite the distribution of food, observers estimated that some 200 people died of starvation and exposure during the Yali concentration (Buell, 1930, 338; Macaulay, 1985, 143).

The preceding offers only a short summary of some of the terror that confronted the civilian population of northern Nicaragua during the war years of the late 1920s and early 1930s. There is no clear accounting of the number of Nicaraguans who were killed, tortured, arrested, or relocated before the 1933 cease-fire was signed. After the war was over, Sandino noted that "the number of peasants killed by the marines or Guardia, on the land, and by air, no one knows nor can it be calculated" (Román, 1983, 131). Despite the tidal wave of death and destruction precipitated by the Guardia, Sandino was not defeated at the war's end, and his support, both military and political, was as great as ever. However, while Sandino was not defeated, neither was the Guardia. The war ended as a military stalemate. As the Marines left Nicaragua in 1933, command of the Guardia was turned over to Anastasio Somoza García. In 1934, Somoza had Sandino assassinated, and by 1936 he had seized control of the government. Somoza, and the Guardia, were now ruling Nicaragua.

Guardia Terror: The Continuing War against the Nicaraguan People

From its beginnings, the new regime was based on coercion and corruption. As the U.S. embassy noted in a report dated December 2, 1939:

> The government of the day, which is a purely military dictatorship, is held in power only by command of the Guardia. The members of the Guardia feel themselves apart from the civilian populace. . . . The

unpleasant picture painted above is far from complete. It represents a Government ridden from top to bottom with graft. (NARA, 1939, microfilm 817.00/8736)

For years most Guardia members concerned themselves with graft, and corruption became institutionalized. Besides being the military, the Guardia were also the police, customs, and immigration officials. As one observer remarked, "each rank carried with it a guaranteed fringe income, with the lowest . . . making a few córdobas from on-the-spot fines and senior officers growing fabulously rich" (Black, 1981, 51). The International Commission of Jurists noted that "the National Guard were paid very low salaries, but were all assured extra income from payments by those engaged in drug traffic, smuggling, gambling, alcohol and prostitution" (Fragoso and Artucio, 1981, 19). By the 1970s, top Guardia positions could bring in $20,000 per month from corruption.

Beyond preying on the Nicaraguan population, the Guardia also had their own stores, schools, and hospitals. They were privileged members of society: in their minds, the new elite. For many Nicaraguans, especially the poor, membership in the Guardia was seen as the only means of social mobility. The Guardia became almost a separate caste within Nicaraguan society, and these privileges flowed as long as the Somozas stayed in power. As a result, loyalty to the Somozas became paramount and therefore no effective dissension could be tolerated. Opposition that could not be bought off or marginalized had to be silenced. After the departure of the U.S. Marines in 1933, Nicaragua remained an occupied country, but now the occupying force was its own army. The tactics of repression that the Guardia learned from the Marines during the war against Sandino would be expanded and refined.

While there were always opponents to the Somozas, opposition expanded after the 1956 assassination of Somoza García and the success of the Cuban Revolution. In 1961 the FSLN began its low-level guerrilla war. Many sectors of the Nicaraguan population, including business organizations, political parties, trade unions, and religious groups, also moved into open opposition. By the late 1970s, the Somoza regime and its Guardia Nacional were despised by the vast majority of the Nicaraguan people. In 1978 an insurrection, including fighting in the streets of Nicaragua's cities, was initiated to overthrow the Somoza regime.

As opposition increased, so did repression. Execution, torture, and arbitrary arrests became commonplace, almost routine. While the full scope of these atrocities has never been documented, human rights organizations did issue a number of reports. For example, the Inter-American Commission on Human Rights (I C H R) of the Organization of American States (O A S) accused the Nicaraguan government of being "responsible for serious attempts against the right to life," stating that "many persons were executed in a summary and collective fashion." Furthermore, government forces were "also responsible for the death and serious abuse, arbitrary detention and other violations of human rights of peasant groups." The list of charges continued, including violations of the freedoms of expression, religion, assembly, and so forth (Inter-American Commission on Human Rights [herafter: I C H R], 1978, 77–78).

During the 1970s, the Guardia executed an undetermined number of Nicaraguans. Doris Tijerino, an active Sandinista, described the almost casual manner of these murders. As she was being arrested in the capital city of Managua, she noted that the Guardia also took a boy, an innocent bystander, from a neighboring house. "Then they grabbed that boy and started pistol-whipping him. The boy stumbled and, without even knowing who he was, they began shooting and filled him full of bullets" (Randall, 1978, 96).

Many times individuals were "disappeared," grabbed by the Guardia and never seen again. Disappearances and executions were especially common in rural areas. Sources from the Roman Catholic Church in Nicaragua listed over two-hundred peasants who disappeared in only one province between May 1974 and January 1977. Another church document listed forty-four peasants (twenty-nine children, eleven adult women, and four adult men) who were executed by only one Guardia patrol in January 1977. A third document, signed by two Franciscan fathers, described another patrol that killed more than twenty-five peasants. This last document was a letter to the Guardia's commander in the northern zone. In this letter the priests plead with the Guardia commander that the "wave of terror and fear" needs to be stopped, and they itemize the executions:

> On 9 December [1976], the . . . patrol, without warning, destroyed the home of Gloria Chavarría . . . and killed her, her three grown-up daughters and two children. All these people were completely defenseless. (Amnesty International, 1977)

When in September 1978 the urban insurrections started, the response of the Somoza regime was to unleash the full force of the Guardia against the urban centers. Thousands were killed over the following months. Following the failure of the first insurrection in September, the Guardia launched what they termed Operation Mop Up, in an attempt to eliminate all opponents. The I C H R sent a delegation to Nicaragua in October 1978 to investigate charges of widespread human rights abuses. The delegation reported:

> All the proof gathered by the Commission has led to the conclusion that the Nicaraguan National Guard's actions during the phase called "Operation Mop-up" were marked by complete disregard for human life, that they shot numerous people, in some cases children, in their own homes or in front of the same and in the presence of parents and siblings. (I C H R, 1978, 43)

The commission then published some of the testimonies that its delegates had received. One survivor testified that the Guardia entered her house:

> They took the first three young men to a wall on the other side of the street, with their hands over their heads, and they killed them right then and there. Then they made three other young men leave, among them my 18-year-old son, and when they were coming out of the door with their hands over their heads, the soldiers that were in the street machine-gunned them about their faces and chests. (I C H R, 1978, 49)

Death also came from the air, as Somoza ordered his air force to bomb the cities. The I C H R (1978, 33) noted that it was

> totally convinced that the Nicaraguan National Guard was not only using its firepower indiscriminately causing a great number of casualties and tremendous suffering to the civilian population, but that it also ordered the people to remain inside their houses before the bombing, without even allowing them to evacuate, thus violating a basic humanitarian norm.

One example should suffice in describing this aerial terror against the defenseless civilian population. One woman told the commission's delegates:

> A plane flew very low, it seemed as if it was coming straight at us, and fired some rockets that hit my daughter's shoulder and my husband who was carrying her. Everywhere I looked I could see the heart and

intestines of my child; she was in pieces, destroyed. My husband, who had already lost his arms, took about thirty steps, with blood spouting everywhere, until he fell dead. He had a wound in the chest; he had a part of a still-smoking rocket stuck in his leg. The left leg was bare to the bone. (ICHR, 1978, 33)

The Nicaraguan Red Cross estimated the death toll in September 1978 as 5,000, with another 10,000 wounded, while a research center in Costa Rica raised the estimates to 7,000 to 10,000 dead and 20,000 wounded. The greatest death toll was in the town of Estelí, where estimates of civilian deaths ranged from 500 to 2,500 out of a population of approximately 30,000 (Wheaton and Dilling, 1980, 42; ICHR, 1978, 8; Centro Victor Sanabria, n.d.). The Guardia commander in Estelí at the time was Colonel Gonzalo Martínez, whose attendance at various SOA classes is discussed above.

Human rights abuses did not end with murder. Many people were detained and then tortured. Various human rights organizations document in detail the different tortures to which Nicaraguans were subjected, which ranged from the physical to the psychological. To heighten their fear and disorientation, hoods were placed over the prisoners' heads during torture sessions. The 1981 International Commission of Jurists' report on the Somoza regime listed some of its most common torture techniques:

Torture was regularly used in the interrogation of political prisoners. Common practices included blows, hanging from the wrists, electric shocks, immersion of the head in water, hooding or blindfolding, exhausting physical exercises, keeping naked detainees in air-conditioned rooms at very low temperatures, and food and drink deprivation. . . . In many cases, prisoners died as a result of torture. The nails and eyes of some victims were pulled out while others had their tongues cut off. (Fragoso and Artucio, 1981, 24)

Doris Tijerino described in detail how she was tortured once she was arrested. The abuses began immediately. She was hooded, stripped and beaten. Then:

they took a bench, a seat without a back, and put me on it totally naked, made me stand on tiptoe leaning a little forward with knees bent as if to sit down. . . . They told me to feel with my hands because underneath me was a bayonet. . . . And when I'd fall I'd be skewered on it. . . . Later they told me they were going to give me electric shocks. . . . They applied [them] . . . to my tongue, my nipples and rectum. (Randall, 1978, 100)

She was tortured for thirteen days and would remain in jail for two years.

The Guardia also routinely raped women prisoners. One peasant woman, Amada Pineda, described how she was raped and tortured. For three days Guardia members raped her: "My legs were black and blue, my thighs, my arms. I had bruises all over me." She was raped seventeen times. Then the Guardia threatened to throw her from a helicopter, and finally, "they took the other prisoners and tortured them in front of me. They beat them. They burned them. They half-buried them in ant hills" (Randall, 1981, 80, 87–88). These tortures were not random acts but encouraged by the highest ranks. For example:

In September 1978, . . . Anastasio Somoza Portocarrero . . . explained to his boys how they should proceed with captured Sandinista prisoners. He chose four prisoners at random, and slowly slid his knife between the fingers and toes of the four victims. He then sprinkled them with gasoline and set them on fire, alive, saying: "this is what should be done with these sons of bitches." (Fragoso and Artucio, 1981, 19)

Son of the dictator Somoza Debayle, Somoza Portocarrero established the Escuela de Entrenamiento Básico de Infantería (Basic Infantry Training School, EEBI) after he returned from training at Fort Leavenworth, Kansas. Somoza Portocarrero's "boys" were the soldiers of the EEBI. While it started as a training program, the EEBI became the elite Guardia unit and was seen by many as the power base for the next generation of Somozas. It was their training chant, quoted at the opening of this chapter, that proudly announced they were tigers who drank the blood of the people.

Conclusions

The Somoza family dictatorship remained in power until the summer of 1979. After a widespread insurrection, Anastasio Somoza Debayle fled Nicaragua on July 17, 1979. The final triumph over Somoza had dearly cost the Nicaraguan people: "40,000 dead—1.5 percent of the population, some 100,000 wounded, 40,000 children orphaned, 200,000 families left homeless, and 750,000 dependent on food assistance" (Wheaton and Dilling, 1980, 76). The OAS estimated that 35,000 had been killed in the final ten months of the Somoza regime, most of them in indiscriminate bombings of the cities by the Guardia (ICHR, 1981, 155).

By 1979 the repressive nature of the Somoza regime was clear to the world. For the first time in its history, the OAS passed a resolution denouncing an incumbent government based on its human rights violations and demanding the "immediate and definitive replacement of the Somoza regime." The resolution noted:

> The people of Nicaragua are suffering the horrors of a fierce armed conflict that is causing grave hardships and loss of life. . . . The inhumane conduct of the dictatorial regime governing the country . . . is the fundamental cause of the dramatic situation faced by the Nicaraguan people. (ICHR, 1981, 2–3)

A new "government of national reconstruction," led by the FSLN, was created in July 1979. Among its first acts was the abolition of the Guardia Nacional. While many of the Guardia leaders escaped Nicaragua, nearly 6,500 former Guardia members and collaborators were captured and then tried for their human rights violations. About 3,500 were convicted for a range of crimes ranging from rape and torture to murder. The maximum sentence was thirty years imprisonment, since the new government had abolished the death penalty (ICHR, 1981, 168).

This fifty-year history raises questions about U.S. policies. The Guardia Nacional was a creation of the United States, and even after the U.S. Marines were withdrawn in 1933, the culture of indifference toward the human rights of the civilian population that they initiated would continue unabated. Regular U.S. aid made it possible for the Somozas and the Guardia to function. While turning a blind eye and continuing aid, for nearly fifty years the U.S. government acquiesced in the ongoing repression of the Nicaraguan people. Even when the Carter administration finally raised the question of human rights violations, direct aid was not ended until the regime's downfall was all but certain. By 1979, at the moment when Somoza's defeat became obvious, the United States still tried to perpetuate the Guardia Nacional as the best institution to "preserve order."

After 1979, the relationship between the United States and the new Nicaraguan government quickly soured. By 1980, an armed counterrevolutionary movement (generally known as the Contras) had begun to be organized. Of the eight individuals identified by the Central Intelligence Agency as the military leaders of the first contra organization, Legión 15 de Septiembre (15th of September Legion), seven were graduates of the School of the Americas (Central Intelligence Agency, 1998). These seven attended a total of thirty-four classes and two were honor students. By 1981, under President Ronald Reagan, U.S. aid began to flow to this reconstructed Guardia, and the war for Nicaragua was renewed. The legacy of terror and human rights violations that had started in 1927 would continue.

NOTES

1. This chant was part of the training at the Escuela de Entrenamiento Básico de Infantería (Black, 1981, 54–55).

2. Richard Millet, in testimony to the U.S. Congress, estimated a total of U.S. aid to Nicaragua of more than $296 million between 1946 and 1976 (U.S. Congress, 1978, 5). In addition, in 1977 and 1978 Nicaragua received about $40 million in aid. These numbers reflect direct U.S. government aid and do not include indirect aid, such as loans from the Export-Import Bank of the United States, Inter-American Development Bank, World Bank, International Monetary Fund, and so forth. Between 1970 and 1978 Nicaragua received another $500 million from these sources (Bendaña, 1978, 40).

3. The first numbers are from the statement submitted by Miles D. Wolpin to the House of Representatives (U.S. Congress, 1976d, 94, footnote 2). The second figure is from Bendaña (1978, 40). Since these figures are from two separate sources, I am not sure if they compare all of the same aid programs. The report by Bendaña (1994) includes the dollar amount of all military aid programs including grants, loans, as well as the cost of training programs. The Carter administration drastically cut some of the military aid programs. For example, in 1977 only $15,000 in direct grants was given (as compared to $536,000 in 1974). However, military sales on credit in that year equaled $2.5 million (as compared to zero in 1974). By 1979 direct military aid was finally ended.

4. This figure comes from SOA documents, which are posted on the web page of the human rights organization School of the Americas Watch (www.soaw.org).

Among these documents is a country-by-country listing of each student and the classes they attended; all the discussions of s o a attendance are based on these documents. From 1946 through 1973, students from twenty Latin American countries attended the s o a. Nicaragua, a country with one of the smallest populations in the region, had the largest number of students, comprising 14 percent of the total. This number is from documents supplied to the U.S. Senate by the Department of Defense in 1973. Ken LaPlante, Senior Advisor and Analyst for Western Hemisphere Affairs, Core Processes, Inc., provided copies supporting DAMO-SSR, the Army G-3. LaPlante had been an instructor at the s o a and is now one of its archivists. The School of the Americas was formally closed in January 2001 and replaced with a new school, the Western Hemisphere Institute for Security Cooperation.

5. Cuartel General de la Guardia Nacional de Nicaragua, Comunicado No. 36, 11 August 1978. The names of all the students at the s o a, and the classes they attended, are available from the School of the Americas Watch web page. Thanks to Richard Millett for sharing this document with me.

6. From 1943 through 1972, 10,899 students from twenty Latin American countries attended the i a a f a (information drawn from documents supplied by Ken LaPlante).

7. The source for this information, Bob Wirt, is a former member of the Eighth Special Forces Group, First Special Forces, Fort Gulick, Panama (personal communication, May 22, 2002).

8. Knut Walters (1993, 214) has charted the Guardia's size from 1946 (with 3,635 members) to 1956 (4,391 members). The U.S. Arms Control and Disarmament Agency (1975, 1982) lists the size as remaining steady at 6,000 members from 1965 until 1977. By 1978 the Guardia had grown to over 7,000 (Rudolph, 1982, 245). These figures do not distinguish between the Guardia units involved in combat activities and those that had nonmilitary responsibilities, nor do these numbers include paramilitary units. By 1978 there were about 4,000 paramilitaries (Rudolph, 1982, 245). Johnson (1985, 60) suggests that, by 1979, total Guardia strength was 14,000, but many of these recruits were "teenage conscripts who had received a two-week crash course" to prepare them for combat.

9. The official records of the Guardia Nacional during the war against Sandino were taken by the Marines and deposited in the United States. These consist of tens of thousands of pages, including contact and patrol reports, intelligence reports, internal memorandums, and so on. This collection is now part of the n a r a, Records of the United States Marine Corps, Record Group 127.

10. Aurelio Osabas Izaguirre, Instituto de Estudio de Sandinismo, interview number 056. The Instituto de Estudio de Sandinismo (i e s) conducted more than one hundred interviews in the early 1980s. In 1990 the i e s changed its name to the Instituto de Historia de Nicaragua; as the research was conducted under the old name, however, I continue to refer to it in that way.

BIBLIOGRAPHY

Amnesty International. 1977. *The Republic of Nicaragua*. London: Amnesty International Publications.

Bendaña, Alejandro. 1994. *La Mística de Sandino*. Managua: Centro de Estudios Internacionales.

————. 1978. "Crisis in Nicaragua." *NACLA Report on the Americas* 12, 6 (Nov. –Dec.): 2–42.

Black, George. 1981. *Triumph of the People: The Sandinista Revolution in Nicaragua*. London: Zed Press.

Buell, Raymond L. 1930. "Reconstruction in Nicaragua." *Foreign Policy Association Information Service* 6, 18 (12 November): 332–38.

Central Intelligence Agency. 1998. *Allegations of Connections between CIA and the Contras in Cocaine Trafficking to the United States* [online]. Report 96–0143–IG. Washington, DC: Central Intelligence Agency [cited 10 January 2003]. Available from www.odci.gov/cia/publications/cocaine/index.html.

Centro Victor Sanabria (Research and Documentation Area). n.d. "Presentation of the Third Report on Human Right in Nicaragua, Nicaraguan Septembre [sic]: '10 or 20 Guernicas.'" San Jose: Centro Victor Sanabria Research and Documentation Area.

Fragoso, Heleno Claudio, and Alejandro Artucio. 1981. *Human Rights in Nicaragua: Yesterday and Today*. Geneva: International Commission of Jurists.

Grossman, Richard. 1996. "'Hermanos en la Patria'," Nationalism, Honor and Rebellion: Augusto Sandino and the Army in Defense of the National Sovereignty of Nicaragua, 1927–1934." Unpublished Ph.D. diss., University of Chicago.

Instituto de Estudio de Sandinismo. 1980s. *Interviews*. 055-1-2, 11.

Inter-American Commission on Human Rights (I C H R). 1978. *Report on the Situation of Human Rights in the Republic of Nicaragua: Findings of the "On-site" Observation in the Republic of Nicaragua, October 3–12, 1978*. Washington, DC: Organization of American States.

————. 1981. *Report on the Situation of Human Rights in the Republic of Nicaragua*. Washington, DC: Organization of American States.

Johnson, Major Paul J. U.S. Army. 1985. "Military Assistance and the Development of Officer Professionalism: Lessons from Nicaragua, 1961–1979." Unpublished Master's Thesis, U.S. Army Command and General Staff College.

Jonas, Susanne. 1976. "Nicaragua." *NACLA Report on the Americas*. 10, 2 (February): 2–40.

LaFeber, Walter. 1984. *Inevitable Revolutions: The United States in Central America.* New York: W. W. Norton.

Macaulay, Neill. 1985. *The Sandino Affair.* Durham: Duke University Press.

Millett, Alan R. 1980. *Semper Fidelis: The History of the United States Marine Corps.* New York: Macmillan.

Millett, Richard. 1977. *Guardians of the Dynasty.* Maryknoll, NY: Orbis Press.

National Archives and Records Administration (NARA). 1927. Microfilm, U.S. Department of State. Washington, DC: U.S. Department of State.

———. 1928. *Records of the United States Marine Corps, Record Group 127.* Washington, DC: U.S. Department of Defense.

———. 1929. *Records of the United States Marine Corps, Record Group 127.* Washington, DC: U.S. Department of Defense.

———. 1931. *Records of the United States Marine Corps, Record Group 127.* Washington, DC: U.S. Department of Defense.

———. 1932. *Records of the United States Marine Corps, Record Group 127.* Washington, DC: U.S. Department of Defense.

———. 1937. Microfilm, U.S. Department of State. Washington, DC: U.S. Department of State.

———. 1939. Microfilm, U.S. Department of State. Washington, DC: U.S. Department of State.

Ramsey, Russell. 1996. "50 Years of Service to American Liberty" [online]. *Adelante* (fall) [cited 16 January 2004].

Randall, Margaret. 1978. *Doris Tijerino: Inside the Nicaraguan Revolution.* Vancouver: New Star Books.

———. 1981. *Sandino's Daughters: Testimonies of Nicaraguan Women in Struggle.* Vancouver: New Star Books.

Reiman, Elisabeth, and Fernando Rivas Sanchez. 1988. *Los Tigres Vencidos.* Buenos Aires: Ediciones Reunir.

Román, José. 1983. *Maldito Pais.* Managua: Editorial Pez y Serpiente.

Rudolph, James D. 1982. *Nicaragua, a Country Study: Foreign Area Studies, the American University.* Washington, DC: Headquarters, Department of the Army.

United States Marine Corps Historical Center (USMCHO). 1928. Personal Papers: Harold Utley. Washington, DC: United States Marine Corps Historical Center.

U.S. Arms Control and Disarmament Agency. 1975. *World Military Expenditures and Arms Transfers, 1965–1974.* Washington, DC: Department of State, Government Printing Office.

———. 1982. *World Military Expenditures and Arms Transfers, 1970–1979.* Washington, DC: Department of State, Government Printing Office.

U.S. Congress. 1976a. *Human Rights in Nicaragua, Guatemala, and El Salvador: Implications for U.S. Policy.* Hearings before the Subcommittee on International Organizations of the Committee on International Relations, House of Representatives, Ninety-fourth Congress, second session, June 8 and 9. Washington, DC: Government Printing Office.

————. 1976b. *Statement of Fernando Cardenal, Society of Jesus (SJ).* Hearings before the Subcommittee on International Organizations of the Committee on International Relations, House of Representatives. Washington, DC: Government Printing Office.

————. 1976c. *Statement submitted by Don Etchison.* Hearings before the Subcommittee on International Organizations of the Committee on International Relations, House of Representatives. Washington, DC: Government Printing Office.

————. 1976d. *Miles D. Wolpin Statement.* Hearings before the Subcommittee on International Organizations of the Committee on International Relations, House of Representatives. Washington, DC: Government Printing Office.

————. 1978. *Rethinking United States Foreign Policy toward the Developing World: Nicaragua.* Hearings before the Subcommittee on International Developments of the Committee on International Relations, House of Representatives. Washington, DC: Government Printing Office.

Walter, Knut. 1993. *The Regime of Anastasio Somoza, 1936–1956.* Chapel Hill: University of North Carolina Press.

Wheaton, Philip, and Yvonne Dilling. 1980. *Nicaragua: A People's Revolution.* Washington, DC: Ecumenical Program on Central America and the Caribbean (EPICA) Task Force.

Williams, Dion. 1930. "The Nicaragua Situation." *Marine Corps Gazette* 15, 3 (November): 19–22.

Wolpin, Miles D. 1972. *Military Aid and Counterrevolution in the Third World.* Lexington, MA: D.C. Heath & Co.

Zimmermann, Matilde. 2000. *Sandinista: Carlos Fonseca and the Nicaraguan Revolution.* Durham: Duke University Press.

CHAPTER 4

The Culture and Politics of State Terror and Repression in El Salvador

ALDO A. LAURIA-SANTIAGO

Introduction

In an attempt to gain an understanding of the phenomenon, the practice of state terror could be seen simply as a result of the confrontation between powerful state-based actors and their opponents—occupying a realm in which the exercise of power by the state's repressive machinery follows a political logic of elimination and suppression. Torture, massacres, beatings, and rapes, then, would all be but side effects of a regime's efforts to remain in power by obliterating its opposition. The practice of state terror, however, also points to the existence of important ideological and cultural dimensions that come to form part of a country's unique political terrain. These cultural, historically structured aspects of the practice of state terror must be examined as part of the causes, contexts, and effects of the phenomenon of state repression.

In the context of this volume, the principal idea presented in this chapter holds that explanations of state terror that rely on functional or instrumental arguments alone do not suffice to explain the practice of violent repression, torture, and murder by states and their agents. Until recently, it was these categories that characterized most studies of state terror, violence, and torture in El Salvador. That is, discussions of state terror in the Central American context before the 1990s did not look beyond characterizations of a given regime and the functions of its institutions, considering the state's repressive practices for the most part in the limited context of immediate political conjunctures and confrontations.

Although these aspects are necessary elements to recognize in any examination of state violence, they still fail to account for the form that this violence

and repression has taken—its national and local, cultural and historical determinants. This chapter will argue that the literature on repression in El Salvador has overlooked important aspects of how the country's history, culture,
and local class relations affected the formation of its repressive practices during the early 1980s.

This chapter is driven by two motivations. The first is the need to study in
comparative perspective one of Latin America's bloodiest campaigns of terror and state-based repression. Second is the need to have a better understanding on its own terms of the origins of this sort of violence, as part of efforts to recover its hidden aspects.[1] We not only need to study the intended
goals of official repression but also to contextualize what are often treated as
unproblematic, objective, and transparent categories, while making space for
the conceptions and ideological constructs of the agents and victims of state-
based terror. This endeavor suggests a contextualized definition of terror:
state-based repression needs to be interpreted through the definitions, uses,
and goals articulated by the terror victims and agents themselves. This approach, similar to that provided by Taylor and Vanden (1982), avoids the for-
malistic debates of mainstream political science and ascribes greater importance to the local context of the violence.

While most considerations by political scientists of state terror and repression get bogged down in definitional, abstract, and circular considerations—
with case materials used to test a priori and ahistorical propositions—Taylor
and Vanden (1982, 107) propose a contextual approach to the study of state
terror and violence: "Instead of addressing the definitional and perceptual
problems, we observe the case in its entirety and reserve the right to qualify
terrorism on the basis of events." Our challenge is to sketch more clearly than
has been the case in the past the cultural–historical formation of the national
and regional contexts in which state terror occurs.

An emerging literature (initially dominated by political scientists but now
also including anthropologists) has begun to provide systematic case-study,
comparative, and theoretical examinations of state violence and repression
in Latin America. Little in this vein, however, has been published on El
Salvador—mostly because before the early 1990s scholars balked at the risks
of carrying out field research on repression at the same time that many in
El Salvador sought to leave behind the worst aspects of the period of civil war
in the 1980s (Sloan, 1984; Taylor and Vanden, 1982; Petras, 1987; Livingstone, 1984; McClintock, 1985; Millet, 1981).

The massive state repression that was part of the civil wars in El Salvador and Guatemala led political scientists to question some of the traditional assumptions about political violence as being instrumental (in part because it was apparent that increased repression, at least under certain conditions, enhanced the ability of rebels and opposition organizations to both recruit for and legitimize their struggles). More recently, however, there have been discussions of how the intense practice of state terror did undermine the long-term ability of rebel organizations to win support in the cities. Nonetheless, the calculus of terror and its impact does belong among the forces and processes that determined the outcome of the revolutionary civil war during the 1980s.

In addition, the centrality of state terror to these conflicts has encouraged scholars to question some of the rigid and ahistorical categories commonly relied on in their disciplines. Among political scientists, Brocket (1989) has challenged conventional methods of testing repression as a clearly definable "dependent variable." He argues that traditionally the tendency had been to consider government as a neutral force or, in the words of McCamant (1984, 91), "as an antiseptic process where all is clean and fair." Ironically, after decades of authoritarian rule in much of Latin America and extensive discussions among political scientists about regime type and transitions, the very glue of these regimes—fear, repression, and terror—was long left unexamined.

An overview of the literature on the origins and practice of government repression and how it relates to events in El Salvador during the 1970s and 1980s will help us to clarify the problem, while highlighting the more useful aspects of different approaches. The purpose of this review is not to deny the partial validity of these approaches, but to clarify the conceptual space for examining how national and local culture and history might be a necessary part of studying state terror and repression.

The literature that provides the foundation for an in-depth examination of state terror in El Salvador can be grouped into five categories. The first group denounces state terror as a violation of human rights as described in international human rights agreements, wartime treaties, and so forth. This literature is fairly straightforward in its orientation and tends to homogenize and dehistoricize the violence itself; its goal has been to end the violations by means of international pressure and/or suspension of the outside support that is held to be morally, politically, or materially responsible for the actions of the Salvadoran government.

This literature has usually been written quickly after the occurrence of acts of repression, and it rarely assumes a wide, retrospective sweep. The writings included in this group range from systematic reports on an event or a violator to more participatory narratives of events themselves. They are useful sources when one is seeking deep narratives of the practice and consequences of state repression and terror, but they often do not attempt or are not able to provide contextual information concerning events (America's Watch, 1985; Nairn, 1984; Navarro, 1981; DeYoung, 1981; Hochschild, 1983; Petras, 1980; Guerra, 1979).

The most important exceptions to these limitations have been the investigations and reports that resulted from the ending of the civil wars in both Guatemala and El Salvador (Comisión para el Esclarecimiento Histórico, 2000; Comisión de la Verdad, 1993). These materials provide evidence, numbers, narration, and a human dimension to the practice and results of state terror. However, the narrative, testimonial character of the sources used in this literature tends to foment the assumption that the evidence speaks for itself. Its appeal is based on presumably universal and self-evident moral standards.

The second approach examines repression in the context of popular-democratic or revolutionary struggles by various sectors of a population and the local regime's attempts to suppress challenges to its power. Its emphasis is on the conjunctures of the confrontation. Generally functionalist, it attempts to explain violence and repression in terms of the immediate functions of the institutional responses and needs of a threatened regime.

This approach assumes a response mechanism, mediated perhaps by other factors, through which repressive agents weigh the need for repression in relation to popular challenges. The violence unleashed by the regime is then seen to be in direct relation to the intensification of the popular challenge. Much of this literature, produced by the Left, activists, and often the victims of repression themselves, glosses over important local and cultural factors in its need to produce a denunciatory—and mobilizing—effect. It is however understandable, for example, why the social and cultural origins of El Mozote as a community were not considered to be of primary importance, when both the Salvadoran and U.S. governments denied the very occurrence of this massacre (Danner, 1994; Binford, 1996; Comisión de la Verdad, 1993).

The third group of writings on state terror can be loosely termed "instrumentalist." Instrumentalist writings purport to uncover the hidden logic and goals of state repression. They are guided by approaches to state terror, such as Gurr's, that argue state terror, by definition, has to be instrumental or goal oriented. In Petras's formulation, state repression is thoroughly instrumental: its sole intention is to physically eliminate the members of popular organizations challenging the status quo. The purposeful or unintended creation of a culture of fear does not appear as a major component in this type of analysis.[2]

The fourth group of writings emphasizes the institutional capabilities of the state and its agencies and often allows for discussions of the political culture of the state or its components (Dunkerley, 1982; McClintock, 1985). McClintock, who provides the only in-depth history of the country's state-security agencies, ties the modernization of El Salvador's repressive apparatus between the 1950s and 1970s to U.S. aid and support. In his view, security-oriented, anticommunist-minded programs sponsored by the United States since the late 1950s are to be held responsible not only for the technical capabilities of the Salvadoran state at the time the civil war broke out in 1980. They also are seen to have contributed to the rigid ideologies of anticommunism, national security, corporate loyalty, and professional secrecy that formed the philosophical framework for the repression of the civil war period.

In this literature, the role played by neocolonial allies has been crucial to establishing and maintaining repressive capabilities, technologies, and ideologies—practices that in the Salvadoran case enhanced the ability of the military as an institution to retain its influence over politics and society (Williams and Walter, 1997). It is undeniable that the United States (and to a lesser extent other states such as Israel, Argentina, and Guatemala) played a critical role not only in enhancing the military and repressive apparatuses of the Salvadoran state during the late 1970s and early 1980s but also in affecting the course of the civil war and particularly Salvadoran responses to critical junctures in the war.

Finally, the fifth approach to the study of state terror stresses the pervasive influence of larger issues of political economy and government economic policy. Pion-Berlin (1984) argues that one of the main indicators of repression, the increase in the number of victims of extrajudicial killings in the Argentine case he cites, was a direct result of the government's implementation of orthodox, economic-stabilization policies. Hence, he rejects the proposition of a correlation between regime type and the level of repression. For Pion-Berlin, an increase in state repression is not necessarily tied to actual political challenges or regime-specific responses. Rather, it is an outgrowth of cross-national issues in political economy in which preemptive action against losers in the stabilization policy is deemed necessary in order to counter potential opposition to government policies.

Petras reaches similar conclusions when discussing El Salvador. He ties the increase in state terror and repression to the unsuccessful implantation of a "new economic model," obstructed by a strong antigovernmental social movement (Petras, 1987, 315, 317, 331).[3] Mason and Crane (1989) also tie a likely decrease in government repression to the successful implementation of a counterinsurgent agrarian reform during 1980, a relationship, however, that is not clearly supported by the evidence.

All of these approaches help us to understand aspects of the shifting dynamics of political confrontation and how they might produce motivations and contexts for state-based repression. Identifying the structural elements that conditioned the Salvadoran government's massive violence toward segments of the country's population is indeed critical to any discussion of state terror (Gurr, 1986).

In this regard, one thing that makes El Salvador unique in the comparative study of state repression in Latin America is the concurrence within the society of all the structural elements that might be seen to generate a violently repressive state. At their worst, writings produced from these perspectives emphasize conjunctural analyses that consider only momentary shifts in the balance of forces or that simply reproduce narratives by the victims of state terror and repression. They do not, however, tie these insights into an examination of the larger historical production of culture in El Salvador, overlooking the crucial mediating roles of perceptions, local politics, the historical formation of state cultures, class relations, identities, and iconographic continuities that are necessary for the deep, ethnographic study of state violence.

Origins of Repression: Impeding Reform and Constructing a Nation

Of the many structuring moments that have left their mark on El Salvador, the 1932 western uprising and massacres have provided political—and most certainly—iconographic material for the construction of the Salvadoran state and polity.[4] For many, the structural violence of the 1970s and 1980s finds its roots in the earlier period of repression. The demonstrative power of the 1932 massacres originated in an "unnecessary" display of repression: the rebels

were defeated, but their audacity required the minting of an exemplary les-
son that would help to consolidate the newly emergent military regime of
General Maximiliano Hernández Martínez.

The massacres began as and remained an icon of the state's power over
subordinate groups, especially indigenous peasants and farmers.[5] For elites,
middle sectors, and the state, the massacres were a necessary evil to contain
the primitive horde of communists ready to challenge the very institutions
that brought progress to the nation—in their view, bestiality and civilization
were useful rhetorical polarities in the "educational" campaigns and government propaganda that followed the suppression of the revolt and the extensive, but brief, terror that followed.[6] Additionally, although we lack studies
that carefully analyze the persistence of images, language, and political constructs drawn from the 1930s into the 1940–1979 period, it is clear that, at
the very least, the events of 1932 both legitimated and codified in a rigid way
an elite authoritarian discourse, providing a concrete footing to the military's
claim to be the nation's best guarantor of order and progress.

During the 1970s the memory of the 1932 revolt and massacres, and a particular reconstruction of their history, served to legitimate the Left's revolutionary culture.[7] The Left's umbrella organization, the Frente Farabundo
Martí para la Liberación Nacional (F M L N), explicitly drew the connection between the radicalization of the 1970s and the events of 1932 by naming itself
after Farabundo Martí, one of the leftist leaders during the 1932 revolt. A similar, if more rigid, construction applied to the persistence of ideology of war at
any cost within state agencies and a sector of the country's economic oligarchy: the figure of General Hernández Martínez, who is known to have
given his field commanders and civilian militias a free hand in the repression
of 1932, was similarly brought back in the name of one of the death squads of
the late 1970s.

Yet, as a result of a lack of research into the political history of the country
and its cultures of class, the military, and community, no clear, direct line has
been drawn to connect the events of 1932 to the more recent period. In fact,
it is important to recognize in this regard the existence of important discon-
tinuities in the form and ideology of state rule during the 1950s and 1960s
that contrast with the conditions seen in both the earlier and the later periods. For more than four decades, until the mid-1970s, El Salvador did not witness levels of state-sponsored violence that would be reminiscent of 1932 or
that would prefigure the violence of the late 1970s and early 1980s.

In effect, the continuity resides in the minds and ideologies of participants in the repression and not in any institutional lineage. Thus, in the 1970s and 1980s an elite and state-centered view of the 1932 events provided the state an echo chamber, a language, and a confirmed justification for what was perceived as the necessary solution to the problems of social and political mobilization from below. Even as late as 1989, members of the Salvadoran elite spoke in terms of the thousands of lives it would take to end the war and stabilize the country, thereby reviving the idea of "the necessary massacre" even after the butchery of the early 1980s and a decade of war.

The regimes of the 1970s repeatedly hoped that massacres would produce the desired and expected silence, but their attempts contributed instead to the radicalization of significant sectors of the once reformist or inactive opposition. For the early years of the conflict, those expectations were repeatedly disappointed: the increasingly frequent massacres led only to an escalation of the confrontation and the successful creation of rebel recruits.

There is disagreement about exactly when the qualitative escalation of violence and repression took place. It is not difficult to trace the quantitative changes on a chart, but to evaluate qualitative differences that might signal a change in attitude or disposition from the regime is more problematic. Various authors identify different moments as key to the qualitative heightening of the violence. Some point to the massacre that followed the fraudulent elections of 1972, while others point to the confrontations between the Bloque Popular Revolucionario (the Popular Revolutionary Bloc, BPR) and the government during May 1979.[8]

McClintock cites as representative of a notable escalation in the use of state violence a 1974 invasion of a hamlet in San Vicente during which twenty peasants organized by the Federación Cristiana de Campesinos Salvadoreños (FECCAS) were either killed or kidnapped by members of the Salvadoran National Guard. In 1975, moreover, two thousand university students were attacked while demonstrating against government expenditures related to the Miss Universe pageant held in El Salvador that year. At least thirty-seven people were killed by machine-gun fire in that incident (McClintock, 1985, 172–73).

The February 1977 massacre in which people protesting the electoral fraud committed by the military were repeatedly attacked with a clear intent for bloodshed is also considered a turning point (McClintock, 1985, 183). The willingness to take on the Catholic Church, as evinced by early attacks by the

Union Guerrera Blanca (White Warrior's Union) death squad against church workers and priests, was a further sign of how far the hard-core rightists within the state security agencies, as well as within sectors of the elite, were willing to go in order to avert any reforms and impede popular organizing and demands.[9]

There is some disagreement about how exactly to characterize the military regimes that ruled El Salvador for much of the twentieth century. After 1948, the military were able to provide some stability to the forms and practice of rule. Different military regimes employed rhetorics of reform, nationalism, modernization, and constitutionalism that reflected their desire to be seen to defer, at least ritually, to the niceties of a constitutional, electoral process.

This deference was based, at least partially, on the need to legitimize the military's informal but very close alliance with the agro-industrial sectors of the Salvadoran elite. In addition, the maintenance of the formal—although often farcical—elements of an electoral, constitutional democracy allowed for sufficient, and often considerable, support from below. The alliance between the oligarchy and the military was shifting and tension-ridden and usually involved a substantial amount of autonomy for the military as a political force. Indeed, the image of the military as an autonomous and even a reformist institution had some weight during the 1950s and early 1960s.

In concrete terms it is unlikely that either the economic modernization that began in the postwar period or the state's rationalization of political control and security functions changed much of the deeper, ideological constructs that remained so strong in Salvadoran politics through the 1980s. This is especially true outside of the handful of large cities: in rural areas and small villages, more than in urban areas, peasants and workers interacted directly with the security forces as a part of their daily life and work. The literature on Salvadoran political culture has emphasized the importance of the countryside, especially regarding the establishment of rural unions and peasant organizations during the 1970s, but we still lack studies of how the state ruled the country's villages, hamlets, and farms.

Building on this appearance of stability, the "modernization" of the Salvadoran state and its security functions took place during the late 1950s and 1960s—when the military and other state agencies increased their intelligence and policing capabilities. Salvadoran military elites took advantage of U.S.-sponsored programs driven by a desire to contain revolutionary movements in the wake of the Cuban Revolution, a trend documented by other chapters in this volume. These preparations included complex schemes involving communication networks, central filing systems, civilian contacts, paramilitary organizations, and secret groupings within the military itself.

By the early 1970s, a Creole version of national security had been enhanced by its insertion into what was billed as a hemispheric and global struggle against Communism, while the technological basis for a strong, repressive, and militarized state had been secured. By that time, the Salvadoran state had intelligence and repressive capacities that might have seemed beyond any reasonable calculus of need, even considering the possibility of war with its neighbors. Indeed, the state was prepared and predisposed to confront an enemy that did not yet exist.

Beyond these new elements, a clear continuity existed with the practices of previous decades in the social function of the Salvadoran National Guard. Established early in the twentieth century as a rural police force, by the 1970s the National Guard had become an icon of governmental authority and power in the countryside and was responsible for most of the violence against rural workers and peasants before 1979. The increasingly disruptive and displacing effects of the temporary labor offered by the Salvadoran cotton, coffee, and sugar plantations made this force even more necessary to police the lives of seasonal migrant workers. Beginning early in the century, both the urban police forces and the National Guard were under the control of the military commanders of each department and these, in turn, responded to the departmental governors, who usually both held the purportedly civilian governorship as well as serving as the district's military commander.

These historical elements strongly limited the alternatives available to those fighting for political change and social reform. Reformist and inclusive alternatives emerged in the early 1960s, 1972, 1976, and 1979, but with near-automatic certainty, the reactionary, hard-line tradition prevailed—usually with the use of force and with the resulting entrenchment of the more reactionary factions. In these years reformist, electoral, populist, and social-democratic alternatives to the exclusivist, authoritarian rule of the military emerged, but by different means—electoral fraud, massacres, a state of emergency, or the murder or exile of prominent leaders—the regime foreclosed any chance of the institutionalization of a new political order.

The political developments of the 1970s altered the balance of forces significantly enough to escalate the functioning of the machinery of repression. The regime that emerged from the 1977 electoral fraud was, more clearly than in the past, under the influence of the most reactionary elements of the army and security agencies. Violence spiraled upward throughout the two-year presidency of General Carlos Humberto Romero (1977–1979), as security forces attacked the growing popular organizations and the military capacity of the revolutionary Left increased.

In particular, the worst violence was directed at rural organizations, base communities, peasant and farm-worker groups sponsored by the Catholic Church, and lay and church organizers themselves. Rural unions had been made illegal in 1932, and the government barely tolerated the informal rural associations, which often attempted to operate as unions. Sometimes the killing of peasants was tied to conflicts with local landowners; at other times the mere act of organizing activities with a popular ideology of liberation was perceived as a threat and repressed. The extreme and increasing impoverishment of whole sectors of the rural population, growing inequalities in income and land tenure, the marginalization of increasing numbers of rural workers but, especially, the culture of intransigence of the landholding elite—stronger apparently among its middle sectors—all contributed to the society's polarization and predisposed El Salvador toward radical political confrontation.[10]

By 1979 heightened levels of state-sponsored repression convinced reformist junior officers in the military—and clearly the U.S. government as well—that Romero had no control over the actions of his security agencies and, therefore, needed to be removed before the situation got further "out of hand" and opened the door to a leftist success. The July 1979 victory of the Frente Sandinista de Liberación Nacional in Nicaragua played an important role in the perception of the pressing need to bring the spiraling violence and popular mobilization under control by other means.

Between October 1979 and February 1980, state violence ebbed but did not stop. Reformist politicians and officers struggled to bring the security agencies and government policy under their control, but actual state power had been substantially decentralized, a precondition for the next years of even worse carnage. Between October 1979 and 1982 the center of gravity of the state itself shifted from the traditional executive and was restructured more clandestinely. It fragmented into diverse centers of power, including, notably, regional military commands. In El Salvador in the early 1980s, there no longer appeared to be a single central point of political power or authority.

One of the peculiarities of El Salvador's reign of terror is that despite the fact that it was so extensive, systematic, and, indeed, terrifying, its general

Table 4.1 *Political Violence in El Salvador, 1972–1987*

	Administration			
Categories	Molina 1972– 1976	Romero 1977– 1979	JGR[1] Oct. 1979– 1984	Duarte 1984– 1987
Initiated by Government				
Political killings	37	461[2]	41,769	5,660
Disappearances	69	131	3,805[3]	380
Executions of priests	2	4		
Wounds by Security Forces	78	88		
Prosecutions or arrests for political offenses	113	477		1,348
Other terrorist acts	9	15		
Initiated by Insurgents				
Killings of Security Personnel	24	58		
Killings of Paramilitary Personnel	18	74		
Wounds in guerrilla attacks	11	14		
Attacks	31	60		
Kidnappings of elite notables	8	161		

1. The Junta de Gobierno Revolucionario (JGR) resulted from the overthrow of General Romero in October 1979. It provided a military-dominated vehicle for the negotiation of a new United States–dominated regime and the pursuit of repressive counterinsurgent policies.

2. By another estimate 1,476 people were killed by security agencies or death squads during this period (Instituto de Derechos Humanos, 1988, 196–97).

3. Does not include 1979.

Sources: Adapted from López Vallecillos, 1979, and Instituto de Derechos Humanos, 1988.

outlines and especially its quantitative aspects were relatively well documented. To a certain extent, this is a reflection of the level of U.S. involvement in the country, based in U.S. attempts to create a political regime in El Salvador based on something other than the military and the traditional oligarchic elite. This increased U.S. role resulted in a massive documentary record from U.S. agencies, as well as closer scrutiny by U.S.-based human rights and solidarity organizations.[11]

Furthermore, compared to other repressive contexts in Latin America, the strength of the Salvadoran opposition in the context of a continued and

successful guerrilla war allowed for more open, if fluctuating, spaces for recording human rights violations. Salvadoran and foreign organizations were
able to document extensively the different types and most flagrant incidents
of state repression and terror.[12] Salvadoran and international organizations
have monitored closely the violations of human rights, while journalists, activists, and academics have used various means to obtain "inside" accounts
and confidential information from U.S. government agencies involved in
official programs for support of the Salvadoran government.

Organizing Terror and Repression

Beginning with the December 1931 coup that brought to power General
Hernández Martínez, through more than seven decades the Salvadoran state
developed under the control of the military. During the 1960s, as part of an
increasing hemisphere-wide concern over communist-sponsored revolution
led by U.S. programs and ideology, El Salvador developed highly sophisticated state-security agencies that later facilitated the successful practice of
massive state terror. The Sistema Nacional de Inteligencia (SNI; later, Agen-
cia Nacional de Servicios Especiales de El Salvador, ANSESAL), a centralized
intelligence unit controlled by the executive and tied to the security forces
(the Treasury Police, National Police, National Guard, and Border Police), directed intelligence gathering within the country.

Besides coordinating efforts between the different branches of the security apparatus, SNI/ANSESAL also developed a large right-wing paramilitary
and vigilante branch known as the Organización Democrática Nacionalista
(ORDEN). Both institutions were under the directorship of the National
Guard's General José Alberto "Chele" Medrano, a "hero" and prominent veteran of the 1969 Honduras campaign (in which El Salvador invaded its
neighbor) and the reputed founder of the death squads.[13] With anywhere
from 65,000 to 100,000 grassroots members, ORDEN recruited government supporters directly in the countryside, particularly among better-off
peasants (Cabarrús, 1983, 174–96).

ORDEN also recruited from those who had been identified as parts of a
possible cadre when they ended their military service. The old neighborhood
patrols, in existence since the nineteenth century, provided recruits with
local knowledge and contacts. By the mid-1970s ORDEN was a powerful or-
gan of "enforcement terrorism" and acted as an official rival to independent
peasant and rural worker organizations. Local class and political forms and

relations, however, played a determinant role in the action and organization of these institutions (Cabarrús, 1983).

This mobilized, integrated displacement of the state's repressive functions to intermediaries is one important element that distinguishes state terror in the 1980s in Central America from the experiences of the countries of the Southern Cone in the same period. And it is precisely this nexus that calls for the close analysis of local culture and class relations, as local agents and intermediaries pursued a variety of their own agendas, interpretations, and priorities.

Although the Junta de Gobierno Revolucionario (J G R), the interim government that emerged from the October 1979 coup, ordered the disbandment of o r d e n, the networks of this organization continued to provide the basis for less visible and perhaps less "formal" practices of repression, including the strengthening of *orejas* (extensive networks of local spies). The well-known Mano Blanca (White Hand) death squad also emerged from within o r d e n, influenced by similar groups in Guatemala (Nairn, 1984, 20, 28; McClintock, 1985).

Nairn documents the ties between the U.S. Central Intelligence Agency (c i a) and its local assets, including General Medrano, which continued well after 1979. The c i a practice of giving lists of people deemed subversive to a n e s a l is further evidence of the planning that went into some of the repression carried out by state agents. When threatened with disbandment, the entire top infrastructure and intelligence database of o r d e n and a n e s a l was picked up and moved into the army's headquarters. Roberto D'Aubisson, perhaps the best-known leader of this and later right-wing organizations such as the Frente Nacional (f n) and the Alianza Republicana Nacionalista (Nationalist Republican Alliance, a r e n a), had begun his career as a National Guard officer assigned to a n e s a l by way of his close relations with General Medrano, founder of o r d e n and long time-director of the National Guard.

According to testimony provided by members of these units and military officers, the accepted view was that most of the killings and torture were planned by officers with very detailed intelligence. Agents were given lists of people to abduct and bring back for interrogation. The prevailing attitude was that few would make it out alive, while much of the torture was aimed at making the victims unidentifiable rather than extracting information from them.[14] Information on supposed subversives was received from both above and below, from centralized information gathering and from "the leading citizens of the community," many of whom are still—to this day—willing to justify the levels of violence as necessary to maintain the social order.[15]

The machinery of repression, however, was also dispersed and decentralized. Every garrison and combat unit had a death squad within it composed of people who had proven themselves ruthless and trustworthy and who were often recruited formally and put on a generous payroll (Nairn, 1984, 22; Bonner, 1984, 328–29). Killers for hire also abounded within the security forces, and higher officials operated as a kind of protection and racketeering Mafia.

Privately controlled death squads existed, although their targets were linked more closely to land-related issues and to the elimination of the opposition movement's important leaders. The Union Guerrera Blanca, for example, first known as FALANGE (Fuerza Armadas de Liberación Nacional-Guerra de Exterminación), was reportedly established by two business groups (Frente Agropecuario de la Región Oriente and Asociación Nacional de la Empresa Privada) to counter the growing ability of the Left to retaliate after the execution of rural leaders. This group would carry out executions that were deemed more sensitive or that might not be taken on by government agencies directly (Dunkerley, 1982, 103–04).

Many aspects of the practice of repression in El Salvador were highly organized. The common image of mysterious and independent death squads, free-lancing violently on behalf of the status quo, is misleading. In fact, uniformed members of the Salvadoran army carried out the overwhelming majority of the killings. After 1980, with pressure put upon the Reagan administration in Washington to force the Salvadoran military to comply with human rights requirements, the language of the Salvadoran regime itself promoted the convenience of invisibility.

Table 4.2 *Military and Police Forces in El Salvador before 1980*

Regular Armed Forces	16,000
National Guard	6,000
National Police	5,000
Treasury Police	5,000
Customs Police	2,000
Municipal Police	2,000
Paramilitary Groups	40,000

Source: Instituto de Derechos Humanos, 1988.

President Reagan and the U.S. State Department insisted that the violence came from fringe elements on the left and right, and that the government itself was not responsible for any gross human rights violations. This rhetoric filtered down in El Salvador and promoted the invisibility of the state agencies in many of their actions, leading them to make further use of the "death squad cover" and thus draw less attention to the regime. Factionalism within the military itself and their shifting alliances and conflicts with the president, the national assembly, and so forth also promoted the practice of secretive killings.

Although every major military base or garrison had interrogation facilities, important "suspects" were taken to the headquarters of the National Guard or the army for further questioning and torture. Groups within the security forces also had safe houses or clandestine prisons. El Playón became notorious as an open dump for the bodies of those tortured at nearby air force and cavalry headquarters. People were usually picked up in their houses at nighttime, during the strict shoot-on-sight curfew that began early in 1980 and lasted almost without interruption for three years. This curfew provided both the cover as well as the justification for many killings and illegal arrests or abductions. There is evidence also that the security forces had mobile torture vans, which would at least partially explain the many disfigured bodies dumped on rural roadsides.

The array of torture methods were as brutal as any, and involved practices that clearly went beyond the extraction of information, a confession, or the physical neutralization of the victim. The attack on sexual organs, even after the victim's death, decapitation—apparently practiced in a slaughterhouse with specialized equipment—were methods of torture that established their own goals and justification and provided the security agencies and rightist groups with iconic power far beyond the "tactical" elimination of people perceived as activists or revolutionaries. Ultimately, the repeated public display of tortured and disfigured bodies was a method of terrorizing the living (a point made also by Torres, this volume).

Contexts to the Practice of Terror

The use of terror has varied in El Salvador in relation to larger factors, some more obvious than others. Between 1977 and 1981 almost every demonstration held by the Left and popular organizations was attacked, including funeral marches for the victims of previous attacks. Before 1979, uniformed personnel carried out the killings, but after 1979 the tendency was to use well-placed, plainclothes snipers from atop government buildings. Most massacres took place in the countryside. Usually guardsmen occupied entire hamlets or towns, and local leaders and others would either be killed or disappear.

These practices continued after the war began in 1980 and became part and parcel of the counterinsurgency practices of the army, especially its elite U.S.-trained battalions. Similar urban barrio invasions took place in these years: uniformed treasury police and national guardsmen would surround a neighborhood and men in plainclothes would round up people, usually with lists in hand, driving them away or executing them shortly thereafter. The selection of victims by the security forces in these cases depended as much on "hardcore" intelligence as on purely contextual elements, ranging from the identification of victims based on kin relations to the whim of agents bent on exercising their power arbitrarily. The U.S. military and CIA implemented a counterinsurgency program in El Salvador based on the Vietnam-era Phoenix Program designed to identify and "eliminate" rebel leaders and other sympathizers.

The CIA operative who did the initial counterinsurgency work in El Salvador was Felix Rodriguez, a Bay of Pigs veteran notorious for his involvement in the support of the Contras in Nicaragua and the capture and execution of Che Guevara. U.S. General Paul Gorman, who commanded the U.S. forces in Central America in the 1980s, described Phoenix-like programs as "a form of warfare repugnant to Americans, a conflict which involves innocents, in which non-combatant casualties may be an explicit objective" (*Boston Globe*, July 10, 1984). Peasants who had not left a rebel-controlled zone during the early years of the war were perceived by the military to be actual or potential FMLN supporters. Peasants and workers were also identified individually as activists or sympathizers. Apparently, the use of collective punishment was less evident in marginal urban areas, where victims were identified individually more often than in the countryside.

At another level, actual or suspected leaders of organizations related to the Left, the activist Catholic Church, the peasant organizations linked to the Left, the Christian Democratic Party, and so forth were taken, tortured, and killed. Most notable were the assassinations of the Archbishop of San Salvador Oscar Romero, the leaders of the Frente Democrático Revolucionario (FDR),[16] agrarian reform administrators, peasant leaders of the rural sector of the BPR, and the dean of the national university, but the count of "notable" killings is so long that it blends into the larger mass of victims.

In addition to these notable killings, thousands of other people were tortured, killed, or disappeared. Accounts of the arbitrary and personally motivated use of violence abound (often targeting women: soldiers killing their ex-girlfriends or their rape victims). Although many of the killings can be traced not only to an attempt to physically eliminate people thought to be associated with opposition and activist social groups, state agencies also looked to instill fear in all potential opponents, regardless of any specific behavior that could be identified as dangerous (Corradi, 1992). A practice that reveals the underlying culture of terror within the state agencies was the killing of circus workers as "antisocial" elements by the Maximiliano Hernández Martínez Brigade. This same death squad also took responsibility for the murder of the F D R leaders in 1980 (Bonner, 1984, 330).

In general terms, however, most of the killings and torture took place in the context of an escalating confrontation between supporters of the regime and its challengers. After about 1977, the chronology of repression in El Salvador reads like a chronicle from hell. This escalation in violence resulted from a perceived threat to both the basis of state power and the privileges of the economic elite, whose most prominent and powerful sectors (such as agro-capitalists) had been traditionally allied with rightist elements in the military.[17] The terror at first contributed to the radicalization of the initially peaceful opposition and provided enlarged recruitment and justification for the consolidation of the F M L N and its guerrilla war against the government. Later, however, it limited the spaces for political action outside of armed opposition, paralyzing both F M L N -linked and autonomous popular movements.

One condition that contributed to the drastic increase in political violence during the early period of the J G R (October 1979 to summer 1980) was the simultaneous intensification of pressure from two opposite sides. At the same time that the popular organizations were transformed by the violence and their remnants began to dissolve into rebel armies, the U.S. embassy deployed its "reformist" policies, tying economic and military support to the nationalization of banking and coffee exports and the regime's acceptance of U.S.-designed agrarian reform. Once the Social Democratic members of the J G R resigned—by February 1980—the ability of the United States to influence the government increased.

At this point, the United States began to promote a package of reforms aimed at increasing the autonomy of the state and its interventionist powers over the economy. Forming part of the U.S. government's efforts to create a stable "center" in El Salvador that had begun with the October 1979 coup that brought the J G R to power, these policies forced the "fascist" sectors within the military and elites to accept the presence of civilian politicians, such as future president José Napoleón Duarte, in the government. These reforms challenged the power of large landowners, but they were closely tied as well to the political goals of the counterinsurgency programs that also began to be instituted in those months. Ironically, these counterrevolutionary reforms fueled the repression rather than halting it.

The agrarian reform program was born in the middle of these battles and quickly turned into a new battleground itself, often facilitating the repression of the more militant and organized sectors of the rural working class and peasantry. The implementation of the reform's first phase, affecting the larger estates, was carried out by the military during 1980. Many times the military would tell the members of the new cooperative organizations to elect their leadership and then move to execute or arrest them. The thoroughly repressive and militarized character of the agrarian reform led to a strike by the land surveyors charged with putting the reform into practice, who were also violently attacked by the army.

The U.S.-supported policy of forcing a problematic agrarian reform on the country's wealthiest landowners resulted in a wave of violence directed against the reform's intended beneficiaries. In this context, however, the larger argument of this chapter is important: the violence had as much to do with the frustrated elite's desire for revenge as for any strategic desire to demobilize the peasant movement.

Targets of Terror

At least half of those killed during the repression of the early 1980s were peasants, which in Salvadoran usage includes rural workers as well as smallholders and tenant farmers. This figure roughly parallels the presence of rural workers nationwide: estimates suggest that about 60 percent of the population was engaged in "rural" economic activities at the time. However, occupational information is available for only about half of the victims, considering that residents of remote rural areas would have more difficulty locating their relatives or friends, or providing this information to urban-based human rights organizations. Consequently, it is likely that an even greater percentage of those killed were peasants than this first estimate suggests.

Table 4.3 *Political Prisoners in El Salvador, 1981*

Occupation	Men	Women	Total
Peasants/Farmers/Day Laborers	26		26
Urban Workers/Tradesmen	79	4	83
Students	43	14	57
Professionals	4	3	7
Teachers	5	1	6
Merchants	4	2	6
Street Vendors	2	3	5
Journalists	3		3
Foreigners	1		1
Domestic Workers		1	1
Housewives		1	1
Total	167	29	196

Source: Instituto de Derechos Humanos, 1988.

It is also likely that the few hundred assassinations of government informants and supporters claimed by leftist groups are accounted for as either
victims of political violence in general or simply as part of the overall body
count from the war. Although the activities of groups on the Left are harder
to discern than are those of the paramilitaries or death squads, especially
once the civil war advanced, they were the only groups to provide information on how many assassinations—*ajusticiamientos* in their terms—they had
carried out (Cabarrús, 1983, 293). In the final report on human rights issued
as a result of the 1992 Peace Accords, the Left was held accountable for only
a small percentage (about 4 percent) of noncombat deaths.

When comparing the data on killings for the entire country with the data
on political prisoners held in the three principal jails (Mariona, Santa Tecla,
and de Mujeres), differing patterns emerge (see Table 4.3). Of those held for
political crimes, the greatest majority stood accused of "active" crimes, rather
than "passive" memberships or organizing activities. The great majority had
been held (by December 1981) for more than six months and many for more
than a year (the law then stipulated that they could only be held for 180 days
without trial). Many had their trials *indefinido* ("not scheduled") or *estancado*
("delayed"), and military judges visited most whose process had some official
status. Table 4.3 presents the occupational/class breakdown of the men and
women cited as political prisoners (as reported by the Comité de Madres y
Familiares de Presos y Desaparecidos 'MOAR').

Although this chapter focuses on the violent, extralegal aspects of the Salvadoran repression, data on more "legal" practices engaged in by the regime help us to put state violence in perspective. For instance, evidence of the class distribution of those held as political prisoners shows that rural workers were more likely to be killed in massacres than arrested for political offenses. More than 50 percent of those killed were peasants, while this group accounted for only 12 percent of those arrested in 1981. This finding is explained in part by the fact that most massacres, especially after 1979, took place in the countryside.

In 1980 seventeen massacres with 1,294 victims were reported to the archbishop's office. In 1981 the number increased to twenty-seven with 4,500 victims and, in the first half of 1982, there were fifteen reported massacres with 885 victims (Instituto de Derechos Humanos, 1988, 205, 209). The practice of massacring peasants requires closer examination, especially regarding the justifications put forward by the military, as well as the responses of survivors.

Mass killings must be approached in terms that go beyond those provided as justification for them: that those killed were actual or potential supporters of the FMLN, or—on the other hand—that the armed forces and security agencies practiced this kind of repression simply because they were murderous, unrestrained, or unprofessional. The ideological continuities that exist within elite and popular conceptions, linking events in the 1970s and 1980s to the 1932 massacre, as well as the roles that constitutional, legal, and juridical institutions and ideologies have played in relation to the repressive practices discussed here, deserve further attention.

Culture, History, and Local Context: A Proposal

Repression as massive, persistent, and characterized by systematic torture and violence as that which took place in El Salvador cannot be considered solely in utilitarian, functional, or even conjunctural terms but rather requires an ethnographic and historical examination of its contextual and cultural determinants. In the introduction to this chapter I proposed that a "deep" examination of state repression needs to transcend the emphasis on political economy, structural-functionalist, and rational-instrumental approaches that until recently prevailed in the literature. I suggested that the examination of state terror and repression had to be related to ideological, cultural, and iconographic elements that had shaped its agents and victims alike.

It is, in this view, not sufficient to explain the repressive practices of a state simply in terms of its own bureaucratic or ideological goals or needs. Studies of state repression and terror must go beyond examining any one actor's assessment of the balance of forces to pose deeper questions about the contradictory contexts from which state violence emerges, the assumptions and origins of the agents of violence, why the violence takes one shape instead of another, and how it is understood, experienced, and responded to by those involved.

Since the demise of Latin America's military regimes and the end of the civil wars in Central America, scholars have begun to pay more attention to the effects and practice of state terror, especially in the Southern Cone. This literature focuses for the most part on the establishment of cultures of fear, of the silence produced by state terror, while also examining the origins of state violence and repression. Few studies, however, have approached the ethnographic and historical analysis of repression that I am proposing here.

That said, the trend in the scholarly community is certainly toward increasingly more complex examinations of state terror that move beyond the descriptive or functionalist approaches outlined earlier (Knisely Huggins, 1991; Rotker and Goldman, 2002; Rupesinghe and Rubio Correa, 1994; Koonings and Kruijt, 1999; Corradi, Weiss Fagen, and Garretón Merino, 1992; Waldmann, Reinares, and Laitin, 1999; Rosenberg, 1991).[18] While state violence can be approached as instrumental or goal-oriented, in the context of a confrontation between state-based and insurgent contenders we must also consider how the practice of state terror is mediated by ideological and cultural constructs that escape the rationality, functionality, or instrumentality of the state's political objectives—and which might also reflect larger, historical processes (Corradi, 1982). The practice of terror is closely tied to the historic and daily-life ideological constructs of social control and state violence as they have emerged in El Salvador during the last century.

This outlook proposes, at the very least, that practices of violence and state repression are mediated by the construction of identities and ideologies whose origins do not entirely reside within the rationality of state actors nor within the functionality of the capitalist mode of production. Engagement with this view requires a quasi-Geertzian approach, what Lüdtke (1979, 176)—a prominent proponent of the integration of the study of daily life and class culture with the study of state practices—calls the "deep study of repression."

In his study of state violence in early nineteenth-century Prussia, Lüdtke advocates its linkage to the socialization of workers and citizens early in the development of capitalist social relations. His interest is in examining how "traditional," "external," or overtly violent forms of domination and social control from the early nineteenth century "protruded" into the social and political dynamics of the early twentieth century. These forms of domination and social control, he finds, were intertwined with modern, ideological, and "merely" economic forms of control and regularization. In this view, modern capitalism had to develop "step by step with the forms, contents, and practice of state domination and authority that had arisen in an agrarian, pre-bourgeois context" (Lüdtke, 1979, 183).

Although the main thrust of Lüdtke's argument is not readily applicable to the experience of El Salvador, his study is nonetheless helpful in its proposals for the location of the study of state violence. The historical section of Lüdtke's article examines how "organized state power in the form of physical violence repeatedly affected a broad spectrum of daily activities, above all among the 'lower classes,'" and so physical violence demands to be approached "as a constitutive element of daily life" (Lüdtke, 1979, 186). The methodology he only partially spells out calls for examining the "daily arrangements" of concrete subject–state relations (Lüdtke, 1979, 186–87).

The implications of Lüdtke's approach for the kind of examination I am proposing here are threefold. First, it forces us to reconsider the institutional linkage between state "violence" in a general sense and the more distinct notion of "terror," but it also exposes the distinctions that must be made when examining actual examples of both types of coercion. Second, his approach helps us to locate some initial empirical starting points: in order to correctly examine what appears to be merely conjunctural and purely "political" phenomena— such as the repressive "waves" of the 1975–1985 period in El Salvador—a larger, more expansive net must be spread to include such things as the daily, local-level interaction of police, residents, and temporary migrant laborers, places of work and leisure, and local personal and ideological affinities between landowners, police, members of the National Guard, and so forth.

These considerations, moreover, must also be combined with an analysis that considers the regional political and agrarian history of El Salvador, something that is always lacking in studies of this period. Finally, Lüdtke's call reminds us that whatever the apparent immediacy or autonomy of specifically political or "anti-insurgent" repression, the entire institutional, practical, and ideological formation of state–subject power relations is the necessary and proper setting for such research.

In order to account for the forms assumed by both official and semi-official state repression, we need to reconsider recent Salvadoran history in the context of local, ideological, and daily-life structures. A recent exchange between two anthropologists who have written extensively about repression and violence in El Salvador provides some important insights in this regard. While their exchange focuses principally on the justification and effects of guerrilla violence and the effects of popular participation in antistate violence, the exchange provides an important opportunity to highlight the need for cultural and historical research that addresses events predating the civil conflict of the 1980s (Bourgois, 2001; Binford, 2002).[19]

In this debate, Binford (2002, 205) calls for the study of "the social and cultural mediations through which individuals and groups come to comprehend political violence and their roles in it" as a means of avoiding what he sees as Bourgois's oversimplified claim that mass participation in antistate violence (war making) during the 1980s created a culture of violence and insensitivity in El Salvador. While Binford focuses on critiquing Bourgois's claim by contextualizing both popular participation in revolutionary violence during the 1980s and the post–civil war political terrain, the argument could also be extended to the period before the 1980s. Indeed, the very fact that Bourgois sees El Salvador's high homicide rate in the 1990s as a reflection of the war obscures the larger question, in that El Salvador *before* the civil war started in the late 1970s had extremely high homicide rates as well.

Indeed, while Bourgois is correct to suggest that all Salvadorans experienced a distinct culture of violence in recent decades, to claim that the creation of that climate was the result of revolutionary violence alone is not acceptable. In response to Bourgois's claims, Binford proposes a framework for research on violence: "discussions of both wartime and postwar Salvadoran social relations need to go beyond generalized claims about the metamorphosis of violence from one domain or form to another (political to everyday, for instance); it must engage both dominant structural relations and institutional forms, and the social and cultural mediations through which their effects are transferred downward, as well as the ways in which those structures and institutions respond to and are shaped by resistance and struggles of subordinate groups" (Binford, 2002, 208).

Stanley (1997) provides an example of a style of analysis that brings to light the kinds of complex layering and mediating structures present in the internal workings of the security agencies. He shows how rightist officers implicated in the death-squad activities of the early 1980s forced other officers to participate in indiscriminate killings in order to make them complicit and so to neutralize their ability to oppose such practices. Recognition of this pattern of forced complicity helps to explain at least partially the "overflow" of violence and would not be visible without the careful interview material gathered by the author. Similarly, Binford's ethnography of the 1981 massacre at El Mozote demonstrates how the repression of rural people developed a logic of its own: El Mozote, he finds, could well have been portrayed by the Salvadoran government and its sponsors in the U.S. Agency for International Development as a model village of successful commercial farmers who would have welcomed counterinsurgent reformism. Instead, El Mozote's residents were subjected to the most implacable repression by the army. The origins and effects of this sort of "cultural" and political blindness of the military also require further research and clarification.

The empirical materials reviewed in the previous sections are not entirely adequate for the kind of research that this chapter suggests. First of all, we need to take a closer look at the repressive practices themselves within their more immediate context, including the language and images employed by state agents and their allies. Such an approach would also involve examining the larger ideological elements at work in the changing constructions of the Salvadoran nation, among both elite and popular sectors. A closer examination of the conception of mass–nation relations beginning with the 1932 massacre and other political upheavals (the 1944 and 1948 revolts, for example) would also be necessary.

Additionally, we would need to consider the "local" sources of repression, especially outside of San Salvador and in rural areas. Violence was deeply connected to local fields of power that often included civilians (neighbors, landowners, and so on), as well as military or paramilitary forces, and was mediated by local ethnic, religious, agrarian, ideological, and personal conflicts. Therefore, the study of repression must involve not only national institutions and ideologies but also local communities and their histories. Similarly, the study of local, gender- and class-specific notions of respect, identity, honor, and humiliation—especially in the countryside—would also be important aspects of the kind of research proposed here.

We would then have to relate these ideas more closely to the more conjunctural elements outlined above, emphasizing the formation of distinct Salvadoran "political cultures" and the ideological and institutional constraints that mediated state actors' perceptions of threat and their responses. In the end, this approach would provide a clearer, more complete understanding of the experience of terror and governmental repression in terms of both the shared and contested cultural and ideological forms that have emerged historically in El Salvador. It would reveal the state as an amalgam of culturally determined and negotiated practices and conceptions, rather than simply a mechanical assemblage of function and structure.

NOTES

1. Between 1978 and 1984, approximately 1 percent of the Salvadoran civilian population was killed. Another 25–29 percent of the population was displaced either internally or externally by the counterinsurgency and repression, as well as by the unexpected consequences of the establishment of emigrant and transnational networks of Salvadorans in the United States (Zolberg, Suhrke, and Aguayo, 1989, 212).

2. A few authors familiar with the operation of security agencies have drawn parallels between the violence of the Salvadoran Left and the government's repressive practices. Gabriel Zaid (1982), a Mexican writer and "social critic," accused the Left in El Salvador of forming part of the same authoritarian, militaristic, and repressive tradition that shaped the practices of the government.

3. It is misleading to understand the violence carried out by the Salvadoran government against its population in terms of the implementation of a new economic or accumulation model, as Petras does. While the stabilization measures and structural reforms (in banking, export control, the coffee trade, the agrarian sector, and so on) that were implemented from 1980 to 1989 might constitute a reformist, state-centered accumulation model, the greatest source of opposition to these programs came not from the Left but from sectors of the economic elite.

4. See Alvarenga (1996, 1998) for a discussion of the use of intermediaries in the policing of communities before 1932. For a recent interpretation of the revolt, see Lauria-Santiago and Gould (2004).

5. The intent here is not to disavow recent research that has shown that a paternalist and limited attempt to protect indigenous people and peasants from abuse was implemented in the western departments after the massacres of January and February. For a discussion of these aspects, see Ching and Tilley (1998) and Ching (2003).

6. Anderson's classic book *Matanza* (1969) exposes aspects of this thinking among members of the elite and state actors.

7. For an examination of the contradictions and silences involved in these practices of memory, see Gould (2001) and Lauria-Santiago and Gould (2004).

8. The BPR was the largest of the popular organizations of the late 1970s, organizing tens of thousands of workers, students, and peasants.

9. Most notable was the opposition mobilized by these sectors to the relatively mild Transformación Agraria proposals put forth in 1976 by the administration of Colonel Arturo Molina.

10. Instituto de Derechos Humanos, 1988, 53.

11. The National Security Archive (1989, 1995) has published thousands of U.S. government documents relating to policy in El Salvador during the 1980s. They are available online and in microformat. See also http://www.chadwyck.com/products/pt-product-DNSA.shtml).

12. Most important among these organizations are the Tutela Legal (later Socorro Jurídico), an office of the Archdiocese of San Salvador, and the independent human rights commission, Comisión de Derechos Humanos. As useful are the monthly accounts, documentary sections, and analysis provided by the Jesuit Universidad Centroamericana (U C A), the target of the latest high-visibility murders by the Salvadoran armed forces. In two important publications, *Estudios Centroamericanos* (López Vallecillos, 1979) and *Proceso*, the course of the civil war has been closely documented.

13. Medrano was accused of carrying out massacres of peasants when he led the invasion of Honduras by Salvadoran forces in 1969.

14. The "anonymizing" of the victims of terror also sends a message to the living that the victim could have been anyone, since their identity remains unknown.

15. See Petras (1987, 329); Jeffrey Paige, personal exchange in San Salvador, 1990.

16. A Social Democratic leftist party allied to but separate from the F M L N.

17. See Paige (1997) for a discussion of the politics of different sectors of the Salvadoran elite during the 1980s, especially its most right-wing sector.

18. Historians of Latin America have not yet begun to research repression and state violence, but recent literature on criminality is clearing the path toward examinations of state cultures of violence and law. See, for example, the essays in Salvatore, Aguirre, and Joseph (2001) and Aguirre and Buffington (2000).

19. For a summary of recent trends in violence in El Salvador, see Programa de las Naciones Unidas para el Desarollo (2002).

BIBLIOGRAPHY

Aguirre, Carlos A., and Robert Buffington, eds. 2000. *Reconstructing Criminality in Latin America.* Wilmington, DE: Scholarly Resources.
Alvarenga, Patricia. 1996. *Cultura y Ética de la Violencia: El Salvador 1880–1932.* San José: EDUCA.
———. 1998. "Auxiliary Forces in the Shaping of the Repressive System: El Salvador, 1880–1930." Pp. 122–150 in *Identity and Struggle at the Margins of the Nation-State: The Laboring Peoples of Central America and the Hispanic Caribbean,* eds. Aviva Chomsky and Aldo Lauria-Santiago. Durham: Duke University Press.

America's Watch. 1985. *With Friends Like These: The America's Watch Report on Human Rights and U.S. Policy in Latin America*, ed. Cynthia Brown. New York: Pantheon.

Anderson, Thomas P. 1969. *Matanza: El Salvador's Communist Revolt of 1932*. Lincoln: University of Nebraska Press.

Binford, Leigh. 1996. *The El Mozote Massacre: Anthropology and Human Rights, Hegemony and Experience*. Tucson: University of Arizona Press.

————. 2002. "Violence in El Salvador: A Rejoinder to Philippe Bourgois's 'The Power of Violence in War and Peace.'" *Ethnography* 3, 2 (June): 201–20.

Bonner, Raymond. 1984. *Weakness and Deceit: U.S. Policy and El Salvador*. New York: Times Books.

Bourgois, Philippe. 2001. "The Power of Violence in War and Peace: Post-Cold War Lessons from El Salvador." *Ethnography* 2, 1 (March): 5–34.

Brocket, Charles. 1989. "Cycles of Protest and the Impact of Repression in Central America." Paper presented at the fifteenth International Congress of the Latin American Studies Association, Miami.

Cabarrús, Carlos Rafael. 1983. *Génesis de una Revolución*. Mexico: La Casa Chata.

Ching, Erik. 2003. "Patronage and Politics under Martínez, 1931–1939: The Local Roots of Military Authoritarianism." In *Landscapes of Struggle: Politics, Society, and Community in El Salvador*, eds. Aldo Lauria-Santiago and Leigh Binford. Pittsburgh: University of Pittsburgh Press.

Ching, Erik, and Virginia Tilley. 1998. "Indians, the Military and the Rebellion of 1932 in El Salvador." *Journal of Latin American Studies* 30: 121–56.

Comisión de la Verdad. 1993. *De la Locura a la Esperanza: La Guerra de 12 Años en El Salvador*. San José: Departamento Ecuménico de Investigaciones.

Comisión para el Esclarecimiento Histórico. 2000. *Guatemala: Causas y Orígenes del Enfrentamiento Armado Interno*. Guatemala: F&G Editores.

Corradi, Juan E. 1982. "The Mode of Destruction: Terror in Argentina." *Telos* 54 (3): 61–76.

Corradi, Juan E., Patricia Weiss Fagen, and Manuel A. Garretón Merino, eds. 1992. *Fear at the Edge: State Terror and Resistance in Latin America*. Berkeley: University of California.

Danner, Mark. 1994. *The Massacre at El Mozote: A Parable of the Cold War*. New York: Vintage Books.

DeYoung, Karen. 1981. "White Hand of Terror: How the Peace Was Lost in El Salvador." *Mother Jones* 6 (June): 26–36, 45–48.

Dunkerley, James. 1982. *The Long War: Dictatorship and Revolution in El Salvador*. London: Junction Books.

Gould, Jeffrey L. 2001. "Revolutionary Nationalism and Local Memories in El Salvador." Pp. 138–171 in *Reclaiming the Political in Latin American History: The View from the North*, ed. Gilbert Joseph. Durham: Duke University Press.

Guerra, Tomas. 1979. *El Salvador: Octubre Sangriento*. San José: Centro Victor Sanabria.

Gurr, Ted Robert. 1986. "The Political Origins of State Violence and Terror: A Theoretical Analysis." Pp. 45–71 in *Government Violence and Repression: An Agenda for Research*, eds. Michael Stohl and George A. Lopez. Westport: Greenwood Press.

Hochschild, Adam. 1983. "Inside the Slaughterhouse." *Mother Jones* 8 (August): 18–43.

Instituto de Derechos Humanos. 1988. *La Resistencia*. San Salvador: Instituto de Derechos Humanos de la Universidad Centroamericana.

Knisely Huggins, Martha, ed. 1991. *Vigilantism and the State in Modern Latin America: Essays on Extralegal Violence*. New York: Praeger.

Koonings, Kees, and Dirk Kruijt. 1999. *Societies of Fear: The Legacy of Civil War, Violence and Terror in Latin America*. London: Zed Books, Ltd.

Lauria-Santiago, Aldo A., and Jeffrey Gould. 2004. " 'They Call Us Thieves and Steal Our Wage': Towards a Reinterpretation of the Salvadoran Rural Mobilization, 1929–1931." *Hispanic American Historical Review* 84, 2 (May).

Livingstone, Neil C. 1984. "Death Squads." *World Affairs* 146: 239–48.

López Vallecillos, Italo. 1979. "Rasgos Sociales y Tendencias Políticas en El Salvador (1969–1979)." *Estudios Centroamericanos (ECA)* 34, 372–373 (Oct.-Nov.): 863–84.

Lüdtke, Alf. 1979. "The Role of State Violence in the Period of Transition to Industrial Capitalism: The Example of Prussia from 1815 to 1848." *Social History* 4: 175–221.

Mason, T. David, and Dale A. Crane. 1989. "The Political Economy of Death Squads: Toward a Theory of the Impact of State-sanctioned Terror." *International Studies Quarterly* 33: 175–98.

McCamant, John F. 1984. "Governance without Blood: Social Sciences Antiseptic View of Rule; or, The Neglect of Political Repression." Pp. 83–98 in *The State as Terrorist: The Dynamics of Governmental Violence and Repression*, eds. Michael Stohl and George Lopez. Westport: Greenwood Press.

McClintock, Michael. 1985. *The American Connection: State Terror and Popular Resistance in El Salvador*. London: Zed Books, Ltd.

Millett, Richard L. 1981. "The Politics of Violence: Guatemala and El Salvador." *Current History* 80: 70–88.

Nairn, Allan. 1984. "Behind the Death Squads." *The Progressive* 48: 20–29.

National Security Archive. 1989. "El Salvador: The Making of U.S. Policy, 1977–1984" [microfiche online]. Washington, DC: National Security Archive [cited 28 January 2003]. Available from http://www.gwu.edu/~ nsarchiv/nsa/publications/elsalvador/elsalvador.html.

——. 1995. "El Salvador: War, Peace, and Human Rights, 1980–1994" [microfiche online]. Washington, DC: National Security Archive [cited 28 January 2003]. Available from http://www.gwu.edu/~ nsarchiv/nsa/publications/elsalvador2/.

Navarro, Vicente. 1981. "Genocide in El Salvador." *Monthly Review* 32: 1–16.

Paige, Jeffery M. 1997. *Coffee and Power: Revolution and the Rise of Democracy in Central America.* Cambridge: Harvard University Press.

Petras, James. 1980. "The Junta's War against the People." *The Nation* (20 December): 671–74.

———. 1987. "The Anatomy of State Terror: Chile, El Salvador and Brazil." *Science and Society* 51: 314–38.

Pion-Berlin, David. 1984. "The Political Economy of State Repression in Argentina." Pp. 99–122 in *The State as Terrorist: The Dynamics of Governmental Violence and Repression,* eds. Michael Stohl and George Lopez. Westport: Greenwood Press.

Programa de las Naciones Unidas para el Desarollo (PNUD). 2002. *Indicadores sobre Violencia en el Salvador.* San Salvador: Programa de las Naciones Unidas para el Desarollo.

Rosenberg, Tina. 1991. *Children of Cain: Violence and the Violent in Latin America.* New York: W. Morrow.

Rotker, Susana, and Katherine Goldman. 2002. *Citizens of Fear: Urban Violence in Latin America.* New Brunswick: Rutgers University Press.

Rupesinghe, Kumar, and Marcial Rubio Correa, eds. 1994. *The Culture of Violence.* Tokyo: United Nations University Press.

Salvatore, Ricardo D., Carlos A. Aguirre, and Gilbert M. Joseph. 2001. *Crime and Punishment in Latin America: Law and Society since Late Colonial Times.* Durham: Duke University Press.

Sloan, John W. 1984. "State Repression and Enforcement Terrorism in Latin America." Pp. 83–98 in *The State as Terrorist: The Dynamics of Governmental Violence and Repression,* eds. Michael Stohl and George Lopez. Westport: Greenwood Press.

Stanley, William. 1997. *The Protection Racket State: Elite Politics, Military Extortion, and Civil War in El Salvador.* Philadelphia: Temple University Press.

Taylor, Robert W., and Harry E. Vanden. 1982. "Defining Terror in El Salvador: 'La Matanza.'" *Annals of the American Academy of Political and Social Science* 463 (September): 106–118.

Waldmann, Peter, Fernando Reinares, and David D. Laitin. 1999. *Sociedades en Guerra Civil Conflictos Violentos de Europa y América Latina.* Barcelona: Paidós Estado y Sociedad.

Williams, Philip J., and Knut Walter. 1997. *Militarization and Demilitarization in El Salvador's Transition to Democracy.* Pittsburgh: University of Pittsburgh Press.

Zaid, Gabriel. 1982. "Enemy Colleagues." *Dissent* (Winter): 13–40.

Zolberg, Aristide R., Astri Suhrke, and Sergio Aguayo. 1989. *Escape from Violence: Conflict and the Refugee Crisis in the Developing World.* New York: Oxford University Press.

CHAPTER 5

Caught in the Crossfire

Militarization, Paramilitarization, and State Violence in Oaxaca, Mexico

KRISTIN NORGET

> I left my house, looking for work, saying to my wife that I would arrive home in the afternoon. Eight agents dressed in civil attire arrested me. . . . Later, again the torture, the blows, the insults. I felt as if I was going to faint; electric shocks in different parts of my body, the same questions: Who was Captain Sonia? They insisted I knew him, that I worked with him. I said to them, "Señores, I don't know anything, I can die or wait the time that you want and I won't tell you anything because I just don't know." They answered me, "You son of a bitch, you have to talk, it's your last chance, you rat. The order was to throw you out of the airplane, but we wanted you alive; you have to talk sooner or later. I can cut your balls off, shoot you, inject you, and leave you disgraced the rest of your life, you will die slowly." After a long while someone gave the order to stop the punishment, then spoke to me softly, making the same questions, as if we were friends. Every day I trusted them less, because they told me that I was practically dead in life, that outside no one cared about me, about my disappearance. (Luna Gasca, 2002; translation by author)

Introduction

This account of the grisly torture he endured, at the hands of anonymous "agents," is the testimony of Eugenio López (a pseudonym), a 26-year-old Zapotec subsistence farmer from the region of Loxicha, a municipality of indigenous Zapotec towns in the low mountains toward the Pacific coast of the southern Mexican state of Oaxaca. The Loxicha region is one of the most impoverished of this state that is, itself, probably the poorest, most rugged, and most ethnically diverse in the country. Since 1996, a brutal, low-intensity war has been waged here against the local population by a government that fears a repetition of the Zapatista insurrection that erupted in early 1994 in the neighboring state of Chiapas.

As I write this essay, six years after the onset of the worst period of repression, eighteen Loxicha men are still incarcerated in Oaxaca City (Oaxaca de Juárez). Some of them were sentenced to thirty to forty years imprisonment on suspicion of belonging to an insurgent guerrilla group. Currently they are undergoing a hunger strike to pressure the federal government to pass an amnesty law that would secure their freedom. They are not the only victims of this long-enduring, state-sponsored repression. The repression's effects have had ramifications throughout the Loxicha region, touching profoundly the lives of women and men, young and old. The violence has displaced hundreds of Loxicha families. The people fear the intimidating presence of the military in the region and the members of the paramilitary groups who collude with it.

What factors motivate this militarization? What strategies condone its ruthless practices and allow the Mexican government to construe them as a necessary remedy to purported threats to national security? How does the Loxicha case relate to current key shifts in national, and indeed transnational, levels of power orchestration? The Loxicha situation is just one reflection of the present political and social climate in Mexico, a nation showing the severe contradictions and pains of an unprecedented period of rapid transition. The unfolding of Mexico's "militarized democracy" (North American Congress on Latin America [hereafter: NACLA], 1998) has involved a delicately balanced construction of a semblance of a "rule of law" on the one hand and unchecked political violence on the other. Extensive training of Mexican military and police bodies in counterinsurgency and "low-intensive" warfare techniques has catalyzed this violence. It includes terrorizing suspects and civilians by destroying property and threatening them with death, as well as with physical torture, rapes, arbitrary arrests, imprisonments, disappearances, and assassinations.

The Mexican government has had a hand in more than the incidents discussed previously. The trade agreements and neoliberal economic restructuring policies inaugurated by the administration of President George H. W. Bush in the late 1980s and early 1990s have been tied to maintaining firm U.S. and Latin American military alliances. Today, Washington uses the war on drugs to justify a mounting American military presence in Mexico and throughout Latin America. Thus, it continues to support the region's militaries through training, joint-operations programs, and by supplying arms and other military equipment (NACLA, 1998, 15). Beginning as far back as the end of the Cold War, the U.S. government has increasingly pressured various police and military bodies in Mexico to take a prominent role in tackling drug trafficking, "terrorism," insurgency, immigration, and refugee flows. To a degree unprecedented in the nation's history, this pressure has forced Mexico to expand the army's role into domains customarily reserved for the civilian police.

This chapter explores how Loxicha may serve as a window onto the broader issues raised by an emerging consolidation of geopolitical power across North America. Frameworks of such magnitude can be problematic in their tendency toward producing only generalities. However, a failure to acknowledge the actual extension of existing interrelations and complicities limits our ability to discern, in turn, the alignment of interests that may be motivating them. A broad analytical framework also facilitates understanding of the ways and extent to which, through these networks, power is exercised and reinforced by means of an escalating political violence and its institutionalization.

This chapter explores this extension of power relations, while describing as well the legitimation strategies practiced within Mexico's state-sponsored violence, especially as it is seen in the form of militarization. With a focus on the recent Loxicha region's tragic history, this chapter examines the links in Mexico between militarization, transnational economic interests, and modes of violence that target particular social groups.

Context

The gradual implementation, since the 1980s, of neoliberal "structural adjustment" policies in Mexico has taken place concurrently with efforts at social, liberalist democratization. In the Mexico of the late twentieth and early twenty-first centuries, not every member of society has benefited from the sanguine promises of the neoliberal, economic project. With the gradual privatization of state enterprises, deregulation and opening of the country to foreign investment, an end to internal subsidies, the establishment of an ostensibly open trading zone by means of the North American Free Trade Agreement (NAFTA), and drastic cuts in spending on education and public health care, the divide between rich and poor has opened ever wider. Today, roughly half of Mexico's 93 million people live at or below the poverty level. From 1988 to 1998, the number of Mexicans living in extreme poverty rose dramatically from 14 million to 22 million.[1] Those most negatively affected by these economic trends are the country's rural and indigenous populations, who are hugely dependent on subsistence agriculture and small-scale service and commercial activities.[2]

For the last two decades, discontent and opposition (inspired by policies resulting in continual economic crises), an eroding social welfare safety net, and corrupt and authoritarian practices on the part of members of the Mexican government have together given rise to an energized civil society. Despite various repressive measures deployed by the government, popular resistance and protest have proliferated as democratic struggles have spread to more social arenas.

Among the important actors in this new political landscape are armed insurgent groups. These groups have emerged in response to what they view as the flagrantly corrupt and authoritarian political system that benefits Mexico's relatively tiny elite to the exclusion of the country's many economically marginalized social sectors. In this exclusionary political climate, the indigenous Ejército Zapatista de Liberación Nacional (Zapatista Army of National Liberation, EZLN) chose the date marking Mexico's entry into the league of "first world" economic players (the enactment of NAFTA on January 1, 1994) to suddenly thrust the plight and concerns of the most marginalized social sectors—the indigenous peoples concentrated in the south of the country—to the center of the national social and political consciousness. The Mexican government responded instinctively in traditional authoritarian manner, sending in hundreds of troops to Chiapas and gradually, over subsequent months, implementing a program of low-intensity warfare in the region.

This comprehensive counterinsurgency plan included, among other measures, the training and operation of an array of paramilitary groups to destroy the Zapatistas and their civilian bases of support, control and censorship of the media, and military occupation of particular regions within the state of

Chiapas. The paramilitaries established roadblocks and permanent bases, intimidated local populations by regular patrols through communities, took over community lands, and attempted to frustrate the work of human rights and nongovernmental organizations (Willson, 1998, 3). While paying lip service to initiatives toward reconciliation and the establishment of a lasting peace in the region, the government worked to eliminate the Zapatistas. Over time, the federal government sent more military units to entrench themselves further in the Chiapan countryside, especially in the impenetrable Lacandon Forest, the suspected center of EZLN operations and sympathies.

Violence is a way of enforcing definitions of the nation-state, as is particularly apparent in periods when those definitions are under threat. The EZLN appeared on the scene when the Mexican state was at a vulnerable point, about to assert itself as a credible trading partner and political ally on the international scene. The enactment of the agreement was to mark the crowning achievement of NAFTA's main promoter, then president Carlos Salinas de Gortari. The spellbinding sight of hundreds of indigenous workers—sporting balaclavas and with handkerchiefs across their faces—proclaiming "¡Ya basta!" (Enough!), eclipsed the president's glory. The eruption of public opposition to the Salinas administration exposed, in spectacular fashion, the contradictions of the neoliberal state's development agenda.

Next to the EZLN, the Ejército Popular Revolucionario (Popular Revolutionary Army, EPR) is one of the largest armed insurgent groups currently at large in Mexico.[3] Since the Zapatista uprising, both national and international public interest has been focused on Chiapas but, as the activities of the EPR demonstrate, mobilization of armed insurgent groups is occurring throughout the country. Along with Guerrero, Oaxaca is one of two states where EPR guerrillas have been most active and government repression of suspected group members the most severe.

The Mexican government appears to have instituted the low-intensity counterinsurgency strategy because it considers it to be the most effective way to destroy these groups and other militant rural movements. In this plan, the state's aim is to obtain information at all costs. At the same time, authorities seek to debilitate the political or peasant-based organizations they suspect are linked to these guerrilla movements. By means of a carefully conceived plan of long-term militarization, harassment, and physical and psychological torture, fundamentally economic objectives are being enforced on what have been customarily the margins of the social and political arena. Indigenous communities serve as proxies for a vilified social category of "guerrillas" or "delinquents" whose aims challenge the very legitimacy of the state.

Unfolding Repression: The Loxicha Case

On August 28, 1996, the EPR emerged simultaneously as a military force in seven Mexican states. Members of the group carried out a series of armed raids to protest political detentions, assassinations, and disappearances perpetrated by the Mexican state. In Oaxaca, the E P R launched their first major attack at three sites far removed from one another.[4] At one of those locales, just outside the resort town of Huatulco on the Pacific coast, a violent confrontation between the army and the E P R took place. Seven members of the E P R and armed forces and two civilians died, and several others were wounded, making the Huatulco uprising the most severe of all the attacks across the country (Frumin and Ramirez, 1998, 14). The event was fateful for the Loxichas also. One of the two dead E P R members was a resident of the town of San Agustín, the seat of Loxicha's municipal government, near Huatulco.

The state and federal authorities' response demonstrated their resolve to show the E P R—and indeed any form of popular resistance—what they were up against. On September 25, 1996, a major operation was launched in the Loxichas, focused on the town of San Agustín (population 3,000), by some five hundred agents of the preventive police,[5] state judicial police, federal judicial police, and military integrated forces. In their zealous hunt for E P R members, these police and military groups arbitrarily arrested local men, including *campesinos* (peasant farmers), teachers, elderly men, and minors. Many of these men experienced beatings and other forms of physical torture. Homes in Loxicha communities were ransacked, their owners' belongings trashed or stolen. The twenty men arrested in the raid were blindfolded, taken to military camps or hideouts, threatened with death, and made to sign blank sheets that were later filled in with confessions.

The September operation was only the beginning of the Loxicha region's state of terror. Another large-scale invasion took place on November 7, 1996, some three months after the initial E P R attacks. At 3 : 00 A.M. about five hundred national army, federal transport police, preventive police, and even, according to the testimony of several witnesses, agents of the U.S. Federal Bureau of Investigation (F B I) carried out the operation. Nineteen people were detained and, once again, torture and prosecution followed these arbitrary arrests. According to detainees' testimonies, two individuals—dressed in black and wearing leather jackets and caps bearing the insignia of the F B I— headed the entire operation. The written testimony of one prisoner specified that the suspected F B I agents were tall of stature, and had North American facial features and a minimal command of Spanish. Other Loxicha men arrested concurred with his observations. While much ambiguity surrounds the F B I agents' involvement, representatives from the organization Global Exchange have confirmed the presence of F B I members in Oaxaca City at the end of 1997 (Frumin and Ramirez, 1998, 18).

Brian Willson reports that on December 9, 1996, the F B I, which maintains one of its largest foreign offices in Mexico City, held training sessions in Oaxaca for members of the police forces of Chiapas and other states. These training sessions occurred just thirteen days before a December 22 massacre at Acteal Chiapas, in which local police forces were implicated (Willson, 1998, 11). The synchronicity of these events points strongly to a central U.S. role in the training for military and police and so to the implementation of terror in the Loxicha region.

Over the course of the initial series of invasions into Loxicha territory that followed the EPR attacks, a total of over 138 Loxicha men were arrested, including members of the Loxicha municipal authority. Arrests were carried out without warrants and, in many cases, were accompanied by excessive violence. Human rights organizations received reports of women and children beaten and terrorized, people being violently evicted from their homes, and thefts and harassments creating a climate of fear in the communities. Detainees themselves were subject to constant threats of death and simulated executions. Later they attested to physical torture, including beatings, electric shocks, and food deprivation.

Often the torture was aimed at coercing self-incriminating statements from prisoners concerning EPR membership, or extracting testimony implicating neighbors, relatives, or friends. Many of the detainees spoke only Zapotec, yet they were not given access to a translator. In addition, some forty cases of extrajudicial executions have been associated with the period of repression. Many of these took place during operations conducted by the judicial police or followed the detainees' torture (Human Rights Watch, 1999a).

After being held incommunicado for short periods in military camps or other holding sites, Loxicha men were taken directly to prisons, while others were "disappeared" for periods ranging from a few days to eighteen months.

During these disappearances, the only way family members knew if their missing relative was living or dead was when he suddenly "appeared" in a prison somewhere in the state. From the resort town of Huatulco, many of the arrested men were transferred via small airplane to prisons in the states of Oaxaca, Hidalgo, and Mexico. Eleven of the detainees ended up in the infamous maximum-security prison, Almoloya, in the city of Toluca. Imprisoned an hour from Mexico City and six hours from Oaxaca, detainees at that location were effectively cut off from their family members and their communities.

Over the next year, from autumn of 1996 to the autumn of 1997, the military presence throughout the Loxicha region was intensified. The military erected checkpoints at main road intersections and bases or encampments outside communities, often occupying lands without permission. They conducted daily patrols through the villages, deepening the climate of fear and intimidation. Caravans of human rights activists and observers traveling to the Loxicha area were harassed and threatened, often by police of ambiguous affiliation. Estimates from 1997 place the number of Mexican army troops alone in the Loxicha region at 5,000.

Groups referred to by the Spanish acronym BOM (*bases de operaciones mixtas*, or integrated forces) carried out the militarization. These groups included agents of the army, preventive police, and the state and federal judicial police forces. In addition, members of the Airborne Special Forces group regularly patrolled the area by helicopter. After visiting the Loxicha region in 1997, leading human rights representative Mata Montiel declared this zone as the most militarized and repressed in the country (Frumin and Ramirez, 1998, 14). The repression did not stop with the initial round of arrests. Between 1996 and 2000, a total of some 150 Loxicha residents were detained. Many were subsequently liberated due to a lack of evidence against them, or proof of improper proceedings during their arrest. Following the passage of an amnesty law by the Oaxacan state congress—benefiting prisoners accused of crimes that fell within Oaxaca state jurisdiction—others were freed at the end of 2000.[6] While the number of arrests has declined over the years, the military still occupies the Loxicha region. Acts of violence and intimidation continue and, as mentioned previously, today—over six years later—some eighteen men remain in prison.

The Loxicha case demonstrates how in the Mexican political sphere a particular social group's members can be constructed as dangerous suspects, which then justifies the political violence and severe human rights abuses committed against them. It is a technique in the larger strategy of the Mexican state to pull out all stops and quash any murmur of political opposition that could endanger the emerging politico-economic order.

Militarization in Mexico: The Drug War and Counterinsurgency

Two intertwined, yet contradictory, tendencies characterize today's Latin America. On the one hand, there are resurgences of civil society, struggles toward democratization, and related more general pressures to open up political systems. On the other hand, there are concerted efforts to contain, or eliminate, manifestations of social mobilization and opposition. The result is a problematic situation referred to by McSherry (1998) as a "guardian democracy": under these conditions, the military is charged with a significant role in governance and public security, with the effect of cloistering civil society and limiting the space allowed for the public expression of political opposition.[7] In Mexico, the army has become a formidable political force.

How has this situation come about? In part, political liberalization and the rising importance of internal security issues have had an impact on the relationship between civilians and the police and army. This trend, moreover, is happening in tandem with the erosion of the hegemonic party system (signaled by recent electoral defeats of the long-dominant Partido Revolucionario Institucional) and of traditional practices of patronage. Finally, civilians are unable to secure their grasp on political institutions and resolve problems within these new conditions (López-Montiel, 2000, 79). In short, the military's ascendance as an important social actor is enabled by a pervasive political uncertainty and instability in the current period of transition. In the course of these developments, the army has slipped into a still ambiguous niche within the larger apparatus of political power.

Yet this is not the entire story. The United States supports this militarization process in order to extend its network of control in Mexico and across Latin America. This expansion of U.S. influence is felt to be necessary to guarantee stability, order, and social control for the establishment and growth of a free-market, corporate economy throughout the entire region. McSherry explains that today's U.S. security doctrine reaffirms the role played by the military forces during the Cold War (McSherry, 2000, 27).

Blurring the line between internal security and national defense, this new security paradigm strengthens Mexico's military, security, and intelligence forces. Historically, throughout Latin America these forces have been the most prominent obstacles to democratization, popular social movements, and civilian institutions. The militarization of Mexico has been especially flagrant and conspicuous since the Zapatista uprising began on January 1, 1994. Indeed, in the wake of the Chiapas conflict, the country's military budget was increased by more than 40 percent (Willson, 1998, 2).

In addition, the United States has had a vested interest in helping Mexico to eliminate the insurgents. The Mexican government drastically devalued the peso in December 1994, as foreign investors' view of the EZLN's continued presence (in late 1994 and 1995) helped to undermine confidence in the Mexican economy and in its government. This sagging confidence in the strength of Mexico's financial sector eventually led to a serious economic crisis that required a bailout by the United States. The EZLN's activities eroded the image of a stable political system promoted by Mexico's elites. Thus, the Zapatistas discouraged foreign investment and threatened the safety of the U.S. financial interests already established in the country, while at the same time the specter of substantial political instability in Mexico threatened to promote increased illegal migration to the United States.

Aside from the conspicuous increased presence of the military in urban locales, the militarization process has involved a deployment of soldiers in small towns, on highways, and in rural mountainous regions in a number of southern states. The Loxicha zone, for instance, is just one of several militarized areas in Oaxaca state. This ubiquitous presence of soldiers is justified by recourse to arguments concerning the need to maintain "public security" and combat drug trafficking. The areas that are most militarized are those where insurgent armies are believed to be most active.

From 1986 to 1999, the Mexican armed forces grew from 170,000 to 240,000 members (Ai Camp, 1999, 131). Active members are currently estimated at 175,000. Most are involved in anti-drug-trafficking campaigns, containment of guerrilla groups in the countryside, participation in policing programs, and in activities the government considers "social services" (López-Montiel, 2000).[8] In addition, under the administration of President Vicente Fox Quesada (who took office in December 2000), army officers have been appointed to prominent positions of power within the government.

A notable example is Mexico's current federal state prosecutor, Rafael Macedo de la Concha, who has a long career history in the national armed forces, including representing the Mexican government and the Department of National Defense before the U.S. State Department in issues related to arms and drug trafficking. He now occupies the rank of brigadier general of military justice. Many human rights and civilian organizations consider that Macedo's deep entanglements with the national armed forces compromise his capacity to act as a neutral party in addressing alleged instances of the military overstepping its bounds.[9]

The normalization of the pervasive military presence in Mexico is striking. Over the past decade, it has become customary, for example, to see armed soldiers acting as security guards in banks, patrolling city streets and rural communities, or manning checkpoints along highways and rural roads. This process, most conspicuous in Chiapas after the Zapatista uprising in 1994, is still visible throughout the country, especially in southern states like Oaxaca. Distinctions between the role of the military and that of the police are blurry and ambiguous. In Mexico, as elsewhere, civilian authorities are turning to the armed forces to take on a number of nonmilitary tasks that together lead to the militarization of domestic safety and security and a growing tolerance of paramilitary behavior.

U.S. Involvement in Mexico's Militarization

U.S. military operations in Mexico have a long history. Since 1836, there have been at least eleven documented military interventions (Willson, 1998, 1). Now, as Mexico becomes more and more absorbed into a regional neoliberal economic order and furthers its implementation of NAFTA, security linkages between the countries have both solidified and expanded.

In the decades after the Mexican Revolution of 1910, successive governments gradually reduced the military's allocation in the federal budget. At the beginning of the 1980s, however, this trend was reversed, when Mexico began to look to the United States as its primary arms provider. Thus, even before NAFTA became effective in 1994, the U.S. influence over Mexico's security forces was already climbing steadily. Between 1982 and 1990, Mexico leased, purchased, and received as aid more military equipment and services from the United States, under all categories of assistance,[10] than in all of the previous thirty years. Between 1984 and 1993, Mexico received ten times the number of U.S. arms than it had amassed from 1950 to 1983. During this time, U.S. government officials declared their apparently innocuous desire to cultivate Mexico as a "secure, stable, and friendly neighbor," and to expand its influence over the Mexican military.

Through 1993 and 1994, military supplies flowing to Mexico from the United States became even more varied and vast, in large part responding to the requirements of the campaign against drug trafficking. At the beginning of the 1990s, the United States started sending a number of helicopters to the Mexican attorney general's office (which controls the war against drugs) and to the Mexican armed forces. Then came the 1994 Zapatista uprising, which was a wake-up call for U.S. government advisors on Mexico. The EZLN, they concluded, was a grave threat to the internal stability of Mexico and, indirectly, to investor confidence in the national economy. The United States jumped swiftly to the Mexican army's aid, as U.S. helicopters were used in Chiapas to move Mexican soldiers to areas of conflict (Willson, 1998, sec. I, 6).

Not long thereafter, exchanges began between the Mexican and U.S. governments about the need for Mexico to develop a counterinsurgency-trained military force to deal with the Zapatistas. As a result of these discussions, the so-called Rainbow Task Force was formed just before the Mexican elections in the summer of 1994 and was assigned to this specific task. Not coincidentally, a couple of months later, President Bill Clinton issued export licenses for $64 million's worth of additional military equipment, plus $14 million for aerial forces to fortify Mexico's ground-based security forces (Willson, 1998, sec. I).

When Ernesto Zedillo followed Carlos Salinas as president in December 1994, he placed the army at the forefront of the war on drugs. A mere three weeks after his formal installment as president, the value of Mexico's currency declined precipitously, and the viability of the Mexican economy was further eroded. The famous January 13, 1995, "secret" Chase Bank memo that was leaked to the press demanded the annihilation of the Zapatistas owing to the threat the rebels posed to investor security.[11] Just seventeen days later, President Clinton engineered a contentious $50 billion bailout package to rescue the Mexican economy.

Zedillo's military offensives in Chiapas against the Zapatistas were designed to placate the Clinton administration and the international financial community. Later in 1995, Zedillo requested from Clinton's government military equipment valued at $237 million, ostensibly for use in the drug war (Willson, 1998, sec. IV, 4). In October of that same year, then Secretary of Defense William Perry paid a visit to the Mexican army's elite armed forces and announced a new security agreement between the two countries.

Declassified documents from the U.S. State Department and the Pentagon, which appeared in the Mexican daily *El Financiero*, revealed the leading role of the U.S defense establishment, from as early as January 1995, in directing Mexico's military and counterinsurgency strategies against the Zapatistas (Willson, 1998, sec. I, 5). The Mexican army's large-scale invasion of eastern Chiapas in February 1995, for example, relied on United States–supplied military hardware and support. U.S. spy planes were used in these efforts. The documents also reveal that the United States intended to continue to increase armaments and training for the Mexican military. By 1999, documents report, there were to be several thousand Mexican elite troops trained in what were referred to as "anti-narcotics operations."

These events had broader implications. Mexico's October 1994 counterinsurgency plan (termed Chiapas '94) was launched in early 1995. Following this plan, under the protective wing of the Mexican military and public security forces the first paramilitary group was recruited in northern Chiapas. At this point, the military offensive against the EZLN had moved into a new stage. On Zedillo's orders, the army moved into zones under Zapatista control, pushing the guerrillas further into the jungle near Guatemala. The government employed the concept of a low-intensity war (*guerra de baja intensidad* or GBI), a plan conceived by the Pentagon in the 1980s, as the preferred strategy to deal with their opponents. The aim was to wear down the Zapatistas through intelligence activities, psychological warfare, and "control of populations" in a prolonged war of attrition (Fazio, 1996, 48) without attracting international attention by resorting to a short-term, severe show of military force.

Thus, the flow of equipment and expertise from the United States to its southern neighbor steadily rose between 1995 and 1997. In April 1996, the defense chief of Mexico, General Enrique Cervantes Aquirre, visited U.S. Secretary of Defense Perry in Washington. They signed another milestone accord that included the transfer of an additional $50 billion's worth of military equipment and an intensification of training (Willson, 1998, sec. I, 8).[12]

Training has always been an important aspect of U.S. military aid to Mexico. Pentagon records indicate that between 1981 and 1995, 1,448 Mexican soldiers received training in the United States under the International Military Education and Training program and the Foreign Military Sales program (Sierra Guzmán, 2000, 202). Intensified U.S. training of Mexico's varied armed forces was precipitated by the Pentagon's doubts, expressed in

January 1995, that the Mexican military had the strength to combat the Zapatista insurgency. When the EPR's insurrection erupted in seven southern states in August 1996, the U.S. government's doubts were further strengthened.

Shortly after this "new" rebel army publicly declared its existence, the U.S. ambassador to Mexico, James Jones, declared to the Mexican press on September 9, 1996, that the United States was ready to provide Mexico with yet more equipment and training. That is, they would supply whatever was needed to purge the country of "terrorists." Since that time, training has become a key aspect of military relations between the two countries. Today, Mexico sends more military personnel to U.S. training programs than to those of any other country, thereby magnifying U.S. influence over the military (Willson, 1998, sec. I, 8).

The Mexican government's decision to put the army at the head of the drug war is itself a convenient rationale for a continued U.S. military presence in Latin America. By providing training, arms, and logistical support, the United States has encouraged use of the Mexican armed forces in counter-drug operations (Sierra Guzmán, 2000, 201). No noticeable reduction in the flow of drugs into the United States has occurred as a result of these changes, however, despite the millions of dollars the U.S. military has spent toward increased surveillance and antinarcotics efforts in Mexico (Willson, 1998, sec. I, 6; Sierra Guzmán, 2000, 199). Mexico remains a primary supplier of heroin, methamphetamine, and marijuana for the U.S. market and the transit site for over half the cocaine sold in the United States (NACLA, 2002, 14). Furthermore, Mexican military officers in the highest echelons have been accused of collusion with drug cartels.[13]

Much uncertainty surrounds the amount of funding and material support channeled to the Mexican army to fight the drug war. There is the suspicion that much of the military aid given to Mexico—ostensibly to fight drug trafficking—has been diverted to "internal security" and used to combat and contain armed insurgency movements in southeast Mexico, especially in the states of Guerrero, Chiapas, and Oaxaca (Sierra Guzmán, 2000, 201). Through the 1996 accord between the United States and Mexico, training of Mexican security forces in the United States has escalated dramatically. In the summer of 1996, many thousands of Mexican military personnel began training at seventeen bases in the United States. Noteworthy are the types of training sites used by members of Mexican military and security forces: six-hundred Mexican military officers, for example, received training at the infamous U.S. Army School of the Americas between 1946 and 1994.

In addition, U.S. Army Special Forces (Green Berets), based at Fort Bragg, North Carolina, considered the "nerve-center" of low-intensity war training, conduct the most specialized training courses in sophisticated counterinsurgency methods. Among those trained at Fort Bragg was General Mario Renán Castillo, who directed counterinsurgency efforts in Chiapas in 1996 (Fazio, 1996, 52). From 1996 onwards, U.S. training of Mexican soldiers was further enhanced with the field instruction of more than 1,500 members of the specialized Airborne Special Forces groups in 1997, which are known to have participated in the Loxicha raids in Oaxaca (Willson, 1998, 9).

In 2001 alone, 857 Mexican officials received specialized training in the United States. Official documents indicate that the numbers of officials trained rose 37 percent in the two years beginning in 2000 (Cason and Brooks, 2002, 3). United States–Mexico military training continues to be justified as part of the war on drugs. López-Montiel (2000), however, notes that the military and police commonly accuse each other of selling protection to drug-trafficking organizations, stealing confiscated drugs, and notifying drug dealers in advance when they are in danger of being raided.

Documents from the U.S. Congress reveal that in 1997, the Clinton administration channeled "anti-narcotics funds" of $8 million to Mexico, a significant leap from $2.2 million in 1996 (Sierra Guzmán, 2000, 202). Official U.S. government documents from 1999 indicate that the Mexican army purchased more than $62 million worth of U.S.-manufactured armaments in that year alone (U.S. Department of State, 1998; Arronte, Castro Soto, and Lewis, 2000, 208).

The continuous and escalating flow of arms and personnel between the United States and Mexico raises serious issues regarding human rights accountability. The official legitimacy that protects state and federal police bodies and the armed forces allows them to operate in conditions of utter impunity. Cases of summary executions, rapes, and physical abuses at the hands of government troops are commonly documented (Amnesty International, 2001; Human Rights Watch, 1999b).[14] Yet, it is in the context of the psychological war—an aspect of low-intensity warfare using terror—that human rights violations are especially acute.

The "Shadow State"

Economic globalization has induced the emergence of what Gledhill calls "shadow states": "new forms of state power and governmentality that are connected in important ways to the continuing regulatory powers of Northern governments and the interventions of transnational capital" (Gledhill, 1999, 199). In Mexico, an important dimension of the shadow state is the presence of intimate links between the activities of police and politicians on the one hand and illegal activities such as drug trafficking on the other. Some Mexican political elites have successfully solidified their power by sustaining an influence with the illegal economy's upper echelons, especially those of the illicit drug industry (Astorga, 1999; Fazio, 1996, 33–34).[15] Gledhill concludes that the "war against drugs" may be, in fact, part of a struggle to guarantee the neoliberal, economic model's perpetuation in Latin America. This model of development has encouraged considerable transnational economic investment in "legitimate" business (for example, financial services, resorts, and hotels) in which powerful political networks reputed to be involved in drug trafficking and money laundering also participate.

Beyond the corruption of the body politic, drug production and the campaign against it are deeply imbricated in local, national, and transnational economic and power relations. Violence related to the drug trade has become bound up with struggles over political control, natural resources, and counterinsurgency efforts against southern guerrilla groups (Weinberg, 2002, 18–19). The Lacandon forest area in Chiapas, for example, is also the home of vast natural resources that enhance the region's strategic value (Fazio, 1996, 41).

For Fazio, U.S. keenness to "continentalize" the Mexican economy—by means of encouraging privatization of its gas and oil industries, water, electric energy, railways, ports and airports, and highways and telecommunications—dovetails with the U.S. political-military order's aims to undermine the sovereignty of the Mexican federation. While the degree of this collusion of interests is debatable, eliminating natural resources from consideration as a factor fueling the militarization process would appear to be fundamentally naïve.

In Oaxaca, the main areas of conflict between the armed forces and armed insurgent groups are the state's most militarized, and they lie within regions that have either a geostrategic importance or else harbor significant natural resources. The Isthmus of Tehuantepec has strategic significance for the World Bank, the International Monetary Fund, and large transnational corporations as the center of the Plan Puebla-Panama. This multinational development project aspires to create a railway and road bridge across the isthmus that will serve as an alternative to the Panama Canal, as well as establishing an industrial belt encompassing maquiladoras and tourism facilities, and based on a more efficient exploitation of resources.[16] Likewise, the Loxicha region has been reputed to harbor significant mineral deposits. Military presence in these areas thus partly supports the efforts of greater national and transnational interests toward gaining exclusive access to resources and territories that are presently within the legal dominion of the indigenous peoples who inhabit these zones.

From this perspective, justifying its decisions by reference to the requirements of the war on drugs, Mexico has merged its national security strategy with that of the United States. The new transnational politico-economic system that is being created through this combined effort has been founded on critical social and economic shifts that have stretched the gap between Mexico's rich and poor. The safeguarding of the new system, moreover, is being delegated more and more into the hands of a Mexican military infrastructure trained and outfitted to a significant extent by the United States.

Paramilitarization

The trend in recent decades toward the encouragement of property privatization in Latin America has been matched by a growing privatization of the means of violence. The federal counterinsurgency plan of October 1994 reportedly included the training and operation of paramilitary groups charged with decimating the Zapatistas and their bases of support through campaigns of murder and intimidation. Paramilitaries have been regarded as responsible for a number of killings, including the horrific 1997 Acteal massacre. Since 1995 (when paramilitaries in Chiapas were first recruited, trained, and armed), a dozen such groups have reportedly been operating in the state (Hidalgo Dominquez, 2000).

In January 1997, the Oaxaca state government led by Diódoro Carrasco formulated a counterinsurgency plan to deal with the E P R. The document declared that the military annihilation of the E P R was impossible and prioritized instead intelligence actions that could operate to isolate, both politically and socially, the members of the "strategic command" of the E P R and their supporters (Castro Soto, 2000, 74). The creation of paramilitary groups has been one of the most terrible elements of this low-intensity or "dirty war." Paramilitarization represents the emergence of a campaign of systematic terror through particularly brutal means of a constant and omnipresent nature: intimidation, searches, raids, arbitrary roadblocks, interrogations, torture, burning and stealing property, ambushes, kidnappings, rapes, and assassinations. In Oaxaca, many of these groups are found in urban and rural indigenous zones. Sometimes, as has been common in Chiapas and the Loxicha region, their presence and the climate of terror they create have forced people to flee their homes and communities to seek refuge elsewhere.

Customarily, new members of paramilitaries are recruited from within local populations, often by taking advantage of existing divisions within communities. Incentives for joining are financial, but the power and status that such an affiliation promises are also significant attractions. Recruiting individuals from the local region as paramilitaries blurs the distinctions between perpetrators and victims (Zur, 1998). By this means, state officials and representatives of the federal government can keep their moral image clean and sustain the impression that unrest is rooted in local conflicts.

As in Chiapas, paramilitary presence in southern states like Oaxaca and Guerrero, where the government views insurgent mobilization to be particularly threatening, is also common. In Oaxaca, and the area of Loxicha in particular, paramilitary groups have played key roles in militarizing and waging "low-intensity" conflict. During the 1980s, members of Loxicha communities organized themselves and succeeded in driving out the area's local political bosses (*caciques*), who had exploited and harassed them for decades. Nevertheless, after the appearance of the EPR in 1996, these *caciques* managed to return. They reasserted their control over the region partly by hiring paramilitary groups or "white guards" (*guardias blancas*)[17] to terrorize and subdue the local population.

Many Loxicha men detained in 1996, for example, were not surprised that members of the security forces that carried out the raids on their communities were related to the area's former *caciques*. Although dressed as federal police or hooded, these agents were recognized as the same hired gunmen who had worked for *caciques* before being expelled from the Loxicha zone. During the security forces' raids, such paramilitaries regularly colluded with the state judicial police and the Mexican army by identifying individuals to arrest. These paramilitaries also have been involved in murdering many Loxicha residents (Human Rights Watch, 1999c).

Like other military and police forces, paramilitaries operate with complete impunity, given protective cover by local elites. Their practices often have the complicity of military and security forces. Severe human rights abuses have gone unpunished, and both within and outside of Mexico, there is much less awareness of the Loxicha case of state repression than that of Chiapas. In part, this testifies to the efficacy of the state and federal authorities' propaganda campaign to justify their actions in the Loxicha region. Through rumor, manipulation of the media, and influence over other sources of public representations, this ideological campaign is staged on the bodies, hearts, and minds of indigenous peoples.

Manufacturing Consent: Torture and Identifying an Enemy
Violence is visible and invisible, both material and symbolic. The litany of violent acts the Loxicha prisoners have been accused of committing—murder, terrorism, kidnapping, sabotage, robbery, arms trafficking, conspiracy, assault and battery, and rebellion, among others—amounts to a sadistic projection of the heinous crimes committed against them by the authorities. Yet the nature of state-authorized violence deployed against the prisoners is aimed at something beyond punishment, beyond instilling fear, and more than a brutal assertion of the perpetrator's authority. Acts of ongoing torture endured by the indigenous detainees, and especially by the "disappeared" Loxicha men, can be read at a deeper level.

The Oaxacan government's 1997 counterinsurgency plan acknowledged the federal army's direction of all counterinsurgency efforts in Oaxaca. The army's intelligence apparatus orchestrated the state government's actions regarding the content of operations carried out against the guerrillas (Castro Soto, 2000, 79). As part of the tactics of low-intensity war, torture was used both to elicit information and to construct the Loxicha detainees as guerrilla suspects (Stephen, 2000). In these terms, torture is a practice exercised directly on the bodies of indigenous suspects in order to inscribe a particular identity as a subversive; that is, through torture they are branded as someone who poses a threat to the otherwise "peaceful" and "stable" social body.

Customarily, members of the integrated forces raided Loxicha communities in the early morning hours, signaled by rounds of ammunition shot off outside homes to intimidate those within. Members of the judicial police or paramilitaries broke into people's houses and grabbed men from their beds. They beat them harshly and often terrorized other family members, particularly children. Instances of physical and psychological torture reported by the Loxicha men followed such arbitrary arrests, "disappearances," and incommunicado detentions. Blindfolded, the men would be taken to another site where they were beaten further. Some were subjected to asphyxiation torture methods; others endured electrical shocks applied to sensitive parts of the body (Frumin and Ramirez, 1998; Acción de los Cristianos para la Abolición de la Tortura [hereafter: ACAT], 1997).

Often the men were deprived for days of food and water, as well as access to personal hygiene facilities (Human Rights Watch, 1999c). Psychological tortures included constant threats of death to the detained men or threats to beat and/or kill members of their families. Racial insults punctuated many of these threats. Periodically the men would be taken from the small quarters where they were held for further interrogation. This would continue until verbal confessions were exacted about their complicity in EPR activities, or until they signed blank sheets that would later be filled in with their confessions.

These instances of torture and false confessions were used to implicate detainees as members of the EPR. Only rarely, however, did prosecutors or judges show any concern regarding the circumstances in which detainees came into custody, or the torture they testified to experiencing. In many of the most closely documented torture cases, prosecutors neglected to investigate them, despite medical records that indicated the suspects had been tortured (ACAT, 1997).

The goal of state violence is not merely to inflict pain. It is also motivated by "the social project of creating punishable categories of people, forging and maintaining boundaries among them, and building the consensus around those categories that specifies and enforces behavioral norms and legitimates and de-legitimates specific groups" (Nagengast, 1994, 122). As Foucault (1977) argued, one of the key components of the state's technologies of normalization is the important role they play in the systemic creation, classification, and control of "anomalies" in the social body.

The 1997 Oaxaca state counterinsurgency plan declared that the key to winning the battle against the EPR was garnering "the recognition and support of society." One of the plan's policy goals was, therefore, "to legitimize government institutions in the eyes of the people." [18] The challenge for the state, then, became the winning over of public opinion and establishment of the "credibility for government institutions through a new discourse and leadership" (Castro Soto, 2000, 78).

A systematic, carefully concerted, ideological campaign masks the continued persecution of indigenous communities in the Loxichas and elsewhere in Mexico. In part, the low-intensity war conducted in Mexico's southern region operates through figurations of ethnicity. This amounts to a basis of moral and social differentiation through "othering" (Stephen, 2000, 823; Todorov, 1984).[19] Beginning in the 1970s, the ascendance of indigenous peasant organizations put them "on the map" as regional and national political actors. Yet, especially since the EZLN uprising, they remain a stigmatized social group within the larger nation despite more recent coordinated efforts to claim both their rights in the present and redress for a long-standing pathology of social injustice.

The identification of indigenous people as seditious guerrillas fuels existing stereotypes of them as dangerous, primitive, hostile, and subversive, stereotypes that have deep historical roots in the Mexican collective cultural imaginary. This spatialization of individuals is part of the state's control over its population. Mexico's rural spaces in its southern states have become not merely the marginalized zones inhabited by indigenous peoples but bastions of insurgent mobilization that pose a threat to the *estado de derecho* (state of law), the stable social order. Thus, indigenous, insurgent groups are represented as a virus in and on the social body. Essentially, they are dangerous and malevolent and must be rounded up, disciplined, and contained.

Militarization in Mexico and the brutality of the activities associated with it have been justified indirectly by spreading fear among the general population. As a result, the extent of daily violence and social and general insecurity is accentuated, and consequently people are encouraged to see that the only alternative to military order would be chaos (NACLA, 1998). Ironically, many of those authorities perpetrating the violence believe that they are merely fulfilling their "duty," ridding society of a pernicious and well-established threat to societal well-being.

Through games of denial, silence, and distorted perceptions, the state—and the various authorities and forces that represent it—orchestrates a collective violence. This regime of control endorses a particular method of dealing with anyone suspected of involvement in any form of coordinated, antistate mobilization. Rather than being targeted at ameliorating poverty (arguably the root of insurgent mobilization in the first place), the government's actions focus on counterinsurgency maneuvers. The government, and the media, veils the maneuvers with small, publicly funded "development" projects in the Loxicha region.

The government uses language manipulation to underline its justification of militarization, exploiting fears and uncertainties, as well as distorting public awareness and perceptions of the danger that really exists "out there." The largest and most popular media channels, effectively under government control, affirm government declarations, aiming to foment paranoia and dissent among Loxicha inhabitants.[20] Disinformation campaigns are key to this process. Local Oaxaca newspapers have published articles listing names of Loxicha men they claim to be EPR members still at large.[21]

In spring 2002, a banner appearing over a roadway in Loxicha, which blatantly advertised EPR presence in the region, received close coverage by the local written press. Such twisting of representations is complemented by a virtual dearth of media or official information regarding the current situation. These practices form part of the technologies of violence deployed by the state in the context of the war of attrition. Through cruelly gradual and incremental means, the war of attrition is aimed not only at harming the perceived enemy but also its popular support base. Such techniques of violence are carried out in order to hinder testimonies, suppress criticisms, and prevent resistance.

Conclusion

Catalyzed by the explosion of the Zapatista indigenous insurrection and the wave of popular mobilization it entailed, certain Mexican social sectors have built and strengthened civil society and the human rights movement since 1994. However, this has been combined with continued impunity and a steep rise in militarization and counterinsurgency methods intended to stifle or destroy civilian opposition or challenges to the state. This is especially true in the present context of government-induced, neoliberal political and economic reforms.

Since 1996, when armed guerrilla groups such as the EPR became active in Oaxaca and Guerrero, these states have seen increasing violence, militarization, and human rights abuses. As exemplified by the Loxicha region's case, the persecution of presumed members or sympathizers of armed groups has led to harsh repression in indigenous zones of these states. Mexican militarization has included a systematic reign of terror, harmonizing with counterinsurgency and low-intensity warfare that is designed to subjugate whole populations. Through an abundant array of arms, other military equipment and, most conspicuously, military training, the United States has steadfastly supported this process. The continuous U.S. military aid funneled into Mexico has been excused on the basis of the "war on drugs." However, much of the evidence suggests that the U.S. government's true motivation in providing such aid is to assure stability for the Mexican economy. Indirectly, the United States seeks to protect transnational, corporate, economic interests that involve significant and, as yet, largely untapped natural resources. This is especially true for those resources found in rural, indigenous regions of the southern states.

Some analysts believe that the U.S. government has aimed in recent decades to unify all armies in the Americas under its leadership (McSherry, 1998, 2000; Reyes, 2002). The power networks of the "shadow state" operate through the official and more publicly recognized and sanctioned activities of official military and police corps. They also operate through the covert activities of these armed forces, as well as those of the paramilitary groups that collude with them. Recognition of these links requires that attention be paid to broader interests potentially at stake in any instance of state violence.

Within the reign of terror engineered by the Mexican government, paramilitaries represent the state's no-holds-barred stance. Grave human rights violations and brutal acts of psychological and physical torture and killings form part of the repertoire of these and other agents of the so-called low-intensity war. This war of attrition is visited especially on indigenous communities like those of the Loxichas. It is designed to intimidate the civilian population and weaken autonomy by constructing indigenous suspects as threats to internal security. It also exploits the deeply entrenched prejudices and views of indigenous people as dangerous subversives, thus justifying this militarization as the only path to political stability. That this "dirty war" in Oaxaca persists even today—despite abundant evidence amassed by human rights and other independent civilian organizations attesting to its cruel effects—is bleak testimony to Mexico's uncertain journey toward a consolidating and institutionalizing democracy.

NOTES

AUTHOR'S NOTE: I am indebted to Adriana Luna Vasquez, Israel Ochoa Lara, Mexican League of Human Rights Defense (LIMEDDH), Christian Action for the Abolition of Torture (ACAT), Oaxacan Human Rights Network (RODH), Organization of Oaxacan Indigenous Peoples (OPIZ) and, especially, the Loxicha prisoners and families.

1. Between 1994 and 2000, the overall wage decrease was around 20 percent, despite the fact that real wages grew between 1999 and 2000 by just over 1 percent (Salas, 2002, 34.)

2. According to the National Council of Population, the state of Oaxaca ranks third nationally in levels of marginalization: infant mortality rates, minimum salary levels, illiteracy rates, levels of education, and degree of access to potable water and electricity. Loxicha is classified as a "highly marginalized" zone in an already poor state.

3. Reputedly in existence since the 1970s, the EPR formed itself as a political and military entity in May 1996. Since that time, it has carried out military attacks or political acts in seven states (Oaxaca, Chiapas, Guerrero, Tabasco, Puebla, Guanajuato, and Mexico). The EPR's August 1996 attacks, avowedly aimed at the government, were the first major armed attacks. Yet, afterward, the government claimed that several leftist civilian groups, including teachers, were fronts for the EPR.

4. The three sites were Tlaxiaco, sixty miles west of Oaxaca City; La Crucesita, just outside Huatulco, a coastal resort town; and San Pablo Macuilxóchitl, ten kilometers east of Oaxaca City.

5. The preventive police, a corps of 3,000 soldiers created in January 1999 at the end of Zedillo's presidential term, functions effectively as a direct instrument of the Mexican state.

6. The amnesty law also cancelled 250 pending orders of arrest but did not benefit the remainder of the Loxicha prisoners, as their cases were being processed at the federal level.

7. McSherry (1998) identifies six trends visible throughout Latin America: (1) expansion of military presence in civilian institutions, (2) civilian governments' continuing use of authoritarian practices, (3) new internal security and domestic intelligence doctrines and missions for the military, (4) the use of a political intelligence organization, (5) continued impunity for violators of human rights, and (6) acts by paramilitary groups and unregulated private security organizations.

8. Where I worked in Oaxaca, for example, such activities on the part of members of the armed forces may include providing inoculations or distributing fertilizer or foodstuffs.

9. These organizations included the Inter-American Commission on Human Rights (Paternson, 2001), the Red Oaxaqueña de Derechos Humanos (based in Oaxaca City), and Amnesty International.

10. These categories were foreign military sales, commercial sales, excess defense sales, and sales under the International Military Education and Training program (Willson, 1998, section I, p.2).

11. The Chase Bank memo is reproduced on the following website: http://www.webcom.com/~ lpease/collections/hidden/chase-memo.htm.

12. The Pentagon prioritized the training of rapid-reaction units, instructing them in espionage, air assault, and drug interception (Sierra Guzmán, 2000, 202).

13. For example, at the beginning of President Salinas's term in 1988, the antinarcotics team of the federal judicial police was held responsible for severe human rights violations and collusion with drug traffickers (Sierra Guzmán, 2000, 203; see also Willson 1998).

14. Amnesty International (2001) and Human Rights Watch (1999a) were among the organizations collecting extensive testimonies of such Mexican military abuses. Currently, military authorities investigate and prosecute army abuses; owing to this arrangement, serious abuses go unpunished.

15. The most powerful Mexican drug traffickers appear to have had tight relations with high-ranking politicians.

16. Alfonso Romo, president of the multinational but Mexico-owned agro-industrial conglomerate Grupo Pulsar, oversees the Plan Puebla-Panama. He is also on the board of the nongovernmental organization Conservation International, which lobbies for "conserving" forests like the Chimalapas and the Selva Lacandona in Chiapas. In these cases, the effect of decreeing such zones ecological reserves is the disenfranchisement and even displacement of indigenous communities in those areas, enhancing the possibilities for the exclusive control of the areas and their resources by multinational interests.

17. *Guardias blancas* emerged in Chiapas during the state governorship of Samuel León Brindis (1958–1964), who gave them official status in 1961 by means of a decree that permitted cattle ranchers to carry arms and hire "private police."

18. From the counterinsurgency plan, "Oaxaca: The Conflict and the Project," as quoted in Castro Soto (2000, 75).

19. "Othering," as used here, is a concept developed primarily by postcolonial scholars. Tzvetan Todorov (1984), for example, describes how the Spanish "othered" the indigenous peoples of the so-called New World. They assumed the indigenous peoples were radically alien in every way and, therefore, justified their horrific abuse and genocide during the colonial period.

20. The enormous and hugely popular Televisa, for example, is a national, near-monopolistic, progovernment, private television network.

21. See, for example, "Documenta Gobernación 239 Eperistas 'Activos' en Oaxaca" (*Tiempo*, 16 de enero, 2002, p. 5).

BIBLIOGRAPHY

Acción de los Cristianos para la Abolición de la Tortura (ACAT). 1997. *La Tortura en México: 1996, Casos de Tortura Política.* Mexico City: Acción de los Cristianos para la Abolición de la Tortura.

Ai Camp, Roderic. 1999. *Politics in Mexico: The Decline of Authoritarianism.* New York: Oxford University Press.

Amnesty International. 2001. "Mexico: Casos de la Tortura: Clamor para que se Haga Justicia" [online]. London: Amnesty International [cited 2 April 2003]. Available from http://www.edai.org/centro/infos.html.

Arronte, Ernesto Ledesma, Gustavo E. Castro Soto, and Tedford P. Lewis, eds. 2000. *Always Near, Always Far: The Armed Forces in Mexico.* San Francisco: Global Exchange.

Astorga, Luis. 1999. "Drug Trafficking in Mexico: A First General Assessment" [online]. Paris: UNESCO, Management of Social Transformations Discussion Paper No.36 [updated 27 March 2003; cited 2 April 2003]. Available from http://www.unesco.org/most/astorga.htm.

Cason, Jim, and David Brooks. 2002. "Recibieron Capacitación en E.U. 857 Militares Mexicanos en 2001." *La Jornada*, 21 May, International ed., p. 3.

Castro Soto, Gustavo. 2000. "The Counter-Insurgency Strategy in Oaxaca." Pp. 73–80 in *Always Near, Always Far: The Armed Forces in Mexico*, eds. Ernesto Ledesma Arronte, Gustavo E. Castro Soto, and Tedford P. Lewis. San Francisco: Global Exchange.

Fazio, Carlos. 1996. *El Tercer Vínculo: De la Teoría del Caos a la Teoría de la Militarización.* Mexico City: Joaquín Mortiz.

Foucault, Michel. 1977. *Discipline and Punish: The Birth of the Prison*, trans. Alan Sheridan. New York: Pantheon Books.

Frumin, Amy, and Kristen Ramirez. 1998. *The Untold Story of the Low Intensity War in Loxicha: Human Rights Violations in the Sierra Sur of Oaxaca, Mexico* [online]. Unpublished manuscript San Francisco: Global Exchange, 1998 [cited 2 April 2003]). Available from http://www.globalexchange.org/campaigns/mexico/mil/loxichaSummary.html.

Gledhill, John. 1999. "Official Masks and Shadow Powers: Towards an Anthropology of the Dark Side of the State." *Urban Anthropology* 28 (3–4): 199–251.

Hidalgo Dominquez, Onécimo. 2000. "Paramilitarization in Chiapas." Pp. 111–30 in *Always Near, Always Far: The Armed Forces in Mexico*, eds. Ernesto Ledesma Arronte, Gustavo E. Castro Soto, and Tedford P. Lewis. San Francisco: Global Exchange.

Human Rights Watch. 1999a. *Systemic Injustice: Torture, "Disappearance," and Extrajudicial Execution in Mexico* [online]. New York: Human Rights Watch [updated 2002; cited 2 April 2003]. Available from http://www.hrw.org/reports/1999/mexico/.

———. 1999b. "Torture and Extrajudicial Execution in Oaxaca State," sec. VI [online]. New York: Human Rights Watch [updated 2002; cited 2 April 2003]. Available from http://www.hrw.org/reports/1999/mexico/Mexi991-06.htm.

———. 1999c. "The Loxicha Region: Abuses in the Search for EPR Suspects," sec. VI [online]. New York: Human Rights Watch [updated 2002; cited 2 April 2003]. Available from http://www.hrw.org/reports/1999/mexico/Mexi991-06.htm#P799_216619.

López-Montiel, Angel Gustavo. 2000. "The Military, Political Power, and Police Relations in Mexico City." *Latin American Perspectives* 27 (2): 79–94.

Luna Gasca, Adriana. 2002. "Tortura en Sobrevivientes de la Región Loxicha." In *Oaxacan Human Rights Network: Third Annual Report*. Oaxaca de Juárez: Red Oaxaqueña de Derechos Humanos.

McSherry, J. Patrice. 1998. "The Emergence of 'Guardian Democracy.'" NACLA 32 (November-December): 16–19.

———. 2000. "Preserving Hegemony: National Security Doctrine in the Post-Cold War Era." NACLA 34 (3): 26–27.

North American Congress on Latin America (NACLA). 1998. "Militarized Democracy in the Americas: Faces of Law and Order." NACLA 32 (3): 15.

———. 2002. "Profile: Mexico. Drug Economies of the Americas." NACLA 36 (2, September/October): 14.

Nagengast, Carole. 1994. "Violence, Terror and the Crisis of the State." *Annual Review of Anthropology* 23: 109–36.

Paternson, Kent. 2001. "Transferred from Military: Human Rights Groups Scrutinize Mexico's New Attorney General." *Jinn Magazine*, 16 February [online; cited 2 April 2003]. Available from http://www.pacificnews.org/jinn/stories/6.29/010216-transferred.html.

Reyes, Leonarda. 2002. "El Pentágono Quiere a México en su Comando Norte." *Proceso* 1321 (February 24): 43–46.

Salas, Carlos. 2002. "Mexico's Haves and Have-nots: NAFTA Sharpens the Divide." NACLA 35 (4): 32–35.

Sierra Guzmán, Jorge L. 2000. "Mexico–United States Relations and Drug Trafficking." Pp. 199–208 in *Always Near, Always Far: The Armed Forces in Mexico*, eds. Ernesto L. Arronte, Gustavo E. Castro Soto, and Tedford P. Lewis. San Francisco: Global Exchange.

Stephen, Lynn. 2000. "The Construction of Suspects: Militarization and the Gendered and Ethnic Dynamics of Human Rights Uses in Southern Mexico." *American Ethnologist* 26 (4): 822–42.

Todorov, Tzvetan. 1984. *The Conquest of America: The Question of the Other*, trans. Richard Howard. New York: Harper-Perennial.

U.S. Department of State, Office of Resources, Plans and Policy. 1998. *Congressional Presentation for Foreign Operations, Fiscal Year 1999*. Washington, DC: Government Printing Office, March.

Weinberg, Bill. 2002. "Drugs, Guerrillas and Políticos in Mexico." NACLA 36 (2): 18–19.
Willson, S. Brian. 1998. *The Slippery Slope: U.S. Military Moves into Mexico* [online]. San Francisco: Global Exchange [cited 2 April 2003]). Available from http://www.globalexchange.org/campaigns/mexico/slope/.

Zur, Judith. 1998. *Violent Memories: Mayan War Widows in Guatemala*. Boulder: Westview Press.

CHAPTER 6

Bloody Deeds/Hechos Sangrientos

Reading Guatemala's Record of Political Violence in Cadaver Reports

M. GABRIELA TORRES

Introduction

In the more than thirty years of Guatemala's civil war (the 1960s to 1996), politically motivated violence became an integral part of the functioning, governance, and maintenance of the state (Jonas, 2000; Nelson, 1999; Falla, 1994). Violence and terror, epitomized in highly public assassinations, ruthless massacres, and unsolved disappearances, became the favored political tools for Guatemala's military and political elites (McCleary, 1999).

The success of violence as a political tool was such that today in Guatemala politically motivated violence has come to be understood as a "cultural fact"—that is, violence has come to be unquestionably quotidian, perceived, at least by social scientists and popular journalists, as somehow both "natural" and "cultural" (Nordstrom, 1997). Briefly, many Guatemalans hold the belief that political violence is an integral, historically inherited, and ultimately inevitable part of commonplace conceptions and practices of the everyday (Torres-Rivas, 2000), and the fear and suspicion that accompany political violence have become a way of life (Sluka, 2000).

This chapter follows Nordstrom's suggestion that, precisely because violence has become perceptually naturalized into culture, it must be studied within the cultural contexts of its construction and practice as a "persistent and enduring dynamic" (Nordstrom, 1997, 123). I will argue that the naturalization of political violence into a cultural fact was produced, in part, through the creation and promotion of a language or pattern of political violence that—while it generated terror—at the same time obfuscated the political economy of its own production.

In Guatemala over the course of the civil war, the increasingly complex documentation and resulting bureaucratization of violence made possible the development of counterinsurgency policy aimed not at eliminating a small guerrilla movement but rather directed at controlling the general population. Establishing control of the population secured an advantageous political and economic position for the country's military elite—the Guatemalan armed forces—and its political allies, represented by the Comité Coordinador de Asociaciones Agrícolas, Comerciales Industriales y Financieras (Coordinating Committee of Agricultural, Commercial, Industrial and Financial Associations, CACIF) (McCleary, 1999; Falla, 1994). Through an analysis of both the marginal and mainstream documentation of violence, this chapter aims to give a brief insight into the ways in which Guatemala's military and political elites authored terror and violence in a repetitive and orchestrated display of fear-inducing images and texts.

One of the principal means through which generalized fear was created in Guatemala throughout the period known as "the violence" (la Violencia, 1978–1984) was through the display of images and descriptions in newspapers of cadavers and public assassinations. During this period, cadaver reports appeared almost daily.[1] I aim to show how the parade of cadaver reports and public assassinations documented in newspapers throughout la Violencia are patterned. The patterns revealed by cadaver reports, moreover, indicate the presence of an organized system of counterinsurgent state-sponsored violence that—in addition to seeking the death of particular targets—was intended to create a sense of generalized fear throughout the Guatemalan population. Building on the work of Scarry (1984) and Feldman (1991), in this chapter I propose to begin to disentangle the political meanings of the tortured body.

Although this chapter deals with the public display of cadavers, it is important to note that—in the Guatemalan case—there is much documentary evidence to suggest how tortured and murdered bodies were produced. Prior to looking at the meanings of the display of bodies, it is important to briefly highlight some insights into the everyday functioning of counterinsurgency that have been gained from the study of internal military documents.

The high level of organization and bureaucratization of Guatemala's counterinsurgency machine is most evident in a leaked log of one particular death squad's counterinsurgency activity between 1983 and 1985.[2] The document, intended for internal use only, does not explicitly state that the squad's activity occurred within the military institution. Nevertheless, the records kept in the document do evidence deep structural links between the 183 kidnappings, assassinations, and tortures for which this squad was responsible and the activities of other military departments, such as Military Intelligence (G-2).

What Doyle (1999) has called the "death squad diary" provides chilling insight into the bureaucracy behind kidnapping, torture, and murder carried out in the name of ridding the country of an armed insurgency. While the death squad diary sometimes admits to the murder of individuals in its logs (usually attributed to third parties or justified by escape attempts) and to the acquisition of information from individuals, no mention is ever made of the use of torture techniques. Even in a document meant only for internal use, a concerted effort was made to achieve a state of "plausible deniability"—as neither explicit written records nor bodies that could be traced to the perpetrators were intended to be left behind. The concealment of murder and torture practices through codes in an internal document stands in contrast to the numbers of publicly displayed tortured cadavers that are the subject of this chapter.

In part because murder and torture are concealed in internal records, the repetitiveness of newspaper reports of violence might have been intended to have several effects on readers similar to those Pentecost (2002) documented in her study of the effects of war photographs in Northern Ireland. Despite the richness of the archival data used in my study, the effects that the records had on their readers cannot be drawn from the newspaper records themselves. My interpretations are based, instead, on a series of informal conversations on the subject of my research project with Guatemalan academics, human rights activists, and militants during my fieldwork, as well as from remembered conversations on political violence with Guatemalans in exile in Mexico, Canada, and the United States during the 1980s.

Cadaver Reports and the U.S. Role

Guatemala's violent past is not entirely home grown. Because of a long-standing geopolitical interest in the country, as well as an interest in the curtailment of communist-inspired movements in its region of influence,[3] U.S. military and diplomatic personnel have been documented, at best, to have been fully aware of the atrocities committed by Guatemala's bloody military regimes and, at worst, to have been active supporters through the provision of military guidance, training, and financing for those atrocities (Jonas, 2000, 128).

In addition to a public admission of past wrongdoings in 1999 by then President Bill Clinton, documents written during la Violencia also demonstrate the detailed knowledge that U.S. intelligence agencies had about Guatemala's counterinsurgency machinery (Jonas, 2000, 157). In a Central Intelligence Agency secret cable written in 1983, U.S. officials discuss the reappearance of cadavers, which they openly identify as products of an apparent reemergence of el Archivo, the special forces branch of the Guatemalan presidential guard:

> Over the past few months, kidnappings, particularly of students and educators, have increased in numbers and bodies are again appearing in ditches and in gullies. Showing the telltale signs of rightist hit squad executions similar to those common under the previous regime [of General Romeo Lucas García]. . . . Ambassador's Comment: I am firmly convinced that the violence described in paragraph three is Government of Guatemala ordered and directed violence and not "right wing violence" and that these were not "rightist hit squad executions" but again executions ordered by armed services officers close to president Rios Montt. (Central Intelligence Agency, 1983, 2)

This cable clearly shows that U.S. officials were sufficiently versed in Guatemala's language of violence to understand who was responsible for particular cadavers' appearances and how signs on bodies were connected to the counterinsurgency machinery.

Yet, as was previously mentioned, U.S. involvement in Guatemala was not limited to knowledge of the design and practice of la Violencia but also included financial and military support to the country's successive military regimes. Despite a curtailment of overt military aid to Guatemala beginning in 1977 (and lasting until 1984), due to the military's excessive human rights abuses, U.S. policymakers retained an active interest in the country, compiling assessments of those abuses and of their practitioners (Doyle, 2000). U.S. military support to Guatemala's military included the training of police and military officers, ground troops support, and arms and ammunition sales, particularly in the periods preceding and following the height of la Violencia (Perera, 1993; Jonas, 2000).

While the United States continued economic assistance to Guatemala during la Violencia (albeit at reduced levels),[4] the country received negligible levels of direct military assistance. However, commercial sales of munitions and lethal or potentially lethal equipment by U.S. companies to the Guatemalan government and military continued during la Violencia, totaling $120.5 million during that seven-year period (United States General Accounting Office [hereafter: U S G A O], 1986). After the U.S. Congress lifted its restrictions on support, Guatemala again began to receive direct military assistance. In 1986, the first full calendar year of reinstated direct assistance, such aid totaled $10.3 million (U S G A O, 1986).

Collecting Cadaver Reports

As part of a larger archival research project,[5] I examined all issues of the national daily *Prensa Libre* published in the period 1978–1984 and collected all the cadaver reports discussed in this daily newspaper, which during la Violencia had the country's largest circulation. In this chapter, I have chosen to highlight individual records that are either exceptional within the broader body of accounts or that are representative of the narratives found in the newspaper. It is important to note that the cadaver records discussed here represent a very small percent of the total number of people killed during the civil war.

It is estimated that from 1978 to 1984, 80.4 percent of the overall count of victimization cases (including assassinations, rapes, and disappearances) were not reported in the press (Comisión de Esclarecimiento Histórico [hereafter: C E H], 1999).[6] Broken down by presidential terms of office: in the period 1978–1981, 67.9 percent of cases were not reported in the press; in the period 1982–1983, 80.2 percent of cases were not reported in the press; and in 1984, 55.1 percent of were not reported in the press. The lack of coverage reinforces the suggestion that throughout la Violencia the press was constrained from publishing the effects of counterinsurgency. The press appears to have been particularly constrained in this regard during the period in office of General Ephraín Ríos Montt (March 1982–August 1983).

The reports of civil war–related deaths in *Prensa Libre* emphasize individual violent deaths, while the deaths of the majority of the people who were killed in massacres were minimally discussed in the newspaper. Reports of massacres that did appear in *Prensa Libre* were, for the most part, coverage of mass killings that were attributed with ease to guerrillas or convincingly portrayed as a result of conflicts internal to indigenous communities.[7]

This chapter is based on the discourse and statistical analysis of nearly 3,000 cadaver reports.[8] I have chosen to highlight for the first section examples of cadaver reports that can be considered representative of at least 60 percent of my sample. The final section on women and gender contains examples of out-of-the-ordinary or exceptional cadaver reports; these excerpts were chosen specifically because they serve to show the boundaries of violent acts in Guatemala. By showing the margins of Guatemala's violent record (the socially unacceptable and the blatantly grotesque) as well as the mainstream, we gain a better understanding of how systematic politically motivated violence was constructed and negotiated in the process of becoming a part of the collective imaginary of Guatemalan society. The implicit editorial acceptance of the representative cadaver reports and the subtle rejection of the unusual or offensive accounts make visible the social processes through which a public record of the violence was constructed.

Before entering into the analysis in earnest I would like to highlight a personal apprehension in constructing and presenting this study. This chapter is difficult to write because even in my best attempts at academic deconstruction I cannot escape thinking of—or perhaps more specifically, imagining—the suffering and physical pain of torture and decapitation, as well as the fear, loneliness, and indignity that must surely have been felt by the people (and their families) whose life stories are reflected here. It is also difficult to write because of my awareness that the act of analysis and writing about these tortured bodies is itself an act of objectifying the pain that was felt. In doing so I fear I may contribute in some form to the process of externalization and perhaps even minimization of the individual and the societal significance of human suffering.

Having expressed my trepidations, I would like to suggest that the detailed reading of and writing about human suffering implied by cadaver reports was not intended by their authors. Representing the horror of the cadaver in newspaper stories was perhaps only meant as a coded type of fear-mongering. Deconstructing the codes, reading the details, and reframing this bodily evidence of pain, therefore, may serve to show more about its authors than they would wish to show. It is in the spirit of contributing to the unmasking and deconstruction of the fear-producing state and its tactics that I now wish to delve into the accounts of death that follow.

Representative Cadaver Reports in Historical and Social Context

The representative cadaver reports found in the newspapers are of male cadavers with some signs of torture but not substantial excess, found in unremarkable rural or urban locations. In terms of style and language, there seems to be a strong link between the representative cadaver reports and the reports made by justices of the peace (*jueces de paz*). When a dead body is found, and particularly in cases where there is evidence of foul play, the Guatemalan Procedural Penal Code requires that a legal affidavit be made by a justice of the peace in situ prior to the relocation of the body to the morgue or any other interment or disposal of the body.[9] While currently this preliminary report is preferentially made by a medical examiner, during the historical period in question the report of the body's location, the circumstances of the find, an inventory of the body's wounds and garments, and a preliminary assessment of the cause of death were all recorded by a justice of the peace.

Cadaver reports appeared in *Prensa Libre* throughout the period 1978–1984 but with greater frequency in 1978–1981 and 1983–1984. From March 23, 1982, until the end of June the same year (the period of the military junta), fifty-seven cadaver reports and seven massacre accounts appeared in *Prensa Libre*. Those figures represent an average of just over nineteen cadaver reports per month, which coincides with the average of twenty cadaver reports per month seen during the preceding presidential term of General Romeo Lucas García (in office July 1978 to March 1982).

Ball, Kobrak, and Spirer (1999, 41) estimate that the total number of politically motivated killings and disappearances—both publicly reported and unreported—that occurred during Lucas García's nearly four-year term in office was just under 9,000, whereas during Ríos Montt's sixteen-and-one-half-month term the number of politically motivated killings and disappearances is estimated to have been just over 12,000. Seen as a monthly accounting, these figures represent an increase of nearly 300 percent in the number of politically motivated killings when Ríos Montt's term is compared to Lucas García's term (Ball, Kobrak, and Spirer, 1999). Nevertheless, the number of cadaver reports that appear in *Prensa Libre* during Ríos Montt's term in office is 171, making the average count just over twelve per month, which is a substantial decrease (approximately 40%) from the number of cadaver reports that appeared in *Prensa Libre* during the terms in office of both Lucas García and the military junta.[10]

Studying the distribution of cadaver reports through time is particularly interesting because the period of fewer cadaver reports coincides closely with the presidency of Ríos Montt—during which the greatest number of crimes linked to political violence occurred.[11] It is important to note that most victims of violence during this period were from rural areas and of indigenous origin, killed mainly in larger-scale massacres that were previously uncommon (Proyecto Ínterdiocesano de Recuperación de la Memoria Histórica [hereafter: REMHI], 1998a).[12]

The implications of this coincidence are varied and cannot be fully explored here. Nevertheless, the data substantiate two simultaneous probabilities. First, the reduction in the public representation of death during the Ríos Montt period might be precisely attributable to some form of military directive targeted at constraining press coverage of the human costs of its counterinsurgency campaigns. This probability is borne out partly by the increase in military-sponsored pro-counterinsurgency public advertisement during this period and by repeated complaints of tightened controls on the freedom of the press.[13]

Second, reports of mass killings might have had an undesired effect on newspaper audiences: whereas a report of an individual death can be reasoned away as the fate of an individual involved in unsavory practices, a criminal killing, or simply common crime, accounts of mass killings of rural laborers are much more difficult to explain away. One cannot help but wonder, in addition, if the reaction to mass killings on the part of the general population, and in particular on the part of members of the economic elite, would not have been significantly more forceful if the victims had been of ladino origin.[14]

As the REMHI (1998b) report points out, the display of tortured bodies through cadaver reports might have been intended to create uncertainty among their viewers. Almost as a rule, cadaver reports do not identify a perpetrator of murder or torture, yet they offer various degrees of detail of the signs of violence on the body. The REMHI publication *Guatemala: Nunca Más* calls this type of fear-inducing strategy "terror by example," where fear and uncertainty are created through the sheer disregard for human life that is demonstrated in the display of a tortured cadaver (REMHI, 1998b, 8). Despite the evidence of wounds, however, such displays are not accompanied by elaborated explanation of the causes of the violence, thus creating a diffuse, almost intangible sense of insecurity. Because no perpetrator of violence is mentioned and because the reader is unsure as to why the victim has been killed, it is impossible for the reader to definitively exclude herself or himself from the probable target group.

In addition, the examples of cadavers might have acted as warnings of the potential consequences of undesired associations and behavior. While government, insurgent, or army sources are seldom pinpointed as perpetrators of the assassinations, readers clearly associated the deaths with some type of involvement in the armed conflict. As letters and comments from family members of the disappeared show, Guatemalans during the period of la Violencia considered any type of political activity as potentially lethal, since someone could construe it as taking a side in the conflict, thus making oneself physically vulnerable (*Prensa Libre*, 28 April 1983, 13).

A third potential effect of the parade of cadavers and assassinations is the double effect of naturalizing violence as a disruptive but ever-present daily occurrence. Because of the sheer excess of detail in the many reports, the constant repetitive gruesomeness of the killings, and their unending extent, violence of this type lost what we might call shock value (Pentecost, 2002). Nevertheless, at the same time, the details of violence, particularly for politically involved Guatemalans, became codes of the direction, intensity, and potential spread of violence.

In the late 1980s, Guatemalans in exile often read cadaver reports as deeds of particular death squads. The modus operandi enacted on each cadaver was read as a form of signature. The torture signs inscribed on the bodies and described in cadaver reports allowed readers to speculate as to which agency (police, army, presidential guard, and so on) might be to blame for a crime, instead of simply reading each report as a further sign of increasing violence. Thus, as violence became more naturalized and everyday, its practical utility—the reasons why readers found reports useful or interesting—also changed.

Modus Operandi and Torture Signs:
Establishing and Naturalizing Fear
The marks left on dead bodies which suggest a modus operandi (scars, decapitations, maiming, skewering, burns, and so on) are, in Feldman's words, narratives of violence that are "invested in material artifacts and relations that have a story telling capacity on their own" (Feldman, 1991, 14). Both the stories that are told by these necrographic maps—or what I would like to call

inscriptions—and the ways and means through which these cadaver reports found their way into newspapers tell as much about the authors of violence as they tell us about the acts of violence themselves. Yet, these inscriptions are not only signs that tell us of the power relationship between the cadaver and that person's victimizer; they are also signs or signatures that, by their publication in newspapers, need also to be seen as texts created with a wider audience in mind.

The cadaver reports might also be read as purposeful attempts at creating terror to encourage social immobility. Generalized suspicion and the practice of "systematic not knowing" or "ignoring" or "not remembering," even of things such as the blatantly public and constant record of violence, became key elements of survival through social immobility. That is, terror was meant not only to threaten probable opponents, or to destabilize society, but also to discourage even the possibility of conceiving or speaking of any anti-elite or antigovernment action. Death, after all, could come at any time and be perpetrated by a wide range of actors.

Siebert (1996) discusses how this type of silence or immobility can be a key element in the maintenance of an enveloping power. What I am proposing here is that while the cadaver record was impossible to ignore, and the daily readings imply themes still more broad than those I suggest here, the enforced practice of both reading/seeing and yet not knowing these records was a seemingly contradictory but nevertheless efficient way to manage survival in the volatile climate of the civil war. Guatemalan readers of cadaver accounts needed to practice not knowing to show their loyalty to the state, which was run on the all-too-familiar mentality, "you are either with us or against us."

According to testimonials published in *Guatemala: Nunca Más*, the appearance of bodies with signs of torture, combined with the impossibility of seeking aid from civil or judicial authorities, was a significant factor in developing a climate of terror of such an advanced and pervasive degree that it led to the complete disorganization of the daily functioning of many families (REMHI, 1998b). Because cadaver reports were intended to induce fear, naturalize political instability and violence, and disrupt the everyday social life of Guatemalans through a constant display of power, they stand as clear examples of what Scarry calls the "unmaking of the world" (Scarry, 1984, 56). Scarry suggests that the process of torture and unmaking—detailed in the cadaver reports—not only disrupts society but inevitably results in the bolstering and fetishization of state power.

According to Scarry, the state's power is seen through the tortured body because it is through the very act of torture that a body's political meaning is appropriated by the violent state (Scarry, 1984). Feldman challenges Scarry on this point, suggesting that violence can serve to invest the tortured body with political meaning principally because these bodies become evidence ("texts"), both of acts of defiling and the power dimensions encoded within the act of defilement itself (Feldman, 1991). As a result, Feldman suggests that tortured bodies must be seen as encoding the entanglements of power (exercised through varied combinations of violence-wielding institutions, agents, and political technologies and rituals), not merely *re*presenting the power that made them so but also possessing a clear political meaning in and of themselves.

The case of Guatemala serves to reinforce Feldman's reconceptualization of the meaning-laden tortured body. The bodies remembered in the cadaver reports analyzed here were meant to unmake the world for their audience. The reports are indeed laden with intended political meaning that reifies the state while prescribing citizen behavior and demonstrating the state's vast power. Yet, the cadaver reports seen here are also fraught with unintended meaning, because they give insights into the identities, strategies, and motives of the perpetrators of violence, while they also unmask the institutions and the technologies that the state used to exercise and expand its power.

The signs of torture inscribed in these cadaver reports are symbols of the systematization and organization of procedures, processes, and institutions involved in the application of counterinsurgency violence. In its analysis of the terror-inducing strategies, *Guatemala: Nunca Más* notes that state-sponsored Guatemalan military and paramilitary forces were responsible for 85 percent of all cases of torture in this period (REMHI, 1998b). The repetitive and organized appearance of the same signs of torture in the cadaver reports is evidence of an established pattern or language through which violence was expressed for both public consumption and for consumption by state-sponsored violence agents.

Through analysis of these data, I have been able to establish that military and quasi-military organizations [15] instituted a series of recognizable, lasting patterns of torture and death. These patterns served multiple purposes: to conceal the individual identities of violence practitioners; to alert violence practitioners of counterinsurgency victims, operations, and potential targets; to allow for a high degree of mobility and flexibility in carrying out counterinsurgency goals; to spread the specter of terror literally across the national territory through the careful use of public and private spaces for torture and detention; and most important to the state's long-term goals, to foment a fear of the unimaginable combined with tangible consequences for dissent in the general population.

As was noted before, each excerpt from a cadaver report reprinted here narrates a partial life story. Despite the variety of interpretations that can be made of these reports, I propose that the publication of these stories of death served counterinsurgency efforts by reconfiguring the Guatemalan nation through the display of torture. The tortured bodies can be *reviewed* in light of their fetish potential. Axel (2001) posits that tortured bodies created by states for nation-building purposes can be seen as fetishes both in the Marxian and Freudian senses of the word. For Axel, the tortured body acts to constitute the relationship between the state and its citizens, and the tortured-body-as-fetish highlights the viewer's knowledge of the simultaneous difference and similarity between the "reader/citizen" and the "object/noncitizen" in his or her gaze (Axel, 2001, 32).

I propose that cadaver reports were constructed so as to draw readers in by highlighting the relationship of difference and similarity between readers/ citizens and the unexplained, discarded, and mutilated, rejected noncitizen body. While readers were drawn in, the tortured body's meaning and the probable explanation of death repulsed them, primarily because of the reader's need to define themselves as different from those who had been so violently expelled from the nation. In fact, this back and forth between repulsion and attraction, similarity and difference, may be related to the impossibility of expressing pain and suffering through language (Scarry, 1984).

The Typical Cadaver Report

Prior to exploring the margins of violence, it is important to become familiar with the structure of typical cadaver reports. The most common and straightforward report type contains elements found in the following account taken from page 5 of the issue of *Prensa Libre* published on 29 March 1978:

The cadaver of an unidentified man was found yesterday morning in an empty lot near kilometer 33 on the highway to the Atlantic in the jurisdiction of the town of Agua Caliente with fifteen bullet wounds and signs of torture.

First, most cadaver reports *re*present "unidentified" (and therefore name-less men) who were, as the cadaver reports themselves detail, buried as "XX." Paradoxically, this nameless quality allows cadavers greater representability than would a named murder victim. By not knowing the victim's name or his-tory, it is impossible for readers to exclude themselves from belonging to the victim's group (subversive, student, indigenous, and so forth), and as a result, the reader cannot gain distance from the threat of violence.

Second, cadaver reports always discuss the location of the body's discov-ery. Location was marked most often by cross streets and the city zone or the kilometer mark closest to where the body was found. This element of the cadaver report might be due to the legal requirements around each cadaver find, but they also give readers specific information of the spread of violence and perhaps even of the authors of violence themselves. Even seemingly ba-nal elements of information in a newspaper report could contain crucially relevant social meaning for the intended audiences. A third relevant element found in cadaver reports is at least a minimal description of the nature of the wounds, which is again in congruence with the cadaver find affidavit. Read-ers and report authors interpreted wound types as signs much in the same way as locations.

Finally, although not present in the sample report shown here, cadaver re-ports often detail specific pieces of clothing worn by a cadaver or a cadaver's state of undress. Descriptions such as the following were common: "he wore only yellow briefs and a green corduroy jacket. Besides the cadaver, there was a pair of light-blue pants, as well as shoes and black socks" (*Prensa Libre*, 11 October 1978, 15). This degree of minutiae, or set of ostensibly insig-nificant details, is in part a result of the elements that make up the legal records kept on cadavers (from which the published newspaper reports bor-row). Nevertheless, I posit that for the reader such insignificant details on each cadaver might also have served to establish a type of empathy based on sharing everyday details of living.

Women, Margins, and Gendering State-sponsored Violence

Cadaver reports of women victims are unusual and make up less than 10 per-cent of all cadaver accounts collected. This difference is in part due to the comparatively small number of women openly assassinated during the civil war, but it may be attributed as well to a methodological difficulty.[16] In practice, it is difficult to assess whether female victims (of assassinations, rapes, beatings) suffered politically motivated abuse or a form of domestic abuse. More often than not, newspapers detailed horrific accounts of beatings and assassinations for which the victim's husband, boyfriend, or father had been apprehended.

Through conversations with human rights advocates, it became clear that sometimes the victim's relatives were accused of what was in fact a politically motivated crime. Thus, my definition of what constitutes a politically motivated crime against women may result in the underreporting of the counterinsurgency's effects on women. Although I collected all published records of violence against women in *Prensa Libre*, I chose to classify as political violence only records where torture was evident and where no individual had been identified as either a culprit or a suspect.

Despite the small sample and these methodological difficulties, there does appear to be a specific story of violence, with broad theoretical implications, that is told by the cadaver reports of female victims. In Guatemala, as in most instances of political violence, the victim's gender plays a pivotal role in determining the type of torture, the way that bodies are disposed of, and the extent and type of reporting that is made of violated cadavers.[17] In this section, I will attempt to characterize how women were portrayed in cadaver reports, highlighting the gender-specific necrographic maps and the significance of these signs to the role of women in the restructuring of the Guatemalan nation through violence (Malkki, 1995).

> YOUNG WOMAN. Under the Rio Seco Bridge, kilometer 127 of the route from Rio Bravo to Tiquisate, a cadaver of a young woman, around 26 years of age, was found. She was shot to death after having been tortured. The unknown woman was 1.5 meters tall, had white skin and, as a detail that could lead to her identification, she had two gold crowns on her upper teeth. (*Prensa Libre*, 20 June 1978, 2)

This cadaver account bears strong resemblance to the straightforward account of the typical male cadaver. The location in which the body was found and the signs of torture on the body suggest a pattern that is common in all politically motivated crimes. Two details stand out in this account: there is an implicit request for a recognition attempt, and her skin color and gold crowns suggest a particular socioeconomic standing. These elements—the implicit request for identification and details suggesting the cadaver's class or economic background—are unusual among male cadaver reports and seem to be more common in those accounts describing female victims.

> The cadaver of a woman cruelly assassinated and buried as an unknown. . . . The body was found completely nude on Sunday afternoon.
> (*Prensa Libre*, 5 April 1979, 12)

This account again bears close resemblance to the straightforward male cadaver accounts, where the deceased has been buried as an unknown person and where nudity and the accompanying qualifier "cruelly assassinated" would typically signal that the body was of a victim of state-sponsored torture. With the body of a woman, this seemingly typical description may signal a form of torture often reserved or emphasized for female victims: rape. In Guatemala, rape was typically associated with two types of violations: massacres, evidence of which are not seen in detail in the cadaver analysis, and capture by state or parastatal authorities (CEH, 1999).

The accounts that follow detail evidence of rape associated with capture and the torture of victims by state or parastatal actors. These accounts substantiate my assertion that there is a difference in the meaning of the necrographic maps inscribed on female bodies. In addition to the preferential use of women in sexual crimes for counterinsurgency purposes, there are differences in the ways that bodies are marked and in the way that women's bodies are reported on.

> Miss Gladys Gutiérrez Flóres, 25 years old, who was kidnapped last Thursday by three men driving a car close to the Central Square of the Capital City, was found close to Police Stand no. 3 suffering from nervous shock and with both hands and feet tied . . . she left the National Palace and was walking toward a bus that would take her home to 6th Street and 5th Avenue in the Capital City's Zone 1 when two men descended from a car into which she was forced. She stated that while they were on the highway leading to Antigua Guatemala one of the men took out a hypodermic syringe and gave her an injection that made her lose consciousness. (*Prensa Libre*, 13 February 1978, 2)

This account and the one that follows are both eyewitness accounts from survivors of assassination attempts. Although eyewitness accounts are rare, when they do appear they shed light on the processes of torture. Miss Gutiérrez Flóres was kidnapped, drugged, and tied up in a way that suggests she was tortured. The tying of hands and/or feet was common among tortured and over-killed bodies. What is particularly interesting in this account is the location of her body after the kidnapping ("close to Police Stand no. 3"), the location of her capture ("she left the National Palace"), her public identification in the newspaper account, and the use of some type of injected drug in her abduction. These signs are meaningful only through a conjecture of probabilities that, although not substantiable, may serve to shed light on the processes by which cruelty was inflicted, recorded, and publicly extended.

While the victim's identity is defined, the type of victimization that was committed against her is vague, unresolved, and open to speculation, both because she was injected with a drug that obscured her memory of the events and because she was not killed. What happened during her capture is a question that begs to be asked. Furthermore, while authorities often kidnapped people in public places, the National Palace and Guatemala City's central square are the country's ultimate public spaces, making her capture symbolic, at least in terms of its public record. Finally, cadavers were not usually found near law-enforcement locales, and the finding of the victim near Police Stand no. 3 raises the profile of her discovery and draws public attention to her fate.

Was the account of Miss Gutiérrez Flóres's torture designed to be simultaneously ambiguous and public? What was the intention of the perpetrators? What was the effect of the account on its readers? The answers to these questions are not found in the public record. Nevertheless, we can estimate that this type of account could evoke fear in the minds of readers: a fear of unwarranted, imminent capture that can take place anywhere, a fear of unspeakable and unknowable torture, and a fear of the shame that public identification could bring.

Female bodies would be the appropriate sites for the creation of such fears. The intimidation of the female body—the unknown defilement and subsequent public disrepute—exists, after all, in the context of pro-Catholic Spanish-American Guatemalan society.[18] According to Linda Green in *Fear as a Way of Life*, rape was both a method of counterinsurgency and "a gendered way in which the military attacked the social fabric of family and community life" (Green, 1999, 32; see also REMHI, 1998b, 216).[19] The violation of the social fabric implied by rape is often hinted at through the subtle editorial commentary of newspaper articles, as in the following extract:

> Meanwhile the kidnappers also removed Miss Estrada from the vehicle by force. She was crying because of what they had done to her brother. One of the villains—it was said—tried to rape her, but she defended herself by biting his face and hands. This angered the kidnapper who then shot her various times until he thought she was dead. (*Prensa Libre*, 1 May 1979, 8)

Miss Estrada's account is another eyewitness testimony of typically female-cadaver necrographic maps. In this account, the assailants, having made the victim watch the assassination of her brother, attempted to rape her. Rape was used as part of the psychosexual troop control mechanisms where sexual access to victims was often touted as a benefit of being a soldier at war (REMHI, 1998b).[20] *Guatemala: Nunca Más* (REMHI, 1998a) details how rape was differentially used as a method of torture on different types of captives and how the choice whether to rape a victim or not was based on a cost-benefit analysis of whether it would aid or detract from obtaining popular acceptance. Gang rape and rape in general were preferentially used on women considered guerrillas (REMHI, 1998b).

One such instance is detailed in a horrifying account documented by the Commission for Historical Clarification (CEH). A soldier described the following in the case of a woman who was captured with her son and suspected of being a guerrilla: "[W]e found a woman, 'You are a guerrilla,' said the sub-lieutenant . . . they called the boys and said, 'there is meat guys,' and then they came, took the girl, took away her youngster and everyone raped her, in a mass rape, and then they killed the woman and the child" (CEH, 1999, 34). The CEH also documents that prostitutes were used in training Guatemalan soldiers to familiarize them with the practice of rape in the context of war (CEH, 1999).

Newspaper reports, however, rarely use the word *rape* in cadaver or eyewitness reports; rather, *ultrajar* is most commonly used in cadaver accounts to mean rape. The typical English translation of *ultrajar* would be "to spoil," "to disarrange," and/or "to abuse." This discrepancy in interpretation could indicate a particularly Guatemalan (Central American) idiomatic use of the word that conveys the societal importance accorded to the purity (and conversely) the defilement of the female body. In testimonials of rape collected by the CEH, victims also avoided using the word *rape (violación)*.

Instead, rape survivors and their families choose to use verbs with subtexts similar to those attached to the verb *ultrajar.* Thus, victim survivors and their families used "to be with," "to pass through"(*"pasar con"*), or "to use"(*"usar a"*) when they referred to rape (CEH, 1999, 21). The avoidance of the term *rape*, both in newspapers and in everyday language, is not remarkable on its own; rather, the words that are used as replacement are noteworthy. *To spoil, to disarrange, to pass through*, and *to use* are all terms that explicitly (although perhaps not consciously) recall an act where a body was misused and, more specifically, where the victimizer's act is seen as so abnormal or inordinate that its consequences and implications are evidently unmentionable to the degree that they remain unnamed.

Despite the fact that the topic of rape was itself taboo and that editorial chastisements tended to accompany reports suggesting rape, most cadaver reports concerning female bodies detail rape as part of the necrographic maps, as is shown in the following disturbing excerpts:

> The cadaver of a woman approximately 30 years old was found yesterday at the bottom of the Belice Bridge precipice, Zone 6 [Guatemala City], with evidence of various blows and signs of having been strangled. According to our reporters it is believed that the woman in question could have been kidnapped by unknown men, who after having raped her, strangled her, and threw the cadaver in the aforementioned place. (*Prensa Libre,* 9 May 1978, 2)

Again, an unknown woman's cadaver is disposed of under a bridge and, like other accounts already looked at, her body shows multiple signs of torture. This report is unusual in that it uses the word "rape" (violación) to describe the evidence of sexual assault. It is also unusual in its suggestion of the process suffered by the victim: first kidnapped, then raped, then strangled, and finally dumped in a precipice. This implication is surprising because it can be interpreted as an attempt to guide the reader's interpretation of the necrographic maps. This implies that signs of beatings, rape, and strangulation may have been so systematically and consistently found on other bodies in eyewitness accounts that it has become a pattern readily recognized by the authors who covered the violence inflicted on cadavers.

The second cadaver report where the term "rape" is explicitly used is accompanied by defacement (for the purposes of making recognition impossible). This type of defacement was commonly found in cadavers killed by military or paramilitary forces who attempted to limit the identification of the people they killed. This type of rape, termed "national security rape" by Falcon (2001), is conceived to be a result of the hypermasculinization of a militarized environment where rape becomes a tool to shame women and men considered to be outside the bounds of acceptance.

Making these rapes public was part of the process of national security rape itself, as the viewing of the rape by an intended audience is part and parcel of such a politicized act. In this case, although they attempted to obscure the victim's identity, the assassins wanted their act to be public, thus placing the woman prominently near the University of San Carlos just before the morning rush hour.

> The cadaver of a lady approximately 23 years of age was found yesterday on 31st Street and 10th Avenue, Zone 12 [Guatemala City], El Bosque Residences, at 6 am. Its face and cranium were completely destroyed, making a full identification impossible. . . . [She was] nude and showed clear signs of having been raped, said the volunteer firemen. (*Prensa Libre*, 11 April 1983, 19)

Rape has been identified by the United Nations Commission on Human Rights as a preferred weapon of war. The prime objective is to "exercise power and control over another person" through the degradation, shame, and humiliation of the victim (Falcon 2001, 31). Placing this young woman's body to be seen by commuters in Zone 12 of Guatemala City in particular, and by the national audience of newspaper readers in general, completes the exercise of power that was begun on the victim's body.

The final cadaver reports in this section on women and gender are perhaps the most gruesome in detail and in their implications.

> A WOMAN'S CADAVER WAS FOUND: It was noted that the woman was 1.60 meters tall. The cadaver was already in an advanced state of decomposition. It showed multiple blows and a hole in the abdominal region. . . . Two days earlier, the remains of an also unidentified man

had been found very close to where the cadaver of the lady was found.
(*Prensa Libre*, 26 October 1982, 40)

This account shows evidence of evisceration of the type commonly practiced by the Guatemalan military on pregnant victims of rape. As documented
by my own previous research as well as in the pages of *Guatemala: Nunca Más*
(REMHI, 1998b) and *Memoria del Silencio* (CEH, 1999), the removal of the
fetus from the body of a pregnant woman was a common precursor to the
assassination of both women and men during a massacre. The symbolic appropriation of the community's future, or symbolic obliteration of communal
hope, often followed the rape or defilement of the same woman and was often
completed by placing the cadaver on display so that it would be seen by those
about to be massacred.

More specifically, the body was placed to be seen by those in a position to
read the clues after the fact. While the previous cadaver report does not expand on the reasons or nature of the "hole" in the abdominal region, it is possible for the reader to understand the pieces of evidence offered in the account. These include the decomposed state of the body and the previous find
of a cadaver in the same location, which evinces the context within which this
woman was violated and assassinated.

The local justice of the peace, upon starting the necessary judicial proceedings, looked for the victim's clothes nearby, and found a skirt and
a blouse, as well as an apron in a nylon bag and shoes that were styled
like sandals. She had blows on different parts of her body. The authorities reported that the woman was brutally raped and then branches
from a coffee bush were inserted into various regions of her body.
(*Prensa Libre*, 5 April 1979, 12)

On their own, the woman's apron and sandal-like shoes imply an occupation, socioeconomic standing—domestic worker—and perhaps in the
Guatemalan context, where young indigenous women primarily hold this occupation, even an ethnic identity (Nelson, 1999). There was a predominance
of extreme forms of violation of the nude bodies of indigenous women similar to the type detailed here. The forced insertion of branches into a woman's
body was common during massacres and in displays made by soldiers prior to
mass assassinations. As evidenced by testimonies I collected from refugees,

and in a growing number of academic accounts, spearing and disemboweling women was done to incite fear during massacres of primarily indigenous populations (Green, 1999; REMHI, 1998a; Torres, 1995; Falla, 1994).

In this case, however, the solitary body of an unidentified woman in a perpetual state of violation stands as evidence of the degree to which life, and particularly indigenous life, was publicly defiled in Guatemala. As Nelson (1999, 326) has stated, the disdain for indigenous life, and particularly indigenous female life, was temporarily extended by counterinsurgency where "probable insurgents" of all extractions were treated "like Indians—expendable, worthless, bereft of civil and human rights." Yet, even in the realm of counterinsurgency violence, I suggest indigenous women in particular were dealt an unusually cruel hand.[21] *Memoria del Silencio* puts it thus: "In the case of Mayan women, armed violence was added to gendered violence and ethnic discrimination" (CEH, 1999, 14).

As this section illustrates, the tortured female was a particular site for the rewriting of the Guatemalan nation-state. Women, as the culturally ideal vessels of the Guatemalan family, were not killed as often as were men. In the instances in which women were killed, however, their cadavers showed evidence of mutilation and rape, implying that divergence from expected behavioral norms was punished more heavily for women than for men precisely because the moral costs of "defilement" were higher.

The tortured bodies of women victims were designed to draw others into the cloak of shame and secrecy commonly associated with rape. The torture and rape of women, even if editorially condemned by newspapers, still drew the eyes of the public away from the victimizers and onto the victims, because editorial condemnation rested on *re*viewing the violated body and never on finding the culprit of the violation.

The focus of rape is, by default, on the victims rather than on the victimizers, and it reinforces feelings of vulnerability that the agents of politically motivated violence hoped to instill. This sense of insecurity is further reinforced by playing up the silences commonly associated with rape in two ways: first, since the rapists were the authorities, they had unquestioned immunity (REMHI, 1998b); thus, making rapes public would not bring the perpetrators to justice.

Second, because the rapists were the authorities, the physical safety of both the victims and their families depended on keeping rapes secret. Building on the violence, shame, and secrecy commonly associated with rape, the designers of Guatemala's counterinsurgency policies attempted to force women and men—both indigenous and nonindigenous—into a symbolically subservient role through which military immunity and authority could remain unquestioned. Victims were caught in a double bind, where public claims of rape by authorities would mean adding a threat to their lives, already burdened by the pain and shame of the rape itself. It is in this space of silence that the voices of the tortured female cadavers from beyond the grave remind readers of their own potential deaths and of the unspeakable yet systemic actions of their assassins.

Conclusion: Cadavers and Cultures of Violence

This chapter has attempted to examine the processes through which political violence becomes "cultural fact" (Nordstrom, 1997). I have argued that the patterns of violence alluded to by both typical and marginal cadaver reports unveil an organized system and bureaucracy of violence. Guatemala's bureaucracy of violence relied on the documentation and public display of its actions that intended not only to eliminate particular people but also to create generalized fear. Fear, created primarily through the display of victims in public spaces (such as the pages of newspapers), was instrumental to the armed forces' efforts to shield themselves from recognition in their role as agents responsible for violence.

The widespread societal fear and instability that political violence induced in Guatemala is a direct result of the obfuscation both of the authors of this violence and of the processes by which victims lose their identity and become nameless yet ever-present cadavers, at least for the reading public. In the process of making violence quotidian, "natural," and "cultural," the Guatemalan armed forces relied on the creation of a recognizable discourse of violence. This discourse is suggested by the patterned and continuous appearance of cadaver reports, and it is expressed through both the signs of torture left on bodies and the strategy of the display of cadaver reports. This language of violence suggests a systematic and underlying practice. When cadavers appear without reference to their murderers—and when violence is constructed exclusively within the realm of culture and society—the political and economic aims of the violence's authors are inevitably obscured.

The recognition and deconstruction of the processes and patterns through which violence becomes "cultural" or "natural" allows for an understanding of state-sponsored political violence beyond popular explanations of such violence as a given "fact" of a "sick society." By recognizing the patterns through which violence became integrated into perceptions of Guatemalan "culture," it is possible to shed light on how a particular political and economic elite in control of the apparatus of the state designed and carried out a plan for social change—a plan with definite and publicly overt political, economic, and social goals.

NOTES

1. The arbitrary executions and torture which cadavers evidence make up only 38.4 and 18.81 percent respectively of the types of human rights violations that occurred during la Violencia (CEH 1999, 89).

2. The National Security Archive put the document they term the "death squad dossier" into electronic form for public use on May 20, 1999. Kate Doyle, director and senior analyst of the National Security Archive's Guatemala Documentation Project, has suggested the infamous el Archivo secret intelligence division of the Guatemalan presidential guard produced the "death squad diary" (Doyle 1999, 53).

3. See Immerman (1982), Gleijeses (1991), and, more recently, Doyle (2000).

4. U.S. economic assistance to Guatemala was reduced from 1976 levels ($37 million) to just over $2 million in 1977 (U.S. General Accounting Office, 1986). Between 1978 and 1984, Guatemala received an average of $18.6 million in economic assistance per year, with the lowest levels of assistance received being during the term in office of General Romeo Lucas García (USGAO, 1986). After aid restrictions to Guatemala were relaxed, U.S. economic assistance rose to approximately $80 million in each of the two years 1985 and 1986 (USGAO, 1986).

5. Social Sciences and Humanities Research Council of Canada, York University, and the Ontario Graduate Scholarship Program provided funding for this project. Malcolm Blincow, Liisa North, Teresa Holmes, and Ana Torres provided comments that aided in drafting this paper. I obtained copies of *Prensa Libre* thanks to the staff of the resource-sharing department at the University of Toronto Libraries.

6. The CEH was established as part of the formal peace process through the Oslo Accords (1994) in order to document the violence that took place during the civil war.

7. For example, the massacres of principally civil-defense-patrol members in Batzul, Chajul, and Quiché in May 1982 and in Chacalté, Chajul, and Quiché in June of that same year were both reported in *Prensa Libre* and attributed to guerrilla activity (*Prensa Libre*, 20 May 1982, 46; *Prensa Libre*, 16 June 1982, 4). According to REMHI (1998a, 36), Guatemalan guerrilla groups were responsible for approximately

3.16 percent of all massacres perpetrated during la Violencia. While some of these massacres authored by the Guatemalan armed forces were represented in *Prensa Libre*, the coverage tended to suggest that internal conflict, guerrilla activity, or the influence of the Catholic Church was to blame for the incident (REMHI, 1998a, 38; *Prensa Libre*, 1 June 1978, 2, 6, 7; *Prensa Libre*, 2 June 1978, 5; *Prensa Libre*, 3 June 1978, 2, 11).

8. Cadaver reports were indexed and coded using four variables: the cadaver's condition when found, the cadaver age, the cadaver gender, and the location of where the cadaver was found. The cadaver's condition when found was further coded as marked by up to four of twenty-eight possible characteristics.

9. See the Guatemalan *Código Procesal Penal* (1973), sec. 5, art. 195 (*Levantamiento de Cadáveres*).

10. It is interesting to note that, during both the term of the military junta (March 1982–June 1982) and Ríos Montt's term in office (June 1982–August 1983), 9 percent of the cadaver reports that appeared in *Prensa Libre* involved victims who were identified as either police officers or members of the military.

11. The Guatemalan military's public relations machinery does seem to have been involved in creating an image of a numerical reduction of politically motivated violence in the post–Lucas García period (*Prensa Libre*, 7 January 1983, 43). Most victims of violence during this period were killed in massacres. Of the 410 massacres documented in *Guatemala: Nunca Más* (REMHI 1998a), 296 took place in the 1981–1983 period, when cadaver reports were relatively rare. The massacres that occurred during this period (when cadaver reports were not published) represent, using the most conservative estimates, the deaths of at least 19,000 people (REMHI 1998a). Ball, Kobrak, and Spirer (1999, 75) estimate that during Lucas García's term in office there were an average of seventy-eight politically motivated deaths and disappearances per month. This figure skyrockets to 2,223 victims in March 1982 and 1,813 victims per month for the first four months of Ríos Montt's term in office.

12. The REMHI report was sponsored by Guatemala's Catholic Church and directed by the late Bishop Juan Gerardi (assassinated two days after the findings' presentation) in an effort to aid in the reconciliation efforts envisioned within the scope of the peace process.

13. Guatemala's treatment in the foreign press was of great national concern for sustaining both the agendas of the military (including free reign in counterinsurgency) and of the national elites (mainly tourism and attracting foreign investment) (*Prensa Libre*, 25 October 1982, 11).

As Ríos Montt consolidated his power, limitations on the freedom of the press became more blatant. In July 1982, he restricted the press from publishing material that could "cause confusion or panic or could aggravate the situation" (*Decreto-Ley 45–82*, 1 July 1982, art. 15). As a result, he made the Presidential Secretary of Public Relations the origin point of all such information (*Prensa Libre*, 7 July 1982, 4).

14. While primarily ladino political activists were the targets of the selective assassination counterinsurgency strategies in the 1970s, ladinos were never subject to mass killings in the same degree or scope as the targeting of indigenous residents of the departments of Quiché, Huehuetenango, or Baja Verapaz (Torres-Rivas, 2000, 130). Statistically, the CEH found that 83.33 percent of all victims of political violence in the period 1962–1996 were Mayans and 16.51 percent were identified as ladino (CEH, 1999, 102).

15. Within the armed forces, groups involved in the technical aspects of the practice of violence included members of the state presidential guard, the military commands stationed in any of the eighteen military zones, the special forces (including the infamous Kaibiles and the guard of honor), civil affairs officers, members of the armed forces' Department of Information and Public Relations, and the Directorate of Intelligence—responsible for the design and orchestration of the violence. Other commonly active counterinsurgency forces were the national police (in particular the sixth command and the detective corps), the Guardia de Hacienda, and the Mobile Military Police Corps (REMHI, 1998b; CEH, 1999). Counterinsurgency strategies also employed commissioned forces such as the civil defense patrols (CEH, 1999, 102).

16. The victim statistics used by the CEH estimate that only 25 percent of all victims of violence whose sex is known were women. Further clarifying this statistic, *Memoria del Silencio* (CEH, 1999) also states that women comprised 23 percent of documented arbitrary execution and torture victims. In stark contrast, *Memoria del Silencio* points out that women made up 99 percent of all victims of sexual crime (CEH, 1999, 19). The REMHI (1998a, 52) report estimates a smaller number of total female victims, putting them at only 10 percent of the total number of torture victims, a figure that does not include sexual crimes.

17. See Barstow (2000), Green (1999), and Aretxaga (1997).

18. Rape was seen as an assault not only on the woman who was victimized but also as an assault on the dignity of the woman's husband or partner and her family in general, because of the shame that was associated with this type of violation (Green, 1999).

19. *Memoria del Silencio* states that rape, particularly in indigenous areas, resulted in "breaking marriage and social ties; generating social isolation and communal shame; provoked abortions, infanticide and obstructed births and marriages within these groups, thus facilitating the destruction of indigenous groups" (CEH, 1999, 14).

20. See Cynthia Enloe (1993), in *The Morning After: Sexual Politics at the End of the Cold War*, which also discusses the use of rape as a socializing strategy for new recruits.

21. Because of rape's association with massacres, it is estimated that close to 90 percent of all rape victims were of indigenous descent (CEH, 1999, 23–29).

BIBLIOGRAPHY

Aretxaga, Begoña. 1997. *Shattering Silence: Women, Nationalism, and Political Subjectivity in Northern Ireland*. Princeton: Princeton University Press.
Axel, Brian Keith. 2001. *The Nation's Tortured Body: Violence, Representation and the Formation of a Sikh Diaspora*. Durham: Duke University Press.

Ball, Patrick, Paul Kobrak, and Herbert F. Spirer. 1999. *Violencia Institucional en Guatemala, 1960–1996: Una Reflexión Cuantitativa*. Washington, DC: American Association for the Advancement of Science.
Barstow, Anne Llewellyn. 2000. *War's Dirty Secret: Rape, Prostitution, and Other Crimes Against Women*. Cleveland, OH: Pilgrim Press.

Central Intelligence Agency (CIA). 1983. *Secret Cable* (Declassified February 1998). Document 18. Washington, DC: National Security Archive, Georgetown University, February.
Comisión de Esclarecimiento Histórico (CEH). 1999. *Las Violaciones de los Derechos Humanos y los Hechos de Violencia*, vol. 2, *Memoria del Silencio*. Guatemala City: American Association for the Advancement of Science.

Doyle, Kate. 2000. *The Guatemalan Military: What the U.S. Files Reveal*. Electronic Briefing Book No. 32. Washington, DC: National Security Archive. Available from online database at Georgetown University.
———. 1999. "Death Squad Diary." *Harper's Magazine* 298 (1789): 50–55.

Enloe, Cynthia. 1993. *The Morning After: Sexual Politics at the End of the Cold War*. Berkeley: University of California Press.

Falcon, Sylvanna. 2001. "Rape as a Weapon of War: Advancing Human Rights for Women at the U.S.-Mexico Border." *Social Justice* 28 (2): 31–51.
Falla, Ricardo. 1994. *Massacres in the Jungle: Ixcán, Guatemala, 1975–1982*. Boulder: Westview Press.
Feldman, Allen. 1991. *Formations of Violence: The Narrative of the Body and Political Terrorism in Northern Ireland*. Chicago: University of Chicago Press.

Gleijeses, Piero. 1991. *Shattered Hope: The Guatemalan Revolution and the United States, 1944–1954*. Princeton: Princeton University Press.
Green, Linda. 1999. *Fear as a Way of Life: Mayan Widows in Rural Guatemala*. New York: Columbia University Press.

Immerman, Richard H. 1982. *The CIA in Guatemala: The Foreign Policy of Intervention*. Austin: University of Texas Press.

Jonas, Susanne. 2000. *Of Centaurs and Doves: Guatemala's Peace Process*. Boulder: Westview Press.

Malkki, Liisa. 1995. *Purity and Exile: Violence and Memory and National Cosmology among Hutu Refugees in Tanzania*. Chicago: University of Chicago Press.
McCleary, Rachel M. 1999. *Dictating Democracy: Guatemala and the End of Violent Revolution*. Gainesville: University of Florida Press.

Nelson, Diane M. 1999. *Finger in the Wound: Body Politics in Quincentennial Guatemala*. Berkeley: University of California Press.
Nordstrom, Carolyn. 1997. *A Different Kind of War Story*. Philadelphia: University of Pennsylvania Press.

Pentecost, Debrah. 2002. "War Photojournalism and Audiences: Making Meaning from Tragic Moments." Ph.D. thesis, School of Communication, Simon Fraser University, Vancouver.
Perera, Victor. 1993. *Unfinished Conquest: The Guatemalan Tragedy*. Berkeley: University of California Press.
Proyecto Interdiocesano de Recuperación de la Memoria Histórica (R E M H I). 1998a. "Impactos de la Violencia." In *Guatemala: Nunca Más*, vol. I. Guatemala City: Oficina de Derechos Humanos del Arzobispado de Guatemala.
———. 1998b. "Los Mecanismos del Horror." In *Guatemala: Nunca Más*, vol. II. Guatemala City: Oficina de Derechos Humanos del Arzobispado de Guatemala.

Scarry, Elaine. 1984. *The Body in Pain: The Making and Unmaking of the World*. New York: Oxford University Press.
Siebert, Renate. 1996. *Secrets of Life and Death: Women and the Mafia*. London: Verso.
Sluka, Jeffrey, ed. 2000. *Death Squad: The Anthropology of State Terror*. Philadelphia: University of Pennsylvania Press.

Torres, M. Gabriela. 1995. "Return to the Land: A Study of Changes in Gender Relations and Ethnic Identities from the Perspective of Guatemalan Refugees." Master's thesis, Anthropology, Latin American Faculty of Social Sciences (F L A S C O - Ecuador), Quito.
Torres-Rivas, Edelberto. 2000. "Prólogo: La Metáfora de una Sociedad que se Castiga a sí Misma." In *Guatemala: Causas y Orígenes del Enfrentamiento Armado Interno*, ed. Commission for Historical Clarification (C E H). Guatemala City: F & G Editores.

United States General Accounting Office (U S G A O). 1986. *Military Sales: The United States Continuing Munitions Supply Relationship with Guatemala*. Washington, DC: Report to the Chairman, Subcommittee on Western Hemisphere Affairs, Committee on Foreign Affairs, House of Representatives.

CHAPTER 7

U.S. Militarization of Honduras in the 1980s and the Creation of CIA-backed Death Squads

JOAN KRUCKEWITT

Introduction

Of the five countries that comprise Central America, Honduras and Costa Rica have been known as "exceptions" to the general patterns because they have not had the high levels of political violence and repression that historically have characterized Guatemala, El Salvador, and Nicaragua. In these three countries, the governments have traditionally met civil society's demands for reform with repression, while the governments of Honduras and Costa Rica have traditionally met such demands for reform with flexibility, concessions, and, occasionally, accommodation.

Yet, in the early 1980s, Honduras became less of an apparent exception as its government began to engage in political violence and repression. In the years from 1980 to 1988, some 174 people permanently disappeared in Honduras (National Commissioner for the Protection of Human Rights in Honduras, 1994), while about the same number "temporarily" disappeared. Why did Honduras lose its supposed exceptionalism and experience this sudden increase in repression? And why, a few years later, did the incidence of repression decline? Did Honduras return to its exceptionalism?

In this chapter I will argue that human rights abuses in Honduras occurred due to the intentional militarization of the country by the United States. The militarization, supported by massive amounts of U.S. aid, caused a shift in the balance of power within Honduras. The militarization strengthened the armed forces who, during a seventeen-year period of military regimes

(1963–1980), had already established their dominance over the country's civilian political forces.

Furthermore, the actions of U.S. political leaders strengthened the position of hard-liners within the Honduran military. The U.S.-backed militarization of the country came hand in hand with demands for the Honduran military to turn control of the government over to civilian forces, but military leaders made a pact with civilian forces whereby both sectors would enjoy U.S. aid if the military remained in de facto control (Hammond, 1991, 79). In the late 1970s, the Carter administration had kept military hard-liners in check by demanding political and judicial reforms to go along with U.S. aid, but in the early 1980s the Reagan administration, which began the militarization, dropped demands for those reforms.

Human rights abuses, including disappearances, began to occur when military hard-liners came to power, applying a Honduran-style doctrine of national security to the country. As in Guatemala, El Salvador, and Nicaragua, the use of repression, instead of concessions and reform, became the norm, and Honduras lost its "exceptionalism." Repression and human rights abuses declined when hard-liners were removed from power and replaced by "nationalist" officers. Gradually, the country began to demilitarize and the military-political pact unraveled. By the end of the 1980s, as regional conflicts subsided, there was external and internal pressure for all Central American governments to democratize. In Honduras, civil society demanded a return to the norm, the exceptional role that Honduras, along with Costa Rica, had previously played in Central America. The balance of power that was established in the 1980s changed Honduran institutions, however, and the military, formerly the country's main political power, became part of the country's economic elite.

The Honduran "Exception"

Guatemala, El Salvador, and Nicaragua have been called "reactionary despotic regimes," because traditional sectors of power in those countries had long been intransigent, meeting demands for modernization and reform with repression. Opposition groups, who believed that the only way to break this intransigence was through violence, resorted to armed struggle (Weeks, 1986, 61). Honduras is said to have avoided this pattern because the traditionally dominant social sectors (particularly economic elites who based their power on land ownership and agro-exports), instead of being intransigent, often compromised with oppositional views.

This distinctiveness from its neighbors came as a result of the country's particular economic, political, and military histories, which allowed reform, instead of repression, to be the norm. Economically, Honduras was differentiated by its small population and lack of the extensive inequality in land distribution that characterized other Central American countries. Politically, Honduras had a weak local economic elite and a powerful foreign economic elite (centered in the banana trade and in mining companies), but the two sectors acted independently and had few common interests. Lastly, the Honduran military did not develop as a tool of the economic and political elites but rather as an independent institution. It was not a repressive force (unlike most other Central American armies), but rather one that guaranteed political stability in the country, had some popular support, and was regarded by civilian sectors as a mediator during political conflicts (Hammond, 1991, 4).

Beginning in 1946, with the signing of a military agreement between the two countries, the United States established and operated military schools in Honduras (Hammond, 1991). U.S. instructors professionalized and trained Honduran soldiers, uniting the country's disparate rural militias into five field battalions, the country's first "real army." In 1954, the U.S. and Honduras signed another military assistance pact. In 1957, the Honduran armed forces and civilian leaders modified the constitution to make the armed forces an independent, autonomous force with a secret budget (Bowman, 2002, 164). Beginning in 1963 and lasting nearly two decades, military leaders ruled the country through a series of coups.

In 1975, when officers demanded greater roles in decision making, the military created the Consejo Superior de las Fuerzas Armadas (Superior Council of the Armed Forces, CONSUFFAA), a consulting body of nineteen officials. Over time, the Superior Council became the ultimate authority in the country, deciding broad matters of national policy (Salomón, 1992, 10). In 1978, for example, it began to ask cabinet ministers to provide briefings about regional programs and budget allocations—not out of concern for the programs but rather to track the amount of money flowing into each commander's region (Hammond, 1991, 59).

Regional Conflict

By late 1979, Honduras, a small country of some 4 million people, was surrounded by turmoil. In Nicaragua, leftist Sandinista guerrillas had just overthrown the forty-five-year dictatorship of the Somoza family, staunch U.S. allies. Guatemala and El Salvador were engulfed in civil conflicts that were spilling over their borders. In the United States, the Carter administration attempted to head off a conflict in Honduras similar to those of its neighbors by courting the country's military government. At the same time, to keep the Honduran military in check, Washington demanded political reforms, including a return to civilian rule and respect for human rights.

In March 1980, General Policarpo Paz García, the leader of the Honduran Armed Forces Superior Council, visited the United States (*Latin American Weekly Report*, 7 March 1980), where he met with the former commander of NATO, General Alexander Haig, executives of the Sikorsky helicopter company, and President Jimmy Carter, who praised Honduras for its announcement of upcoming elections. The Carter administration emphasized that U.S. aid was conditioned upon the next president of Honduras being a civilian (Hammond, 1991). A statement from Washington read:

> The U.S. is prepared to support the Honduran government with economic and security assistance because of its commitment to reforms, economic development and free elections. (Reuters, 3 March 1980)

While Washington stated that its objective in Honduras was to strengthen democracy, newspaper columnist Jack Anderson saw a different objective:

> The Administration apparently has chosen Honduras to be our new "Nicaragua"—a dependable satellite bought and paid for by American military and economic largess. (*Washington Post*, 23 March 1980)

Back in Honduras, the military drew up a secret pact with civilian sectors that would guarantee the military's continued political dominance. This pact restricted the powers of the president and further increased the powers of the military (Hammond, 1991, 98).

President Ronald Reagan Draws the Line on Communism
When President Ronald Reagan took office in January 1981, his objective regarding Central America was to stop communism from spreading:

> Reaganite images of the international arena identified the Soviet Union
> as the central source of trouble. . . . Alongside this analysis went a be-
> lief that regional problems and conflicts were intimately linked to the
> Soviet global threat, and that the "New Cold War" would be fought out
> in Central America, the Middle East and Southwest Asia as well as in
> Europe. It was the USA's duty to support the forces of freedom in such
> conflicts, and this view became formalized in the "Reagan Doctrine,"
> identifying the President with the need to resist and roll back commu-
> nist expansion in the third world. (Hogan, 1990, 264)

The Reagan administration viewed Central American conflicts not as domestic issues, caused by poverty, lack of economic opportunities, or inequality, but as East/West issues in which the United States and the Soviet Union
(or its proxy, Cuba) were fighting for political and economic influence. Viewed
through this Cold War lens, Washington believed that the Sandinistas and
other leftist guerrilla movements threatened the stability and safety of the
United States. To combat this threat, Washington implemented what was
termed the Reagan Doctrine, whereby not one country would "turn communist" during President Reagan's term in office. According to this doctrine,
communism itself (as represented by the Sandinistas) would be overthrown,
and the threat of communism (as represented by Salvadoran and Guatemalan
guerrillas) would be contained (Hogan, 1990).

In order to accomplish these objectives without sending U.S. troops to
Central America, Washington militarized the region by supporting the
Nicaraguan counterrevolutionaries, or "Contras," to confront the Sandinistas,
and preparing the Salvadoran army to wage warfare against the guerrillas in
that country (some of this training and support would later take place in Honduras). Along with militarization, Washington promoted elections in the region, and, to make its goals easier for leaders of the countries to accept (both
politically and economically), Washington infused the countries' traditional
structures, especially the military, with massive amounts of economic aid (see
Table 7.1). By 1985, Honduras was the eighth leading recipient of U.S. military
and economic aid in the world (*Washington Post*, 16 December 1984).

Table 7.1 *Authorized U.S. Assistance for Grants and Loans to Honduras,*
1979–1989 (in Millions of U.S. Dollars)

Fiscal Year	Total Loans and Grants	Military Aid	Economic Aid[1]
1979	32.3	2.3	29.1
1980	66.8	3.9	53.1
1981	37.3	8.9	36.4
1982	112.6	31.3	80.7
1983	154.3	48.3	106.0
1984	172.6	77.4	95.0
1985	298.4	67.4	229.0
1986	198.1	61.1	136.6
1987	259.8	61.2	197.8
1988	198.1	41.2	156.9
1989	130.5	41.1	88.1

1. Includes support for military infrastructure.

Source: Latin American Studies Center, University of California at Los Angeles.
1995. *Statistical Abstract of Latin America*, Vol. 31, Part 2. Los Angeles: Latin
American Studies Center, UCLA, table 2812.

The militarization of Honduras, therefore, was part of Washington's larger plan to pacify the region. The Reagan administration's new role for Honduras in Central America was as a bulwark against communism, to prevent "regional conflicts and potential infiltrations" of supplies to Salvadoran and Guatemalan rebels (Volk, 1981, 124), and to be the staging base for the Contras. Before national elections were held in Honduras in the fall of 1981, Hammond notes, the armed forces struck a deal with the Liberal Party that their leader, Roberto Suazo Córdova, would win the presidency if his government guaranteed the military's continued autonomy. Suazo Córdova agreed to these conditions and won the 1981 presidential election (Hammond, 1991, 92).

Joint Military Maneuvers

In October 1981, U.S. and Honduran troops held joint military maneuvers for the first time. Between 1983 and 1985, more than 12,000 U.S. military personnel participated in similar joint maneuvers (Bowman, 2002, 229). U.S. money and U.S. personnel, including National Guard units, built airport runways, army bases, radar stations, tank traps, fuel depots, ammunition storage facilities, and military warehouses across the nation—all ostensibly to protect Honduras from Nicaragua. After maneuvers in August 1983, about 1,800 U.S. soldiers remained in Honduras, most of them stationed at Palmerola airfield (now called Soto Cano airbase).

Palmerola hosted "a field hospital, a base logistic echelon, a helicopter company with thirteen aircraft, and a 300-man intelligence unit that . . . [carried out] frequent reconnaissance missions over El Salvador . . . in support of Salvadoran counterinsurgency operations" (Rudolph, 1984, xxxii). Sixty U.S. personnel operated a radar site near Tegucigalpa, 150 Marines ran another site near the Gulf of Fonseca (which links Honduras, El Salvador, and Nicaragua), and 150 personnel, mostly from U.S. Army Special Forces, were stationed at the Regional Military Training Center (Centro Regional de Entrenamiento Militar, CREM) (Rudolph, 1984, xxxii), a facility where U.S. troops later trained Salvadoran and Honduran soldiers.

The joint U.S.-Honduran exercises provided both a cover for the funneling of arms to the Contras and a lucrative source of income for the Honduran military (Bowman, 2002, 229). The Honduran army falsified end-user certificates for weapons and ammunition in the international arms market and passed the weapons to the Contras (*Latin American Regional Reports*, 14 February 1986). Money for the arms came from the U.S. Congress, from the illicit fund-raising operations coordinated by Lieutenant Colonel Oliver North, and from a plethora of private and quasi-governmental groups in the United States. The Honduran army channeled both arms and money to the Contras, keeping a hefty cut as payment for those services.

Under Washington's tutelage, Honduras's traditional enemy, El Salvador, became its newest ally. Washington pressured Honduras to patch up the border quarrel with El Salvador that had erupted into war in 1969, and pushed the Honduran military into cooperating with the Salvadoran military, where, in joint operations in 1980, the two armies massacred hundreds of Salvadoran refugees fleeing along the Río Sumpul and Río Lempa (*Sunday Times of London*, 22 February 1981).

Honduran military operations against Salvadorans were met "tit for tat with terrorist actions in Honduras" by Salvadoran guerrillas (Rosenberg and Shepherd, 1986, 144), who retaliated by targeting Honduran institutions, including robbing banks, and kidnapping Hondurans for ransom. The militarization fostered by the United States did not promote democratization but instead undermined the country's own security and "led to all the things that Honduras wanted to avoid: instability, violence and repression" (Rosenberg and Shepherd, 1986, 146).

Balance of Power Shifts toward Military Hard-Liners

While the Carter administration had both courted the Honduran military and restrained it by putting conditions on the granting of U.S. aid, the Reagan administration dropped demands for political and judicial reforms as it emphasized Honduras's "military participation in the regional conflict" (Volk, 1981, 127). On March 9, 1981, two months after taking office, President Reagan ordered the expansion of covert operations to provide training, equipment, and related assistance to cooperating governments throughout Central America in order to counter what was said to be foreign-sponsored subversion. In these efforts, the U.S. Central Intelligence Agency (c I A) employed "non-Americans," including Argentine trainers who were sent to Honduras. Some of the Argentine trainers had helped run government death squads in Argentina that had already disappeared thousands of people (see Armony, this volume).

Colonel Gustavo Álvarez Martínez, a young, ambitious Honduran hardliner, had been eagerly talking to U.S. officials for some time about his plans to rid Honduras of its enemies. An honors graduate from the Argentine military academy who had attended military courses in the United States, Peru, and at the U.S. Army School of the Americas in Panama, Álvarez was one of the few Honduran military officers with a professional background. In August 1980, at the time when political dissidents first began to be targeted in Honduras, Álvarez was chief of the Public Security Forces (Fuerzas de Segúridad Publica, FUSEP), the national police apparatus that was under the command of the armed forces rather than an independent police force (Americas Watch, 1982, 9). In the view of Donald Winters, the c I A station chief in Tegucigalpa from 1982 to 1984: "Gustavo Alvarez was very much out of national character—dynamic, firm, uncompromising. He knew where he wanted to go" (*Baltimore Sun*, 11 June 1995).

In early 1981, Álvarez told Jack Binns, the U.S. ambassador to Honduras, that he admired how the Argentine military—who had killed or disappeared more than 10,000 people—had dealt with subversives. He said he would use similar methods in his own country. Binns, a Carter appointee, was shocked, and he cabled his concerns to Washington: "Alvarez stressed theme that democracies and West are soft, perhaps too soft to resist Communist

subversion. The Argentines, he said, had met the threat effectively, identifying—and taking care of—the subversives. Their method, he opined, is the
only effective way of meeting the challenge. When it comes to subversion,
[Álvarez] would opt for tough, vigorous and extra-legal action" (*Baltimore
Sun*, 11 June 1995).

In June 1981, Tomás Nativi, a 33-year-old university professor, was dragged
from his bed and "disappeared." Binns cabled Washington his disapproval:

> I believe we should try to nip this situation in the bud. I have already
> asked [CIA] chief of station to raise this problem obliquely with . . .
> Álvarez (whose minions appear to be the principal actors and whom
> I suspect is the intellectual force behind this new strategy for handling
> subversives/criminals). (*Baltimore Sun*, 11 June 1995)

Binns suggested that the United States stop the violence by withholding
aid to the Honduran military. Instead, in late 1981, the Reagan administration
replaced Ambassador Binns with John Negroponte, a former political officer
in the U.S. embassy in Saigon during the Vietnam War who shared the Reagan administration's zeal to stop communism. "I believe we must do our best
not to allow the tragic outcome of Indochina to be repeated in Central America," Negroponte stated at the time (*Baltimore Sun*, 18 June 1995).

Negroponte and Álvarez shared the same goals. Supported by the Reagan
administration, Álvarez was named chief of the Honduran armed forces on
January 26, 1982, one day before President Suazo Córdova took office. The
new president subsequently promoted Álvarez to brigadier general and
named him leader of the Superior Council. A few days later, Álvarez restructured the military and consolidated his power by exiling officers who had tried
to block his promotion. He also created the Consejo de Seguridad Nacional
(National Security Council, CSN), which was modeled after the U.S. National
Security Council. This body consisted of four civilians and eight military
hard-liners, including Álvarez (Salomón, 1992, 19).

Through the CSN, Suazo Córdova and Álvarez found "a 'legal' way for the
military to 'influence' policy-making" (Hammond, 1991, 106). The actions of
the CSN, the country's most important decision-making body, now superseded
those of the Superior Council. It set the country's foreign policy, formulated
the national budget, and determined official responses to labor unrest
(Aguilar, 1992, 168). Through the CSN, the "armed forces . . . institutionalized

their intervention in political life" (Hammond, 1991, 168) and began implementing the doctrine of national security.

While military hard-liners ruled the country, a quiescent legislature rubber-stamped all initiatives from the CSN. However, an important civilian-military confrontation occurred over the CREM, the U.S. military's training center in the country. Washington wanted a place where Salvadoran soldiers could be trained at a low cost, and in May 1983, during a secret trip to Washington, Álvarez and U.S. officials signed a treaty creating the CREM to serve as a training base in Honduras. When the treaty was announced, legislators in the Honduran congress were appalled at his decision to train Salvadorans, the country's traditional enemy, on Honduran soil (*El Tiempo*, 27 May 1983).

In June 1983, the Reagan administration awarded Álvarez the Legion of Merit for "encouraging the success of democratic processes in Honduras" (*Baltimore Sun*, 11 June 1995). Upon his return to Honduras, Álvarez lectured the Honduran congress for six hours, saying that the CREM would train not Salvadoran soldiers but "students." The legislature's disquiet over the CREM was stifled, as not one legislator dared to debate Álvarez (Hammond, 1991, 110–12). Still, Honduran politicians and nationalistic military officers were humiliated by his agreement to train Salvadoran troops,[1] and the CREM would eventually weigh heavily in the ouster of Álvarez.

The Doctrine of National Security

General Álvarez and other hard-line officers in the Honduran armed forces believed in the National Security Doctrine, which had been developed and implemented in the previous decades in Brazil, Chile, Argentina, and Uruguay. This conceptual frame is defined as

> the systemization of concepts of state, war, national power and national goals that place national security above personal security; the needs of the state before individual rights; and judgment of a governing elite over the rule of law. (Crahan, 1982, 7)

Accordingly, the military sees itself as a neutral force, an autonomous institution that does not represent certain social, economic, or political interests but is instead a force that represents national interests and operates for the common good. It is, moreover, in this view seen to be omnipotent.

The main concern of the state is guaranteeing national security through elimination of societal conflict and subversion, even if this requires unfettered exercise of state power by armed forces and the police. (Crahan, 1982, 7)

A national security state—a state administered by application of the National Security Doctrine—arises when a military sector feels that the state is being attacked by internal or external leftist political forces, and that democratic governments are too weak, inefficient, incompetent, or corrupt to deal with what they perceive to be an onslaught of Marxism. National security regimes believe that their countries are "the last bulwarks of Western civilization against secularism, Marxism, and the communists" (Crahan, 1982, 102). According to national security ideology, the state's enemy is anyone whom the state decides is "subversive." All sources of conflict, including strikes, sit-ins, partisan politics, and mobilizations of traditional organizations, are seen as threats to security.

General Álvarez deemed that the state was under assault, and that Honduras was riddled with enemies. According to the National Security Doctrine (as it was applied in Honduras), the external enemy became identified with the internal enemy; Honduras's national interests became subordinated to Washington's interests, and Washington's enemies became Honduras's enemies. General Álvarez declared:

Nicaragua is attacking Honduras indirectly and is violating Honduran security every day. Therefore, in its ideology and its objectives, Nicaragua is Honduras' enemy. (Rudolph, 1984, xxvi)

Nicaragua, traditionally an ally, had become an enemy in the same way that El Salvador, traditionally an enemy, had become an ally.

To "save" the country from its internal enemies, the armed forces, together with a pliable president and a rubber-stamp congress, pushed through harsh laws that militarized Honduran society. In April 1982, the government instituted Decree 33, an antiterrorism law that established "draconian penalties for crimes against state security" (Schulz and Sundloff Schulz, 1994, 83). It outlawed land seizures (the traditional method that peasants used to pressure for reforms) and classified the machete, the basic farming tool, as a deadly weapon. The government established civil defense committees and set up a hotline to report "suspicious" activity (Americas Watch, 1982, 20, 34–35). The army required citizens to carry identification cards, and then set up arbitrary roadblocks to spot-check the documentation of identity. The notion of "state security" was also extended to attack legal groups such as peasant organizations and workers' unions.

In the past, these groups had been allowed some political space in which to maneuver and, at times, the government had even ceded to their demands for reform, thus relieving political pressure. However, in the 1980s, the army cracked down on these institutions, repressing demonstrations, banning some organizations, and decapitating their leadership. The Honduran government attacked and destroyed the very institutions that had helped save Honduras from violence in its past and, when the government destroyed these reformist groups, the outcome was polarization and violence (Blachman, LeoGrande, and Sharpe, 1986, 137–38).

By the early 1980s, habeas corpus and other judicial guarantees were regularly ignored, and the police and other security forces were operating outside the control of both judicial and civilian governmental authorities. The military's role in society grew ever larger: over the course of the 1980s, in Honduras "the military extended the definition of security interests to include aspects of foreign policy, criminal procedure and immigration and refugee matters" (Americas Watch, 1982, 3).

At the same time, an increasing amount of politically motivated violence—including bombings, bank robberies, and kidnappings—by leftist groups became directed against the Honduran government. Up to this time, significant guerrilla movements had never evolved in Honduras because, unlike reactionary despotic regimes, Honduran rulers had sometimes met demands with limited reforms. However, when military hard-liners came to power, they acted more like reactionary despots and, as a result, several small Honduran guerrilla organizations sprouted in the early 1980s. The Honduran military quickly rooted out the safe houses, eliminated the leaders, and disbanded the movements.

The "Argentine Method"

Álvarez publicly called for what came to be known as the Argentine method (based on disappearances) to deal with subversive threats (América Latina Informe Político, 23 July 1982, 118, as quoted in Amnesty International, 1988), and by 1982 the execution of disappearances had become systematic (Americas Watch, 1982, 5). Table 7.2 shows the increasing number of political assassinations and disappearances that occurred while General

Table 7.2 *Human Rights Violations in Honduras, 1980–1984*

	1980	1981	1982	1983	1984	Total
Political Assassinations						
Hondurans	1	16	16	18	13	64
Salvadorans	0	25	12	5	21	63
Others	0	1	1	2	2	6
Total	1	42	29	25	36	133
Permanent Disappearances						
Hondurans	2	10	24	21	14	71
Salvadorans	0	22	0	1	5	28
Other	0	20	2	3	0	25
Total	2	52	26	25	19	124
Temporary Disappearances						
Hondurans	11	64	33	18	30	156
Salvadorans	0	3	2	0	0	5
Others	0	0	0	1	2	3
Total	11	67	35	19	32	164

Note: From 1980 to 1983 there were 58 political prisoners, of whom 44 were Hondurans, 9 Nicaraguans, and 5 Salvadorans. From January to November 1984, there were 160 political prisoners registered, of whom 16 were sent to court before March 31, 1984.

Source: Committee for the Defense of Human Rights (CODEH), Tegucigalpa, Honduras, 1985.

Álvarez was head of the armed forces. "Political assassinations" refers to those killed outright; "permanent disappearances" refers to people who were picked up by security forces and never seen again. "Temporary disappearances" refers to people whom the security forces secretly held incommunicado for days or months, but who then were released, often under the conditions that they leave the country and not talk to the media.

In Honduras, the first people to disappear were Salvadoran refugees who were suspected of being guerrillas. Soon, however, the victims included Honduran students, labor leaders, teachers, union activists, college professors, journalists, peasant organizers, and alleged leftists or sympathizers of the Salvadoran guerrillas or the Nicaraguan Sandinistas. Between 1980 and 1992, 179 disappearances were recorded, of which the majority occurred between 1980 and 1984 (National Commissioner for the Protection of Human

Table 7.3 *Number of Documented Disappearances in Honduras, 1980–1988*

Year	Hondurans	Nicaraguans	Salvado-rans	Costa Ricans	Guate-malans	Others	Total
1980	1						1
1981	14	3	27	5	2	2	53
1982	17	1					18
1983	16	1	1		1	1	20
1984	14	4					18
1985	7	19					26
1986	4						4
1987	14	8					22
1988	12						12
Total	99	36	28	5	3	3	174

Source: Information compiled from National Commissioner for the Protection of Human Rights in Honduras, 1994.

Rights in Honduras, 1994). The office of the National Commissioner for the Protection of Human Rights in Honduras compiled Table 7.3, which lists fewer disappearances than does Table 7.2, because it only lists incidents with evidence that indicts the security forces for the disappearance.

According to the Honduran human rights commissioner, in general, "the *modus operandi* [of disappearances] consisted of: (1) surveillance and identification of the victim; (2) the victim's prior arrest by FUSEP [the national police], the military, or the DNI [Departamento Nacional de Investigaciones, the intelligence service]; (3) detention of the victim in public or in the person's home with total impunity, by armed men dressed in civilian clothes; (4) the use of official resources and authority to carry out kidnappings and to avoid interference by other security branches; and (5) the total indifference or subordination of any authority that may have witnessed the kidnapping" (National Commissioner for the Protection of Human Rights in Honduras, 1994, 123). In the rare cases where victims reappeared, it was generally due to unusual circumstances such as the status of the victim or the victim's family, or international pressure.

Battalion 3-16, the Death Squad

The leading Honduran death squad, eventually called Battalion 3-16, was first known by different names, including the División de Investigaciones

Especiales (Special Investigations Division, D I E S), the Group of Ten, and the Group of Fourteen. General José Bueso Rosa, General Álvarez's chief of staff, attributed the creation of Battalion 3-16 to the Americans:

> It was their idea to create an intelligence unit that reported directly to the head of the armed forces. Battalion 3-16 was created by a need for information. We were not specialists in intelligence, in gathering information, so the U.S. offered to help us organize a special unit. (*Baltimore Sun*, 11 June 1995) [2]

In August 1980, twenty-five Honduran officers were flown in a private Honduran air force plane to an unpaved desert airstrip in the southwestern United States, where they were met by an agent identified as Mr. Bill and four or five other American instructors and interpreters.[3] Florencio Caballero, an interrogator and kidnapper with Battalion 3-16, recalled:

> We went to a military base. It was so private. There was no TV, no cable, only videotapes. . . . The [Honduran] officers knew where we were. They would say, "here in Texas." It was like a college. We had everything we needed—food, drink, a swimming pool. (*Baltimore Sun*, 13 June 1995)

For six months, members of the C I A and the U.S. Federal Bureau of Investigation, using translators, taught the Hondurans interrogation techniques. The trainers specialized in psychological torture and taught the Hondurans how to use prisoners' weak points and fears against them. Among other lessons, they taught them how to use sleep deprivation and blackmail to extract information.

Back in Honduras, some thirty members of Battalion 3-16 attended counterinsurgency courses taught by Americans and Argentines at an army base outside Tegucigalpa. The advisors instructed them in electronic surveillance, "combat maneuvers, pursuit, torture, explosives, interrogation."[4] In secret testimony before the U.S. Senate Select Committee on Intelligence in June 1988, Richard Stolz, C I A deputy director for operations, confirmed the C I A training:

> The course consisted of three weeks of classroom instruction followed by two weeks of practical exercises, which included the questioning of

actual prisoners by students. . . . Physical abuse or other degrading treatment was rejected, not only because it is wrong, but because it has historically proven to be ineffective. (*Baltimore Sun*, 11 June 1995)

As José Barrera Martínez, a Honduran participant, admits, "The Argentines taught courses on torture" (*Baltimore Sun*, 13 June 1995). Oscar Álvarez, a former Honduran special forces officer and nephew to General Álvarez, remembers:

The Argentines came in first, and they taught how to disappear people. The U.S. made them more efficient. . . . The Americans . . . brought the equipment. . . . They gave the training in the U.S., and they brought agents here to provide some training in Honduras. . . . They said, "You need someone to tap phones, you need someone to transcribe the tapes, you need surveillance groups." They brought in special cameras that were inside thermoses. They taught interrogation techniques. (*Baltimore Sun*, 11 June 1995)

The headquarters of Battalion 3-16 was located in the capital, Tegucigalpa, but units operated elsewhere in the country. In Tegucigalpa, Battalion 3-16 had a secret jail in a military building where the kidnapping and interrogation groups slept. The secret jails were off limits to everyone except 3-16 personnel. A CIA official called simply Mr. Mike, however, visited the headquarters several times a week.

The battalion used several other safe houses, including one where up to thirty kidnapped victims were held at a time. Four men in charge of the executions lived there; these executioners were reportedly serving murder sentences at the central penitentiary when Álvarez selected them for their new duties. The members of Battalion 3-16 obtained information through agents and civilians. Members "tapped telephone lines, trailed victims, and often carried out weeks of surveillance" (*Baltimore Sun*, 11 June 1995). Many of the houses under surveillance turned out to be Contra safe houses or arms warehouses and, notes Caballero, a former member of Battalion 3-16, "when they saw they were Contras, they left them alone."

The members of Battalion 3-16 dressed in civilian clothes and often disguised themselves with masks, wigs, false beards, and mustaches. Armed with Uzi machine guns or pistols, they stalked their victims, kidnapped them, and then sped off in double-cab Toyota pickup trucks with tinted windows and stolen license plates. Many of the kidnappings occurred during daylight, on busy streets. Government personnel rarely intervened. On August 18, 1982, when Germán Pérez Alemán, a union leader, was kidnapped from a busy street in the capital, he fought off his attackers but was beaten and forced into a car. Two military officers in a patrol car witnessed the incident and pursued the kidnappers. When they pulled them over, Lieutenant Segundo Flores Murillo identified himself as an intelligence agent, instructed military officers to say they had not caught up with them, and threatened them. Pérez Alemán was never seen again.[5]

The kidnapped victims were taken to the 3-16's clandestine jails, where they were stripped, bound hand and foot, and blindfolded. The captors taped their eyes. They were then held in basements, bedrooms, or closets. Interrogators questioned them for hours, shouting obscenities, accusing them of terrorism, and threatening they would never see their families again if they did not confess (*Baltimore Sun*, 11 June 1995). Although, during trainings, the Americans had eschewed violence, the CIA advisor referred to as Mr. Mike told Caballero privately that electric shocks were "the most efficient way to get someone to talk when they resisted" (O'Connor, 1994). In addition, General Álvarez told interrogators that psychological torture was not effective; he instructed them to use physical torture instead.

The tortures Battalion 3-16 used included electric shocks, dunking in water, and suffocation. Torturers shocked victims by clipping wires to genitals, navels, ribs, and their backs. Miguel Carias, an architectural draftsman who was held for a week in 1982, remembers: "They started with 110 volts. Then they went up to 220. Each time they shocked me, I could feel my body jump and my mouth filled with a metal taste" (*Baltimore Sun*, 11 June 1995).

Torturers attached electric wires to the breasts and vagina of thirty-eight-year-old Gloria Esperanza Reyes, the wife of a journalist. "The first jolt was so bad I just wanted to die," she reports (*Baltimore Sun*, 11 June 1995). José Barrera, a 3-16 member, remembers such pleas: "They always asked to be killed. Torture is worse than death" (*Baltimore Sun*, 11 June 1995). Barrera has testified that one of the battalion's methods was to strip a male prisoner, stand him on a chair, tie a basket to his testicles, and, as the torturer interrogated the prisoner, fill the basket with stones, then swing it back and forth (*Baltimore Sun*, 13 June 1995).

Torturers tied victims' hands and feet, and then submerged them head first into a barrel of water. Torturers also used the *capucha* (the hood), a piece of rubber cut from an inner tube that covered the mouth and nose and suffocated detainees until they fainted (Shaw and Denton, 1987). Victims were hung from the ceiling and beaten, and torturers raped and fondled women (*Baltimore Sun*, 11 June 1995). Torturers often kept detainees nude, drenched them repeatedly with cold water, withheld food and drink, and threatened to harm family members. According to Barrera:

> We would show them photos of their family. We would say, "We're going to get your mother and rape her in front of you." Then we would make it seem like we went to get the mother. (*Baltimore Sun*, 13 June 1995)

Battalion 3-16 worked with other branches of the military. Before a kidnapping occurred, FUSEP forces cordoned off the area and, in the few cases when it was required that the prisoners "reappear," the DNI assumed responsibility to protect the secrecy of 3-16. When an international outcry developed over the disappearance of Inés Murillo Schwaderer because of her German heritage, she suddenly "appeared" in the DNI jail in Tegucigalpa seventy-nine days after her detention, even though the DNI had ignored several writs of habeas corpus presented to them.

As early as 1982, detainees were routinely killed. When an execution was ordered, the prisoner, already weak from torture and lack of food, was handed over to the execution squad. Prisoners were killed with guns, knives, or machetes, and bodies were buried in clandestine cemeteries, alongside roads, or in construction sites where cement was poured over them. In the early 1980s, before 3-16 became well organized, members of the Nicaraguan Contras often carried out the killings (Amnesty International, 1988, 19).

A Contra identified as Miguel reports that in 1982 he received an order to execute two Hondurans being held by Battalion 3-16, Eduardo Lanza and Félix Martínez. The Contras arranged to meet up with a Honduran army jeep on a highway outside Tegucigalpa, where a soldier handed over two emaciated young men. The Contras forced the men to dig a grave on an isolated hillside, then Lanza was made to lie in it, and one of the Contras tried to kill him with a knife. "'But our man did it badly, as if he was afraid, and the kid screamed,' Miguel recalls. 'There were some houses at the edge of the hill, so four or five bullets were fired into his head using a pistol with a silencer. Then lime was shoveled over him . . . so there wouldn't be a bad smell'" (Drucker, 1986, 25–26). Félix Martínez was also killed.

Americans' Role

In Honduras, the U.S. head of the interrogation instructors, referred to as Mr. Bill, worked with the Honduran trainees for several months in 1982. According to Caballero, the American advisor Mr. Mike led interrogations against Inés Murillo Schwaderer. "At times he would write down his questions so the questioner could ask them," Caballero has said (Drucker, 1986, 25–26). Americans also advised the unit on which victims to put under surveillance (Shaw and Denton, 1987). CIA Deputy Director Stolz confirmed the visit of a CIA officer to Murillo's secret cell. "Mindful of the human rights issue, headquarters inquired about her current condition and asked if formal charges had been brought against her," Stolz testified.[6]

The first public debate over the existence of Battalion 3-16 occurred in August 1982, when Colonel Leónidas Torres Arias, who had been exiled by General Álvarez, held a news conference in Mexico and charged Álvarez with being responsible for the disappearances of leftists (DeYoung, 1982). Both Honduran and U.S. officials dismissed Torres Arias's charges. A senior U.S. official told a journalist, "I don't think the police in Honduras are perfect. That's one issue. But to leap from that to the conclusion that Torres is trying to propagate—that Álvarez is trying to eliminate opposition—is just preposterous" (*Washington Post*, 15 October 1982).

In the 1980s, U.S. officials publicly denied abuses by the Honduran military, condoned death squad activities, and "minimized the extent and seeming systematic nature of the killings" (LeMoyne, 1986). Fearing that knowledge of the human rights abuses would jeopardize Washington's aid to Honduras, and thus jeopardize the Reagan administration's plans in Central America, the U.S. embassy in Tegucigalpa concealed evidence of abuses by the Honduran military from the U.S. Congress, and made false and misleading public statements. When one embassy official attempted to write a truthful human rights report, he was "ordered to remove the damaging information" (*Baltimore Sun*, 19 June 1995).

In October 1982, Ambassador Negroponte wrote in the *Economist*, "It is simply untrue to state that death squads have made their appearance in Honduras" (Negroponte, 1982). Years later, however, one senior State

Department official conceded the U.S. role in the disappearances: "The green light was kill a commie. Everybody was winking and nodding. This fostered an environment where everyone was freelancing and tolerating all kinds of things they shouldn't have. Was it policy? People said no, but you could get away with it."[7]

Yearly human rights reports were required under amendments to the Foreign Assistance Act of 1961 (which restrict Washington from providing military aid to countries whose governments engage in a pattern of human rights abuses), and the reports were prepared under the direct supervision of Ambassador Negroponte. "There are no political prisoners in Honduras," asserted the State Department human rights report on Honduras for 1983, even though embassy officials were aware of the disappearances and clandestine cemeteries and, moreover, had helped two of the "disappeared" to reappear after their kidnappings had become politically embarrassing.[8]

As the disappearances accelerated, U.S. officials attacked those who reported the kidnappings. The State Department repeatedly denounced the Comité para la Defensa de los Derechos Humanos en Honduras (Committee for the Defense of Human Rights in Honduras, CODEH)—the human rights group that did the most to expose the death squads—as "antidemocratic" and, ironically, as a front group for terrorists (National Commissioner for the Protection of Human Rights in Honduras, 1994). The president and founder of CODEH, Dr. Ramón Custodio, highlights the difficult position of his organization at the time:

> We had to endure accusations that, by defending human rights, we were defending extremists, leftists and communists. (National Commissioner for the Protection of Human Rights in Honduras, 1994)

CODEH members often received death threats. Dr. Custodio was threatened, kept under surveillance by plainclothes security forces, and detained and interrogated. The CODEH office where he also lived was firebombed three times (National Commissioner for the Protection of Human Rights in Honduras, 1994, 73–74).

The Ineffectiveness of Habeas Corpus and the Climate of Fear
During the 1980s, habeas corpus, a mechanism of constitutional protection that requires someone holding a person in custody to present the prisoner

before a court, failed to secure the releases of those kidnapped. Detainees were regularly held incommunicado longer than the twenty-four-hour limit established by the Honduran constitution. During the period from 1981 to 1984, Dr. Custodio filed fifty writs of habeas corpus and the security forces disregarded all of them. Many lawyers and judges feared getting involved in such cases because of worries over their own safety. In one case, a judge and a witness to a kidnapping presented a writ of habeas corpus to security officials where they knew the abducted person was being held; both the judge and the witness were then themselves detained.[9]

César Murillo, in searching for his daughter, Inés, was told that "the president of the Supreme Court said he was scared of the army and there was nothing he could do. [The judges] told me to look for her in Cuba" (*Baltimore Sun*, 15 June 1995).

Meanwhile, in the clandestine centers, members of Battalion 3-16 ridiculed attempts to locate the disappeared. According to Caballero:

> What I can tell you now sounds absurd, but the truth is that they laughed at what was being said outside. . . . They said, "They are fools . . . why are they asking about this person when this person is never coming back?" . . . . They were almost sure he [the disappeared person] was going to die, because the cases in which they were set free were exceptional; most were not. Then everyone said, "No, this one is not coming out, so why are they fighting, why do they ask?" (Inter-American Court of Human Rights [hereafter: IACHR], 1987a)[10]

CODEH publicized reports of disappearances through the radio, newspapers, and news conferences. Honduran newspapers, especially *El Tiempo*, reported on the abuses, and relatives ran full-page advertisements with photos of the disappeared and pleas to the kidnappers to release them. "General Álvarez, as a human being, I beg you to free my children," read one ad (30 April 1982). In 1982 alone, some 318 stories were published in Honduran newspapers about human rights abuses (*Baltimore Sun*, 11 June 1995).

Like the Argentine Mothers of the Plaza de Mayo, relatives of the Honduran disappeared marched through the cobbled streets of Tegucigalpa, carrying placards with photos of their sons and daughters. Women, white scarves around their heads, chanted, "Alive they were taken! Alive we want them back!" (*Baltimore Sun*, 11 June 1995). However, by 1982, Americas Watch noted that "abuses have created an atmosphere of fear in the population" (Americas Watch, 1982). Miguel Angel Pavón, head of the San Pedro Sula chapter of C O D E H, testified to the Inter-American Court of Human Rights (I A C H R) in 1987:

> I can say that fear existed everywhere during that time period ... because it was as if a blanket of fear had been thrown over society, and everyone knew who was responsible, but few of us dared to speak out against what was going on. So the repression was systematic, continuous and brutal, and when someone spoke out ... the military and the police ... did something that instilled more fear in the people ... and frankly they succeeded in terrorizing the population.[11] (I A C H R, 1987b)

Álvarez Deposed

In March 1981, General Álvarez made a major political mistake when he pressured the Honduran congress to approve a constitutional change regarding generals' ages, and reduced the size of the Superior Council from forty-five members to twenty-one (Salomón, 1992, 12). By these actions he increased rivalries between the *promociones*, the different generations of officers, and shut out of power the younger, more nationalist groups. These younger officers, alarmed by his increasing autocracy (which blocked their own ascendancy), by his desire to engage in war with Nicaragua, and by his unquestioning subservience to U.S. policy, finally took action. On March 31, 1984, they accused Álvarez of "misappropriation of funds," held a pistol to his head, handcuffed him, and put him on a plane to Miami; his rule was over.[12] Several of his allies were also deposed.

The day after the coup, President Suazo Córdova was summoned to a meeting at the air force headquarters (Hammond, 1991, 114), where he was told the military was in charge. On April 4, 1984, Honduras's congress ratified General Walter López Reyes as the new head of the armed forces. To insure that a single officer would never override them again, the Superior Council stripped the new chief of many of the powers Álvarez had accumulated. It disbanded the C S N and reinvested itself with the authority to make national policy. The Superior Council returned to its traditional collegial nature by which, in time, military officials were assured of being promoted and of receiving the business opportunities that promotions offered.

The new leaders of the armed forces were not ideologues but nationalists with business acumen. They realized how important Honduras's geopolitical position was to the United States and, in order to continue Honduran support for the Contras' activities, they renegotiated their arrangements with Washington. They signed a new treaty that eliminated the hated C R E M, and they cut a favorable new financial package. Moreover, the Honduran military awarded itself remunerative "business contracts" with the Contras, supplying weapons and supplies at a price that included a substantial profit for themselves (Bowman, 2002, 229).

Under López Reyes, the armed forces took a more moderate view toward social and economic problems in the country. During June 1984, shortly after Álvarez was removed, labor unrest increased, but leaders from the armed forces met with labor and peasant unions and encouraged dialogue rather than confrontation. Thus, the military began a return to its traditional role of mediator, and the civilian sectors returned to their traditional roles of seeking the military's intervention to solve their problems.

When López Reyes took power, he was faced with increasing international and domestic pressure to deal with human rights abuses. The military continued to deny that their forces were involved but, after Álvarez was removed, the leaders of Battalion 3-16 were replaced, although the unit was not disbanded. Table 7.3 indicates that the numbers of disappearances fluctuated after 1984, when Álvarez was deposed.

The Inter-American Court Case and Return to "Exceptionalism"

On July 29, 1988, in San Jose, Costa Rica, the Inter-American Court of Human Rights determined that Honduras had violated the American Convention of Human Rights by carrying out a "systematic" practice of disappearing individuals during the period from 1981 to 1984 (I A C H R, 1987/1988, par. 147). The case established new precedents in international law in that, despite the tens of thousands of state-sanctioned disappearances that occurred in Latin America during the 1960s, 1970s, and 1980s, it was the first case in which an international court decreed that a state was responsible for disappearances (Grossman, 1992, 363; Drucker, 1988, 290), thus setting a new standard and guideline for human rights law. Members of international human rights organizations hailed the judgment as a warning to Latin American militaries that they no longer had impunity to violate human rights. "The Court established the important principle that disappearances are a crime against humanity and, therefore, governments have an affirmative duty to investigate, prosecute, and punish them" (Americas Watch, 1989, 72).

In August 1987, under pressure from domestic and international forces, the five Central American countries signed the Esquipulas II Peace Plan (for which Costa Rican President Oscar Arias Sánchez won a Nobel Peace Prize). Within the United States, support for the Reagan administration's policies in Central America faltered, and the U.S. Congress voted against additional military aid for the Contras. The Contras and the Sandinistas entered into peace talks. As Washington was forced to back off from arming the Contras, aid to Honduras declined and demilitarization began. During the U.S. militarization, the Honduran armed forces had profited on a scale that, up to that time, had been unimaginable. As millions of uncharted dollars surged into the area, the Honduran military profited from arms transfers, corruption, and from the myriad business opportunities that the U.S. militarization afforded them.

In addition, just as U.S. economic aid began to dry up, the military began profiteering from drug money—as Honduras became a major transshipment point for cocaine (Rosenberg, 1988, 143). At the end of the 1980s, the armed forces emerged as the country's new economic elite. In January 1988, a military official told the Inter-American Court that Battalion 3-16 had been "permanently recessed" in 1987. Many of the officers who had commanded it, however, were still part of the active military force.

Conclusions

What were the legacies of Honduras's U.S.-led militarization during the 1980s? Politically, even as Honduras held regular presidential and legislative elections and had a civilian chief executive, the Honduran military dominated political affairs. Although this dominance cannot be attributed solely to the U.S.-sponsored militarization, as the armed forces had already established their primary influence during seventeen years of rule before the 1980s, the militarization of society contributed to the strengthening of the military as an institution and, in particular, to a strengthening of the positions of hard-liners within the military. The Honduran hard-liners and Washington during the Reagan administration shared the same goal—to rid Central America of communists and other leftists—and, backed by U.S. political support and flush with massive amounts of U.S. aid, the hard-liners made a pact with civilian leaders that allowed them to carry out repressive policies unfettered. In a country without a tradition of political violence, human rights violations occurred unabated because they fit into the political goals of the Honduran leaders, which in turn matched the political goals of their backers in Washington.

Economically, the armed forces emerged during this period as a new elite, using financial windfalls gained during the 1980s to become one of the most important sectors for financial investment in the country. Combining this economic prominence with de facto control of political power, the military emerged from the period of U.S.-led militarization as the most powerful sector in the country, with few checks or balances to restrain them. In time, the armed forces returned to their traditional role of mediator, of opting for reform over repression, and Honduras returned to the role of an "exception" among the countries of Central America. As the subsequent careers of the members of the main death squad, Battalion 3-16, shows, however, even after the process of militarization had subsided and begun to reverse, the military still had impunity in matters of human rights.

NOTES

1. In 1983, 700 Honduran troops and 1,500 Salvadoran troops were trained at the CREM (Rudolph, 1984).

2. Years later, General Álvarez admitted U.S. participation in the death squad. "The CIA trained my people in intelligence," he told a reporter. "They gave very good training, especially in interrogation" (O'Connor, 1994).

3. Sworn testimony of Florencio Caballero at the IACHR, Public Hearing, October 6, 1987 (IACHR, 1987a).

4. Testimony of José Barrera Martínez, quoted in National Commissioner for the Protection of Human Rights in Honduras, 1994.

5. Testimony concerning the abduction of Germán Pérez Alemán was presented by Florencio Caballero at the IACHR. See National Commissioner for the Protection of Human Rights in Honduras, 1994, 144.

6. Censored transcript from Richard Stolz's secret testimony before the Senate Select Committee on Intelligence in June 1988 (as reported by the *Baltimore Sun*, 13 June 1995).

7. O'Connor, 1994.

8. *Baltimore Sun*, 11 June 1995. In 1986, when the *New York Times* first published reports of CIA involvement in killings by the secret unit, the newspaper received an official reaction from the U.S. government: "Michael O'Brien, a spokesman for the U.S. Embassy in Honduras, issued a prepared statement drafted with the aid of State Department officials in Washington. The statement said: 'There is no connection between specific professional training which may have been provided by the U.S. Government to Honduran security forces and charges that Honduran security personnel subsequently may have engaged in improper activity. At no time has there been any United States Government involvement in supposed death squad activities'" (*New York Times*, 14 February 1986).

9. Testimony of Miguel Angel Pavón to IACHR, September 30, 1987, as cited in Asociación Centroamericana de Familiares de Detenidos-Desaparecidos (hereafter: ACAFADE), 1988, 30.

10. IACHR testimony of Florencio Caballero as cited in ACAFADE, 1988.

11. On January 14, 1988, some three months after testifying before the IACHR, Miguel Angel Pavón was gunned down in Tegucigalpa (allegedly by members of Battalion 3-16).

12. After being deposed, Álvarez moved to Miami, where he worked as a consultant to the Pentagon in "low-intensity warfare," as well as to the RAND Corporation, and he became an evangelical preacher. In April 1988, after having a dream that urged him to return to Honduras to preach the gospel, he moved back to Tegucigalpa. A Honduran human rights group, Comité de Familiares de Detenidos-Desaparecidos en Honduras (COFADEH) filed charges against Álvarez for violations of human rights, but the charges were dropped when clerks lost the papers (Barry and Norsworthy, 1990, 30). Álvarez shunned protection from his friends in the military and preached on street corners, saying, "My Bible is my protection" (*Baltimore Sun*, 11 June 1995). On January 25, 1989, Álvarez's vehicle was ambushed three blocks from his house and he was killed by a hail of gunfire. His bible was on the dashboard. The U.S. embassy blamed leftist forces, but Álvarez's family suggests that he may have been killed by his former military colleagues (Schulz and Sundloff Schulz, 1994, 250; *Washington Post*, 26 January 1989; *Baltimore Sun*, 11 June 1995).

BIBLIOGRAPHY

Aguilar, Ernesto Paz. 1992. "The Origin and Development of Political Parties in Honduras." Pp. 161–74 in *Political Parties and Democracy in Central America*, ed. Louis W. Goodman, William M. LeoGrande, and Johanna Mendelson Forman. Boulder: Westview Press.

Americas Watch. 1982. *Human Rights in Honduras: Signs of the Argentine Method.* New York: Americas Watch.

————. 1989. *Honduras: Without the Will.* New York: Americas Watch.

Amnesty International. 1988. *Honduras, Civilian Authority–Military Power: Human Rights Violations in the 1980s.* London: Amnesty International Publications.

Asociación Centroamericana de Familiares de Detenidos-Desaparecidos (A C A F A D E). 1988. "Informe: 44 Periodo de Sesiones de la Comisión de Derechos Humanos de la Onu, Guinebra, Suiza (Feb-Mar)." San Jose: Asociación Centroamericana de Familiares de Detenidos-Desaparecidos.

Barry, Tom, and Kent Norsworthy. 1990. *Honduras: A Country Guide.* Albuquerque: Inter-Hemispheric Education Resource Center.

Blachman, Morris, William LeoGrande, and Kenneth Sharpe. 1986. *Confronting Revolution: Security through Diplomacy in Central America.* New York: Random House.

Bowman, Kirk. 2002. *Militarization, Democracy, and Development: The Perils of Praetorianism in Latin America.* University Park: The Pennsylvania State University Press.

Crahan, Margaret. 1982. *Human Rights and Basic Needs in the Americas.* Washington, DC: Georgetown University Press.

DeYoung, Karen. 1982. "Honduran Colonel Who Denounced Chief Finds Nervous Refuge." *Washington Post*, 16 Oct.

Drucker, Linda. 1986. "A Contra's Story." *The Progressive*, August.

————. 1988. "Governmental Liability for 'Disappearances': A Landmark Ruling by the Inter-American Court of Human Rights." *Stanford Journal of International Law*, Fall: 289–322.

Grossman, Claudio. 1992. "Disappearances in Honduras: The Need for Direct Victim Representation in Human Rights Litigation." *Hastings International and Comparative Law Review* 15 (3): 363–89.

Hammond, Captain Tony. 1991. "The Role of the Honduran Armed Forces in the Transition to Democracy." Master's thesis, University of Florida, Gainesville.

Hogan, Joseph, ed. 1990. *The Reagan Years.* Manchester: Manchester University Press.

Inter-American Court of Human Rights (I A C H R). 1987/1988. Transcripts, Manfredo Velásquez case [online]. San Jose, Costa Rica: Inter-American Court of Human Rights [updated 2001; cited 31 March 2003]. Available from http://www.corteidh.or.cr/public_ing/index.html.

————. 1987a. Sworn testimony of Florencio Caballero at the I A C H R, Public Hearing, 6 October.

————. 1987b. Testimony of Miguel Angel Pavón to I A C H R, Public Hearing, 30 September.

LeMoyne, James. 1986. "C.I.A. Accused of Tolerating Killings in Honduras." *New York Times*, 14 February, foreign news, sec. A, p. 1.

National Commissioner for the Protection of Human Rights in Honduras. 1994. *The Facts Speak for Themselves: The Preliminary Report on Disappearances.* New York: Human Rights Watch.

Negroponte, John D. 1982. "Letter to the Editor." *The Economist* 23 October.

O'Connor, Anne Marie. 1994. "Who Was 'Mike' and What Was He Doing in a Honduran Torture Cell?" *Atlanta Journal and Constitution*, 13 March, foreign news, sec. A, p. 21.

Rosenberg, Mark. 1988. *Honduras in the Central American Conflict: Trends and Recent Developments.* Miami: Latin American and Caribbean Center, Florida International University.

Rosenberg, Mark B., and Philip L. Shepherd. 1986. *Honduras: Perspectives on Critical Issues.* Boulder: L. Rienner Publishers.

Rudolph, James (ed.). 1984. *Honduras: A Country Study (Foreign Area Studies, The American University)*, 2nd ed. Washington, DC: Department of the Army.

Salomón, Leticia. 1992. *Política y Militares en Honduras.* Tegucigalpa: Centro de Documentación de Honduras.

Schulz, Donald E., and Deborah Sundloff Schulz. 1994. *The United States, Honduras, and the Crisis in Central America.* Boulder: Westview Press.

Shaw, Terri, and Herbert H. Denton. 1987. "Honduran Death Squad Alleged." *Washington Post*, 2 May.

Volk, Stephen. 1981. "Honduras: On the Border of War." *NACLA Report on the Americas* 15: 122–37.

Weeks, John. 1986. "An Interpretation of the Central American Crisis." *Latin American Research Review* 21 (3): 53–64.

CHAPTER 8

"No Hay Rosas Sin Espinas"
Statecraft in Costa Rica

ANNAMARIE OLIVERIO AND PAT LAUDERDALE

Introduction

During the 1970s and 1980s, largely through images transmitted world-wide, state terror became almost synonymous with Latin America. Death squads, *desaparecidos* ("the disappeared ones"), and unstable, elite oligarchies appeared to be the normal elements of Latin American political and social control. Indeed, repressive actions were so prevalent that numerous Latin American "specialists" declared that state violence was simply a shared cultural legacy, a part of the cultural heritage of the region (Koonings and Kruijt, 1999; Bauer, 1992; Rosenberg, 1991; Wiarda, 1982; Zea, 1965). From the autocratic rule of the Aztec, Mayan, and Incan nations to the brutal Spanish invasion in the 1500s, state development seemed to have been characterized primarily by repression, violence, and military power. It has even been suggested that the Spaniards, in addition to their own forms of terror and mass slaughter, learned many strategies of domination and brutality from the large indigenous nations of the area. Thus, the level of terror conducted by the state in the latter half of the twentieth century is often considered to be consistent with its history: terror ostensibly is inherent in Latin American political culture. Such claims, however, are either gross simplifications or misleading stereotypes that ignore both historical patterns of hegemony and external pressures on state formation (Perez, 1981).

The experience of Costa Rica, despite that country's own problems with various forms of state domination, violence, and repression, presents a significant challenge to such simplifications and stereotypes. While surrounding states were characterized by military rule, Costa Rica abolished its formal army in the late 1940s, promoted civilian control of its security forces, and encouraged international research and teaching regarding peace. However, as the title of this chapter suggests, "there are no roses without thorns." International pressure, as well as the nature of modern states and now dominant forms of globalization, threaten continually to encroach on the autonomy of small Costa Rica.

Contrary to the cultural heritage theory just outlined, we suggest that terror and violence are more closely related to the development of the modern state, specific global influences, and the process of "democratization" than they are to a "cultural inheritance" of Latin American societies. Modern technologies of control and terror are integral to the centralization of the state, to homogenization, and to dominant forms of globalization. Although its experience has been less bloody than elsewhere in Latin America, Costa Rica has also had to manage such pressures and difficulties, surrounded geographically by political and social instability and buffeted by influences from external forces (from, for example, the geopolitical machinations of the Reagan administration). Thus, in explicating this case as a challenge to the cultural heritage theory, we include a brief historical analysis of Costa Rica prior to and following 1948. Before focusing more specifically on Costa Rica, however, it may be useful to examine the essence of the modern state, and its ostensible "democratic" transition, to better understand the relevant structures and processes of domination, repression, and violence.

The Art of Statecraft and Terror: A Symbiotic Relationship

In order to understand structures of terrorism and violence, their logic and coherence, we must first examine the structure of the state. Past research on the relationship of the state to terrorism has projected the state's role as simply reactive to "terrorist" challenges, while policy concerns have focused on implementing an increasingly repressive system of social control (Emerson, 2002; Alexander and Swetnam, 2001; Whittaker, 2001; Nacos, 2000; Hoffman, 1999; Grosscup, 1998; Reich, 1998; Stohl, 1988; Lesser and Tellis, 1996; Bell, 1994; Wilkinson, 1986, 1990; Cooper, 1985; Jenkins, 1985; Laqueur, 1977). Most modern states, for example, define terrorism as a type of political violence that undermines the legitimacy of the state. Moreover, whether practiced by the state or by a group challenging the state's position, terrorism typically is characterized in terms of psychological motivations, economic deprivation, and ideological politics.

The concept of terrorism as it is used and understood in contemporary research and media texts emerges from eighteenth and nineteenth century political literature criticizing the "mobilization of the masses" (Oliverio, 1997, 1998; Stehr, 1994; Burke, 1982 [1790]). Inherent in the concept are the historical and philosophical referents of that time, such as orthodox concepts of the nature of man, the nation-state, and political sovereignty. Two hundred years later, these views continue to dominate contemporary knowledge and politics related to terrorism. As Carnoy (1984, 4) notes:

> In the United States, we are particularly tied to certain of these traditions as if little has changed during the last two hundred years. But the issue of the State has become much more complex, and with this increased complexity, we need theories that deal with it adequately and accurately.

Some scholars have attempted to define the concept of terrorism more precisely than it was formulated in the past, hoping to overcome the more obvious ideological and historical problems that have been contained within it. Gibbs (1989, 333), for example, suggests that terrorism should not be equated with or misunderstood as "fear of terror," which he defines as the state's use of this tactic, a process conceptually distinct from terrorism. While he presents a compelling argument for the development of a theory of terrorism stated in terms of systemic control, his analysis does not consider the rhetorical component of terrorism as inextricably related to the state, the art of statecraft, and the production of injustice (Oliverio, 1997).[1]

Throughout history, as is abundantly evident in Costa Rica and other areas of Latin America, social movements and protest groups have consistently appealed to the state either directly or indirectly to establish systematic and equitable laws and practices by which people can live. While the state may have appeared to comply rhetorically, its inherent political structure has typically lent itself to processes of standardization and not equity, uniformity and not diversity, co-optation and not community. Such a reality begs the question: Is terrorism intrinsic to the establishment of modern states, which rhetorically invoke stability and order as the intended outcome even of violent actions?

An approach that examines this "structure" of state terrorism highlights and questions structures of domination and violence inherent to modern states, from tyrannical to liberal democratic ones. Tyrannies, at one end of the continuum, represent total control by the state, as is the case in a monarchy or through the rule of a despotic leader. Liberal democratic regimes, at the other end of the continuum, approximate a form of political organization in which the citizens, at large, have the greatest power to organize, protest, and elect leaders. A democratic regime is also significant in its protection of human and civil rights and "offers the most peaceful and effective way for the diverse groups to negotiate satisfactory answers to inevitable ethnic and regional cleavages, interest group conflicts, and ideological differences" (Gershman, 1990, 9).

Yet, democracies vary around the world and, as a result, levels of open political discussion and compromise among diverse groups differ widely from society to society. In countries with extreme social cleavages, democratic rhetoric typically is used to obfuscate reactionary forces. Liberal democracies have varied, for example, in their definitions of what actions should be termed terrorism. Typically, the term *terrorism* is invoked by the state at times when competing interests are great and compromise is viewed as threatening or a sign of weakness, especially when those definitions are set by more powerful liberal democracies (Oliverio, 1998).

Democracy

Given the political context for the emergence of democracy in ancient Greece, where the majority of the people were not citizens, it is understandable how different political regimes can employ this term to their own ends.[2] Whether it is the dynastic rule of the Somoza family in Nicaragua or the liberal political leadership characteristic of Costa Rica, modern Latin American states were founded upon elitist hierarchical structures. Thus, democratic stability rooted in historical, social, political, and economic conditions nonetheless manifests inherent political limitations, which, of course, vary by degree. Limitation is the essence of the modern state, as the state itself is maintained by means of its rigid, hierarchical structure and practices of formal social control.

Although the evolution and development of the democratic state in Costa Rica has followed a different path than in its neighbors, the country's processes of democratization have been neither uniform nor violence-free. Examination of the case of Costa Rica in comparison with those of other Latin American states, however, indicates that a variation in U.S. foreign policy toward the country appears to have had a greater impact than any other factor on the course of democratization and the evolution and development of states with differing degrees of terrorism (Halebsky and Harris, 1995; Zarate, 1994). Of course, the paradox of this finding is that during the Cold War period changes in U.S. foreign policy in Latin America, including that related to Costa Rica, had the greatest impact on the degree of violence and terrorism employed by those Latin American states (Zarate, 1994; Lauderdale, 1986; Lincoln and Lauderdale, 1985).

Hegemony

Rather than simply bemoan the paradoxical rhetoric of democratic stability in relation to its historical practices and manifestations in Latin America, it is important to understand that largely discursive relationship. While in prison, Antonio Gramsci (1971) attempted to understand similar paradoxical processes via his examination and development of the theory of hegemony. Gramsci noted at this time that hegemony is produced via the practices of "institutions and organizations whose task it is to influence common sense" (Augelli and Murphy, 1988, 24). Institutions such as education, media, religion, law, and medicine, among many governmental organizations, are involved in a process of generating and presenting information that appears simple and devoid of any intrinsic political agendas or philosophical critiques. Rhetorically, for example, the idea of democracy as "government for the people, by the people" has come to stand for a universal, political ideal of freedom, equality, equity, and justice for all. Such a simplified concept becomes endlessly repeated until it becomes part of a common, normal, "taken-for-granted," rarely questioned facade. From this perspective, democracy in practice can have little or nothing to do with democracy in rhetoric. Indeed, the rhetorical ideal has not been practiced historically, neither in the Greek city-states from which the concept emerged, nor in most modern manifestations.

Another important issue elucidated by a hegemonic analysis, especially as it relates to Costa Rica, is the state's claim to establish democracy by abolishing distinctions among people that are determined by birth, social rank, education, and occupation. Declaring these as nonpolitical distinctions, and so viewing the diverse elements that compose the real life of a nation only from the standpoint of the state, the state proclaims legal equality for every member of society. The state, nonetheless, does allow the existence, development, and institutionalization of social differentiation through inheritance, private property, education, and occupation. Far from abolishing such differences, the state only exists so far as they are presupposed (Inverarity, Lauderdale, and Feld, 1983). International development and business agreements that promise to provide assistance in the development of infrastructure, education, and agriculture are unilaterally made by the state, usually without "the voice of the people." Despite the state's rhetorical claims to be providing equitable solutions for its people, how can equity be implemented in a state based on hierarchy, domination, power, and transcendence to a specific standard, including a standard condoned by a "western ideology" (Fanon, 1987 [1961])? [3]

When we consider the symbiotic relationship between the modern state and terrorism, it is clear that Costa Rica's experience with state violence was prompted primarily by outside forces, similar to the experience of other Latin American countries. The Spanish conquest and the systematic subjugation of the indigenous populations of Costa Rica began in the 1500s shortly after Christopher Columbus arrived on the Atlantic coast near present-day Limón. In order to appreciate more fully the circumstances that led to Costa Rica's unique political culture, it is important to provide a brief history of the area.

Costa Rica's Political History: Cracks in the Hegemonic Facade

Two distinct historical views dominate discussions of the development of Costa Rican political culture. The first examines Costa Rica as a "rural democracy." In this view, Costa Rica's colonial experience is considered to have been modest and mostly egalitarian. Since there were few precious metals and relatively few Indians, the early Spanish had little from which to build economic wealth, and therefore settlers had to work the land themselves. Thus, the present pacifist, democratic, political, and social institutions seen to characterize the country were founded on the basis of what might be termed a rural egalitarian society (Wilson, 1998; Alfaro, 1989; Pacheco, 1961).

A second view, based on more recent research, notes the crucial role of social stratification in the country's political development. This view claims that the colonial social structure in Costa Rica was not egalitarian but rather complex and highly structured (Nef, 1995; Stone, 1989, 1991; Vega Carballo, 1989; Gundmundson, 1983). The surviving native population was enslaved through a system called *encomiendas* (forced patronage) and was not allowed to gain (or regain) autonomy or buy property (Helmuth, 2000; Paige, 1997). Political governance and positions of authority were given to the conquistadores and to the hidalgos, the noble elites. Resolution of critical political issues in the area was controlled by a small group of families, descendants of Spanish nobility who held a monopoly on political and social power. Urban commercial centers were also better developed than earlier historical accounts describe (Gundmundson, 1986). Even though there were relevant differences among the experiences of the Spanish in Costa Rica, it is clear that their social and economic organization, and their political structures based on domination, emulated the state structures of their mother country, Spain, while mirroring as well other colonized areas of Latin America.[4]

Between its declaration of independence from a regional Central American federation in 1838 and the drafting of a new constitution in 1948, Costa Rica underwent a series of military coups punctuated by liberal or reformist phases. The military coups brought about great loss of life as well as a serious depletion of public finances and materials. In addition, a cholera epidemic killed 10 percent of the population in 1856. Mandatory military service was difficult to maintain, as agricultural laborers were always needed. Public debt was high, as was taxation. Despite the obvious role the military played in maintaining the dominant oligarchical and patrimonial system, extreme poverty worked against its establishment as a central institution of political rule. Once a coup ended, the military reverted to its previous role as a ceremonial prop for national celebrations (Vega Carballo, 1989).

Costa Rica's more "democratizing" historical periods, on the other hand, were based largely on the influence of decentralized political structures; they were built on a lack of exports rather than on consolidated wealth, foreign aid, economic production, or a centralization of the state (cf. Zarate, 1994; Pastor, 1989; Skidmore, 1989; Dahl, 1971; Frank, 1967; Lipset, 1959). Furthermore, out of the constant regime changes from military coup to liberal reforms, more "flexible," transparent, and accountable state structures gradually emerged. Whether through protests, elections, or the creation of new political parties, Costa Ricans became active political participants, often at the expense of their domestic stability.

Domestic stability in Costa Rica, unlike in the United States and most other nation-states, is not measured in terms of how long an elected (or appointed) government is in power. Rather, it is measured according to a government's level of tolerance for ambiguity, for the free flow and serious consideration of ideas from its citizens, and for the representation of diverse interests. Old governments are relatively easily dissolved and new ones are readily formed. For the most part, Costa Ricans believe that moral and national issues are not necessarily connected. These issues, therefore, cannot be represented in a uniform way. As participants in a nation-state, Costa Ricans prefer to be able to express their various opinions, interpretations, and individual interests while "camping on the same territory, held together by habit and utilitarian motives," rather than out of a sense of national fervor (Romano, 1984, 25).[5]

One of the most interesting factors in Costa Rica's democratic development was the sustained growth of its national education system. As early as 1823, public education was defined as the principal foundation for human happiness. The steady growth of public education occurred regardless of the type of regime in power. The Constitution of 1869 declared compulsory state-sponsored primary education for both women and men of all class levels. As Vega Carballo (1989, 47) notes:

> By the 1860s, the advantages of popular access to knowledge and even compulsory education were fully appreciated in Costa Rica. Education implied improvements in labor productivity and contributed to the formation of a collective mentality that made it possible for society to be self-administered without resorting to state repression.

In 1882, a newly formed Liberal government used the education system as "an effective substitute for the harsh and repressive methods of controlling the population and resolving conflict within the political system" (Vega Carballo, 1989, 47).[6]

Consider such a change in Costa Rica from a hegemonic perspective. The process of asserting and maintaining hegemony via wars of position and maneuver is neither linear nor simplistic, particularly in the face of international economic dependency and political relations, and the first half of the twentieth century in Costa Rica illustrates this point. Before the military as an institution was finally abolished in the period 1948–1949, Costa Rica saw the return in 1917 of military dictatorship under General Federico Tínoco Granados. Although his rule lasted only thirty months, Tínoco had the support of many of the Costa Rican elites, mostly owners of coffee plantations who opposed the economic and taxation reforms of the previous government. Those policies had been based on a system of direct, progressive taxation, so that nationals and foreign guests paid taxes: that is, rich and poor alike were taxed according to their income level. While the U.S. president, Woodrow Wilson, refused to recognize Tínoco's regime as a legitimate government, the United States communicated its intent not to restore the previous leader, despite his more liberal and reformist ideals, claiming he was a German sympathizer.

For his part, Tínoco attempted to adopt a pro-U.S. foreign policy, but Wilson defined Tínoco's coup d'état as an "illegal and unconstitutional act" (Murillo Jimenez, 1989, 67). Although politicians and diplomats in the United States encouraged Wilson to recognize Tínoco as a matter of political expediency (also noting Costa Rica's proximity to the Panama Canal), Wilson remained steadfast. He proceeded to isolate the Tínoco regime diplomatically by enlisting a similar political stance from Europe and the rest of Latin America, including Costa Rica's neighboring countries. As Tínoco received more and more international pressure, his national support suffered, and Costa Rica's internal strife, conflict, and poverty increased (Murillo Jimenez, 1989, 66).

As a military regime, Tínoco's administration utilized repressive tactics (an eventual factor in its own demise), especially toward those who publicly opposed it. Opposition to Tínoco and his regime grew stronger, as did riots and demonstrations organized mostly by teachers and students. Tínoco's military officials resorted to beating the rioters, often to death, to disperse the crowds. They also closed parks and other public areas in order to prevent further protests, but the turmoil only increased. The Costa Rican protesters accused Tínoco and his brother of being "bandits" and organized behind a rebel leader who had fled to Nicaragua, while another protesting faction organized in Panama also rose against the president. The protests, moreover, were exacerbated by the arrival of a U.S. warship in Limón, as well as the imminent threat of intervention by Nicaragua.

Although initially the Wilson administration in Washington did not give orders for its military forces to disembark, the Costa Rican regime finally gave in to U.S. pressure in May 1919, and in August 1919 Tínoco went into exile. The Costa Rican economy had already been severely damaged by the economic conditions created by World War I, but it was the U.S. policy of "nonrecognition" and economic isolation that had led most directly to the breakdown of Tínoco's regime. Tínoco's brother, who was supposed to take over the leadership after a brief interim government, was promptly and mysteriously assassinated, and the temporary government that followed oversaw elections that brought to power Julio Acosta García (who had been supported by Nicaragua). The U.S. administration recognized Acosta as the legitimate leader of the country (Murillo Jiminez, 1989).

In the 1920s, Costa Rica was governed by an oligarchical regime that controlled the production of coffee, bananas, and beef. Such rule brought about severe deprivation among people in the middle and lower classes. While oligarchs governed the central and western areas of the country, the United Fruit Company largely controlled the east coast. Workers were subjected to prejudice, extreme poverty, and harsh conditions, and they were prevented from organizing into unions (Zarate, 1994). In essence, until the 1940s, the development of the state and the dominant political culture was characterized by a variety of changes, often influenced heavily by the United States.

Costa Rican Statecraft since 1948

In the preceding discussion, four varying interpretations of Costa Rica's democratic state development have come to light. The first highlights Costa Rica's "simple" colonial history as the key to understanding its egalitarian and stable structure. The second emphasizes the nature and strength of the various political leaders and interests during the period following independence. The third explanation points to Costa Rica's predominantly laissez-faire economic development in the coffee, banana, and beef industries. The fourth explanation points to the absence of a formal military. In an attempt to better understand the influence of U.S. foreign policy in Costa Rica, particularly with regard to the fourth interpretation, two crucial historical periods need to be examined: the revolution of 1948, in which the suppression of a rebellion provided the opening for a renewed assertion of the dominance of constitutional rule and abolition of the army, and the crisis of remilitarization as a result of the Nicaraguan Contras' war against the Sandinistas in the 1980s (see Lauderdale, 1986).

The type of statecraft for which Costa Rica is famous today arose, for the most part, in the latter half of the twentieth century. International politics (U.S. foreign policy, for example, toward Costa Rica) had a significant impact on the country's democratic stability. The neighboring countries of Guatemala and Nicaragua were also affected by such policies; their experiences internationally, however, were very different from those of Costa Rica. In an examination of these two crisis periods of 1948 and the 1980s, it becomes evident that the disparity in the politics experienced within these three states had less to do with each one's colonial and postcolonial domestic history than with the dominant nature of its state structure and with the roles played by international and global politics.

Indeed, seen in terms of domestic dynamics, the development of political and social systems in Costa Rica was not significantly different from the experiences of its neighbors. For nearly forty years between 1824 and 1899, Costa Rica was ruled by one of several military dictatorships. Despite a significant number of independent, subsistence farmers, wealthy families ruled the country, and limited, often fraudulent, political processes (including elections) characterized the state. Additionally, its rich indigenous, cultural heritage was repressed and exploited. Blacks and other "minorities" were marginalized, segregated, and often stigmatized. With respect to coffee production, for example, Paige (1997, 232) notes the dismissive attitude Costa Rican processors had toward their "cheap labor":

> "I think all the Indians like to do is drink *chicha*. The Indians don't do much work and they are not very intelligent. And they were very cheap workers," said another older processor. For most of the processors, the absence of what they saw as a racially inferior Indian lower class, which would inevitably be exploited by dominant Europeans, was the foundation of Costa Rica's rural egalitarianism. For most of those interviewed the racial inferiority of the indigenous population of the Americas was an accepted fact and racial stratification an inevitable consequence of that inferiority.

Yet, with the absence of a large Indian population, divisions were less pronounced than in neighboring countries. As a result, the dominant European population simply dismissed the relevance of other races. State violence was unnecessary, moreover, since a relatively small population of "inferior" people provided ready and expedient forms of cheap labor. This attitude toward a democratic system of government is not unlike that of the ancient Greeks.

Throughout the first half of the twentieth century, the ruling oligarchies in Costa Rica that controlled economic production along with the United Fruit Company were periodically confronted by opposition from collectivist or communist organizations. In this regard as well, until the 1940s Costa Rica's historical development had more similarities with that of its Central

American neighbors than it had differences (Helmuth, 2000; Wilson, 1998; Paige, 1997; Zarate, 1994).

In contrast to its response to trends at the time in neighboring Central American states, the administration of President Harry S. Truman played a role in Costa Rica during the 1948 revolution that was characterized by non-interference. As a result, Costa Rica, in turn, was able to resolve many of its more critical domestic conflicts before the rigid Cold War politics of the 1950s emerged. At the time of the 1948 revolution, in its international relations the United States still adhered to the Good Neighbor Policy adopted by the administration of President Franklin Delano Roosevelt in 1933. As Zarate (1994, 38–39) notes:

> It is clear that the Good Neighbor Policy was a sincere attempt to mend the rift between the United States and Latin America. Roosevelt and his officials, like Secretary of State Cordell Hull and Undersecretary of State Sumner Welles, were extremely well liked and respected in Latin America because the United States treated its Latin neighbors like equals in a cooperative and consultative manner.

The Good Neighbor Policy was codified in September 1947 with the signing of the Inter-American Treaty of Reciprocal Assistance at the conclusion of a hemispheric security conference held in Rio de Janeiro, where twenty-one American republics agreed to implement their first mutual defense treaty. It was further reinforced in April 1948, when these same countries signed the Organization of American States charter in Bogotá, Colombia. This charter was the equivalent of a United Nations agreement for the Western Hemisphere that would provide security from political "posturing" (Zarate, 1994). This policy was so successful at the time that U.S. diplomats defined some of the more radical popular political demands as "liberal" rather than communist, despite the growth of communist sympathies in the region. Fourteen of the twenty-one republics present were governed through democratic process, and it appeared there was no reason to expect that the rest would not simply fall into place behind them.

By means of the 1948 revolution, Costa Rica already had negotiated its own necessary reforms and counter-reforms (Halebsky and Harris, 1995; Zarate, 1994). In fact, the Costa Rican revolution really began in the early 1940s and is better described as a long, protracted period of conflict, disputes,

and negotiation among the various political and ideological factions, culminating in the constitutional reforms of 1948 and 1949. By the late 1940s, the
leading Costa Rican politicians, José Figueres Ferrer and Teodoro Picado,
were aware that the United States would be deeply involved in particular issues. As Zarate (1994, 35) notes:

> In this sense, domestic actors had a limited range of possible action
> with parameters defined by the [U.S.] State Department. Costa Rica's
> transcultural reference to the United States and the intellectual forma-
> tion of the dominant class are two elements of this type of influence.

Additionally, despite the formation of a communist organization in Costa Rica,
anticommunist sentiment as it was promoted by the United States was not the
major issue at this time. Competing factions within Costa Rica did not polar-
ize by allowing this sentiment to dominate ideological politics and, as a result,
anticommunist policy did not flourish until after 1948. This is a significant historical condition for Costa Rica, as U.S. foreign policy had changed significantly by the time Dwight Eisenhower gained the U.S. presidency in 1952.
Even during the Truman era at the end of the 1940s, when Cold War sentiments began to solidify, the international policies of the United States were
focused on Europe and South Korea. Zarate (1994, 39) further indicates that

> most important, . . . the Truman administration still drew distinctions
> between leftist parties and Communist parties: "Distinctions between
> extreme leftist parties and communists are often fluid. [Therefore], we
> should caution against [labeling] leaders as communists."

By the time Eisenhower replaced Truman in office in 1952, the international
precedents set by previous U.S. administrations had begun to be ignored or
replaced with strict Cold War positions. Communists, in this new view, were
often defined as those who opposed or challenged the existing order or even
those who simply sympathized with the Soviet position. Thus, the experiences
of Guatemala, Nicaragua, and El Salvador during their reformation and
counter-reformation periods, which occurred in the 1940s and 1950s, were
increasingly enveloped in the Eisenhower administration's strict Cold War
stance, and Washington proceeded to strengthen Central American militaries
and authoritarian regimes to fight against purported Communist invasions

or uprisings. Opposition to the repressive states in these countries (such as the rule of the Somozas in Nicaragua or Salvador Castañeda Castro in El Salvador) was defined as communism and, usually, destroyed. With the advent of the 1950s, the Good Neighbor Policy in Latin America had officially ended, and the Cold War had become firmly established. Yet, Costa Rica managed to continue to benefit from the former U.S. foreign policy in managing its own domestic political and ideological conflicts while escaping the many ravages of Cold War politics.

In addition to its ability to resist the Cold War-era pressures of the United States, another significant element in Costa Rica's political stability is the absence of a formal military (Lauderdale, 1986). The main reasons cited for the success of Costa Rica's 1948–1949 demilitarization reflect both domestic and foreign-policy concerns. That is, on the one hand, it is said that the threat of communism was not yet firmly established in the international arena at this time and Central America was not an area of international focus either by the United States or by the rest of Latin America. Moreover, it is believed that Costa Rican governments were already so clearly dependent on U.S. policies and programs for their domestic survival that they felt secure that the United States would support and defend the country should international aggression occur. On the other hand, it is said that Costa Rican government leaders, working in particular through the courts, were in the process of creating and implementing a series of additional innovative "checks and balances" on state machinations (Lauderdale, 1986, 240).[7]

Thus, for Costa Ricans, it was thought to be obvious that expenditures for a professional military were unnecessary and the resources could be used more prudently. In addition, the civilian security forces that were established after 1948 have not had a consistent professional military to threaten their existence. Thus, historical timing, isolation from international affairs, and flexibility of the Costa Rican state appear to be three significant reasons that helped Costa Rica to establish and extend a more democratic government and abolish its military, as compared to its Central American neighbors (Zarate, 1994; Lauderdale and Cruit, 1993; Lauderdale, 1986).

While the demilitarization of the late 1940s is a significant variable in the development of the Costa Rican state, the power of the United States to influence change in other countries was more clearly evident in the 1980s when remilitarization of the country appeared inevitable (Lauderdale, 1986; Lincoln and Lauderdale, 1985). Between 1982 and 1986 the Reagan administration increased expenditures to "strengthen" the Costa Rican police force. At this time, Costa Rica was undergoing severe economic instability because of austerity measures imposed by international lending organizations, and it was second only to Israel in the amount of its international debt.

Economic problems were exacerbated when the U.S. State Department further advised that if Costa Rica did not form an army, the United States would withdraw its assistance. The issue of aid is complicated by the "commonly held belief that economic assistance and military assistance constitute a real polarity in U.S. foreign aid." Rather than representing opposite options for U.S. policymakers, however, "ostensible 'non-lethal' economic and humanitarian assistance are critically integrated into an overall strategy of warfare" (Brenes, 1986, 5; Lauderdale, 1986; Lincoln, 1985). The Costa Rican leader, Luis Alberto Monge Álvarez, was besieged by economic crises. He recognized the threats of paramilitary insurgencies, the growing drug trade, and possible aggression from Nicaragua, and so he requested and accepted a certain amount of intervention by the Reagan administration. However, Monge also reinforced Costa Rica's neutral position by denying the U.S. administration permission to conduct maneuvers in Salinas Bay (on the border of Nicaragua and Costa Rica), and he rejected a U.S. invitation to send police trainees to a military training camp in Honduras. The Reagan administration continually pressured Monge to join the coalition against Nicaragua, but Monge refused. Invoking Costa Rica's constitutional agreements and protections in meetings with representatives of the Reagan administration, Monge saw that the country's sovereignty remained largely intact.

The formation at this time of a Cuban-supported insurgency movement, called la Familia, as well as the militant Revolutionary Movement of the People, provided additional indications of a hegemonic crisis in Costa Rica that would likely lead to more ardent state sanctions and social control. Because of their Cuban support, the United States and certain Costa Rican political interests defined these groups as "terrorist," placing more pressure on the local government to accept U.S.-sponsored military and political intervention. Yet, the Costa Rican government resisted U.S. military action against these groups. Moreover, the U.S. military, fearful of repeating in Costa Rica its mistakes leading to the Cuban Revolution of nearly three decades before, kept its distance from the Costa Rican situation.

During the Contras' war against the Sandinistas in Nicaragua and the subsequent Reagan administration, however, U.S. military aid to Costa Rica increased from none in 1980 to $9 million in 1985. Working under the Reagan Doctrine that targeted supposed communist expansionism in the Western Hemisphere, the U.S. State Department was able to develop in Costa Rica a military presence (out of a civil security force) that did not exist prior to 1979.[8] This aid was defined within the U.S. Military Assistance Program as targeted for police professionalization, but the funds were also used for ships with nuclear weapons, M-60 machine guns, river- and oceangoing patrol boats, small aircraft, and Hughes 500E helicopters (Lauderdale, 1986).

While the Costa Rican government tolerated this intervention, its members also pointed out that such military activities were in direct conflict with the Costa Rican constitution. The Costa Rican opposition also noted that while military aid might lead to short-term solutions, the long-term consequences could be greatly worsened by the enhancement of conditions for military coups and an infrastructure for war (Lauderdale, 1986; Farer, 1985). In these years, nonmilitary aid also increased, from $16 million in 1980 to $400 million in 1986 (Lauderdale, 1986). As Zarate (1994, 37) notes, at this time "Green Berets were sent to train 'lightning battalions,' C-130 transport planes shipped new supplies and trainees, the USS Iowa used Costa Rican ports, and thirty Tomahawk missiles were sold to the neutral country."

The main reason cited by the U.S. administration for the proposed expansion of the Costa Rican military was the ostensible threat posed by the Sandinistas' military power and "expansionist ideas" in Nicaragua. The *Tico Times* (1985, 5) noted that in the early 1980s for the first time since the army was outlawed in 1949, U.S. Army Green Berets trained a battalion of Costa Rican civil guardsmen at a newly created, U.S.-sponsored camp near Costa Rica's northern border. The training camp was created after Costa Rica had politely but firmly declined several U.S. offers of military assistance the year before, but when it had become increasingly concerned about the threat posed by Nicaragua. Even José Figueres, former president and ambassador, decided to visit Nicaragua on a "one-man" peace mission. Figueres had been outspokenly critical of the administration's hard anti-Sandinista line for several months. However, the Nicaraguan state responded by intensifying its national furor. President Monge, in the meantime, urged the passage of the "neutrality law" that forbade Costa Rican territory from being used as a territory for "any belligerent party." The passage of this law called for Costa Rica to isolate itself from regional conflagrations.

The attempted militarization of Costa Rica prompted a few domestic and international protests. Costa Rica's resistance to U.S. pressure became more pronounced when President Oscar Arias Sánchez took office in 1986 and began to work diligently to bring about peace in Central America. Then, also in 1986, the Iran–Contra scandal erupted. As Zarate (1994, 51) writes:

> Arias met with Congressional Democrats and made political allegiances with leaders like Speaker of the House Jim Wright to ensure U.S. friendship even if he confronted the Reagan administration in regard to the peace process in the region. His alliances in the Congress emboldened him to expel all military personnel who were connected to the support of the *contras*, including the Green Berets, and he revealed and assumed control of the Santa Elena airstrip in the North. In his most defiant moment, Arias sponsored the Central American Peace Accord of 1987, for which he received the Nobel Peace Prize, despite severe criticism from the United States. Arias' defiance was punished by the Reagan administration when his visit to Washington was cancelled and replaced by a visit from President [Vinicio] Cerezo of Guatemala.

Clearly, the Reagan administration played a key role in Costa Rica's stabilization and destabilization during the 1980s. The Costa Rican government was prudent enough to realize that it needed to maintain as much neutrality as possible so that it would not fall prey to destabilizing and conflicting interests, whether local or international, as was the case in neighboring countries. In short, during this very crucial time, the U.S. administration played a dominant role in the attempted militarization of Costa Rica, as it was in the process of extending militarization in most of the rest of Central America. The experiences of other Central American countries, unfortunately, were marked by massive bloodshed and war.

In general, during the 1980s, the amount of outside resources allocated for military expansion increased rapidly, not only in Costa Rica and the rest of Latin America, but also in many other parts of the world. Militarization often is viewed as increasing economic predictability, as the military, like the state itself, is organized hierarchically. In essence, militarization of the state has become interrelated with the predictability emerging from the increasing rationality of the world economy. As a small and "developing" country, Costa Rica has without question been attempting to create a more predictable economy, yet that is an especially difficult task during periods of instability (Lauderdale, 1986, 241).

The different definitions of nonmilitary aid also have created heated disputes. The boundary between military and nonmilitary aid is ambiguous, since nonmilitary aid often has included assistance from the U.S. Army Corps of Engineers and components of the U.S. National Guard. Debates rage over the activities of these outsiders, with disclaimers from groups inside and outside Costa Rica that point to new bridges, roads, and communication systems, while their opponents point to these developments as part of the construction of a growing infrastructure for war (Lauderdale and Cruit, 1993).

These conflicts and forms of aid have led to perplexing levels of dependency for Costa Rica. Even today, Costa Rica continues to resist U.S. attempts to create a military presence while at the same time attempting to promote peaceful relations with its neighbors. In 1997, for example, the United States drafted a plan to allow its officials to patrol Costa Rican territory with ships and airplanes to target drug smugglers. Laura Chincilla, the Public Security Minister in Costa Rica, claimed that these "U.S. forces would be allowed to chase and search boats and airplanes suspected of smuggling drugs." She also added that "Costa Rican observers would be aboard every boat to authorize specific operations and *maintain respect for national sovereignty*" (Nunez, 1997; emphasis in original).

More recently, at a security summit held in 2001 in San Jose, Costa Rica, the administration of President George W. Bush declared Mother Nature [sic] as a serious threat to "economic sustainability, regional stability, and emerging democracies throughout the Americas" (*Tico Times*, 11 May 2001). According to Robin Rosenberg, Deputy Director of the North–South Center, a U.S. foreign-policy think tank, environmental problems in the hemisphere undermine democracy and prosperity more than any other type of security threat. The military's concern is that environmental problems will result in avoidable security issues, such as border conflicts, insurrections, and economic deterioration. U.S. Major General Gary Speer, Deputy Commander in Chief of the U.S. Southern Command, stated that "militaries must be prepared not only to respond to natural disasters, but also to prevent environmental issues from becoming a source of conflict" (*Tico Times*, 11 May 2001).

Costa Rica's minister of the environment and second vice-president concluded the 2001 conference by stating, "In the past, irreversible damage has been done to the environment by people who wanted to make a better world through war." She proceeded to note examples where U.S.–Costa Rican "drug patrols" could do more to protect the environment: by policing illegal fishing and poaching off the Isla del Coco, reducing numerous forms of contamination as well as continuing to defend other parts of the ecosystem. Again, as the United States under the Bush administration continues to look for justifications for the build-up of military resources, the Costa Rican government continues to define its parameters diplomatically, asserting its independence and resisting threats to the neutrality for which the country has become famous. Of course, "developments" such as the attempt to implement a Central American "free-trade" agreement, with potential member states meeting again in the United States in 2003, led to more systemic dependency problems, not only for Costa Rica, but for the region as a whole.

Conclusion and Suggestions for Future Research

In attempting to refute claims that Latin America's experience with death squads and governments killing their own people is simply indicative of the region's cultural heritage, it is important to examine the case of Costa Rica. Costa Rica's relative stability, the evidence suggests, is more a consequence of politics—the country's systemic ties with other states, for example—and of the development of state structures than it is a question of cultural heritage. The state structures imposed by early colonists are indeed the political forebears of modern state structures. Additionally, terrorism is often invoked in the art of statecraft when a state's order, stability, and/or expansion are threatened. This was the criticism leveled by the nobility at the democratic movements of the eighteenth and nineteenth centuries that sought to include "the masses."

Researchers often give superficial attention to examining the nature of political structures, while ideological concerns take precedence and hegemonic practices dominate. "Democracy" is ideologically (and historically and comparatively) the best choice in providing for human and civil rights, freedom, and protection, all the more so when it is compared to a regime of dictatorship that offers only extreme social control. When states are in the process of formulating or changing their national and global identity, their political and economic structures, and implementing reforms, state terrorism often is a practice intrinsic to the establishment of order and stability. State terrorism is an extreme manifestation of political practices based on hierarchy and domination. Thus, it should not be surprising when ostensibly democratic states behave paradoxically, particularly the United States. The United States is in a critical position nationally and globally. Its state processes came about through violent, revolutionary means (defined by the British state as "terrorism") and its political/cultural legacy paradoxically includes such practices when diverse, conflicting, political perspectives are produced, and particular historical moments become sites of intense struggle. Terrorism is the means by which violence is practiced and disguised as governmental social control when the state privileges domination, rigid hierarchy, uniformity, centralization of power, and exploitation. Equity and diversity, for example, are ignored or suffocated.

In the case of Costa Rica, it appears that its democratic development stems from its political history, such as its unique state innovations and flexibility, and its agility in resisting systemic ties to states that became violent. In essence, whether the issue is state terrorism or democracy, we suggest that future research will profit from an emphasis on the construction and expansion of state structures, economic dependency, and relations within the world system rather than on issues of cultural heritage.

NOTES

1. The state, in contrast to the government, can be operationally defined as the political apparatus that controls and often dominates society. Terrorism, as a practice of statecraft, usually is a crucial part of the construction of modern states. When diverse, conflicting, political perspectives are produced and at particular historical moments become sites of intense struggle, the art of statecraft has often invoked terrorism. Terrorism becomes an intrinsic practice of states as unbridled order and rigid uniformity become the structural vehicles by which equity and diversity are replaced with the consolidation of power and exploitation. Local diversity is continually subjected and often sacrificed to global processes of order (Menchú Tum, 1998; Oliverio, 1998, 2000). The latter, of course, is defined by various states as progressive and humane, while local conflicts often are defined as primitive or even savage.

2. The people who were allowed to participate in the democratic process had to be citizens (not unlike today), and those who were allowed citizenry had to be male, Athenian, and property owners. Women, slaves, and anyone not born in Athens could not participate in "democracy" (that is, in the democratic political process). Citizens did participate, since political functioning of the city-state was a regular responsibility of each individual as well as of the collective (Conolly, 1998; Hansen, 1991).

Since the days of the Greek empire, modern states have slowly expanded the definition of citizenry to include women and "minorities" (it is worth noting that often the minorities have a larger population than does the ostensible majority). Universal voting privileges in most Latin American countries did not exist until after World War II. Only propertied men could vote, thus elections often were perfunctory and symbolic. In Costa Rica, women were given voting rights in 1949 (Miller 1995).

3. When these policies are applied they have the ironic consequence of diminishing, if not denying, diversity and equity. Indeed, because of such state policies, certain unique and little-known groups such as the Guaymian and Borucan Indians in Costa Rica often were ignored via state-imposed definitions. As Costa Rica refers (and sometimes defers) to the United States, it suffers some of the unintended consequences of familiar processes of uniformity, institutionalization, and globalization. Its diverse cultural heritage is appropriated by a singular national identity, or what is defined as "mainstream" society.

4. This Spanish political inheritance is, for the most part, what proponents of the "cultural heritage" theories highlight. The Spanish system was characterized by domination (an elite, aristocratic class, for example, was hierarchical and repressive, demanding submission), supported by a particular form of the Catholic Church (one that was also hierarchic, elitist, and repressive) (Wiarda, 1990; Zea, 1965). The development of death squads, after hundreds of years of this type of rule, therefore, should not be surprising under these conditions. However, other scholars have noted that the development of democratic institutions in a society is not easily predicted from analysis of the society's "preconditions" (cf. DiPalma, 1990; Dahl, 1971). Indeed, factors such as the role of foreign influences appear to have had a greater impact on political environment and state development (Lauderdale and Amster, 2000; Frank, 1967; cf. Huntington, 1984, 1991). These external factors would appear to be critical in Costa Rica and, most likely, in other Latin American countries, as well.

5. For a detailed discussion, with regard to the Italian state, of the "flexibility" of state structures, see Oliverio (1998). Both Italy and Costa Rica have endured authoritarian regimes as well as challenging particular U.S. state interventions. Both societies have maintained friendly, long-standing political and economic associations with the United States, yet their "development" of democratic institutions has been significantly different from what is seen in other societies also supported by specific U.S. presidential administrations.

6. In addition to public education, public health care is another area in which the Costa Rican government has been instrumental and quite effective. Indeed, the level of health care in Costa Rica is often compared to that of the Scandinavian countries; the difference, of course, is that the Costa Rican systems of education and health care were developed despite national poverty, unlike in the former countries (see Lauderdale and Cruit, 1993).

7. Victor Pérez Vargas, Director of the Judicial Review of the Supreme Court of Costa Rica and Professor/Director of Private Rights at the University of Costa Rica, has noted that the Supreme Court justices also constructed a series of creative responses to the Reagan administration's attempts to develop a southern front to attack the Nicaraguan Sandinistas in 1985. In addition, Professor Pérez was a central figure in the use of diplomacy to curb the aggressive proposals of the U.S. State Department when Luis Tambs was appointed U.S. ambassador to Costa Rica in the summer of 1985.

8. Under the Carter administration, international aid was focused on a unique human rights program, which helped to strengthen, for example, Costa Rica's education, social welfare, and health programs. Under other presidential administrations, human rights programs largely have been facades that, rather than giving attention to personal rights and individuals' security, have focused instead on surveillance or ignored crucial environmental problems whose solution is essential to the health of all living things.

BIBLIOGRAPHY

Alexander, Yonah, and Michael S. Swetnam. 2001. *Usama Bin Laden's al Qaida: Profile of a Terrorist Network*. Ardsley, NY: Transnational Publishers.

Alfaro, Carlos Monge. 1989. "The Development of the Central Valley." Pp. 9–12 in *The Costa Rica Reader*, ed. Marc Edelman and Joanne Kenen. New York: Grove Weidenfeld.

Augelli, Enrico, and Craig Murphy. 1988. *America's Quest for Supremacy and the Third World: A Gramscian Analysis*. London: Pinter Publishers.

Bauer, Brian S. 1992. *The Development of the Inca State*. Austin: University of Texas Press.

Bell, Bowyer J. 1994. "The Armed Struggle and Underground Intelligence: Overview." *Studies in Conflict and Terrorism* 17: 115–50.

Brenes, A. 1986. "Peace and War Issues in the Costa Rican Newspapers." Paper presented at the European Psychologists for Peace Conference, Helsinki, Finland, 8–10 August.

Burke, Edmund. 1982 [1790]. *Reflections on the Revolution in France*, ed. Conor C. O'Brien. London: Penguin.

Carnoy, Martin. 1984. *The State and Political Theory*. Princeton: Princeton University Press.

Conolly, Peter. 1998. *Ancient City: Life in Classical Athens and Rome*. Oxford: Oxford University Press.

Cooper, H. H. A. 1985. "Voices from Troy: What Are We Hearing?" Pp. 25–34 in *Outthinking the Terrorist: An International Challenge*. Proceedings of the Tenth Annual

Symposium on the Role of Behavioral Science in Physical Security. Washington, DC: Defense Nuclear Agency.

Dahl, Robert A. 1971. *Polyarchy: Participation and Opposition*. New Haven: Yale University Press.
DiPalma, Giuseppe. 1990. *To Craft Democracies: An Essay on Democratic Transitions*. Berkeley: University of California Press.

Emerson, Steven. 2002. *American Jihad: The Terrorists Living Among Us*. New York: Simon and Schuster.

Fanon, Franz. 1987 [1961]. *Les Damnes de la Terre*. Paris: Découverte.
Farer, T. 1985. "Contadora: The Hidden Agenda." *Foreign Policy* Summer: 59–72.
Frank, Andre Gunder. 1967. *Capitalism and Underdevelopment in Latin America*. New York: Monthly Review Press.

Gershman, Carl. 1990. "The United States and the World Democratic Revolution." Pp. 3–35, in *The New Democracies*, ed. Brad Roberts. Cambridge: MIT Press.
Gibbs, Jack. 1989. "Conceptualization of Terrorism." *American Sociological Review* 54 (June): 329–40.
Gramsci, Antonio. 1971. *Selections from Prison Notebooks*. New York: International Publishers.
Grosscup, Beau. 1998. *The Newest Explosions of Terrorism: Latest Sites of Terrorism in the 1990s and Beyond*. Far Hills, NJ: New Horizon Press.
Gundmundson, Lowell. 1983. "Costa Rica Before Coffee: Occupational Distribution, Wealth Inequality, and Elite Society in the Village Economy of the 1840s." *Journal of Latin American Studies* 15: 427–52.
———. 1986. *Costa Rica Before Coffee: Society and Economy on the Eve of the Export Boom*. Baton Rouge: Louisiana State University Press.

Halebsky, Sandor, and Richard L. Harris (eds.). 1995. *Capital, Power, and Inequality in Latin America*. Boulder: Westview Press.
Hansen, Mogens Herman. 1991. *The Athenian Democracy in the Age of Demosthenes: Structure, Principles and Ideology*. Oxford: Basil Blackwell.
Helmuth, Chalene. 2000. *Culture and Customs of Costa Rica*. Westport, CT: Greenwood Press.
Hoffman, Bruce. 1999. *Inside Terrorism*. New York: Columbia University Press.
Huntington, Samuel P. 1984. "Will More Countries Become Democratic?" *Political Science Quarterly* 99 (2): 193–218.
———. 1991. *The Third Wave: Democratization in the Late Twentieth Century*. Norman: University of Oklahoma Press.

Inverarity, James M., Pat Lauderdale, and Barry C. Feld. 1983. *Law and Society*. Boston: Little, Brown and Co.

Jenkins, Brian. 1985. *The Future Course of International Terrorism*. Santa Monica, CA: RAND Corporation.

Koonings, Kees, and Dirk Kruijt (eds.). 1999. *Societies of Fear: The Legacy of Civil War, Violence and Terror in Latin America*. London: Zed Books.

Laqueur, William. 1977. *Terrorism*. Boston: Little, Brown.

Lauderdale, Pat. 1986. "Social and Economic Instability in Costa Rica: Pre-conditions for Militarization?" *Policy Studies Review* 6 (2): 236–44.

———. 1998. "Afterword." Pp. 147–53 in *The State of Terror*, ed. Annamarie Oliverio. Albany: State University of New York Press.

Lauderdale, Pat, and Randall Amster. 2000. "Local Conflict or Global Order in the Horn of Africa?: The Political Construction of Kinship and Clan." Pp. 1–37 in *Terror and Crisis in the Horn of Africa: Autopsy of Democracy, Human Rights, and Freedom*, ed. Pietro Toggia, Pat Lauderdale, and Abebe Zegeye. London: Ashgate.

Lauderdale, Pat, and Michael Cruit. 1993. *The Struggle for Control*. Albany: State University of New York Press.

Lesser, Ian O. and Ashley J. Tellis. 1996. *Strategic Exposure: Proliferation Around the Mediterranean*. Santa Monica, CA: RAND Corporation.

Lincoln, Jennie. 1985. "Neutrality Costa Rican Style." *Current History* 84: 118–36.

Lincoln, Jennie, and Pat Lauderdale. 1985. "A New Defense Policy for Costa Rica: Constructing Reality and the Policy Agenda." *Policy Studies Review* 5: 220–29.

Lipset, Seymour Martin. 1959. "Some Social Requisites of Democracy: Economic Development and Political Legitimacy." *American Political Science Review* 53: 69–105.

Menchú Tum, Rigoberta. 1998. "Preface." Pp. xiii-xvii in *Searching for Equity: Conceptions of Justice and Equity in Peasant Irrigation*, ed. Rutgerd Boelens and Gloria Davila Assen. Assen, the Netherlands: Van Gorcum and Company.

Miller, Francesca. 1995. "Latin American Women and the Search for Social, Political, and Economic Transformation." Pp. 185–206 in *Capital, Power and Inequality in Latin America*, ed. Sandor Halebsky and Richard L. Harris. Boulder: Westview Press.

Murillo Jimenez, Hugo. 1989. "Tinoco, Wilson and the U.S. Policy of Nonrecognition." Pp. 65–70 in *The Costa Rica Reader*, ed. Marc Edelman and Joanne Kenen. New York: Grove Weidenfeld.

Nacos, Brigitte L. 2000. "Accomplice or Witness? The Media's Role in Terrorism." *Current History* 99 (636): 174–79.

Nef, Jorge. 1995. "Demilitarization and Democratic Transition in Latin America." Pp. 81–107 in *Capital, Power and Inequality in Latin America*, ed. Sandor Halebsky and Richard L. Harris. Boulder: Westview Press.

Nunez, Eric. 1997. "Media Awareness Project: U.S. Military in Costa Rica." *Drug News* 97 (August): 1.

Oliverio, Annamarie. 1997. "The State of Injustice: The Politics of Terrorism and the Production of Order." *International Journal of Comparative Sociology* 38 (1–2): 48–63.

———. 1998. *The State of Terror.* Albany: State University of New York Press.

———. 2000. "Terrorism, the Art of Statecraft and the Horn of Africa." Pp. 32–38 in *Terror and Crisis in the Horn of Africa: Autopsy of Freedom, Democracy and Human Rights*, ed. Pietro Toggia, Pat Lauderdale, and Abebe Zegeye. London: Ashgate.

Pacheco, Leon. 1961. "Evolución del Pensamiento Democrático de Costa Rica." *Combate* 15: 31–43.

Paige, Jeffery M. 1997. *Coffee and Power: Revolution and the Rise of Democracy in Central America.* Cambridge: Harvard University Press.

Pastor, Robert A. 1989. "How to Reinforce Democracy in the Americas: Seven Proposals." In *Democracy in the Americas: Stopping the Pendulum*, ed. Robert A. Pastor. New York: Holmes and Meier.

Perez, Victor. 1981. *La Jurisprudencia de Intereses.* San Jose: Editorial Universidad Estatal a Distancia.

Reich, Walter (ed). 1998. *Origins of Terrorism, Psychologies, Ideologies, Theologies, States of Mind.* New York: Woodrow Wilson International Center for Scholars and Cambridge University Press.

Romano, Sergio. 1984. "The Roots of Italian Terrorism." *Policy Review* 25: 25–27.

Rosenberg, Tina. 1991. *Children of Cain: Violence and the Violent in Latin America.* New York: William Morrow.

Skidmore, Thomas E. 1989. "The Future of Democracy: An Analytical Summary." In *Democracy in the Americas: Stopping the Pendulum*, ed. Robert A. Pastor. New York: Holmes and Meier.

Stehr, Nico. 1994. *Knowledge Societies.* Thousand Oaks, CA: Sage Publications.

Stohl, Michael. 1988. *The Politics of Terrorism.* New York: Marcel Dekker, Inc.

Stone, Samuel Z. 1989. "Aspects of Power Distribution in Costa Rica." Pp. 20–28 in *The Costa Rica Reader*, ed. Marc Edelman and Joanne Kenen. New York: Grove Weidenfeld.

———. 1991. *The Heritage of the Conquistadores.* Lincoln: University of Nebraska Press.

Vega Carballo, José Luis. 1989. "The Dynamics of Early Militarism." Pp. 40–49 in *The Costa Rica Reader*, ed. Marc Edelman and Joanne Kenen. New York: Grove Weidenfeld.

Whittaker, David J. 2001. *The Terrorism Reader*. New York: Routledge.
Wiarda, Howard J. 1982. *Politics and Social Change in Latin America*. Amherst: University of Massachusetts Press.
———. 1990. *The Democratic Revolution in Latin America*. London: Holmes and Meier.
Wilkinson, Paul. 1986. *Terrorism and the Liberal State*. London: MacMillan.
———. 1990. *Terrorist Targets and Tactics: New Risks to World Order*. Conflict Studies no. 236. London: Research Institute for the Study of Conflict and Terrorism (RISCT) and the Center for Security Studies.
Wilson, Bruce M. 1998. *Politics, Economics and Democracy*. Boulder: Lynne Rienner Publishers.

Zarate, Juan Carlos. 1994. *Forging Democracy*. New York: University Press of America.
Zea, Leopoldo. 1965. "Latinoamerica en la Formación de Nuestro Tiempo." *Cuadernos Americanos* 142: 7–20.

PART THREE

◆

SOUTH AMERICA

CHAPTER 9

The Colombian Nightmare
Human Rights Abuses and the Contradictory Effects of U.S. Foreign Policy

JOHN C. DUGAS

Introduction

In the early morning hours of January 17, 2001, a large group of armed men belonging to the right-wing paramilitary group Autodefensas Unidas de Colombia (AUC) entered the village of Chengue in the northern province of Sucre. The paramilitaries forced the villagers to the town center, where they proceeded to kill a number of the village men using axes, machetes, sledge-hammers, and heavy stones to crush their skulls. They subsequently fled, setting fire to the majority of the houses in the village. In the course of this paramilitary incursion, twenty-four men were killed, thirty-five houses were incinerated, and eight-hundred persons were displaced from the area (Defensoría del Pueblo, 2001, 309–10; Wilson, 2001). Although the killing was carried out directly by paramilitary forces, the Colombian military was apparently complicit in the massacre. Survivors recounted that the military provided safe passage to the paramilitaries and "effectively sealed off the area by conducting what villagers described as a mock daylong battle with leftist guerrillas who dominate the area" (Wilson, 2001). Two active-duty marine sergeants were implicated in the Chengue massacre, charged with supplying weapons to the paramilitaries and helping them to coordinate the attack (U.S. Department of State, 2002; Human Rights Watch [HRW], 2002, 132–33).

The 2001 Chengue massacre illustrates several of the arguments advanced in this chapter regarding the relationship between the state and human rights violations in Colombia. First, the ongoing human rights situation in Colombia is atrocious, surpassing even the horrific records of the Southern Cone military regimes of the 1970s and 1980s. Second, the Colombian state is clearly guilty of serious human rights abuses, whether through direct action, complicity in the actions of others, or failure to act. Third, the Colombian state is not the only violator of human rights in the country. Paramilitaries (although often with military complicity) and guerrillas commit the vast majority of the most grave violations of human rights, usually classified as violations of international humanitarian law. Finally, U.S. policy toward Colombia is contradictory, with the efforts of institutions such as the U.S. Agency for International Development (USAID) to promote human rights being undermined by the overwhelming military component of U.S. strategy.

Overview of the Human Rights Situation

Human rights have historically been conceived in relation to the state. Nonetheless, an exclusive focus on the state is insufficient if one seeks to describe accurately the wide range of abuses committed in contemporary Colombia. Today, the majority of political homicides, massacres, kidnappings, and other grave violations of fundamental human rights are committed by nonstate actors, primarily the right-wing paramilitaries and the leftist guerrillas. When committed by nonstate actors, such abuses are considered violations of international humanitarian law, which pertains to *all* armed actors in an internal conflict. In order to provide a complete portrayal of the range of abuses occurring in Colombia, this section describes both state violations of human rights as well as violations of international humanitarian law committed by all of the armed parties.

To begin with, Colombia has one of the highest homicide rates in the world. Over the past five years, the country has averaged over 25,000 killings per year, a disturbingly high level that has worsened in recent years. In comparison, the United States, also a violent country, had a rate of 5.5 homicides per 100,000 persons in 2000, less than one-tenth the Colombian rate (Fox and Zawitz, 2002). It should be noted that the vast majority of homicides in Colombia have no direct political linkage and, thus, although tragic and a source of legitimate concern, are not considered to be violations of human rights or international humanitarian law (Comisión Interamericana de Derechos Humanos [CIDH], 1999, 32). Nonetheless, the number of political homicides is also shockingly high and has increased significantly since 1999. By 2001, some 27 percent of all homicides in Colombia could be considered

Table 9.1 *All Homicides and Political Homicides in Colombia, 1997–2001*

	All Homicides		Political Homicides	
Year	Total	Per 100,000	Total	% Total Homicides
1997	25,379	63	3,730	14.7
1998	23,096	56	3,633	15.7
1999	24,358	59	4,003	16.4
2000	26,540	63	6,987	26.3
2001	27,841	65	7,637	27.4

Source: *Fundación Social–UNICEF*, 2002, Table 10.

Table 9.2 *Breakdown of Political Homicides in Colombia, 1997–2001*

Year	Combat killings		Non-combat killings		Forced disappearances		Total
1997	1,295	(34.7%)	2,098	(56.3%)	337	(9.0%)	3,730
1998	1,495	(41.2%)	1,668	(45.9%)	470	(12.9%)	3,633
1999	1,437	(35.9%)	2,238	(55.9%)	328	(8.2%)	4,003
2000	1,677	(24.0%)	4,632	(66.3%)	678	(9.7%)	6,987
2001	2,094	(27.4%)	4,925	(64.5%)	618	(8.1%)	7,637
Total	7,998	(30.7%)	15,561	(59.9%)	2,431	(9.4%)	25,990

Source: *Fundación Social–UNICEF*, 2002, based on Tables 2, 3, 5, and 10.

political in nature, with over 7,600 Colombians killed in political violence in that year alone (Table 9.1).

Political killings can be differentiated according to deaths in combat between armed actors, deaths occurring outside of combat (of both civilians and combatants hors de combat), and forced disappearances (that is, when an individual is presumed to have been killed, although their body is not recovered). The statistics on deaths in combat indicate that the armed conflict in Colombia has intensified in recent years. The number of deaths in combat increased by nearly 62 percent over five years, from 1,295 in 1997 to 2,094 deaths in 2001 (Table 9.2). Despite the tragic loss of life that direct combat entails, such killings are not formally considered to be violations of human rights or of international humanitarian law.

On the other hand, political homicides that occur outside of combat and forced disappearances are clearly considered violations of human rights and international humanitarian law. The level of such violations in Colombia is

Table 9.3 *Presumed Authors of Political Homicides Committed Outside of Combat,*
Colombia, 1997–2001

Year	Paramilitaries	Guerrillas	State Security Forces
1997	75.9%	20.8%	3.3%
1998	75.7%	22.2%	2.1%
1999	69.9%	28.0%	2.1%
2000	72.4%	19.3%	1.2%
2001	78.2%	17.3%	4.5%
Average	74.4%	21.5%	2.6%

Source: Fundación Social–UNICEF, 2002, Table 7.

appalling. In 2001 alone, over 600 persons were forcibly disappeared (and presumed killed), while over 4,900 persons were blatantly killed outside of combat (Table 9.2). Moreover, such killings have grown at an extraordinary rate in recent years. The number of political homicides committed outside of combat more than doubled between 1997 and 2001 (from 2,098 to 4,925 killings), while the number of forced disappearances increased by 83 percent (from 337 to 618 disappearances). It is worth pointing out that for every fighter killed in direct combat, more than two persons who are not engaged in hostilities are assassinated.

All of the armed actors (state security forces, paramilitary groups, and guerrillas) have committed political killings outside of combat. However, the responsibility for such killings is not divided evenly among the armed combatants. For those cases of political killings in which analysts have been able to determine the author (less than half of all cases), the right-wing paramilitaries are clearly the principal culprit, carrying out 78 percent of all such murders in 2001. They are followed by the leftist guerrilla movements, who committed 17 percent of all political assassinations in 2001, and state security forces, which directly carried out nearly 5 percent of all political killings (Table 9.3). Neither the overall rank orderings nor the percentages themselves changed appreciably in the five-year period from 1997 to 2001. It should immediately be noted, however, that these statistics can be misleading with regard to the state's actual culpability, given that paramilitary forces often act with the acquiescence or the direct assistance of state security forces. This issue is examined in greater detail below.

Table 9.4 *Massacres, Colombia, 1997–2001*

Year	Cases	Victims
1997	114	563
1998	115	685
1999	168	929
2000	236	1,403
2001	186	1,044
Total	819	4,624

Source: Fundación Social–UNICEF, 2002, Table 4.

Certain civilian groups in Colombian society have suffered a dispropor-
tionate number of political killings outside of combat. They include union
members, members of left-wing political parties, members of indigenous
communities, human rights workers, and journalists. Many of these political
homicides take the form of massacres, which the Colombian national police
defines as the killing of four or more persons in the same place during the
same period of time (Fundación Social, 2001, 376). The number of massacres committed annually in Colombia is scandalous, and it has tended to
grow in the past five years, peaking at 236 massacres committed in 2000.
Over 800 massacres took place between 1997 and 2001, which totaled 4,624
killings (Table 9.4). Paramilitary groups are responsible for the vast majority
of the massacres committed in Colombia, although guerrilla forces also commit collective homicides (United Nations High Commissioner for Human
Rights [UNHCHR], 2002, 31). As in the massacre at Chengue, described at
the beginning of this chapter, state security forces have been complicit in several collective homicides, through direct action or acquiescence in the murderous activities of paramilitary forces.

Torture is a grave violation of human rights and international humanitarian law that has been practiced by all of the armed combatants in Colombia's
ongoing conflict. In 2001, the inspector general's office (*procuraduría*) received 29 complaints of torture by state agents (U.S. Department of State,
2002). For the period of January through September 2001, the Centro de Investigación y Educación Popular [CINEP] reported 158 cases of torture by paramilitaries and 40 cases by the guerrillas (U.S. Department of State, 2002). The
internal conflict has also produced a notorious distinction for the country:
roughly half of all kidnappings in the world today occur in Colombia, making
the country the global leader in this violation of international humanitarian

Table 9.5 *Presumed Authors of Kidnappings, Colombia, 1997–2001*

	Paramilitary		Guerrillas		Delinquents		Unspecified		
Year	Number	%	Number	%	Number	%	Number	%	Total
1997	16	(1.0)	979	(58.1)	247	(14.6)	444	(26.3)	1,686
1998	65	(2.1)	2,026	(66.3)	325	(10.7)	638	(20.9)	3,054
1999	159	(4.7)	1,992	(59.6)	360	(10.8)	831	(24.9)	3,342
2000	280	(7.6)	2,110	(63.2)	371	(10.0)	945	(18.5)	3,706
2001	262	(8.6)	1,923	(60.9)	292	(9.6)	564	(23.1)	3,041
Total									
(Avg.)	782	(5.3)	9,030	(60.9)	1,595	(10.7)	3,422	(23.1)	14,829

Source: *Fundación Social–UNICEF,* 2002, Tables 8 and 9.

law (UNHCHR, 2002, 34; Washington Office on Latin America [WOLA], 2002b, 1). In the five-year-period 1997–2001, nearly 15,000 Colombians were kidnapped, the majority of them by leftist guerrillas. In 2001 alone, over 3,000 Colombians were kidnapped (Table 9.5). Another tragic consequence of the conflict has been the forced displacement of hundreds of thousands of persons, primarily from rural areas of the country. In the last ten years, an estimated 1.2 million people have been forcibly displaced, out of a population of forty million (Isacson, 2002a, 1). According to the Consultoría para los Derechos Humanos y el Desplazamiento [CODHES], in 2001 some 342,000 Colombians were forced to flee their homes, the equivalent of 937 persons per day (CODHES, 2002).

The foregoing description, although by no means exhaustive, should suffice to illustrate both the extraordinary crudity of the conflict as well as its multiple origins. All of the armed actors have committed grave violations of human rights and/or international humanitarian law. Having made this point, it must be emphasized that the state has a special responsibility to protect its citizens from such violations and to abstain from partaking in them. Unfortunately, the Colombian state has clearly failed to carry out this obligation.

State Security Forces and Human Rights Violations

The Colombian state security forces have engaged in both direct and indirect violations of human rights and international humanitarian law, primarily in the course of their extended counterinsurgency campaign against leftist guerrilla movements, and to a lesser extent in their fight against drug trafficking.

In principle, such campaigns could be carried out with strict observance of human rights and international humanitarian law. In practice, however, state security agents have engaged in illegal and abusive counterinsurgency and counternarcotics tactics, including torture, extrajudicial killings, forced disappearances, and the creation and support of illegal paramilitary units.

The Colombian military, in particular, has enjoyed a significant degree of autonomy within the state since the establishment of the National Front regime in 1958, especially with regard to policies concerning national security and public order (Dávila Ladrón de Guevara, 1998, 127–74). The relative autonomy of the Colombian armed forces allowed them to develop a counterinsurgency strategy rooted in the principles of the infamous National Security Doctrine, which was characterized by an unyielding Cold War anticommunism. In the Colombian case, as in much of Latin America, international communism was seen as fomenting "internal enemies" who needed to be combated vigorously in defense of national sovereignty (Blair Trujillo, 1993, 112). This perspective, however, promoted military actions that went far beyond fighting armed guerrilla movements and included the repression and killing of civilians on the left of the political spectrum, such as union leaders, social and political activists, and those considered sympathetic to the guerrillas (Richani, 2002b, 42).

The repressive actions of the Colombian military received their staunchest civilian support during the administration of Julio César Turbay (in office 1978–1982), who in 1978 promulgated Legislative Decree 1923, better known as the Security Statute. The Security Statute established media censorship, criminalized social protest, and allowed civilians to be tried in military tribunals (Blair Trujillo, 1993, 132). The use of torture by the military also became widespread during this period. The administration of Belisario Betancur (in office 1982–1986) attempted to reverse the militaristic policies of the Turbay administration by undertaking political reforms and pursuing a policy of peace negotiations with representatives of the guerrilla movements. Nevertheless, the military itself became one of the principal obstacles to a successful peace process, harassing the guerrilla forces and engaging in numerous human rights abuses (Ramírez and Restrepo, 1989, 251–55).

It was during the Betancur administration that there emerged the first clear accounts of military involvement in the creation of paramilitary groups, apparently as a means of continuing their counterinsurgency efforts in a covert manner during the peace process. A report by the inspector general in

1983 charged fifty-nine active-duty military personnel with having links to a paramilitary organization, which was operating in the Middle Magdalena municipality of Puerto Boyacá (Santander) and had committed at least 240 killings (HRW, 1996, 18). Although military officials angrily denied the charges, ties between the military and paramilitary groups became increasingly evident in succeeding years.

The contemporary history of paramilitary organizations in Colombia is complex, in part because these groups have a diversity of origins. Clearly, many originated as part of counterinsurgency strategies implemented by local or regional military commanders. Indeed, until 1989 the formation of such groups was legally supported under a 1968 law that authorized the military to distribute weapons to peasants in order to confront the guerrillas (Gallón Giraldo, 1991, 30). Other paramilitary units, however, began as private self-defense groups organized by large landowners who had grown tired of extortion, kidnapping, and other abuses by the guerrillas. Still others were formed by emerald mine operators in order to establish order in the violent mining zones of the department of Boyacá (Richani, 2000, 40). Finally, some paramilitary groups originated as bands of hired assassins in the service of the major drug cartels. Despite their distinct origins, in the 1980s the various types of paramilitary groups began to merge in practice, becoming offensive (as opposed to defensive) military groups whose sole raison d'être was to struggle against leftist guerrillas (Cubides, 2001, 130–31).

As the paramilitary groups spread throughout the country, they often did so with the explicit support of the military, which cited the 1968 legal authorization to create armed "self-defense" groups. Thus, a 1987 memorandum from the minister of defense informed his subordinates that "the organization, training, and support of self defense groups should be a permanent objective of the armed forces to the extent that [these groups] are loyal and manifest themselves against the enemy" (Americas Watch [AW], 1991, 24). Moreover, the army intelligence command apparently decided in 1987 to coordinate paramilitary activities across the country, summoning paramilitary leaders to meet high-ranking army officers in Bogotá and aiding in the creation of a national network of paramilitaries. Meetings of this network were held in subsequent years, always attended by military intelligence officers (Amnesty International [AI], 1994, 55; HRW, 1996, 22).

Meanwhile, civilian authorities, whose reaction to paramilitary violence had been muted at best, apparently reached a turning point with the January

1989 paramilitary massacre at La Rochela (Santander), in which two judges and ten investigators were murdered while investigating previous paramilitary killings in the region (HRW, 1996, 23). After that massacre, President Virgilio Barco (in office 1986–1990) spoke out openly against the paramilitaries, calling them "terrorist organizations" and noting: "The majority of their victims are not guerrillas. They are men, women, and even children, who have not taken up arms against institutions. They are peaceful Colombians" (Barco, 1990, 360). In April 1989, Barco suspended the norms of the 1968 law that allowed the military to distribute arms to "self-defense" groups. This suspension became permanent one month later, when the Supreme Court declared that it was unconstitutional for the armed forces to distribute arms to civilians (AW, 1991, 26–27). In June 1989, the Barco administration established criminal penalties for civilians or members of the military who recruited, trained, promoted, financed, organized, led, or belonged to paramilitary organizations (HRW, 1996, 24).

Despite these measures, paramilitary organizations flourished during the 1990s, in large part because the armed forces continued to facilitate their activities and refused to cooperate fully either in dismantling the paramilitaries or in judicial proceedings against members of the military involved in the creation or functioning of such groups. The basic strategy of the paramilitary groups, based upon the perceived "success" of Puerto Boyacá in the early 1980s, was to target individuals who constituted the support network of the guerrillas, as well as anyone who was believed to sympathize with them. In accordance with this strategy, the paramilitaries—with backing from sectors of the military—were responsible for the systematic assassination of members of the left-wing Patriotic Union party that commenced in 1986. There was also a clear socioeconomic element of the paramilitary strategy, which consisted of forcibly displacing peasants from their traditional lands in order to increase the holdings of large landowners, many of whom were drug traffickers.

Even as the paramilitary groups were engaged in an array of abuses, often with military complicity, members of the state security forces were directly committing numerous human rights violations. For example, in the early 1990s both the police and the armed forces engaged in a variety of "dirty war" tactics such as torture, disappearance, and murder in their pursuit of the Medellín cartel leaders and their accomplices (HRW, 1992, 57; Bowden, 2001). More frequent still were abuses carried out in the course of counterinsurgency operations. For example, military patrols often forced members of local communities to accompany them as guides or porters. Some army counterinsurgency units employed contract killers (*sicarios*) to carry out the dirty work of killing suspected guerrilla collaborators. Still another disturbing tactic was to murder peasants in cold blood and then to report their deaths as those of guerrillas who had died in combat. The armed forces also frequently engaged in the indiscriminate bombardment of the civilian population during the course of counterinsurgency operations (AW, 1991, 68–71; HRW, 1992, 54; AI, 1994, 43–50). These abuses were further encouraged by the virtual impunity enjoyed by state security forces.

The pattern of impunity was so entrenched that Human Rights Watch called it a conscious "military strategy" (HRW, 1996, 62). The strategy began with strenuous denials that the armed forces had committed any human rights violations. If outside investigations proceeded, the military responded with a variety of obstructionist tactics, including the outright refusal to cooperate with investigators, the tampering with or destruction of evidence, the protection of implicated officers, the harassment of family members and lawyers, and even the killing of eyewitnesses, investigators, and judges (AI, 1994, 85; HRW, 1996, 62–70). Until recent years, the military also insisted that military tribunals have jurisdiction over human rights cases involving members of the armed forces. Such insistence is understandable since military courts have proven to be neither impartial nor even particularly interested in the details of human rights cases. Officers frequently are investigated by their own superiors, who may have ordered them to commit the crimes in the first place (HRW, 1996, 67–68). Not surprisingly, "in the vast majority of cases involving human rights violations the military courts either drop the charges or acquit those implicated" (AI, 1994, 89).

Unfortunately, a new national constitution promulgated in 1991 bolstered impunity by reaffirming the right of military tribunals to have jurisdiction over crimes attributed to state security forces while on active duty (Art. 221). The new constitution also introduced immunity from prosecution for soldiers on the grounds of "due obedience"—that is, lower-ranking officers and rank-and-file soldiers can avoid prosecution for their crimes if they claim that they were obeying orders (Art. 91). Despite this setback, in 1997 the Constitutional Court ruled that human rights violations such as forcible disappearance, torture, murder, and rape could not be considered "acts of service" and should, therefore, be tried in the civilian justice system (Sent. C-358 de, 1997). Since that time, the armed forces have belatedly and reluctantly begun to transfer human rights cases from military jurisdiction to the civilian justice system. This tradition of impunity for direct military violations of human rights has also aided in covering up the record of collaboration between the armed forces and paramilitary groups (HRW, 1996, 67). In general, the state long failed to investigate serious accusations of participation by military officials in paramilitary activities (AW, 1991, 28). This failure became increasingly problematic given the unprecedented growth of paramilitary forces in the 1990s.

During the decade of the 1990s, paramilitary groups—while still collaborating with sectors of the armed forces—also became increasingly autonomous in their structure and organization. The turning point came in 1997, when, under the leadership of Carlos Castaño, paramilitary forces throughout Colombia organized themselves into a national federation, the Autodefensas Unidas de Colombia (United Self-Defense Groups of Colombia, AUC), in order to coordinate their activities. The paramilitaries experienced dramatic growth in these years as reflected in their numbers, their resources, and the intensity of their "military" actions. In 1986, for example, paramilitary groups had perhaps a few hundred members; by 2002, the AUC had approximately eleven thousand armed combatants (Richani, 2002a, 18; Hagen, 2002, 27). With regard to resources, by 2002 their annual income was estimated to be between $200 and $300 million, derived from drug trafficking, money-laundering activities, voluntary contributions, and extortion payments (Richani, 2002a, 18). These resources allowed the AUC to field a well-trained army equipped with state-of-the-art armaments.

Nonetheless, strong ties continue to exist between the armed forces and the paramilitaries. Indirectly, the institutional linkages are extensive, given that at least one thousand former military personnel are currently in the AUC, including at least fifty-three former military officers (Richani, 2002a, 18). Of greater concern, however, is the voluminous evidence detailing direct links between the military and the paramilitary forces. By 2000, Human Rights Watch had documented abundant and compelling evidence linking at least half of Colombia's brigade-level army units (excluding military schools) to paramilitary activity (HRW 2000, 2). As succinctly described by a recent Human Rights Watch report, this relationship has involved

active coordination during military operations between government and paramilitary units; communication via radios, cellular telephones,

and beepers; the sharing of intelligence, including the names of suspected guerrilla collaborators; the sharing of fighters, including active-
duty soldiers serving in paramilitary units and paramilitary commanders lodging on military bases; the sharing of vehicles, including
army trucks used to transport paramilitary fighters; coordination of
army roadblocks, which routinely let heavily armed paramilitary fighters
pass; and payments made from paramilitaries to military officers for
their support. (H R W, 2001, 1)

The nationwide scope of the documented ties between the military and
the paramilitary forces suggests that this relationship does not consist simply
of the aberrant actions of a few isolated military officers. Indeed, human
rights investigators suggest that support for the paramilitaries reaches into
the highest ranks of the armed forces. Nonetheless, the precise nature of the
relationship remains unclear. Support for paramilitary forces is not an institutional position embraced by the military high command. However, there
may well be a coordinated group of influential officers within the military's
leadership who are explicitly committed to supporting the paramilitaries, although such a contention is difficult to prove. In any case, structural factors
have clearly facilitated widespread support on the ground by many local and
regional military commanders. At the very least, there appears to be a conscious effort on the part of many local and regional military officers to "sub-
contract" certain criminal actions to paramilitary forces, thus giving them
"plausible deniability" with regard to the human rights violations perpetrated in their zones.

The current situation of the military regarding the paramilitary forces and
respect for human rights more generally is mixed at best. On the one hand, the
contemporary rhetoric emanating from the highest ranks of the military is
clearly condemnatory of the paramilitaries. In their public pronouncements,
the A U C is routinely grouped with the principal leftist guerrilla organizations,
the Fuerzas Armadas Revolucionarias de Colombia (Revolutionary Armed
Forces of Colombia, F A R C) and the Ejército de Liberación Nacional (National
Liberation Army, E L N), both founded in the early 1960s, as violators of international humanitarian law. Moreover, some local military commanders have
in fact moved to constrain the paramilitaries. Also important is the fact that
some military officers have embraced the issue of human rights with apparent
sincerity. The Colombian Ministry of Defense has instituted a broad program
of training in human rights and international humanitarian law (Ministerio

de Defensa, 2002, 49–51). Not least, the percentage of political homicides committed outside of combat that can be attributed directly to state security forces has dropped significantly, from 54 percent in 1993 to 5 percent in 2001 (Comisión Colombiana de Juristas [CCJ], 1997, 7; see also Table 9.3).

On the other hand, the decline in political killings by state security forces has been more than made up for by the tremendous rise in such homicides committed by the paramilitaries, from 18 percent in 1993 to 78 percent in 2001 (CCJ, 1997, 7; see also Table 9.3). This mirror-image transformation lends some credence to the hypothesis that military units that formerly carried out extrajudicial killings now rely on the paramilitaries to carry out such crimes. Moreover, there continues to be a deep sympathy for the actions of paramilitary units throughout the armed forces. Certainly, the military has not moved to combat the paramilitary forces in any systematic way, a notable lapse given the significant violations of international humanitarian law that the latter perpetrate. Moreover, the military remains tolerant of officers who have worked with paramilitary groups in the past, not only failing to prosecute them but even rewarding them with promotions. Finally, and of greatest significance, the documented collaboration of certain military brigades with the paramilitary forces continues to occur.

In sum, the Colombian military has engaged, both directly and indirectly, in a wide array of human rights violations, which continue to take place. Moreover, the armed forces have both created paramilitary groups and actively collaborated with them in carrying out horrific violations of international humanitarian law. Although such a policy is not the institutional position of the military high command, and much less of the state as a whole, it is also true that high-ranking military commanders have not acted in an energetic fashion to break these ties or to pursue the paramilitary forces with vigor. Nor have they sought to punish the officers or soldiers responsible for directly violating human rights or for collaborating with the paramilitaries in their crimes. No honest appraisal can ignore the heavy burden of responsibility that lies upon the military for the current human rights nightmare in Colombia.

U.S. Policy Contradictions and the Abuse of Human Rights

U.S. policy toward Colombia has been characterized by a deep-seated incoherence. On the one hand, official rhetoric condemns human rights violations by state security forces and provides limited resources to defend human rights in Colombia. On the other hand, the United States has provided massive military aid to Colombia, often to military units that have engaged in egregious human rights violations. In recent years the U.S. Congress has required that the provision of security aid be dependent upon certification that the Colombian government has taken concrete steps to improve human rights. Nonetheless, the administrations of Presidents Bill Clinton and George W. Bush repeatedly circumvented this requirement due to their overriding determination that the Colombian armed forces should be strong enough to carry out effective counternarcotics and counterinsurgency operations. These decisions have sent a clear message to Colombian military officers that human rights violations will not stand in the way of receiving U.S. arms and training.

Support for State Security Forces

The United States has been providing equipment, training, and advice to the Colombian state security forces for over four decades. Indeed, in the 1960s, Colombia became one of the principal recipients of U.S. military aid in Latin America. In 1961, the United States sent its first military training team to Colombia, which soon began to receive U.S. military training in fields ranging from sanitation to counterinsurgency and psychological warfare (Crandall, 2002, 24). Many Colombian officers studied at the U.S. Army School of the Americas (SOA) during the period when its curriculum included "training manuals recommending that soldiers use bribery, blackmail, threats, and torture against insurgents" (HRW, 1996, 93). More than 150 Colombian SOA graduates have been linked to human rights abuses and paramilitary death squads during the 1980s and 1990s (Leech, 2002, 27). Although the United States has provided continual military aid and training since the 1960s, overall levels of such assistance remained relatively modest until the U.S.-declared war on drugs began in earnest.

U.S. policy began to focus intensively on counternarcotics efforts in 1986, when President Ronald Reagan issued National Security Directive No. 221 declaring that drug production and trafficking constitute a direct threat to U.S. national security. With respect to Colombia, the United States began a policy of massive security assistance for the war on drugs in the aftermath of the August 1989 assassination of Liberal presidential candidate Luis Carlos Galán, which was attributed to the Medellín drug cartel. President Virgilio Barco had responded to this killing by declaring war on the cartel, and in September 1989 the administration of President George H. W. Bush provided support for this endeavor by announcing a five-year, $2.2 billion

Andean Initiative. Beginning with the advent of the Andean Initiative and continuing through the present day, the bulk of the counternarcotics aid that the United States has sent to Colombia has been military in nature (Crandall, 2002, 34).

After 1992 most U.S. counternarcotics assistance was channeled to the Colombian national police, which had a less troublesome human rights record than did the military. Nonetheless, during the Clinton administration the armed forces continued to receive various forms of security assistance, including U.S. military training and support in the building of military bases (HRW, 1992, 83; 1993, 134–35, 137; 1996, 83–91). Indeed, between 1989 and 1995, the Colombian military received $322 million in security assistance (HRW, 1996, 83). Several Colombian military battalions and brigades implicated in serious human rights violations received U.S. military aid. This occurred despite the fact that "U.S. officials [were] well aware of military complicity in human rights abuses in Colombia and the dangers inherent in sending them weapons" (HRW, 1996, 86–87).

In 1994, the U.S. Congress sought to ensure that security assistance would not go to abusive counterinsurgency units by mandating that military aid be limited to state security forces that engaged "primarily" in counternarcotics operations (HRW, 1996, 4). In 1996, Senator Patrick Leahy (D-Vermont) introduced legislation that would prohibit international counternarcotics funds from going to specific military units if the "secretary of state has credible evidence to believe such unit has committed gross violations of human rights" (HRW, 1996, 89). Although the so-called Leahy Amendment was directed toward all countries receiving U.S. counternarcotics aid, it was perhaps most relevant to Colombia. Despite the passage of this legislation, the U.S. Department of Defense apparently continued, at least for a while, to train and equip Colombian military units that had not yet been reviewed for human rights abuses (HRW, 1998, 220–21).

By 1998, the United States had increasingly begun to view Colombia as a crisis situation, due to the explosive growth in coca cultivation (in areas largely dominated by the guerrillas) and the increasing number of guerrilla attacks and kidnappings (Crandall, 2002, 147). The Clinton administration chose to address the deteriorating situation in Colombia through what was termed the Plan Colombia, a comprehensive strategy supposedly developed by the administration of the newly elected president, Andrés Pastrana, but in fact largely devised by the United States (Crandall, 2002, 149–50). In principle, Plan Colombia was a multifaceted program designed to eradicate illicit crops, support a negotiated settlement with the guerrilla movements, revive the moribund Colombian economy, and provide aid for judicial institutions, human rights, and alternative development. In practice, however, the bulk of U.S. funding for Plan Colombia went to finance an increasingly militarized war on drugs. Specifically, under the auspices of Plan Colombia, Congress approved $642 million in military and police assistance to Colombia for 2000–2001 (75% of the total aid package for that year).

In addition to greatly ratcheting up overall financial aid, the funding contained in Plan Colombia was given primarily to the Colombian armed forces rather than to the national police. Most of the money went toward the training and equipping of a new counternarcotics brigade within the Colombian army. The financing included the provision of sixty Blackhawk and Huey helicopters to make the brigade air-mobile, so that it could access remote locations of coca cultivation in the country. Underlying this effort was a strategy known as the "push into southern Colombia," in which the newly formed counternarcotics brigade would move into areas of coca production in Colombia such as Putumayo and Caquetá that were dominated by the FARC guerrillas (Tate, 2000, 16–19). According to a White House report, the brigade's objective would be to "establish the security conditions" needed to carry out counternarcotics operations such as aerial fumigation (Isacson, 2002a, 32). In other words, they were to engage in offensive operations against the guerrillas to take control of the area. Thus, under the guise of a counternarcotics strategy, the United States was preparing the Colombian armed forces to engage in counterinsurgency operations.

The administration of President George W. Bush continued to provide support for the Colombian armed forces in the war on drugs, but it expanded the strategy to include neighboring countries through the so-called Andean Regional Initiative (Isacson, 2002a, 35). Of particular significance, in the aftermath of the attacks of September 11, 2001, the Bush administration dropped all pretenses of supporting Colombian state security forces solely for counternarcotics purposes. Rather, key U.S. officials began to reformulate U.S. policy using the rhetoric of "counterterrorism" and referring to the nonstate armed actors in Colombia, particularly the FARC, as terrorist organizations posing a threat to regional security (Isacson, 2002b, 5; Tickner, 2003, 80–81). In February 2002, the Bush administration announced plans to arm and train a new Colombian army brigade, this time in northeastern Colombia, with the explicit purpose of protecting the 480-mile Caño Limón–Coveñas oil pipeline, which is routinely attacked by guerrillas (w o la, 2002b, 9). The legislation approved in July 2002 to support this initiative allows U.S. security assistance to be used "against activities by organizations designated as terrorist organizations," thus officially breaking with the longstanding policy that U.S. military aid to Colombia be utilized solely for counternarcotics purposes (w o la, 2002a, 11).

In the U.S. Congress, opponents of U.S. security assistance to Colombia successfully introduced human rights conditions that needed to be met in order for the military aid contained in Plan Colombia and the Andean Regional Initiative to be released. Most significantly, the conditions mandated that the Colombian military suspend members credibly alleged to have committed serious human rights violations, cooperate with civilian judicial investigations, and take effective measures to terminate their relations with the paramilitary groups. Although the Clinton administration acknowledged that these conditions had not been met, it proceeded to authorize the security aid anyway, twice waiving the conditions on the grounds of the "national security interest" (ai /h rw /wo la, 2000, 2001). In 2002, Congress removed the waiver option in an effort to increase pressure to improve human rights in Colombia. In both May and September 2002, the Bush administration certified that Colombia was making progress on the specified human rights conditions. Such a determination, however, flew in the face of strong and convincing evidence to the contrary presented by Amnesty International, Human Rights Watch, and the Washington Office on Latin America (ai /h rw /wo la, 2002a, b).

Current U.S. policy toward Colombia undermines human rights in several ways. The extensive aerial fumigation of coca crops has destroyed licit food crops and raised significant concerns about its environmental and health effects (w o la, 2002b, 6–7). Studies by the Public Advocate's Office (Defensoría del Pueblo) in 2000 and 2001 underscored health problems associated with the inhalation of the herbicide and contact with human skin (Tickner, 2003, 78–79). The "push into southern Colombia" has had the consequence of exacerbating the already overwhelming tragedy of internal displacement in Colombia, and of furthering the armed conflict by pushing desperate peasants into the arms of the farc or the paramilitaries (Vaicius and Isacson, 2003). Most significantly, however, U.S. policy weakens human rights by greatly strengthening the Colombian armed forces, even as they continue to support or acquiesce in the brutal human rights violations of paramilitary groups.

Support for Human Rights in Colombia

Although U.S. policy has intensified the human rights crisis in Colombia, the U.S. government has simultaneously taken actions to mollify the situation concerning human rights abuses. Indeed, between 2000 and 2002, the United States allocated $343 million for nonmilitary programs, including support for alternative economic development, judicial reform, and direct aid for human rights initiatives (Vaicius and Isacson, 2003). The U.S. State Department and the U.S. Agency for International Development (USAID) have engaged in both rhetorical and substantive measures to promote respect for human rights in Colombia.

The annual country reports on human rights issued by the Department of State have generally described the Colombian situation with accuracy, providing detailed overviews of human rights abuses and relying on both national and international human rights organizations for substantive data. The 2002 report on Colombia (U.S. Department of State, 2002), for example, minces few words in decrying the human rights abuses of both the Colombian state security forces and their connections with the paramilitaries:

> The Government's human rights record remained poor. . . . [G]overn-
> ment security forces continued to commit serious abuses, including
> extrajudicial killings. Impunity remained a problem. Despite some
> prosecutions and convictions, the authorities rarely brought higher-
> ranking officers of the security forces and the police charged with
> human rights offenses to justice. Members of the security forces collab-
> orated with paramilitary groups that committed abuses, in some in-
> stances allowing such groups to pass through roadblocks, sharing infor-
> mation, or providing them with supplies or ammunition. . . . [S]ecurity
> forces also often failed to take action to prevent paramilitary attacks.
> Paramilitary forces still find support among the military and police.

These grim assessments of Colombia's human rights situation have been buttressed in recent years by verbal declarations in support of human rights from the U.S. embassy in Bogotá.

In addition to rhetorical support for human rights, the U.S. government also has undertaken concrete actions to press for human rights improvements. For example, effective pressure from the United States pushed the Colombian national police to improve substantially its human rights performance in the 1990s. U.S. pressure also brought about the decision by the Colombian army in June 1998 to disband its abusive 20th Intelligence Brigade, which was thought to be responsible for much of the violence against Colombian human rights activists (Youngers, 1998, 19). Additionally, in the late 1990s the U.S. government began to revoke the visas of Colombian military officers implicated in human rights violations (Youngers, 1998, 19). In January 2003, the Department of State formally banned U.S. military assistance to Air Combat Command No. 1, citing its failure to adequately investigate a 1998 incident in which a Colombian air force pilot bombed a house where civilians had taken shelter, killing five children and twelve adults (H RW, 2002, 140; Reuters, 2003).

The United States also has sought to undermine the legitimacy of the abusive right-wing paramilitary groups. In September 2001, the Department of State placed the AUC on its list of designated terrorist organizations (H RW, 2002, 139). Equally significant, in September 2002 the U.S. Department of Justice indicted the leader of the AUC, Carlos Castaño, and two of his top henchmen on drug-trafficking charges. The indictment charged the paramilitary leaders with trafficking more than seventeen tons of cocaine into the United States and Europe since 1997 and was accompanied by a request for their extradition to stand trial in the United States (Green, 2002).

U SAI D has provided support for a number of programs to defend human rights in Colombia. Of particular note, it has collaborated with the public advocate to set up a nationwide early warning system (E W S) to alert authorities of impending mass violence or possible egregious human rights abuses. Established in November 2001, the E W S has a central office in Bogotá and fifteen planned regional offices. The information collected by the E W S is assessed by the Public Advocate's Office, which can issue a formal warning and recommend preventative actions to relevant state institutions.

U SAI D also has provided the bulk of the financing for a protection program coordinated by the General Office for Human Rights within the Ministry of the Interior. This program assists individuals whose lives are in danger through both "hard" protective measures for high-risk cases (the provision of armored vehicles, bodyguards, arms, and the armored reinforcement of offices) and "soft" protective measures for lower-risk cases (the provision of cellular phones, self-defense courses, and transportation or moving expenses for threatened individuals). In the first eight months of 2002 alone, the office provided some form of direct protective assistance to 3,874 individuals, including 1,195 trade unionists, 890 representatives of nongovernmental organizations, 644 members of the Patriotic Union or the Communist Party, 570 community leaders, 437 mayors or other local officials, and 138 journalists. Finally, USAID has given numerous small-scale grants to fund the activities of threatened social, labor, and human rights organizations.

Taken by themselves, the actions and programs described above might be judged to have had a positive impact on the situation of human rights in Colombia. Unfortunately, the negative effects of U.S. military aid overwhelm this impact and, indeed, help to foster the conditions under which the continuing abuse of human rights takes place. It must be recognized that the effort to promote human rights in Colombia occurs in a context shaped by the U.S. war on drugs and, more recently, the U.S. war on terrorism, with its support for counterinsurgency operations. The principal activities of U.S. policy in Colombia—providing massive security assistance for counternarcotics and counterinsurgency purposes—are inimical to the goal of promoting human rights, especially given the abusive nature of the Colombian armed forces and their ongoing ties to the vicious right-wing paramilitaries.

Conclusions

The human rights situation in Colombia is appalling, and it has significantly worsened in recent years. The Colombian state is guilty of serious human rights violations, which have occurred through the direct actions of state security forces, complicity in the actions of paramilitary groups, and the failure to prevent abuses. Moreover, U.S. policy contradictions have weakened efforts to promote human rights in Colombia. Although the State Department and USAID have made genuine efforts to promote human rights, such exertions have been undermined by the massive amount of security assistance provided by the United States, which serves to fuel the current epidemic of human rights abuses.

The recently elected administration of Álvaro Uribe Vélez is an additional cause of concern for human rights activists. On August 11, 2002, four days after his inauguration, Uribe used his constitutional state-of-siege powers to declare a "state of internal unrest." Making use of this exceptional situation, Uribe decreed the possibility of special "rehabilitation and consolidation zones" in which military commanders are granted judicial and police powers that supersede those of civilian authorities.

The Uribe administration has also produced misgiving because of its plan to train some 15,000 "peasant soldiers," who will patrol the areas where they live during the day and return to their own homes to sleep at night. This scheme has drawn criticism from the public advocate as well as from human rights activists, all of whom fear that it will expose the families of such soldiers to attacks by illegal armed groups (Hagen, 2003, 68). Of even greater concern is Uribe's design to create an informant network of one million civilians, who are to serve as active collaborators with the military and the police. There is a legitimate fear that paramilitary forces could easily penetrate such a network, providing misinformation to state security forces in an effort to further their attacks on human rights monitors, labor union leaders, and community activists. Moreover, as with the peasant soldiers, there is well-founded concern that the informant network blurs the distinction between combatants and noncombatants, thus exposing civilians to ever-greater risks of being caught up in the armed conflict.

Into the midst of this unpromising situation the United States continues to pour vast amounts of military aid, now no longer limited to counternarcotics operations. In a December 2002 visit to Bogotá, Secretary of State Colin Powell pledged to increase security assistance to Colombia, asserting that the war against Colombian guerrillas and paramilitaries was part of the Bush administration's campaign against terrorism (Weisman, 2002). In January 2003, some seventy U.S. Army Special Forces troops arrived in Arauca to begin training 6,500 Colombian soldiers to protect the Caño Limón–Coveñas pipeline (AP, 2003). Meanwhile, an additional fifteen U.S. trainers were preparing a three-hundred-man commando battalion "to be used to hunt important guerrilla commanders and destroy guerrilla command-and-control centers" (Wilson, 2003).

As the tragedy of human rights violations continues to unfold amidst Uribe's threatening security policies and Washington's insistence on massive military aid, it is necessary to assert forcefully that the protection of human rights should constitute the central pillar of both countries' public policies. The Colombian government cannot use the excuse of the existence of an internal armed conflict to avoid its duty to guarantee the human rights of its citizens. To the contrary, a lasting resolution of the conflict will only be possible when the state effectively upholds human rights. Above all, the executive branch must ensure that state security forces act strictly within the law. When these forces violate human rights or international humanitarian law, the responsible parties must be vigorously prosecuted and punished. To that end, the agencies with responsibility for bringing criminal and disciplinary charges against them—the offices of the attorney general and the inspector general—must be fully financed, offered adequate protection, and staffed with committed public servants. The president must also, in his capacity as commander-in-chief of the armed forces, ensure that all forms of contact and cooperation between the military and the paramilitary forces cease immediately. Moreover, as the principal violators of human rights in Colombia, the paramilitary forces themselves must become the targets of the state security forces' legitimate repressive actions.

For its part, the United States must make the protection of human rights central—not peripheral—to its foreign policy in Colombia. It must vigorously press the Colombian government to take stronger measures to promote and defend human rights. To waive these conditions or to certify "progress" under the current circumstances is disingenuous at best; indeed, it sends precisely the wrong message to Colombian state security forces regarding their need to respect human rights and to disassociate themselves from the paramilitaries. The United States also must take a strong and unyielding public stance on behalf of those threatened by human rights violations—especially human rights activists, labor leaders, journalists, left-wing politicians, and indigenous groups. Finally, and on a more profound level, the United States must reevaluate its approach to fighting drugs and engage in a long-overdue analysis of whether coca cultivation and drug transshipment can ever be resolved by military means.

BIBLIOGRAPHY

Americas Watch (AW). 1991. La "Guerra" contra las Drogas en Colombia: La Olvidada Tragedia de la Violencia Política. Bogotá: Centro de Estudios Internacionales de la Universidad de los Andes/Instituto de Estudios Políticos y Relaciones Internacionales de la Universidad Nacional de Colombia.
Amnesty International (AI). 1994. Political Violence in Colombia: Myth and Reality. New York: Amnesty International.
Amnesty International, Human Rights Watch, and the Washington Office on Latin America (AI/HRW/WOLA). 2000. Colombia Human Rights Certification. New York: Amnesty International.

————. 2001. *Colombia Human Rights Certification II.* New York: Amnesty International.

————. 2002a. *Colombia Human Rights Certification III.* New York: Amnesty International.

————. 2002b. *Colombia Human Rights Certification IV.* New York: Amnesty International.

Associated Press (A P). 2003. "U.S. Envoy Greets Forces in Colombia." *AP Wire,* 18 January.

Barco, Virgilio. 1990. "Intervención por Televisión para Anunciar Decretos de Estado de Sitio contra las Bandas de Sicarios y Grupos de Autodefensa." Pp. 357–362 in *Discursos 1986–1990,* Vol. II, *Paz, Lucha contra el Narcotráfico y Orden Público.* Bogotá: Presidencia de la República.

Blair Trujillo, Elsa. 1993. *Las Fuerzas Armadas: Una Mirada Civil.* Bogotá: Centro de Investigación y Educación Popular (C I N E P).

Bowden, Mark. 2001. *Killing Pablo: The Hunt for the World's Greatest Outlaw.* New York: Penguin Books.

Comisión Colombiana de Juristas (C C J). 1997. *Colombia, Derechos Humanos y Derecho Humanitario: 1996.* Bogotá: Comisión Colombiana de Juristas.

Comisión Interamericana de Derechos Humanos (C I D H). 1999. *Derechos Humanos en Colombia.* 3d. *Informe de la Comisión Interamericana de Derechos Humanos.* Bogotá: Comisión Colombiana de Juristas.

Consultoría para los Derechos Humanos y el Desplazamiento (C O D H E S). 2002. *Boletín 40 Desplazados en la Encrucijada.* Bogotá: Consultoría para los Derechos Humanos y el Desplazamiento.

Crandall, Russell. 2002. *Driven by Drugs: U.S. Policy toward Colombia.* Boulder: Lynne Rienner.

Cubides, Fernando. 2001. "From Private to Public Violence: The Paramilitaries." Pp. 127–49 in *Violence in Colombia 1990–2000: Waging War and Negotiating Peace,* ed. Charles Bergquist, Ricardo Peñaranda, and Gonzalo Sánchez G. Wilmington, DE: Scholarly Resources, Inc.

Dávila Ladrón de Guevara, Andrés. 1998. *El Juego del Poder: Historia, Armas y Votos.* Bogotá: Fondo Editorial CEREC/Universidad de los Andes—Ediciones Uniandes.

Defensoría del Pueblo. 2001. *Gaceta Defensorial Diciembre 2000—Junio 2001,* Vol. I. Bogotá: Defensoría del Pueblo.

Fox, James Allen, and Marianne W. Zawitz. 2002. "Homicide Trends in the United States" [online]. Washington, DC: U.S. Department of Justice, Office of Justice Programs, Bureau of Justice Statistics [updated 21 November 2002; cited 27 March 2003]. Available from http://www.ojp.usdoj.gov/bjs/homicide/homtrnd .htm#contents.

Fundación Social. 2001. *Algo Todavía Ocurrirá: 7 Informes de la Fundación Social a la Comisión Interamericana de Derechos Humanos.* Bogotá: Fundación Social.

Fundación Social-UNICEF. 2002. *Vigía del Fuerte: Boletín sobre la Situación Humanitaria*. Bogotá: Fundación Social–UNICEF, December.

Gallón Giraldo, Gustavo, ed. 1991. *Derechos Humanos y Conflicto Armado en Colombia*. Bogotá: Comisión Andina de Juristas—Seccional Colombiana.
Green, Eric. 2002. *Justice Dept. Indicts Colombian AUC Leaders on Drug Charges*. Washington, DC: U.S. Department of State, Office of International Information Programs, Washington File, 24 September.

Hagen, Jason. 2002. "New Colombian President Promises More War." NACLA *Report on the Americas* 36 (1): 24–29.
———. 2003. "Uribe's People: Civilians and the Colombian Conflict." *Georgetown Journal of International Affairs* 4 (1) (Winter/Spring): 65–71.
Human Rights Watch (HRW). 1992. *Political Murder and Reform in Colombia: The Violence Continues*. New York: Human Rights Watch.
———. 1993. *State of War: Political Violence and Counterinsurgency in Colombia*. New York: Human Rights Watch.
———. 1996. *Colombia's Killer Networks: The Military-paramilitary Partnership and the United States*. New York: Human Rights Watch.
———. 1998. *War without Quarter: Colombia and International Humanitarian Law*. New York: Human Rights Watch.
———. 2000. "The Ties that Bind: Colombia and Military-paramilitary Links." *A Human Rights Watch Short Report* 12, 1B (February): 1–22.
———. 2001. *The "Sixth Division": Military-paramilitary Ties and U.S. Policy in Colombia*. New York: Human Rights Watch.
———. 2002. "Colombia." Pp. 132–141 in *Human Rights Watch World Report 2002*. New York: Human Rights Watch.

Isacson, Adam. 2002a. "Colombia's Human Security Crisis." *Disarmament Forum—Human Security in Latin America* 2: 25–40.
———.2002b. "Colombia after September 11: View from Washington." *Colombia Update* 14: 5–6.

Leech, Garry M. 2002. *Killing Peace: Colombia's Conflict and the Failure of U.S. Intervention*. New York: Information Network of the Americas (INOTA).

Ministerio de Defensa Nacional. 2002. *Informe Anual Derechos Humanos y DIH—2001*. Bogotá: República de Colombia.

Ramírez, Socorro, and Luís Alberto Restrepo. 1989. *Actores en Conflicto por la Paz: El Proceso de Paz durante el Gobierno de Belisario Betancur (1982–1986)*. Bogotá: Siglo Veintiuno Editores—CINEP.
Reuters. 2003. "1998 Bombing Cited as U.S. Decertifies Unit in Colombia." *Reuters Wire*, 15 January.

Richani, Nazih. 2000. "The Paramilitary Connection." *NACLA Report on the Americas* 34 (2): 38–41.

———. 2002a. "Colombia at the Crossroads: The Future of the Peace Accords." *NACLA Report on the Americas* 35 (4): 17–20.

———. 2002b. *Systems of Violence: The Political Economy of War and Peace in Colombia.* Albany: State University of New York Press.

Tate, Winifred. 2000. "Repeating Past Mistakes: Aiding Counterinsurgency in Colombia." *NACLA Report on the Americas* 34 (2): 16–19.

Tickner, Arlene. 2003. "Colombia and the United States: From Counternarcotics to Counterterrorism." *Current History* 102 (661): 77–85.

United Nations High Commissioner for Human Rights (UNHCHR). 2002. "Report of the United Nations High Commissioner for Human Rights on the Human Rights Situation in Colombia." E/CN.4/2002/17, 28 February. New York: United Nations Economic and Social Council.

U.S. Department of State. 2002. *Country Reports on Human Rights Practices for 2001: Colombia.* Washington, DC: U.S. Department of State.

Vaicius, Ingrid, and Adam Isacson. 2003. *The "War on Drugs" Meets the "War on Terror."* Washington, DC: Center for International Policy.

Washington Office on Latin America (WOLA). 2002a. "Colombia Cracks Down." *Colombia Monitor* 2: 1–14.

———. 2002b. "Taking Stock: Plan Colombia's First Year." *Colombia Monitor* 1: 1–10.

Weisman, Steven R. 2002. "Powell Says U.S. Will Increase Military Aid for Colombia." *New York Times*, 5 December, sec. A, p. 14.

Wilson, Scott. 2001. "Chronicle of a Massacre Foretold." *Washington Post*, 28 January, sec. A, p. 01.

———. 2003. "U.S. Moves Closer to Colombia's War." *Washington Post*, 7 February, sec. A, p. 22.

Youngers, Coletta. 1998. "Waging War: U.S. Policy toward Colombia." Paper prepared for the Twenty-first International Congress of the Latin American Studies Association (LASA), Chicago, 24–26 September.

CHAPTER 10

The Path of State Terror in Peru

ABDERRAHMAN BEGGAR

> Then, the questioning begins; and, sometimes, they don't
> control themselves, sometimes they assassinate them.
> Then, there is no problem, because downstairs there is a
> back door. They do not leave by the front door. . . . Of course,
> they take the back door, by way of the incinerator, arrive
> from the back, open the door, walk and arrive at the football
> field, armed with wood and picks. They throw lime and
> kerosene on them, and it is finished, nobody knows.
>
> —Declaration of a former Army Intelligence
> Service agent to an enquiry commission
> composed of members of the
> Peruvian Congress, 2002[1]

Introduction

Peruvian President Alberto Fujimori's resignation from office, his flight to Japan on November 13, 2000, and President Alejandro Toledo's ascension to power marked the end of a period during which the Peruvian state, supported by the armed forces, had adopted a program of repression against intellectuals, unionists, journalists, professors, students, and peasants in the name of antisubversion and antinarcotics campaigns. In Peru in the 1990s, 45 percent of the population lived in poverty, 20 percent were incapable of securing three meals per day, 85 percent were without stable employment, and 25,000 people were killed in political violence in the course of eight years (Paredes, 1997).

What is atypical in the Peruvian case is that, in contrast to the experiences of other Latin American countries, the conditions for terror in Peru are not associated with the era of military governments (1968–1980). Ties with the United States, especially with regard to defense, were not at all encouraging before the last decade of the twentieth century. In Peru, military hegemony ended in 1980 with the organization of the first elections in more than a decade and the victory in the presidential election of a civilian and former president, Fernando Belaúnde Terrey (in office 1963–1968, 1980–1985).

In 1980, however, in the middle of the electoral process, the Maoist organization Sendero Luminoso (Shining Path) decided to strike to mark its position toward this transition. This decision opened a new period in the history of the Andean country, marked by merciless repression (displacements of the population, assassinations, torture, and arbitrary imprisonments) and by a chronic economic crisis. Violence was a golden opportunity for the armed forces to exercise their authority in the name of the antiterrorism fight. For almost twenty years, Peruvian society lived under the pretext of antisubversion and antinarcotics politics, and this era proved to be among the darkest times of the country's history. Internal factors, such as durable alliances between groups of influence, and external factors, including unconditional support by the United States of the status quo, encouraged the military force's participation in establishing and reinforcing the state of terror.

This chapter primarily deals with the Peru of the 1990s, in particular how the United States contributed to a massive militarization of Peruvian society by arming, training, and financing its armed forces, even if these were considered to be completely indifferent or inimical to human rights. The objective is to show how strategic interests (prosecution of the antidrug war) and economic interests (promotion of the free-market model) overrode all others and how U.S. administrations worried little about democratic values as they continuously supported President Alberto Fujimori's government, a regime generally considered a "civil dictatorship."

This period marked the beginning of the post–Cold War era, with Fujimori having been first elected just after the fall of the Berlin Wall. At the same time, it coincided with the birth of a new, more muscular strategy in what the United States called the "war on drugs," which had been initiated in 1971 by the Nixon administration. In fact, when in 1989 President George H. W. Bush gave the order to invade Panama, the United States decided to militarize their antinarcotics policy throughout Latin America. These efforts were directed at destroying coca plant fields, cocaine processing sites, and the transportation infrastructure used in narcotics production and distribution. To some extent, such a strategy came about to fill the vacuum left by the end of the Cold War. It was an opportunity for the U.S. Department of Defense, military planners in the Pentagon, and various other sectors of the military– industrial complex to engage in new missions. This new situation did not favor preserving a fragile Peruvian democracy in a phase of consolidation.

United States–Peru Military Cooperation before the 1990s

With Alberto Fujimori's election in 1990, U.S.-Peruvian relations reached a degree of closeness unequalled since the 1970s. From an economic view-point, prior to Fujimori Peru's military rulers had introduced measures between 1968 and 1980 that the United States had never supported: including the nationalization of some state-owned industries, programs in support of state protectionism, and resistance to the repayment of foreign debts. Indeed, in diplomatic affairs Peru was known for its nonaligned profile and for its solid relations with Socialist countries, in particular with the Soviet Union. The Andean country was well known for its support for Latin American and Third World causes and for efforts to prevent countries in the developing world from falling under U.S. control.

In military affairs, Peru's relationship with the United States had not been strong. Even after the return to civilian governments, during the 1980s the Peruvian military's cooperation with the Soviet Union was so vigorous that in 1989 it purchased more weapons from the Soviets ($2 billion) than from the United States ($264 million) (U.S. Army Intelligence and Security Command, 1992, 41). The exchange with the Soviet Union included training, with a massive presence of Soviet advisers, engineers, and instructors:

> Peruvian Army officers who travel to the Soviet Union receive training in a variety of fields, including intelligence, helicopter maintenance, pilot instruction, ordinance and missiles, armored vehicle maintenance, and supply operations.... A 1987 estimate indicated that over 4,000 persons have been trained in the Soviet Union compared to only 2,800 Peruvian military personnel who have been trained at U.S. facilities since 1976.... The Soviet Union presence in Peru is second only to Cuba in Latin America. (U.S. Army Intelligence and Security Command, 1992, 32)

Even after military rule gave way to civil elections beginning in the late 1970s, the governments of Belaúnde Terrey and Alán García Pérez (in office 1985–1990) were hesitant to accept U.S military assistance, fearing that the primary guerrilla groups, Sendero Luminoso and Movimiento Revolucionario Tupac Amarú (Tupac Amarú Revolutionary Movement, MRTA), would gain legitimacy and popularity from the government's reliance on foreign, North American support.

From a quantitative point of view, at the beginning of the 1990s the Peruvian military ranked as the third largest force in Latin America, after those of Cuba and Brazil. However, catastrophic assessments of the antisubversion fight during the 1980s and the beginning of the 1990s offer proof of its weaknesses. In fact, the Peruvian army had many problems at the time, most notably a lack of training, intelligence, and logistical coordination. The shortage, however, touched even the institution's most elementary aspects, such as the provision of ammunition and clothing:

> Some of the important items needed for the ground forces include personal equipment (boots, load-bearing equipment, fatigues), sufficient ammunition (5.56 mm, 7.62 mm, 9 mm, 60 mm, 81 mm), assault rifles and personal weapons (5.56 mm, 7.62 mm and 9 mm), night vision devices (personal, aircraft), secure radio communications, and transportation (high-altitude helicopters, troop transports, possible HMMWVs [light military trucks] or civilian trucks, e.g., Toyota, Nissan). (U.S. Army Intelligence and Security Command, 1992, 44)

Such material vulnerability, due to constant budgetary cuts, added to corruption and a lack of discipline, explains why the Peruvian armed forces were not able to face the new challenges presented to them in the 1980s. To illustrate this situation, the French monthly magazine *Le Monde Diplomatique* tells a revealing story. According to this report, the Peruvian army could not ensure protection of U.S. civil employees sent to Peru in 1988 to take part in Operation Snowcap, which was intended to control cocaine production sources in Peru, Bolivia, and Ecuador, including Peru's upper Huallaga Valley. Without Peruvian army protection, U.S. personnel had to withdraw in 1989 and return in September 1990 (Klare, 1990). The weakness of Peru's military infrastructure, however, is also explained by another factor: civil governments feared seeing the military return to power during the 1980s. Thus, increasing military capacity was not a priority. Furthermore, the Peruvian military lacked experience. It was prepared for border conflicts with hostile neighbours, especially Chile and Ecuador, rather than for internal nonconventional conflict with armed insurrection.

The Drug War and Military Cooperation with the United States

In the war on drugs, U.S. officials greatly emphasized Peru's importance as the biggest producer of coca leaves in the world. When dealing with public opinion, it is easier to justify an engagement for a problem that concerns everyday life, as we can conclude from the declaration of President George H. W. Bush in San Antonio, Texas, on February 27, 1992:

> Two years ago at Cartagena we formed a regional alliance with Peru, Bolivia, and Colombia to confront the narco-trafficking cartels. . . . First and most importantly, in the United States there are one million fewer cocaine users and two million fewer marijuana users today than in 1988. Drug use among our young people is down 25 percent, a very good sign for the future. (Bush, 1992, 324)

As this speech makes clear, the situation in Peru was regarded by the administration in Washington as affecting the U.S. population directly. The issue, as it was presented publicly, concerned only national security and U.S. domestic interests, however, as Peru's sociopolitical violence itself was not presented by President Bush as a priority. There were two reasons for this omission. On the one hand, the Maoist Sendero Luminoso was isolated from the rest of the world, with no allies in Latin America, China, or the Soviet Union. Moreover, the second leading insurgent movement, the MRTA, had lost all support from its two principal allies, Cuba and Libya, after the 1989 fall of the Berlin Wall.

On the other hand, the war on drugs was not a great priority for the Peruvian government. On the contrary, the drug war posed a major socioeconomic problem for a country where tens of thousands of peasants depended on coca leaves for their economic survival. U.S. assistance to Peru, however, was always welcome, because it gave the armed forces and the government the support they needed to curb the gains of the opposition. In addition, as will be discussed below, the United States, in particular the Central Intelligence Agency

(CIA), played a crucial role in capturing Abimael Guzmán Reynoso, the leader of Sendero Luminoso, as well as in resolving one of the biggest hostage crises of the last century, set in motion by the capture, orchestrated by the MRTA, of the Japanese ambassador's residence in Lima in December 1997.

In the view of both the U.S. and Peruvian governments, the drug war made cooperation with the massive militarization of Peruvian society necessary. It was also used as an excuse to eliminate all the forces considered "subversive" and "revolutionary." The U.S. support that followed the invasion of Panama had the objective, in the words of U.S. Army Colonel John D. Waghelstein, former head of U.S. advisers in El Salvador, "to fight against the terrorists— guerrillas and narco-traffickers in the hemisphere" (quoted in Mariano, 1997, 9). From the beginning of this assistance, one element was clear: the United States was ready to establish a strategic alliance with military forces recognized by human rights organizations, and even the U.S. State Department, as not concerning themselves with the protection of human rights.[2]

The U.S. presence in Peru in relation to the drug war dates from the time of the García administration, beginning with the construction of the largest U.S. base in Latin America, the Santa Lucía, in 1988. This project was intended to foster cooperation between the U.S. Department of State, the U.S. Drug Enforcement Administration (DEA), the Narcotics Affairs Section (NAS) of the U.S. embassy in Lima, the Military Assistance Advisory Group coordinated by the U.S. Department of Defense, and the Peruvian armed forces. Personnel at Santa Lucía totaled about 430, including 32 Peruvians (National Security and International Affairs Division [NSIAD], 1994, letter 1).

The Santa Lucía base was established in the heart of the upper Huallaga Valley, an area considered the center of coca production in the region. The first campaign to target coca production in the valley was Operation Snowcap, launched in 1988, which initiated a new era of cooperation between Peru and the United States (Klare, 1990, 4–5). Its chief purpose was to control the flood of coca paste to Colombian laboratories. Before receiving "three Bell Air Force 212 helicopters, armed with rocket launchers and 12.7 mm machine-guns" from the United States in June 1989, the Peruvian air forces had only twenty-eight Soviet-manufactured helicopters, of which just twelve could operate at the same time (U.S. Army Intelligence and Security Command, 1992, 35). In effect, prior to this weapons acquisition, the Peruvian air forces had almost no control of Peru's airspace. In addition, cooperation with the United States also provided intelligence on airspace movement. This information was used by the Peruvians to shoot down any plane suspected of transporting drugs.

In 1993, the United States left the base to the Peruvian authorities. With control of the base of Santa Lucía, the idea of having a powerful infrastructure and implanting modern technology for military use was born, as the following quote demonstrates:

> In 1988, the United States began to build the Santa Lucia base, which included an airfield, a maintenance facility for 6 to 10 U.S. UH-1H helicopters used for eradication and law enforcement missions, and housing. Because the base was in a highly dense, tropical area with no safe, accessible roads, fixed-wing aircraft (C-123s and C-130s) were supplied by the State Department's Bureau of International Narcotics Matters (I N M) to transport personnel, equipment, and supplies to the base from Lima several times each week. In addition, D E A and Peruvian aircraft used the base for law enforcement operations. (N S I A D, 1994, letter 1)

The nomination in 1995 by President Bill Clinton of General Barry R. McCaffrey to head the Office of National Drug Control Policy introduced a new phase in the U.S. strategy in Peru. General McCaffrey saw only one solution to the problem: total destruction of any connection between coca fields in Peru and the laboratories in neighboring countries, especially in Colombia. The new policy was baptized "airbridge interdiction," and it was an effort to control the points of transit used by drug traffickers.

As these examples suggest, the United States, in support of the fight against drugs, continued to supply all the technology, training, and intelligence for which the Peruvian armed forces had hoped. For example, in fiscal year 1999 the U.S. State Department reserved $29.6 million for the sole purpose of upgrading A-37 aircraft in Colombia and Peru (U.S. General Accounting Office, 2000, 5). From the establishment of the Santa Lucía base in 1988 onward, the Peruvian air forces received intelligence information provided by the most sophisticated U.S. radar. The Iquitos base, which was intended to monitor the movements of drug traffickers in the Amazonian area, is an example of this kind of support:

> In Iquitos—and at one other Peruvian location and two sites in Colombia—[the U.S. Department of Defense] operates relocatable,

ground-based radar sites to provide a surveillance blanket over transit sites along the borders shared by Peru, Colombia and Brazil. . . . Plus, [the Department of Defense] moves the radar units around. For example, two years ago, the Iquitos unit operated by Detachment 4, 24th Operations Group, Howard Air Force Base, Panama, wasn't in Iquitos. "They are positioned to properly interact with other detection assets— interceptor aircraft, tracking aircraft, and relocatable over-the-horizon radars in the Chesapeake Bay area and Texas," [U.S. Army spokesman Lt. Col. Byron] Conover said. . . . Other U.S. resources employed against drug traffickers include high-altitude aerial surveillance, satellite imagery of cultivation areas and radio monitoring. "Our approach is to layer our radar efforts with local capabilities, including air traffic control networks," Conover said. "We take cues from their intelligence sources and from our aircraft overflying the drug zones." Active duty and reserve component Air Force members staff the ground-based radar sites. At Iquitos, six Peruvian enlisted controllers complement 33 U.S. airmen. (Gillert, 1998)

U.S. personnel were to monitor any movement of planes and to inform the Peruvian air forces, who were then directed to intervene to stop or shoot down suspect planes. The operation had the following stages: "a) a ground-based radar detects suspected trafficker, b) early-warning aircraft, such as the U.S. Air Force E-3 and the U.S. Customs P-3B, tracks the target with radar, c) foreign-government forces intercept the trafficker" (U.S. General Accounting Office, 2000, 10).

This strategy became ineffective, however, when about 1988 the traffickers began either to avoid the radar-controlled areas or to ship their cargo by road or river. At this point the idea of additional U.S. assistance was born. Once again the Peruvian armed forces benefited from the situation. They now had control over the river courses and bordering territories, which previously lay outside the reach of the law. At this time, the Iquitos base served as an ideal place for training, intelligence sharing, and tactical orientation:

At a remote outpost along the Amazon River, a small cadre of U.S. Military Advisory Assistance Group members are training Peruvian naval and law enforcement specialists who in turn will train their agencies to battle drug traffickers using the river. Training includes river operations in small patrol boats, of which more than two dozen are being prepared for drug interdictions. Students also learn to conduct jungle warfare and how to stay alive eating various fruits and drawing rainwater stored naturally by certain plants and trees. "We train the trainers," said Army Col. Manuel Fuentes, the assistance group commander based in Peru's capital city, Lima. "They, in turn, train Peruvian naval [including coast guard] and police specialists." The school is still growing and doesn't have its full contingent of students or training resources. When fully operational, Fuentes said, about 60 students will graduate every six weeks. (Gillert, 1998)

This cooperation reached such proportions that in 1999, within the framework of the International Military Education and Training program, 1,300 members of the national police and armed forces were trained in over one hundred programs (U.S. Department of Defence and U.S. Department of State, 2000).

U.S. Assistance and Indifference toward Human Rights Violations

Far from serving a noble cause, the "zeal" of the Peruvian military and police was aimed at the undermining of law enforcement. In the fight against drugs, which was the priority of the U.S. government, the results of Peruvian law enforcement were not encouraging. According to the Townsend Commission, a Peruvian congressional commission formed in July 2001 to investigate criminal charges against Fujimori's regime, "The judicial system in Huallaga is completely bought by the drug traffickers. Only one significant person of the cocaine business has been condemned in Peru in the last five years" (National Security Archive, 2002, 14).

In addition to revealing their remarkably high tolerance for the credibility problems of a close ally, the conduct of the war against drugs shows U.S. policymakers' indifference toward the protection of democratic processes in Peru. For instance, in 1992, during the first year of the Fujimori presidency, the United States gave Peru nearly $95 million in economic assistance and nearly $140 million in military aid. This aid was provided to Peru within the framework of a counternarcotics agreement signed on May 14, 1991. According to Human Rights Watch, this assistance package did not take into consideration the results of the Country Report on Human Rights Practices for 1990 that was prepared by the U.S. embassy and circulated by the Department of State. The 1990 Peru report observed "egregious human rights violations," "summary executions," "torture," and "rapes." In fact, U.S. aid contradicted the agreement signed with the Fujimori government "ensuring that torture, cruel, inhuman, or degrading treatment or punishment, incommunicado detention without charges and trial, disappearances, and other flagrant denials of the right of life, liberty, or security of the person, are not practiced" (Human Rights Watch, 1991, 38). An anti-terrorist law enacted in May 1992 gave special prerogatives to the military and the police forces that put them above all restrictions. They had almost limitless freedom to control what they wanted, to violate the intimacy of the citizens, and to deny all personal freedoms.

The U.S. government became critical of Fujimori following the April 1992 *autogolpe*, a military-supported, self-administered coup d'état, through which the president established a civil dictatorship by dissolving the congress, suspending the constitution, and targeting the opposition. The U.S. reaction was swift, as the Bush administration suspended $200 million in economic and military aid and stopped negotiations over a $1 billion line of credit. U.S. pressure, however, quickly eased. In fact, despite its lack of legitimacy, the Peruvian government had privileged relations with both the Bush and Clinton administrations, receiving the largest portion of the U.S. aid sent to Latin America between 1993 and 1998 (McClintock, 2000).

The absence of a clear U.S. position can be linked to differences within the U.S. government, as is evidenced in two extracts from a declassified U.S. State Department report:

Due to a combative congress that blocked presidential economic and governmental reforms, President Fujimori launched a unilateral political coup in April 1992. (U.S. Army Intelligence and Security Command, 1993, Part II, 49)

In response to a combative congress, a dysfunctional judiciary, an extremely ailing economy, and an increasingly violent insurgency, president Fujimori took over complete control of the government in April 1992. (U.S. Army Intelligence and Security Command, 1993, Part II, 33)

This lack of clarity explains the absence of any reference to respecting human rights as a condition for intelligence sharing between the two countries. In addition to the obvious disjunction between the condemnation of the auto-golpe and the victimization of Fujimori, the respect for human rights as a fundamental principle in any bilateral cooperation is once again absent, as is clear as well in President Clinton's support of aircraft interdiction in Peruvian airspace:

> Pursuant to the authority vested in me by section 1012 of the National Defense Authorization Act for fiscal year 1995, Public Law 103–337, I hereby determine with respect to Peru that: (a) interdiction of aircraft reasonably suspected to be primarily engaged in illicit drug trafficking in that country's airspace is necessary because of the extraordinary threat posed by illicit drug trafficking to the National Security of that country, and (b) that country has appropriate procedures in place to protect against the loss of innocent lives in the air and on the ground in connection with such interdiction, which shall at a minimum include effective means to identify and warn an aircraft before the use of force is directed against the aircraft. (Clinton, 1994)

In his statement, President Clinton seems unaware of the consequences of such cooperation. If we consider his remarks in the context of relations between the United States and Peru, our attention is drawn to the implied definition of two key concepts: *sovereignty* and *national security*. In the first instance, the Peruvian national airspace is constructed as controlled by the United States, and the decision to shoot down an airplane is said to come from American personnel. Thus, we can talk only about "monitored sovereignty." In the second, concerning national security, we might say that it is defined from an egocentric point of view. Explicit or implicit interventionism, as a fundamental principle in the war against drugs, is based on the globalization of the notion of "threat": that is, "my security depends on the perception of the other's security; this recognition empowered me to make it fit my own agenda."

Airbridge interdiction was a disaster and made the United States an accomplice in a series of fatal "errors" that caused heavy casualties. Shooting down suspected planes amounted to extrajudicial executions, without rights to self-defense (Human Rights Watch, 2001).[3] The number of victims remains unclear. According to former Colonel Sewall H. Menzel, in 1991 and 1992, out of 2,000 suspicious flights, 124 planes were shot down (Menzel, 1996).

Moreover, interdiction errors involved U.S. citizens. In 1992, a Peruvian air force plane shot down a C-130 transport plane on a reconnaissance mission for the U.S. Southern Command. The pilot lost his life. Then on April 20, 2001, a small plane—with U.S. passengers (including an infant)—flying in the Amazonian region fell victim to gunfire from a Peruvian aircraft. This incident renewed the debate over this problem in the U.S. Congress. According to the Argentine newspaper *El Clarín*, quoting the chairman of Iquitos airport, the plane had a flight plan, was registered, and the pilot's wife affirmed that the attack occurred "without notice."[4]

The incident revealed a secret side of U.S. cooperation with the Peruvian army. Surveillance of the Peruvian airspace had been contracted by U.S. authorities to a private firm.[5] Indeed, in the April 2001 incident, a Cessna Citation V surveillance plane belonging to a private company located at Maxwell Air Force Base in Montgomery, Alabama, provided the information on the cause of death of both U.S. citizens. This incident shed light on the role of private contractors in the conduct of U.S. foreign policy and added to long-simmering criticisms of the involvement of the United States in Latin America (such as U.S. complicity with dictatorships in Chile, Argentina, and Uruguay, and the role U.S. agents played in political developments in Guatemala, El Salvador, Nicaragua, and Honduras). Questions raised by the media in the United States and elsewhere expressed mistrust concerning the use of private contractors in this type of work.

In London, for example, the *Guardian* characterized the antinarcotics campaign as a "war of mercenaries."[6] Quoting a U.S. official, the *New York Times* noted that "not one person on that [surveillance] aircraft had a commission from the U.S. government to do what they were doing. No one took an oath to the Constitution. They were just businessmen" (Marquis, 2001, 4). The *Guardian* emphasized how some of the contracted companies flouted international law. In this regard, it cited the case of a company based in Virginia, which took part in the fight against drugs in Colombia. After members of one of the main Colombian guerrilla groups, the Fuerzas Armadas Revolucionarias de Colombia (Revolutionary Armed Forces of Colombia, FARC) shot down a police helicopter, personnel from the Virginia company sent to rescue the downed police officers exchanged gunfire with the rebels. This explicitly represented an act of direct interference in Colombian affairs (Borger and Hodgson, 2001, 3).

The April 2001 incident revived an old debate. Indeed, beginning in the 1960s the CIA had hired private companies, with names like Civil Air

Transport Company, Air America, and Intermountain Aviation, for air transport and other aviation services. To give a sense of how large these companies were, Intermountain Aviation alone had a fleet of 200 planes and 20,000 employees. Only when the pilot Eugene Hasenfus was captured in Nicaragua in 1987 did questions begin to be raised concerning the relationship between the CIA and Corporate Air Services and Southern Air Transport, American companies identified by the *New York Times* as CIA subcontractors (Marquis, 2001, 4).

In the Peruvian case, as elsewhere, contracting private companies allowed U.S. civil officials to veil themselves and pass on questionable assignments to private companies. These companies did not have the same responsibilities as did government agencies (Lewis, 1997).[7]

The Antisubversion Fight

Sociopolitical violence in Peru dates back to the 1960s, with the insurrection headed by the Trotskyite Hugo Blanco. The central reasons for the violence were related to land issues. The first Belaúnde administration and the military junta headed by Juan Velasco Alvarado (in office 1968–1974) launched agrarian reforms that, for a time, calmed social agitation but without effectively solving structural problems.

Especially prominent during the 1980s, Sendero Luminoso became one of the most notorious of Peru's armed opposition movements. The movement's birth in Ayacucho, in the heart of the Andes, undoubtedly was related to socioeconomic factors (such as the department being the second poorest in the country). In the beginning, the majority of its members were students, led by Professor Guzmán. Once the movement was in place, new members started joining, especially from shantytowns and other peripheralized sociopolitical sectors. Unemployment and injustice provided the strongest base for the growth of Sendero Luminoso, which quickly became one of the most prominent Latin American armed insurrection groups.

With time, Guzmán's Maoist organization underwent profound changes, forming strong alliances that allowed it to acquire funds and weapons. Presumably, ties with drug traffickers became stronger at this time, as well (Palmer, 1992). Consequently, the group's area of operations expanded beyond the Andes and reached Amazonia. Its main activity consisted of protecting roads and cocaine production points, while securing the strategic control of these areas. Merciless reprisals against all those who opposed it (such as administrators, mayors, soldiers, policemen, workers, and farmers) were at the root of the organization's notoriety. The guerrillas radically changed the lives of ordinary Peruvians, as there were thousands of victims, whole villages displaced, houses destroyed, devastated infrastructure, and extensive minefield expansion.

The other guerrilla movement active at the time was the MRTA. The MRTA's objectives were more clearly political than was the agenda of Sendero Luminoso, and it did not share Sendero Luminoso's methods of generalized violence and elimination. In 1979, MRTA emerged into the public eye when a group of unionists, soldiers, and intellectuals organized against the military government of Francisco Morales Bermúdez, in an attempt to force it to stay faithful to the fundamentals established by the preceding president, Juan Velasco. Velasco had been responsible for a series of social reforms that made his government hugely popular, in spite of his assumption of the presidency through a coup d'état. The MRTA was inspired by Che Guevara's views, with a strategy based on armed resistance and rural guerrilla warfare and a strong commitment to pan-American and internationalist tendencies. For this reason, it created the América Battalion with the Colombian guerilla movement M-19 for a short time in 1985. The MRTA's first operation was an attack on a U.S. Marines security residence in Lima in 1983.

With the arrival in office of the García administration in 1985, the situation deteriorated significantly. Peruvian society sank into violence and also into one of the most serious economic crises of its history. In the lead up to the presidential elections of 1990, the candidates used the economic crisis and the deep fear of Sendero Luminoso as the basis of their campaigns. All the candidates had the same message: put an end to the guerrilla movements and to the economic crisis. Exhausted by the upheavals of the preceding years, Peruvians who lacked confidence in the traditional political system would pay just about any price for a new leader. Thus, Mario Vargas Llosa and Alberto Fujimori dominated the political arena. Both candidates were outside traditional party circuits, and each had stature as an intellectual. Vargas Llosa was a writer famous internationally, and Fujimori was an academic. Their apparent incorruptibility contrasted starkly with García, whose administration was marked by embezzlement scandals and a massacre at El Callao prison, in which the army was given an order to kill some three hundred rioting prisoners. As the situation deteriorated, García fled Peru. The Vargas Llosa and

Fujimori campaigns proposed liberal and dramatic economic programs. When the voting was over, Fujimori had won the election.

Fulfilling his campaign promises, Fujimori implemented a rapid militarization of the country in the name of the antiguerrilla war:

> In 1990 Peru's annual budget for military expenditures was (all figures in U.S. dollars) $1.25 billion. By 1995, this sum reaches $1.879 billion; that is, over $5 million daily. In 1995, military expenditures account for 50 percent of the country's exports. . . . In 1991, 48.7 percent of Peruvians (10,881,131) lived in areas declared as emergency zones. In 1995 it was 58.0 percent (11,300,400), more than 50 percent of all Peruvians. This situation is seen even in the capital city, whose population exceeds 6 million. (Borja, 1996, 3)

In the domain of antisubversive action, U.S. assistance was decisive in two important events. Under the García administration, an antiterrorist service called Dirección Nacional contra el Terrorismo (DINCOTE) was created by the Peruvian government. It was considered ineffective and mired in corruption,[8] however, and the CIA decided not to deal with it and to create a separate cell in its place (see Lane, 2000, 1). The objective of this new force was to capture or kill Guzmán, the leader of Sendero Luminoso, an objective that was finally accomplished on September 12, 1992. In an article published in the *Washington Post*, journalist Charles Lane (2000, 1) recounts the events surrounding Guzmán's capture (an agent with the pseudonym of Superman represents the CIA):

> For months, Superman and personnel brought to Peru by the CIA had trained, equipped, financed and coached the detectives. When the cops needed cars, the CIA paid for them; when they found a Shining Path document in English, Superman translated. And when police radioed headquarters with word of Guzman's arrest, Superman was there to hear the news and join the celebration. Indeed, the U.S. government found out before Peru's then-president, Alberto Fujimori, or his intelligence chief, Vladimiro Montesinos, did. "They were very close to us," Benedicto Jimenez, who commanded the special police unit, said of the CIA, adding: "I think that without that support, it would have been a bit difficult to get where we got." . . . By this time, the Peruvians needed

help not only gaining information but also making sense of the data they had. To address both issues, the CIA set up what the police called an "academy" in DINCOTE headquarters. CIA officers showed the detectives how to analyze, cross-reference and classify documents. Together with an expert from Britain's Scotland Yard, CIA personnel also taught the detectives how to conduct surveillance in disguise. The agency hired Peruvian actors to help undercover officers play the part of, say, a street vendor or homeless schizophrenic. The CIA gave Jimenez's detectives spy gear: telephoto cameras, listening devices, night-vision goggles and a video camera that could be concealed in a briefcase. And the agency rented cars so police could follow suspects from a variety of vehicles. Occasionally, CIA officers stood behind two-way mirrors watching the police question suspects, then advised the Peruvians on their techniques, according to a former senior Peruvian police official.

From this article, we can see the important role the CIA played in training, financing, and providing logistics and operations coordination. They took the leading role in capturing Guzmán and the local police played merely an instrumental role.[9]

The second major event in which CIA involvement was a crucial factor concerned the crisis produced by the seizure of hostages in the Japanese ambassador's residence in Lima that resulted in a siege of the compound lasting from December 17, 1996, to April 21, 1997. The Mexican newspaper *La Jornada* observed that from the first days of the crisis, U.S. and British advisers were present among the Peruvians dealing with the situation ("EU aconseja evitar concesiones, pero no interviene, asegura Burns," 1996). On April 23, 1997, Bob Taubert (a former agent of the U.S. Federal Bureau of Investigation) affirmed in an interview with the Cable News Network that the United States provided training to the Peruvian special unit that freed the seventy-one hostages and killed all fourteen guerrillas. This training was "part of a State Department program to assist police in emerging democratic countries" ("Hostages Freed," 1997). On this same topic, the Lima daily *La República* revealed, "The elite commandos that intervened in the Japanese ambassador's residence and managed the spectacular release of the MRTA hostages used armament of the latest technology that had never been used before in combat in Peruvian territory" ("Comandos Utilizaron," 1997).

The School of the Americas and the Pedagogy of Terror

As mentioned previously, cooperation between Peru and the United States in the antisubversion campaign has not always been respectful of human rights. One aspect of this outcome concerns the U.S. Army School of the Americas (SOA), which was long marked with controversy surrounding its training methods. Between 1946 and 2001, SOA trained 3,997 Peruvians, the majority of whom occupied high positions in the military and police hierarchy.[10]

Among the Peruvian SOA graduates were Vladimiro Montesinos, the former director of the Servicio de Inteligencia Nacional (National Intelligence Service, SIN) and Fujimori's former right-hand man. Montesinos is currently in prison for offenses ranging from assassinations to embezzlement. The *Washington Post* described another SOA graduate, General Nicolás Hermoza Ríos, as the "former head of Fujimori's joint chiefs during most of the 1990s." Hermoza pleaded guilty to taking $14 million in illegal profits from arms deals. He also faced charges of "taking protection money from the drug lords the United States was paying Peru to fight" (Fiola, 2001, 1).

Until it was disbanded in 2001 (to be replaced by the Western Hemisphere Institute for Security Cooperation), SOA had been criticized for teaching its Latin American students methods of torture and interrogation that violated human rights. SOA was also criticized for using instructional manuals that taught counterinsurgent and enforcement methods that when applied would have violated human rights. The SOA training appeared to work well with the Peruvians: their antisubversion activities on the ground closely resembled the methods taught by the SOA manuals.[11]

In SOA training manuals, the antiterrorist pedagogy is generally based on a dangerously simplistic vision of the problem. The suspect is deprived of his or her human nature and the right to defend him- or herself against accusations. This dehumanization corresponds to mystico-phobic stereotypes such as the following:

> Communism is a kind of pseudo-religion, given that it has a founder, a mythology, a sacred book, a clergy, a place of pilgrimage and an inquisition. The founder is Marx; the mythology is communist theory; the sacred book is *Das Kapital*; the clergy are members of the Communist Party; the place of pilgrimage is Moscow; and the inquisition [by] the

state (K G B) and others. ("Revolutionary War, Guerillas and Communist Ideology," cited in Haugaard, 1997, 14, 1–23)

In another formulation, the manuals write, "The terrorist tends to be atheist, devoted to violence" (School of the Americas, 1989a, 263). The enemy is stripped of reason. He or she is made to appear as someone who has been brainwashed or acts under criminal addiction.[12] Considering this situation, under the pretext of antiterrorism, the margin of law disappears: "The C I [Counterinsurgency] agent will have more freedom of action due to the threat that the guerrillas represent, and it is possible that the population becomes more hostile" (School of the Americas, 1989c, 59).

In Peru in the 1990s, the alibi of the antiterrorism war gave the army the opportunity to use force for illicit enrichment, through control of all sectors of society and the resources of the state. This venality at the highest levels of government resulted in an undermining of public morality and a generalized corruption, which ranged from political activities, to actions in the economic, cultural, and social spheres. Violations of physical and psychological integrity, through the use of systemized torture, assassinations, disappearances, reclusion, illegal wiretapping, and blackmail, were quotidian activities. As described in a declassified document from the U.S. embassy: "Fujimori is absolutely committed to destroying Sendero Luminoso and the M R T A within his five year term and is prepared to countenance any methods that achieve this goal. The president is convinced that the only way to eradicate Sendero Luminoso is by physically eliminating the members of the organization; overall government counter-terrorism policy reflects this" (U.S. Embassy, Lima, 1993, 4).

In the S O A scheme, any means, even fear, was acceptable to recruit spies: "if an individual has been recruited using fear as a weapon, the C I [Counterinsurgency] agent must be in a position to maintain the threat." Feelings like the desire for revenge or greed were also exploited. Everyone was welcome, even mercenaries, provided that the person would be effective; it was expected that a person motivated by mercenary intentions would accept work for the government if the compensation were adequate, but any additional methods that might attract the individual should also be explored. Criminals were recruited, as well: "On the other hand, a former criminal who does not sympathize with the cause of the guerrillas could be a good bet to accept to work for the government." Everyone was regarded as a potential informant, to such an extent that even the exploitation of children was encouraged: "The children often are very observant and they can provide precise information about things that they have seen and heard . . . [when] they are questioned in a proper manner" (School of the Americas, 1989c, 12, 25, 24, 26, 21). The implication of this last statement, of course, is to directly involve children in militarized conflict.[13]

In addition to promoting excessive control of the population (School of the Americas, 1989d, 117–19), the manuals encourage the fostering of corruption (School of the Americas, 1989c, 1).[14] Among the places considered as threatening, the university is first on the list: "The universities play a prominent role in the recruitment of terrorists. They introduce Anarchist and Marxist doctrines and many of the student federations are controlled by radicals" (School of the Americas, 1989a, 263). All political parties or organizations that resist the government are also considered threats,[15] a perspective that targets pluralism and all forms of freedom:

> The insurgents are active in the areas of political nominations, political organizations, political education, and judicial laws. They can resort to subverting the government by means of elections in which the insurgents cause the replacements of an unfriendly government official with one favorable to their cause. . . . Also, insurgent leaders can participate in political races as candidates for government posts. (School of the Americas, 1989b, 51)

Grosso modo, the world, therefore, is divided into two categories, the faithful and the traitorous: "In accordance with the sentiments that motivate him, an employee could be trustworthy to his government or become a traitor" (School of the Americas, 1989c, 12). This last category represented a broad part of Peruvian society during the Fujimori decade, since the socioeconomic situation did not promote confidence in the government.[16]

Following his election to the presidency in 1990, one of Fujimori's primary objectives was the removal of Peru from the blacklist, maintained by the International Monetary Fund (I M F), of debtor countries with bad repayment records. The army was present to ensure the application of the structural adjustment program designed to remedy the country's credit situation, and any opposition was considered as dissidence.[17] From the first weeks of the Fujimori government, however, Lima was surrounded by military forces, and strikes and social agitation increased. It was the beginning of a long process known as the "Fuji-shock." During this period, the country experienced a large wave of privatizations with the goal of reducing inflation, public expenditures, and all forms of economic barriers. The I M F imposed a plan of extreme liberalization, lifting customs borders and promoting the disengagement of the state from the economy. Rural areas were the first to fall victim, and small farmers could not withstand the deep crisis. This situation encouraged a "parallel economy" and armed violence, as well as trafficking of various kinds. It increased the gap between the rich and the poor and crushed the middle class. The situation, moreover, worsened over time: according to the Peruvian daily *La República* ("El Perú Después de los Rehenes," 1997), in 1997 the rates of poverty in three principal geographical areas were, respectively, 44.0 percent on the coast, 54.2 percent in the mountains, and 55.2 percent in the forest areas.

In Peru, the antisubversion war reduced the national police force's power in favor of that of the army, which assumed responsibility for all affairs related to terrorism and drug trafficking, leaving the police forces only a rather symbolic role in public security. The military controlled it all, from customs to the treasury and land registers. The military eye was everywhere, taking care of everything.

Conclusion

The programs of the government of President Alberto Fujimori inaugurated the post–Cold War era in Peru, within a Latin American context still resistant to economic neoliberalism and globalization (see, for example, the prominence of the Zapatista movement in Chiapas, the ascension of the Workers Party in Brazil and the rebirth of the Radical Civic Union in Argentina, and so on). It is clear that even after the fall of the Berlin Wall, in dealing with this Andean country the U.S. Cold War mentality did not change. The U.S. government's unconditional support of Fujimori, considered the incarnation of a symbiotic model of authoritarianism and neoliberalism, reveals the contradictions that undermine the presence of the United States in the region. During the 1990s, U.S. policy allegedly supported democracy in Latin America—such support was a leitmotiv of U.S. foreign relations, particularly during the Clinton administration—while, at the same time, it took part in the smothering of an incipient democracy.

Through the actions of the Fujimori administration, supported by the United States, Peruvian society suffered from what is often described as "political cannibalism": negation of institutional and democratic controls, militarization of law enforcement and, therefore, increasing encroachment on civil society. Under the alibis of the antinarcotics war and the campaign against sociopolitical violence, the United States brought the necessary technology, funds, and know-how to foster the creation of a terror state in a country considered geopolitically a key element in the project of a global Pax Americana in the Andes.

NOTES

1. *Townsend Commission* (National Security Archive, 2002, 5).

2. A U.S. State Department (1989, 4) report clearly states: "the military justice code contains no specific language for dealing with cases of killing, kidnapping or torture—only 'negligence' and 'abuse of authority'."

3. In a letter to President Bush, Human Rights Watch emphasizes the illegal aspect of such politics: "The use of firearms is permitted only when the suspect poses an imminent threat of violence to law enforcement officials or others. The leading standard in this area is contained in the Basic Principles on the Use of Force and Firearms by Law Enforcement Officials, which was adopted in 1990 by the Eighth U.N. Congress on the Prevention of Crime and the Treatment of Offenders. Principle 9 prohibits the use of firearms by law enforcement officials except 'in self-defense or defense of others against the imminent threat of death or serious injury' or a 'grave threat to life', and only when 'less extreme means are insufficient'. Mere involvement in criminal activity, or flight from apprehension, is insufficient to justify using firearms under Principle 9 unless there are facts to suggest an 'imminent threat of death or serious injury'. Moreover, Principle 9 proscribes the intentional use of lethal force—the only fair way to characterize shooting at an aircraft—except 'when strictly unavoidable in order to protect life'" (Human Rights Watch, 2001).

4. "Afirman que el avión derribado en Perú estaba registrado y tenía plan de vuelo," (*El Clarín*, 22 April 2001; available from http://old.clarin.com/diario/2001/04/22/i-03601.htm).

5. In fact, hiring private companies is common: "The U.S. government also hires or authorizes private military consultants to train foreign police forces and military troops. According to one source, U.S. companies trained military forces in more than twenty-four countries during the 1990s, including Angola, Bolivia, Bosnia, Colombia, Croatia, Egypt, Equatorial Guinea, Ethiopia, Haiti, Kosovo, Liberia, Nigeria, Peru, Rwanda, and Saudi Arabia" (Amnesty International, 2002, 21.)

6. "Today's mercenaries in the drug war are provided by private companies selling a service and are used as a matter of course by both the state and defence" (Borger and Hodgson, 2001, 3).

7. From Anthony Lewis (1997, 27): "In all these activities the C I A has not been a rogue elephant. It has been carrying out the wishes of the highest U.S. authorities. But the existence of the C I A, operating in secret, allowed those authorities to act as if they knew nothing of the torments inflicted on other people in what we deemed to be our interest."

8. According to the *Washington Post*, "some D I N C O T E agents even posed as terrorists and kidnapped civilians for ransom, according to former D I N C O T E officials" (Lane, 2000, 1).

9. In testimony before the U.S. Senate's Committee on Foreign Relations, historian Donald J. Mabry confirmed this view of the unequal relationship between the Peruvian police and the U.S. forces, saying "another consequence [of that unequal relationship] has been the use of U.S. police and military personnel to perform functions which properly belong to the Peruvian government, that is, to maintain domestic security. Their presence undermines the authority of the Peruvian government, for the message is that the Peruvian government is incompetent to perform the most basic function of any government. Peruvians no more want U.S. police and soldiers in their country than does the United States want Peruvian police and soldiers in the United States. Peru has had little choice. It is such a weak nation that it has had to accept these U.S. personnel as one price for U.S. attention and help" (Mabry, 1990).

10. For a detailed list of Peruvian students who attended the s o A and their links to human rights violations, see the School of the Americas Watch web site at http://www.soaw.org/.

11. The s o A manuals are available at http://www.soaw.org/.

12. "The true terrorist is not a crazy fanatic as is commonly thought. They are hardworking persons that are prepared to give their lives for the cause. Most terrorists desire to live to see that their goals are fulfilled or carried out; to attain that objective they use persons *with* mental problems (crazy people) or common criminals to carry out risky missions such as murders" (School of the Americas, 1989a, 262; emphasis in original).

13. According to the Defensoría del Pueblo, an autonomous Peruvian watchdog organization whose mission is to guarantee respect for constitutional rights, between 1980 and 1996 there were 519 extrajudicial executions and 7,382 disappearances in Peru, 30.6 percent occurring during the second term of President Belaúnde (1980–1985), 41.8 percent during the term of President García (1985–1990), and 26.6 percent during the first six years of the Fujimori government (1990–1996). Among the disappeared, 40 were four years old or younger and 98 were between five and fourteen years old ("Buscan Pruebas de Ejecuciones para Enjuiciar a Fujimori;

Perú Años de Terror Oficial," *La Jornada*, 14 May 2001 [available from http://www
.jornada.unam.mx/2001/mar01/010314/052n1con.html]).

14. "An employee is that person who provides information of value to the intelligence in exchange for some compensation whether in money or some other kind"
(School of the Americas, 1989c, 1). In the s o a manuals, any citizen is a potential "employee," whether an official or a child, elder, or other informant who can be useful to
the intelligence organization.

15. Under the category, "Identities and localizations of persons whose capture and
detention are of foremost importance to the armed forces" is found the entry: "*Political leaders known or suspected as hostile toward the Armed Forces or the political interests
of the National Government*" (School of the Americas, 1989a, 225; emphasis added).

16. In 1990, "more than half of the population lived in absolute poverty" (Lacoste,
1993, 1213).

17. Beginning soon after his electoral victory, Fujimori faced great resistance, resulting in increased social unrest and political violence: "It is estimated that at least
3,452 persons (civilians and military) were killed in terrorist-related violence in 1990,
an increase of over 8 percent from the previous year and 75 percent higher than the
1988 total" (U.S. State Department, 1991, 2).

BIBLIOGRAPHY

Amnesty International. 2002. *Unmatched Power, Unmet Principles: The Human Rights
Dimensions of US Training of Foreign Military and Police Forces.* New York: Amnesty
International, March.

Borger, Julian, and Martin Hodgson. 2001. "A Plane Is Shot Down and the US Proxy
War on Drug Barons Unravels" [online]. *Guardian*, 2 June, Home Pages, p. 3
[updated 2003; cited 12 April 2003]. Available from http://www.guardian.co.uk/
international/story/0,3604,500326,00.html].

Borja, Luis Arce. 1996. "Informe Completo sobre la Guerra Civil Perú: El Abismo de
Fujimori" ("Report on the Civil War in Peru: Fujimori's Abyss"). *El Diario Inter-
nacional*, part 1, 27 (January): 3–4.

Bush, George H. W. 1992. *Public Papers of the Presidents, George Bush—1992*, Vol. 1.
Washington, DC: U.S. Government Printing Office.

Clinton, Bill. 1994. *Presidential Determination #95–99: Resumption of U.S. Drug Interdiction Assistance to the Government of Peru* [online]. Washington, DC: Government
Printing Office, 8 December [cited 2 April 2003]. Available from http://www
.defenselink.mil/news/Jan1998/n01091998_9801094.html.

"Comandos Utilizaron Sofisticados Fusiles FN Herstal P-90." 1997 [online]. *La República*, 28 April [cited 2 April 2003]. Available from http://www3.larepublica .com.pe/1997/ABRIL/pdf28/.

"El Perú Después de los Rehenes: 'Los Desafíos Más Allá de las Encuestas'." 1997 [online]. Wilfredo Haro Neyra, según Alberto Adrianzén. *La República*, 27 April [cited 2 April 2003]. Available from: http://www3.larepublica.com.pe/1997/ ABRIL/pdf27/.

"E U Aconseja Evitar Concesiones, Pero No Interviene, Asegura Burns: Versiones Confusas sobre el Envoi de la Fuerza Delta a Panamá'." 1996 [online]. *La Jornada*, 21 December [cited 2 April 2003]. Available from http://www.jornada.unam.mx/ 1996/dic96/961221/eu.html.

Fiola, Anthony. 2001. "U.S. Allies in Drug War in Disgrace; Arrests of Peruvian Officials Expose Corruption, Deceit." *Washington Post*, 9 May, final ed., Sec. A, p. 1.

Gillert, Douglas J. 1998. "Southern Command Aids Search for Narcotraffickers" [online]. *U.S. Forces Press Service*. Washington, DC: Department of Defense [updated 12 April 2003; cited 12 April 2003]. Available from http://www.defenselink.mil/ news/Jan1998/n01091998_9801094.html.

Haugaard, Lisa. 1997. *Declassified Army and CIA Manuals Used in Latin America*. Washington, DC: Latin America Working Group.

"Hostages Freed: How Peru Did It." 1997 [online]. *US News*, 23 April [updated 2003; cited 2 April 2003]. Available from http://www.cnn.com/WORLD/9704/ 23/peru.how.they.did.it/index.html#2.

Human Rights Watch. 1991 *Into the Quagmire: Human Rights and U.S. Policy in Peru*. New York: Human Rights Watch.

———. 2001. "Peru: Pentagon Urged on Drug Flights" [online]. HRW World Report 2001, letter to President George Bush. New York: Human Rights Watch/Americas [cited 2 April 2003]. Available from http://www.hrw.org/press/2001/07/ perudrug-ltr.htm.

Klare, Michael T. 1990. "Washington et le Risque d'Engrenage en Amérique Latine: De la Guerre Contre la Drogue à la Guerre Tout Court?" *Le Monde Diplomatique*, March, pp. 4–5.

Lacoste, Yves, ed. 1993. *Dictionnaire Géopolitique*. Paris: Flammarion.

Lane, Charles. 2000. "'Superman' Meets Shining Path: Story of a CIA Success; With Agency Aid, Peru Captured Chief Rebel." *Washington Post*, 7 December, sec. A, p. 1.

Lewis, Anthony. 1997. "Costs of the C.I.A." *New York Times*, 25 April, Editorial Desk, sec. A, p. 27.

Mabry, Donald J. 1990. "The Latin American Cocaine Trade." Testimony before the Senate Foreign Relations Committee, June 28. Washington, DC: Government Printing Office. Also available from http://historicaltextarchive.com/sections .php?op=viewarticle&artid=247

Mariano, Aguirre. 1997. "Militarisation de la Lutte Contre le Narcotrafic: La Drogue, Alibi de Washington en Amérique Latine." *Le Monde Diplomatique,* April, p. 9.

Marquis, Christopher. 2001. "Inquiry on Peru Looks at a C.I.A. Contract." *New York Times,* 28 April, Foreign Desk, sec. A, p. 4.

McClintock, Cynthia. 2000. *The United States and Peru in the 90s: Cooperation with a Critical Caveat on Democratic Standards.* Washington, DC: George Washington University, Department of Political Science, June.

Menzel, Sewall H. 1996. "SOUTHCOM in the Andes." *Hemisphere* 6 (2): 38–41.

National Security and International Affairs Division [NSAID]. 1994. *Report to Congressional Requesters: Drug Control—U.S. Antidrug Efforts in Peru's Upper Huallaga Valley.* GAO/NSIAD-95–11. Washington, DC: U.S. Government Accounting Office, December, letter #1.

National Security Archive. 2002. *The Peruvian Townsend Commission Report and Declassified U.S. Documentation* [online]. Electronic Briefing Book No. 72, ed. Tamara Feinstein. Washington, DC: Townsend Commission [updated 26 June 2002; cited 16 May 2003]. Available from http://www.gwu.edu/~ nsarchiv/ NSAEBB/NSAEBB72/#docs.

Palmer, David Scott. 1992. "Peru, The Drug Business, and Shining Path: Between Scylla and Charybdis?" *Journal of InterAmerican Studies and World Affairs* 34 (3): 65–88.

Paredes, Pablo. 1997. "Dictature Civile, Société Militarisée: Le Pérou Otage d'un Pouvoir Autoritaire." *Le Monde Diplomatique* (June): 3.

School of the Americas. 1989a. *Counter Intelligence* [online]. Manual LN324-91. Washington, DC: U.S. Army School of the Americas [cited 2 April 2003]. Available from http://www.soaw.org/new/article.php?id=58.

———. 1989b. *Revolutionary War, Guerillas and Communist Ideology.* Washington, DC: U.S. Army School of the Americas.

———. 1989c. *Handling of Sources* [online]. Declassified manual ODCSINT # 19. Washington, DC: U.S. Army [cited 2 April 2003]. Available from http://www .soaw.org/new/article.php?id=46.

———. 1989d. *Terrorismo y Guerrilla Urbana* [online]. Translation into Spanish of the manual, *Terrorism and the Urban Guerilla.* Washington, DC: U.S. Army [cited 2 April 2003]. Available from http://www.soaw.org/new/article.php?id=83.

U.S. Army Intelligence and Security Command. 1992. *Country Profile: Peru.* Washington, DC: Department of the Army, United States Intelligence and Threat Analysis Center, May.

————. 1993. *Country Profile: Peru*, Part II. Washington, DC: Department of the Army, United States Intelligence and Threat Analysis Center.

U.S. Department of Defense and U.S. Department of State. 2000. *Foreign Military Training and DOD Engagement Activities of Interest* [online], Vol. I. Joint Report to Congress released January 2001, before Congress on 1 March 2000. Washington, DC: U.S. Department of Defense and U.S. Department of State, 1 March [cited 2 April 2003]. Available from http://www.state.gov/t/pm/rls/rpt/fmtrpt/2001/.

U.S. Embassy, Lima. 1993. Comments on Fujimori, Montesinos, but Not Barrios Altos. 22 January, Secret. Washington, DC: Department of State.

U.S. General Accounting Office. 2000. *Drug Control: International Counterdrug Sites Being Developed*. Caucus on International Narcotics Control. Washington, DC: U.S. Senate, Briefing Report to the Chairman, December.

U.S. State Department. 1989. *Human Rights Report: Peru*. Washington, DC: Government Printing Office.

————. 1991. *Country Reports on Human Rights Practices*. Report submitted to the Committee on Foreign Relations Affairs, House of Representatives. Washington, DC: Government Printing Office, February.

CHAPTER II

Turning on Their Masters
State Terrorism and Unlearning Democracy in Uruguay

JEFFREY J. RYAN

Introduction

The actions of the Uruguayan military regime represent one of the least explored and, in some ways, more inexplicable cases of state terrorism to occur during the authoritarian interlude that gripped the Southern Cone during most of the 1970s and 1980s. It is not surprising that Uruguay has been the focus of less attention than have its neighbors. The number of killed or disappeared in Uruguay is estimated in the hundreds, rather than the tens of thousands seen in Argentina. The collapse of democracy was a slow-motion affair in Uruguay, a "coup by quotas," rather than a rapid high-profile drama such as the September 1973 bombing of the presidential palace in Chile. And the Uruguayan regime itself, comprised of a series of fairly anonymous generals, had no widely recognized face, in contrast to the prominent "men on horseback" such as General Alfredo Stroessner in Paraguay or Chile's General Augusto Pinochet.

Nonetheless, the case of Uruguay is distinctive in a number of respects. For one thing, although the regime killed or disappeared a fairly small number of people relative to its regional counterparts, it made such extensive use of imprisonment and torture (particularly psychological torture) that by the mid-1970s Uruguay had the most political prisoners per capita of any nation in the world. A more remarkable distinction, however, might be the nearly absolute lack of indicators that Uruguayan democracy was so imperiled. Only a few years before the imposition of state terror, virtually no one would have thought such a nightmare was possible. The country, known as the "Switzerland of Latin America," had one of the most long-established, vibrant, and stable democracies in the hemisphere. Moreover, the ultimate agent of this democracy's destruction, the military, was almost comically ill equipped to pose a threat. As late as the early 1960s, "prior to heading home in the evenings," Uruguayan soldiers "would change out of their uniforms to avoid being mistaken for bus drivers; one of their main tasks was cleaning up litter on the beaches" (Servicio Paz y Justicia, 1992, xviii).

This chapter will attempt to explain how a traditionally weak, fairly apolitical military with a long history of subordination to civilian authorities eventually turned on both those authorities and society at large, imposing a dictatorship every bit as brutal as those elsewhere in the Southern Cone. While there are a host of internal factors responsible for this transformation, I will focus primarily on three key external influences behind the dramatic role shift on the part of the Uruguayan military. The first is the substantial infusion of resources, in terms of equipment, funding, and training, provided by the United States that sought to "professionalize" the institution as part of a broader U.S. hemispheric-security agenda. The second is the importation of foreign strategic paradigms, most notably the so-called National Security Doctrine and French counterinsurgency philosophy, which gave the military both a cognitive lens through which to view emerging internal "threats" and a rationale for abandoning their commitment to democratic (and human rights) norms.

Lastly, there is the logistical and tactical coordination between the Uruguayan military regime and its counterparts in Argentina, Brazil, Chile, and Paraguay that came to be known as Operation Condor. In essence, the international community provided the Uruguayan military with the means, the logic, and the tactical cooperation necessary to transform itself from an institution committed to serving and protecting the people to one determined to subordinate and terrorize them. What the Uruguayan case makes painfully apparent is that, when the external environment facilitates and endorses a flagrant disregard for human rights, even a long-established democratic culture affords no protection for threatened societies.

Background

As it entered the 1960s, Uruguay had impeccable democratic credentials. In a region where elected civilian rule was often fleeting or elusive, the country was viewed as an oasis of democracy.[1] An extensive social-welfare system—inaugurated by President José Batlle y Ordóñez in the early twenti-eth century—had given Uruguayans one of the highest standards of living in Latin America. Ironically, it was the very progressiveness of this system that ultimately played a key role in democratic rule's collapse.

In the late 1950s and 1960s, a series of economic setbacks exacerbated an already critical deficit crisis, seriously straining the state's capacity to provide the benefits to which its citizens had long been accustomed. The two tradi-tional parties were popularly seen as either unwilling or unable to resolve the crisis, and politics took on an increasingly confrontational and hard-edged tone. In 1967 alone the country experienced more than 700 strikes (Kohl and Litt, 1974, 201). As labor actions by leftist unions escalated, so too did the willingness of the government to resort to the sort of heavy-handed tactics that were all but unknown in Uruguay's recent memory.

It was in this context that an urban guerrilla movement—calling itself the Movimiento de Liberación Nacional-Tupamaros (MLN-T or the Tupa-maros)—emerged.[2] The Tupamaros had their origins in an ideologically di-verse grouping of largely middle-class leftists, whose most important faction was led by sugarcane-union organizer Raúl Sendic. Beginning in the early 1960s, the MLN-T embarked on a gradual buildup of its organization and in-frastructure, periodically "expropriating" money and arms in the process. They did not issue their first communiqué until 1967 and did not begin the armed struggle in earnest until a year later, when they kidnapped a close friend of the president.

Over the next several years, the Tupamaros demonstrated both an impres-sive tactical capacity and a well-developed sense of guerrilla theater. Their as-saults were designed simultaneously to embarrass the regime and bolster their image as crusading and caring idealists. The Robin Hood image culti-vated by the MLN-T through humor and creativity enraged the regime. As the guerrillas proved more daring and the regime less competent, Uruguay ap-peared as a bright red flash on Washington's Cold War radar screen.

The frustrated police and hard-line president Jorge Pacheco Areco (in office 1967–1972) turned to ever-more draconian measures, including repeated suspensions of civil liberties (*medidas prontas de seguridad*), the use of torture, and the creation of death squads. The Tupamaros responded in kind, escalat-ing the level of violence they employed—no one was laughing about the "rev-olution" any more.

A series of Tupamaro assassinations of officials implicated in the torture of prisoners, and the MLN-T's murder of kidnapped U.S. police instructor Dan

Mitrione in 1970, set in motion the final, if slow-motion, disintegration of democracy in Uruguay. The armed forces took power with a figurehead civilian in 1973 (whom they disposed of shortly thereafter) and initiated an eleven-year reign of repression the likes of which had not been seen in modern Uruguay.

While extrajudicial killings and disappearances were infrequent, relative to those carried out in neighboring police states, the use of torture and long imprisonments were both routine and extensive. Precise figures on the number of those seized by the regime are exceedingly difficult to come by, but most estimates suggest that a staggering 50,000–60,000 people, or roughly one in fifty Uruguayans, were detained at some point during the dictatorship. It appears as well that the vast majority of those held by the authorities were tortured. According to the authors of the report titled *Uruguay Nunca Más*, "[T]orture, during the dictatorship years, was widespread and routine and spared only in a few exceptional cases" (Servicio Paz y Justicia, 1992, 78).

A survey of released prisoners—conducted as part of that report—indicates that the victims were primarily male (roughly 80%), young (60% were between eighteen and twenty-nine years old), and residents of Montevideo (approximately 75%). The occupational strata from which victims were drawn are somewhat surprisingly diverse in class terms. Office clerks (25%), professionals (20%), workers (15%), full-time activists (12%), and students (7%) made up the bulk of those imprisoned (Servicio Paz y Justicia, 1992, 324–36).

The first targets of the security forces were the Tupamaros and their supporters. Once the M L N - T had been effectively destroyed as a militant force in the early 1970s, the armed forces widened its campaign to include two organizations with deep roots in Uruguay's political history: the Partido Comunista Uruguayo (the Communist party in Uruguay) and the Confederación Nacional de Trabajadores (C N T), the national labor union federation. Both groups, along with a number of smaller parties and other social organizations, were banned outright by the regime and saw thousands of their members imprisoned.

Eventually, the military broadened its definition of the enemy to include not only those espousing "subversive" ideologies, but also those who spoke out in defense of Uruguayan democracy. Senators, lawyers, and scores of soldiers and police were thrown into jail and tortured for their constitutionalist views. Ultimately, of course, the Uruguayan military itself bears sole responsibility for its intervention in civil society and for its subsequent crimes. Nonetheless, as we shall see, culpability for making the modernized terror apparatus they set up possible lies primarily with outsiders.

Foreign Assistance

Looking at tiny Uruguay in the 1960s, it would have been difficult to identify a country less likely to become a focal point of attention by the hemisphere's sole superpower. With a total national population smaller than most capital cities in the region, a near complete lack of critical resources, and a geostrategic importance that was marginal at best, one would hardly expect Washington to divert much of its finite energies or foreign aid resources there.

Yet when viewed through the magnifying glass of Cold War strategy in general, and the hemispheric National Security Doctrine in particular, Uruguay was transformed from a provincial backwater to a frontline state in the continental struggle against communist subversion. Not surprisingly, this exaggerated vision of both the strategic importance of Uruguay and the gravity of the threat posed by "subversive elements" there resulted in a disproportionately massive infusion of U.S. foreign aid. And while the economic and military assistance provided to Uruguay was only occasionally impressive in an absolute sense, in relative terms the largesse was remarkable.

Between 1950 and 1980, Uruguay received a total of $261.7 million in economic and military loans and grants, ranking it second from the bottom among Latin American aid recipients. This raw figure, however, masks both the priority Uruguay was accorded during some of the critical years within that time span and the enormous impact the aid had, given the country's size.[3]

In the three years leading up to the 1973 *golpe*, the coup d'état that brought the military to power, the United States dedicated an average of 9.5 percent of its total Latin American military-aid budget to Uruguay, and in one year (1970) it was the second largest military aid recipient in the hemisphere. The balance between economic and military assistance, moreover, provides a fairly clear picture of Washington's preoccupation with security issues in the case of Uruguay. Between 1960 and 1976, Uruguay's average rank among Latin American military aid recipients was seventh of twenty-four, while among economic aid recipients it averaged about fourteenth.

U.S. security assistance was provided to both the police and the armed forces and had three primary components: funding, equipment, and training. Most of the aid provided to the Uruguayan police forces was funded through the U.S. Agency for International Development (USAID) as part of its global Public Safety Program. The U.S. Department of Defense was the primary source of assistance to the military; funding was provided through the

Military Assistance Program (MAP), while equipment came either through Foreign Military Sales (FMS) credit financing or the Transfers of Excess Stock program. Additional assistance came through the International Military Education and Training (IMET) program, which will be discussed below.

While the money and materiel provided by the United States was certainly important, most observers point to the foreign training received by the Uruguayan security forces as the most significant external determinant of their transformation from a democratic to a dictatorial orientation. The vast majority of this training was carried out by the United States, although Brazilian and Argentine personnel were thought to have provided some of the more nefarious instruction, particularly in torture techniques.

Initially, most of the U.S. training was designed to "modernize" Uruguay's police forces. From 1964 to 1974, USAID—working through its Office of Public Safety (OPS)—carried out an ambitious program to transform what was perceived to be a rather hapless, ineffective department into a more capable ally in the war against communist subversion. Reports by U.S. advisors reveal a thinly veiled disdain for both the abilities and attitudes of their Uruguayan charges. A 1968 report by USAID officials in Montevideo noted:

> [T]he investigation capabilities and the procedures used by the police are frequently ineffective and are, on occasion, actually counterproductive. . . . [T]he present intelligence unit is not considered capable of coping with the clandestine activities of the Communist embassies and Communist block trade missions that exist in Uruguay, who are engaging in agitation, violence to suit their needs, and in the infiltration of labor, student and other important groups. Uruguay is also being used as a base of operations in this hemisphere by the communists. (Heinz and Frühling, 1999, 316–17)

To be sure, the Uruguayan police at the time were hardly the image of fearsome antisubversive shock troops that their allies desired. Langguth (1978, 240) relates the following anecdote to illustrate how woefully unprepared the local law-enforcement community was for assuming the new role cast for it by Washington:

> When the police chief decided that the children of Jorge Batlle, grandnephew of the great [former president] Batlle, should be protected,

he sent around two policemen armed with .38 Colt revolvers. Batlle spoke with the men and learned that they had never fired their guns. Policemen had to pay for their own ammunition, and these two could not afford the cost. Batlle bought each of them six bullets.

During the early years of the insurgency, the Tupamaros appear to have been equally unimpressed with their adversaries. Indeed, the guerrillas spent a good deal of their time prior to 1973 deliberately humiliating the police. One favorite tactic was a late night visit by a Tupamaro team to an officer's home, where his family was treated to a lecture on the advisability of a career change. Another was a massive jailbreak, such as the 1971 escape of more than one hundred Tupamaro prisoners from a supposedly maximum-security police facility. In 1967, a guerrilla leader noted that only about one in six of the police stationed in the capital "have been trained and equipped for truly military action," and that Uruguay's security forces in general were "sketchily equipped and trained, constitut[ing] one of the weakest organizations of repression in America" (Kohl and Litt, 1974, 233–34).

Alarmed by both the ineffectiveness of the police and their apparent failure to view the communist menace with sufficient alacrity, U.S. advisors set to work devising strategies for shoring up this weak link in the hemispheric-security network. These strategies focused not only on technical capacity building but also on a more intangible reorientation of the police from their traditional law-enforcement role to one focused on internal security. As the U S A I D report cited earlier notes:

> The police, because of the nature of their capabilities and responsibilities, are the primary counter-insurgency force in Uruguay. . . . With the improvement of police services to serve the populace and to keep public order, an automatic strengthening is possible in the overall counter-insurgency machinery. . . . Efforts by U.S. officers to impress the Uruguayans of the dangers of Communism and subversion must be continued so as to awaken additional interests, demands, and support for this important function . . . [U.S.] strategy aims to reorganize this [Intelligence] service and increase the use of modern technology and techniques to detect and apprehend criminal offenders and subversives. (Heinz and Frühling, 1999, 310–11)

The training itself was conducted in a variety of locations in the United States as well as in Uruguay. In all, 173 police officials took part in a total of 276 courses offered in U.S. facilities, with some officials attending up to four different courses. More than half of the classes were offered through the International Police Academy (IPA) in Washington, DC. Another third were carried out at the International Police Services School, also in Washington, where training focused on the administration of police archives (Fernández, 1986, 158). Both of these facilities, according to a number of sources, were at a minimum intimately linked to the Central Intelligence Agency (CIA), if not under the agency's direct control (Agee, 1986; Langguth, 1978).

At the IPA, students received training in a wide range of topics, but the focus was overwhelmingly turned toward issues of internal security rather than general law enforcement. Beyond the perceived practical benefits of U.S.-based training, a key purpose of the program was to produce a cadre of officials who would return to Uruguay as missionaries of American counterinsurgency methods and doctrine. Most of the training carried out at U.S. facilities appears not to have crossed the line of accepted international human rights norms, although that line was frequently skirted within it.

One course did, however, generate a good deal of controversy and is thought by many to be largely responsible for the OPS program's ultimate demise in 1974. This was a course called Investigations of Terrorist Activities, which was conducted at the U.S. Border Patrol Academy in Los Fresnos, Texas. According to information revealed by a congressional investigation, students in the course were trained in manufacturing and using explosives. When asked to account for why such training was either necessary or advisable, OPS officials—who had tried to keep the program under wraps—were at a loss. According to Langguth (1978, 240):

Except for one detail, OPS could have had an unassailable explanation for sending students to Los Fresnos. By now the world had entered upon a time of bombs and bomb threats. Public opinion might have readily accepted the argument that any nation's policemen needed training in the defusing and demolition of bombs. The problem for OPS was that the CIA's course at Los Fresnos did not teach men how to destroy bombs, only how to build them.

At least sixteen Uruguayan officials attended this particular course between 1969 and 1973. It is a disturbing coincidence that shortly after these
graduates returned home, right-wing death squads began adding dynamite
and bomb attacks to their tactical repertoire (Servicio Paz y Justicia, 1992,
199; Heinz and Frühling, 1999, 325–28).

As was noted above, the understandably limited information available indicates that U.S.-based instruction did not exceed "legitimate" (if harsh) standards of law-enforcement operations. What happened in training situations
outside the United States, however, is a different matter entirely. The most
damaging evidence of direct U.S. involvement in human-rights violations in
Uruguay relates to training carried out far from American shores.

Specifically, there is a growing body of data that U.S. advisors were actively
engaged in coordinating and possibly even conducting instruction of
Uruguayan personnel in advanced torture techniques. Some of the information directly linking U.S. personnel with torture comes from sources that
should be considered cautiously, but there is an increasing amount of evidence from declassified U.S. government material that lends credence to the
accounts contained in those sources.

Individuals, who purport to have first-hand knowledge of U.S. involvement
in the torture and murder of civilians in Uruguay, authored two of these accounts. The most well known of these is the book by a former CIA agent,
Philip Agee, which details his participation in various covert operations
throughout Latin America, including his two-year stint in Uruguay in the
mid-1960s. Lesser known is a similar memoir written by Manuel Hevia
Cosculluela, who also worked for the CIA in Uruguay but who turned out to
be a Cuban double agent. In both accounts, OPS official Dan Mitrione plays a
central role. Mitrione was a police instructor who came to Uruguay following
stints at both IPA and in Brazil. In 1970, he was kidnapped by the Tupamaros
and subsequently killed.[4]

Hevia claims that Mitrione's primary mission was to train local police in
more "scientific" methods of interrogation and to provide them with the technology necessary to implement such methods. He recounts being present
at an early training session in which four homeless people were rounded
up as subjects: "There was no interrogation, only a demonstration of different voltages on different parts of the human body, together with the uses
of a drug to induce vomiting—I don't know why or for what—and another
chemical substance. The four of them died." Hevia later reports a lengthy
conversation he purports to have had with Mitrione in which the U.S. advi-

sor laid out a chilling vision of his chosen "art," which was determination of "the precise pain":

> The precise pain, in the precise place, in the precise amount to achieve the effect. . . . When you receive a subject, the first thing to do is to determine his physical state, his degree of resistance, through a medical examination.
>
> "A premature death," he emphasized, "means a failure by the technician."
>
> "Another important thing to know is exactly how far you can go, given the political situation and the personality of the prisoner." Dan was really excited. He needed the kind of audience he had found in me. He continued, "It is very important to know beforehand whether we have the luxury of letting the subject die." It was the only time in all those months that his plastic eyes sparkled.
>
> Finally he concluded: "Before all else, you must be efficient. You must cause only the damage that is strictly necessary, not a bit more. We must control our tempers in any case. You have to act with the efficiency and cleanness of a surgeon and with the perfection of an artist. This is a war to the death. Those people are my enemy. This is a hard job, and someone has to do it, it's necessary. Since it's my turn, I'm going to do it to perfection. If I were a boxer, I would try to be the world champion. But I'm not. Nonetheless in this profession, my profession, I'm the best." (Hevia Cosculluela, cited in Fernández Huidobro, 1973)

In his memoir, Agee documents the role of the CIA's Technical Services Division in supplying sophisticated equipment, including torture devices, to the Uruguayan police. One of the police officials involved, Miguel Angel Benítez, later revealed as a Tupamaro informant, described Mitrione's involvement in one such shipment:

> According to the notes Benítez was keeping, when Mitrione arrived in Montevideo, the police were torturing prisoners with a rudimentary electric needle that had come from Argentina. Mitrione arranged for the police to get newer electric needles of varying thickness. Some needles were so thin they could be slipped between the teeth. Benítez understood that this equipment came to Montevideo inside the U.S. embassy's diplomatic pouch. (Langguth, 1978, 248)

Clearly sources such as double agents, CIA defectors, and guerrilla informants need to be considered with a healthy dose of skepticism. Nonetheless,
a number of more reliable accounts provide fairly persuasive confirmation of
the broad parameters of these stories. The most thorough attempt to explore
Mitrione's activities in Uruguay is the work of former *New York Times* journalist A. Jack Langguth. In his book, *Hidden Terrors*, Langguth's exhaustive research leads him to conclude that Mitrione was indeed directly implicated in
torture training and that Hevia's account is in the main corroborated by other
evidence.

More indirect corroboration can be found in a variety of other sources. For
example, a Uruguayan parliamentary commission investigating reports of
human rights abuses in April 1970 concluded: "The system of mistreatment,
brutality and torture used against prisoners by the police of Montevideo has
become habitual and, so to speak, normal. [This torture includes] the use of
electrical needles" (Weschler, 1998, 106–07). The report specifically notes
the use of the sort of specialized torture equipment other sources describe as
supplied by various U.S. agencies and that most of the documented abuses
occurred in the period following Mitrione's June 1969 arrival in Uruguay.
Similarly, a quote from a torture survivor resonates with strong echoes of
Mitrione's "scientific" method: "You have to understand that these guys were
specialists—the main torturers. They were highly trained in methods of ex-
acting the maximum pain without leaving any significant physical traces—
and, for that matter, without killing the victim in the process" (Weschler,
1998, 126).

Whether or not U.S. personnel were directly engaged in the practice or instruction of torture remains an open question. What is indisputable, however,
is how the U.S. role was instrumental in facilitating Uruguayans' torture
training by third-country "specialists" from Brazil and Argentina. Recently
declassified U.S. government documents are unambiguous in this regard. In
a State Department cable from the embassy in Montevideo to the National Security Council, dated August 25, 1971, U.S. strategy and the rationale behind
it is spelled out in explicit detail. The report is an analysis of current conditions in Uruguay and a set of policy recommendations for the coming five
years. In the section analyzing the political situation, the authors note:

> One of the most effective facets of [U.S. security assistance] programs
> is the training of Uruguayans abroad. Special emphasis should be made

to keep such training at a maximum level. It is especially desirable that such neighboring countries as Argentina and Brazil collaborate effectively with the Uruguayan security forces and where possible we should encourage such cooperation. (U.S. Embassy, Montevideo, 1971, 17)

The report then lists its recommended courses of action in the security realm, with frequent reference to the desirability of shifting the responsibility for training to parties other than official U.S. advisors. Among its recommendations:

Increased Training Abroad—To improve the capacity of Uruguayan services, particularly the Army and the DII,[5] to deal with terrorists every effort should be made to take advantage of opportunities to send Uruguayans to attend courses on such matters abroad.

Detention Procedures—To improve the capability of services to successfully detain, interrogate and imprison suspected terrorists, we should consider the advisability of providing expert advice, preferably through [temporary duty] personnel and utilizing third country specialists if possible, on effective detention procedures.

Strengthening the DII—To improve the intelligence capacity of the DII, U.S. or, if possible, third country agencies should provide training and, where appropriate, organizational and operational counsel. (U.S. Embassy, Montevideo, 1971, 17)

The cable is remarkable for its candor in this and other respects, noting elsewhere, for example, the need for a leftist union to "be broken." More troubling is how it reveals Washington's clear recognition that the training was of such a questionable nature that a discreet distance needed to be maintained between it and the U.S. government. This is nowhere more apparent than in the section on "detention procedures," which urges increased use of private contractors (TDY, or Temporary Duty personnel) and the starkly euphemistic "third-country specialists," for the disreputable business at hand.[6]

Most of these "specialists" had, of course, acquired some of their expertise during earlier training sessions by U.S. instructors, although once trained they tended to refine their techniques through extensive practice.[7] Having helped to create such a cadre of experts elsewhere in the Southern Cone, U.S. officials eventually preferred to play matchmaker in Uruguay. In a sort of perverse student-exchange program, U.S. advisors organized working visits by their Brazilian alumni to assist their less advanced Uruguayan pupils: "Members of Brazil's death squads . . . were brought to the Montevideo Police. Mitrione arranged these meetings. This was typical of the style of the North American [security] agencies: facilitate and encourage coordination between military and paramilitary groups in the region, without appearing in the credits" (Boccia Paz, 2002, 74). Indeed, the Uruguayans were treated to periodic visits by renowned overachievers such as the infamous Brazilian torturer and death-squad founder Sérgio Fleury: "After he shot [Brazilian guerrilla leader] Carlos Marighela in November 1969, Sérgio Fleury of Sao Paulo became celebrated among Uruguayan police. He met with groups of them, on at least two occasions through CIA contacts" (Langguth, 1978, 240).[8]

Argentine specialists got into the act as well, with both the knowledge and presumed support of U.S. officials. Only two days after the aforementioned cable recommended fostering further collaboration among Southern Cone security forces, the U.S. embassy in Buenos Aires informed Washington that such cooperation was already underway. The communiqué describes Argentina's preoccupation with and assistance to its troubled neighbor:

> Argentine authorities have long been distressed over Uruguayan ineffectiveness in combating subversion. . . . GOA [government of Argentina] has sought to strengthen anti-subversive capabilities of GOU [government of Uruguay] through training and counsel, as in case of interrogation team dispatched to Montevideo when Tupamaro Raúl Sendic was captured. (U.S. Embassy, Buenos Aires, 1971, 1–2)

A key to the success of the United States in inculcating its vision of effective internal security practices and in imparting the technical capacity to carry them out was the placement of those so trained in positions of influence. By the early 1970s, seven of the top ten posts in the Montevideo police department were occupied by IPA graduates, more than 1,000 officers had been trained in country, and all 931 members of the investigations division had received in-service training by U.S. advisors with "specific emphasis [given] to upgrading the Division's abilities in the collection and evaluation of information and infiltration of subversive groups" (USAID-Montevideo, cited in Heinz and Frühling, 1999, 314–19). Those local officials who took exception to use of the harsher methods being introduced by these advisors were marginalized and ultimately removed.[9]

Over time, both U.S. advisors and the Uruguayan military and civilian hardliners became increasingly exasperated with the seeming inability of the police to contain the Tupamaro threat. This led to mounting pressure on the Uruguayans to make greater use of the armed forces in the counterinsurgency effort. As Gillespie (1991, 41–42) points out:

> The sophistication and success of the guerrillas in outwitting the Uruguayan police made the calls to bring in the armed forces increasingly difficult to resist. . . . The armed forces had previously been unprestigious and apolitical, but the crisis of the 1960s coincided with exposure to national-security doctrines taught by U.S. advisers and teachers at the Army School of the Americas in Panama. Those doctrines made a fetish out of the need to contain Soviet expansionism in the Third World following the Cuban revolution.

Although calls for deeper involvement by the military became more insistent in the late 1960s, Washington had been pushing for closer collaboration between police and military forces in the fight against "subversives" throughout the region for a number of years. The 1962 course catalog from the U.S. Army School of the Americas (SOA) in Panama, for example, chronicles the early efforts to encourage such collaboration:

> [SOA has] developed a closer relationship with the Inter-American Police Academy in order to form a more potent counterinsurgency team. . . . All courses have undergone major modifications during the past eighteen months in support of the counterinsurgency effort. Not only those courses whose title includes the term counterinsurgency, but every course taught has definite application in the counterinsurgency field. . . . Without exception, the instructor and student are made fully aware of the importance of the total effort which must go into the establishment of internal security and the nation-building effort necessary for stamping out communist-led and communist-fed insurgencies. (Leuer, 2000, 13)

As early as 1967, U.S. military officials were actively discussing establishing an operations center to be utilized jointly by Uruguayan police and
military forces (cited in Heinz and Frühling, 1999, 320). In the August 1971
strategy cable noted earlier, there are a number of references to the need for
a greater military role in antisubversion activities, including the following:

> This effort [to improve Uruguayan counterinsurgency capacity] should
> be coupled with programs to continue to orient the armed forces to-
> ward more effective support of the police on internal security matters,
> and to provide both the police and the armed forces with the materiel,
> or access to materiel, necessary to implement their organizational and
> operational efforts. (USAID-Montevideo, cited in Heinz and Frühling,
> 1999, 16)

Within a month of these recommendations, the military went well beyond
assuming an "effective support" role. On September 9, 1971, President
Pacheco signed a decree granting full responsibility for the "antisubversive
struggle" to the armed forces and ordering the police to "lend whatever collaboration [the military] might require" (Zabalza, 1995, 36).

By the time Pacheco turned things over to the military, they had already
been well prepared. In the years leading up to 1971, the U.S. military training
program for Uruguay had accelerated at a feverish pace. Between 1950—
when the IMET program began—and 1972, a total of 2,119 Uruguayan personnel were trained at U.S. facilities. Yet roughly half of those students were
trained between 1966 and 1972 and fully a third (705) attended courses in
the three years leading up to and shortly after Pacheco's decree (Fernández,
1986, 182).

Furthermore, the balance between students attending more "traditional"
courses offered at facilities within the United States and those sent for more
"specialized" (that is, counterinsurgency) training at the School of the Americas in Panama shifted dramatically during this period. From 1950 to 1964,
only about 17 percent of graduates had trained in Panama, while from 1965
to 1972 the figure jumped to nearly 45 percent. In the first six months of 1971
alone, 45 cadets attended the Internal Security Operations course, 18 took the
Counterinsurgency in Urban Areas course, and five officers were trained in
military intelligence.[10]

By 1972, the U.S. Department of Defense agreed to assign a military intelligence advisor to Uruguay on the basis of the "increased involvement of

the Uruguayan Armed Forces in the urban counterinsurgency efforts of the GOU," although it went on to caution that "the position [should] not be overtly identified as that of intelligence advisor" (U.S. Department of Defense, cited in Heinz and Frühling, 1999, 325). Little of substance changed as a result of the shift in U.S. priorities from supporting the police to backing the military as the principal counterinsurgency force. As with the police, much of the training and technology had already been provided prior to or contemporaneous with the implementation of ever-harsher repression.

In the case of the military, U.S. training continued or even accelerated after the generals had delivered the death knell to democratic rule in June 1973. A total of 710 Uruguayans were trained (319 at SOA) from the time of the coup until the United States cut off military assistance in early 1977, meaning that Washington trained a third as many troops in the four years following the coup as they had in the previous twenty-three years (Fernández, 1986, 182; SOA data). In addition to providing this training, of course, the United States was supplying hefty amounts of funding and equipment to the Uruguayan military. In fact, U.S. assistance actually peaked two years after the coup, reaching $9.2 million—which amounted to a remarkable $428 per soldier.[11]

Once in power, the military amplified and perfected the systems of repression introduced earlier. As with the police, military officers who were reluctant to abandon their commitment to democratic principles and demonstrated insufficient enthusiasm for the new National Security Doctrine model were purged (Rial, 1986, 27). Those who remained set to work realizing the vision of a modern, efficient, antisubversion apparatus that they had been exposed to by their U.S. advisors, as Porzecanski (1973, 68) observes:

> The armed forces' counterinsurgency efforts were based mostly on the systematic use of interrogation and torture. The military was much more thorough than the police in the extent to which it interrogated yet more careful in the degree to which it did so. Broadly speaking, Uruguay's police had become known for their haphazard and brutal interrogation sessions. . . . With the armed forces, interrogation became much more prolonged, systematic, and "sophisticated."

Again, there are disturbing indications of both what this "sophistication" entailed and how it was acquired. The most troubling direct source of information on what sorts of lessons the Uruguayans and others were learning in Panama is the CIA instruction manual used in courses there. A 1963 document, "KUBARK Counterintelligence Interrogation" (KUBARK was the code word for CIA), is a how-to guide for foreign interrogators and was utilized in their training until at least the mid-1980s. There are references throughout to torture techniques and, although there are also scattered disclaimers, it is clear that such methods were considered "acceptable" under certain circumstances. For example, in the section titled, "Legal and Policy Implications," one finds the following telling snippet:

> [P]rior Headquarters approval . . . must be obtained for the interrogation of any source against his will and under any of the following circumstances: 1) If bodily harm is to be inflicted; 2) If medical, chemical, or electrical methods or materials are to be used to induce acquiescence. (U.S. Central Intelligence Agency, 1963, 7)

Elsewhere, in a chapter called ominously, "Coercive Counterintelligence Interrogation of Resistant Sources," there is a detailed description of one approach that seems particularly relevant in the case of Uruguay. One of the most common forms of torture used by the military was the *plantón*, in which prisoners were forced to stand naked and hooded for long periods of time, several days in some instances. Two other forms, *la bandera* (the flag, in which victims were hung by their wrists in a spread-eagle fashion for hours) and *el cabellete* (the horseback, in which prisoners were straddled naked on a metal bar with the feet off the ground), were also frequently employed. In each of these methods, the prisoner was left alone with no interrogator present. The KUBARK manual provides a clue as to where the Uruguayans may have come up with the idea:

> It has been plausibly suggested that, whereas pain inflicted on a person from outside himself may actually focus or intensify his will to resist, his resistance is likelier to be sapped by pain which he seems to inflict upon himself. "In the simple torture situation the contest is one between the individual and his tormentor . . . (and he can frequently endure). When the individual is told to stand at attention for long periods, an intervening factor is introduced. The immediate source of pain is not the interrogator but the victim himself. The motivational strength of the individual is likely to exhaust itself in this internal encounter. . . . As

long as the subject remains standing, he is attributing to his captor the power to do something worse to him, but there is actually no showdown of the ability of the interrogator to do so." (U.S. Central Intelligence Agency, 1963, 93)

As the report on human rights abuses compiled by Servicio Paz y Justicia, a nongovernmental human rights organization, points out, torture in Uruguay was neither random nor senseless, but rather scientific and purposeful:

[T]orture was a policy deliberately planned by the Uruguayan military and police; it was not the aberrant behavior of crazed jailers. In fact, [survivors] interviewed were convinced that the military had studied cycles of increasing suffering and were coordinating and tailoring their torture to particular characteristics of individual prisoners. (Servicio Paz y Justicia, 1992, 88)

In short, by the time the military got down to business, they were not the feeble garbage men in uniform that they had been a decade or so earlier; they were now professional technicians of terror.

Imported Doctrine

It is obvious that without foreign, primarily U.S., assistance, the Uruguayan security forces would have been quite simply incapable of initiating a campaign of terror that was institutionalized, comprehensive, and technologically sophisticated. Yet while this assistance gave the Uruguayan police and military the technical capacity for repression, they still needed some sort of rationale or cognitive framework for exercising this capacity in practice. In effect, the Uruguayan military had been given a hammer—they now needed a justification for using it.

As they inched toward taking power, the armed forces were confronted with a host of decisions that would have been difficult, if not impossible, to take in the absence of a legitimizing paradigm. Lacking one of their own, the generals once more looked beyond their borders for answers. Drawing from a variety of outside sources, the Uruguayans cobbled together their own particular version of the National Security Doctrine so zealously embraced by their military brethren elsewhere in the region. As in the case of local "refinement" of foreign-learned terror techniques, the Uruguayan armed forces took basic elements of preexisting doctrine and adapted them to suit their needs. The primary influence in this process, according to a number of sources, was the French doctrine of *guerre révolutionnaire* developed during the independence struggle in Algeria.[12]

Perelli has persuasively argued that scholars have often misconstrued the role of the National Security Doctrine in precipitating terroristic regimes in Latin America. She suggests that the doctrine was less important as a "coup trigger" than as a post hoc mechanism for resolving contradictions within military institutions that had already embarked on a repressive course. She notes:

> The doctrine not only provided answers to some of the central questions the military were dealing with at the time, but it also had the advantage of simplicity and the aptness of having been created by other military officers who . . . faced a comparable threat. It also incorporated elements vindicating the practices of repression and ritualized destruction of others by providing transcendental goals that justified them. . . . The new doctrine had the important advantage of setting out in unambiguous moral, political and practical terms the problem of control and repression. (Perelli, 1993, 28)

The need for justification was particularly pronounced in Uruguay because of both the democratic culture, which permeated all levels of society—including the armed forces themselves—and the introduction of state terror in a nation that had virtually never known it. By embarking on a path that violated the very essence of their identity, the military needed desperately to redefine and re-vindicate itself:

> In [taking power], they transgressed not only all codes of what Uruguayans had traditionally considered acceptable political behavior, but they also defied the myths that depicted their institution as a Republican all-volunteer force qualitatively different from the intervention-prone armed forces of the region. . . . These factors created high levels of cognitive dissonance among members of the officers' corps. . . . The alacrity with which the doctrine was adopted by Uruguayan officers was contingent upon the magnitude of the transgression that they felt they were performing when they violated the

country's institutional arrangements and installed a regime of terror. (Perelli, 1993, 35–37)

The military also needed to come up with a good reason to continue down that bloody path in the future. In order to utilize the imported paradigm as a justificatory schema, the military faced two tasks. The first was to demonstrate that the conditions of war spelled out in the doctrine were in fact present in Uruguay. To this end, the regime set about documenting the full scope of the specter hanging over the country in near pathological detail. The military presses worked overtime to detail the terrorist crimes being wrought on the tiny but valiant country. Among the titles they churned out were the exhaustive two-volume opus, *Subversion: From the Armed Forces to the People of Uruguay* (Junta de Comandantes en Jefe, 1976), the grim exposé, *UJC: School of Communism* (Dirección Nacional de Información e Inteligencia, 1977), and the indignant *Testimony of a Nation Aggrieved* (Comando General del Ejército de Uruguay, 1978).

The second task involved producing a cogent defense of the indefensible, namely the perpetuation of a state of terror. Here the regime faced something of a quandary. By their own account, they had defeated the guerrillas' armed threat months before they even took over power.[13] Having taken credit for this victory, the military had deprived itself of a key reason for continuing a campaign of repression. In order to remedy this, the armed forces turned to the definitions of threat and enemy laid out in foreign doctrine. Note, for example, the parallels between French counterinsurgency theorist Roger Trinquier's vision of the nature of subversive conflict and the role of the citizenry and the views of the Uruguayan generals a decade later:

> The battlefield today is no longer restricted. It is limitless; it can encompass entire nations. The inhabitant in his home is the center of the conflict. . . . Like it or not . . . he has become a combatant also. Therefore, it is essential to prepare him for the role he will have to play and to enable him to fulfill it effectively on our side. . . . [W]e must have him participate in his own defense. (Trinquier, 1964, 29–30)

> The gravest threat against the body of the nation is the danger of an intrusion of foreign ideologies into the minds of the people. . . . The people must therefore assume the responsibility of their own defense and unmask and destroy the many forms of these types of aggressions.[14]

Tactical Cooperation

A final key external influence in the imposition of state terror in Uruguay is the tactical cooperation extended to the military by security forces in neighboring dictatorships. It is a tragic yet remarkable fact that the majority of Uruguayans who died or were disappeared—as a result of the regime's repressive policies—were killed not inside their native country but abroad. Human rights investigators have been able to document 164 cases of forced disappearance (and presumed death) of Uruguayan citizens from 1971 to 1981. Only thirty-two of these occurred on Uruguayan soil, while the remainder took place outside the country, primarily in Argentina (Servicio Paz y Justicia, 1992, 214).

These disappearances, as well as other atrocities, were carried out as part of a coordinated effort by police states in South America to create what has been called "a veritable game reserve for hunting down anyone these regimes thought objectionable" (Servicio Paz y Justicia, 1992, 262). The undertaking was called Operation Condor and, in addition to the Uruguayan armed forces, involved the security forces of Brazil, Chile, Argentina, and Paraguay (see McSherry, this volume).

As has already been demonstrated, by the time the Uruguayan military took power they had been well equipped, materially and ideologically, to terrorize the population. Condor is thus important principally insofar as it enabled the regime to extend its campaign beyond national boundaries. The cooperation in terms of training noted previously was now simply expanded to the tactical realm. This proved particularly advantageous for the Uruguayan dictatorship in cases where its "enemies" were deemed especially noxious.

The regime, as a rule, tended to be somewhat squeamish when it came to outright liquidation of its opponents—preferring instead to torture and imprison them for years on end without killing them. The juntas next door, however, displayed no such reticence. Thus, when drastic measures were seen as necessary, the Uruguayans preferred that the dirty work be conducted outside the country. This was the case, for example, when two high-profile foes of the regime were assassinated in Buenos Aires in 1976. Senator Zelmar Michelini and Héctor Gutiérrez Ruíz, the president of Uruguay's House of Deputies, had been extremely vocal in condemning human rights abuses in Uruguay, and they were becoming a significant nuisance to the generals. A joint Uruguayan-Argentine military command kidnapped and later murdered both politicians, reportedly at the behest of the highest levels of the government in Montevideo (Martorell, 1999, 147–64; Boccia Paz, 2002, 151–53; Servicio Paz y Justicia, 1992, 266–69).

Although Condor was more or less exclusively a Latin American enterprise, the government of the United States was fully aware of the operation and, at least indirectly, implicated in it. The architects of Condor had become acquainted with each other, after all, primarily through contacts arranged by Washington, particularly through SOA programs. In fact, Condor participants coordinated their operation using U.S. facilities in Panama, as a declassified cable from the U.S. ambassador to Paraguay reveals:

> They keep in touch with one another through a U.S. communications installation in the Panama Canal Zone, which covers all of Latin America. This U.S. communications facility is used mainly by student officers to call home to Latin America but is also employed to co-ordinate intelligence information among the Southern Cone countries. (U.S. State Department, 1978)

The ambassador goes on to suggest that the use of these facilities came as a surprise to him and recommends that it be investigated. Nonetheless, with or without explicitly intending to do so, the United States again provided the technology necessary for terroristic states in the region to carry out their campaign of repression.

Conclusion

Most observers of the tragedy that befell Uruguay during the 1970s and 1980s have concluded that the disintegration of political and civil life leading up to the 1973 coup made the military's intervention all but inevitable. Yet, what is clear from this analysis is that external factors played an integral role in shaping the nature of the regime and, in particular, its use of violence once it had come to power. At the outset of the crisis period, the Uruguayan security forces were simply incapable of the sort of systematized modern repression already underway next door in Brazil and Argentina.

By the time they seized control in 1973, that situation had changed as a result of the training, equipment, and funding they had received from the

United States. Likewise, importing and adapting national security doctrines from foreign strategists gave the Uruguayan military a justificatory logic for retaining power and perpetuating their reign of terror. Finally, the tactical coordination embodied in Operation Condor formalized the integration of Uruguay into a hemispheric network of brutality that was transnational in scope and sophisticated in execution.

NOTES

1. Several first-rate works on the life, death, and resurrection of Uruguayan democracy are available (see, for example, Gillespie, 1991; González, 1993; Weinstein, 1988).

2. A more comprehensive treatment, from the impressive amount of material on the Tupamaros, can be found in Porzecanski, 1973; Fernández Huidobro, 1989, 1999; Gilio, 1971.

3. Figures on U.S. aid are from United States Agency for International Development (n.d.).

4. The 1973 film *State of Siege* by Costa-Gavras is based on this episode.

5. The Directorate of Intelligence and Information (DII) was a counterinsurgency unit within the police that was established at the behest of U.S. advisors.

6. For more on the trend toward the use of private military subcontractors by the U.S. government, see also Beggar, in this volume.

7. Weschler (1998, 62), for example, recounts the testimony of a Brazilian torture survivor whose tormentors exhibited the glee of a student who has surpassed his teacher: "'They said with great pride that in this matter [the development of more ingenious torture methods] they owed nothing to any foreign organizations. On the contrary, they told me, they were already exporting know-how on the subject.'"

8. Caula and Silva (1986, 40–4) report a flurry of exchanges between Uruguayan police and military personnel and their Brazilian and Argentine counterparts in the late 1960s, largely at the instigation of William Cantrell, chief of USAID at the time and reportedly a CIA employee. Virtually all of those participating in these exchanges were later directly implicated in death-squad activity in Uruguay.

9. The most well known case involved Alejandro Otero, director of the DII section with primary responsibility for combating the Tupamaros. According to Porzecanski, Otero was widely viewed as a highly effective and thorough officer who was scrupulous in both his investigative technique and his respect for the human rights of prisoners. His dismissal in January 1970 came about because "his superior officers reportedly . . . disagreed with his practice of being 'soft' on captured guerrillas [while]

Otero was supposedly upset by . . . the introduction and extensive application of torture by fellow police detectives and American police advisor Dan A. Mitrione. . . . Three months after Mr. Otero's dismissal, one of his superior officers, H. Morán Charquero . . . was shot and killed by the guerrillas because of his alleged use of torture on captured Tupamaros" (Porzecanski, 1973, 55). See also Langguth (1978, 248), who suggests it was Otero's confrontation with Mitrione over the torture of one of Otero's female acquaintances that precipitated his removal.

10. Author's calculations using a U.S. Department of Defense (n.d.) database listing all Uruguayan s o a graduates.

11. From 1966 to 1975, the average amount of U.S. military aid per soldier in Uruguay was $332, a figure that dwarfs that in the neighboring police states of Argentina ($110) and Brazil ($70). Author's calculations are based on United States Agency for International Development (n.d.) for military aid and Wilkie (1977) for data on the size of each country's armed forces.

12. Weschler also notes that "when the Uruguayan military went after the Tupamaros in earnest, their models were the French commandos in Algiers, systematically dismantling underground cells one tortured member at a time. They had all read the books of Jacques Massu, commander of the French paratroopers in Algeria. Indeed, they had even studied . . . the film *The Battle of Algiers* as a training exercise. The French were particularly helpful on questions of tactics and justifications for those tactics" (1998, 120–21).

13. In fact, the armed forces claimed they not only destroyed the "seditious military apparatus" but also accomplished the "neutralization of collateral factors which create an environment conducive to the development of subversion" (Junta de Comandantes en Jefe, 1976, 364–5; author's translation).

14. See Junta de Comandantes en Jefe (1976, 13)(author's translation). Elsewhere, one finds a rather curious use of foreign "models" in a book written by former Minister of Justice Fernando Bayardo Bengoa. In elaborating the regime's Orwellian vision of "human rights," Bayardo seeks legal precedent for repressing people on the basis of crimes they might commit (*peligrosidad sin delito*) through reference to both U.S. Supreme Court rulings and Spanish laws from the era of dictator Francisco Franco (see Bayardo Bengoa, 1979).

BIBLIOGRAPHY

Agee, Philip. 1986. *Inside the Company: CIA Diary*. New York: Bantam.

Bayardo Bengoa, Fernando. 1979. *Los Derechos del Hombre y la Defensa de la Nación*, 2nd ed. Montevideo: A. M. Fernández.

Boccia Paz, Alfredo. 2002. *En los Sótanos de los Generales: Los Documentos Ocultos del Operativo Cóndor*. Asunción: Servilibro.

Caula, Nelson, and Alberto Silva. 1986. *Alto el Fuego*. Montevideo: Monte Sexto.
Comando General del Ejército de Uruguay. 1978. *Testimonio de una Nación Agredida*. Montevideo: El Comando.

Dirección Nacional de Información e Inteligencia. 1977. *UJC, Escuela de Comunismo*. Montevideo: Universidad de la República, División Publicaciones y Ediciones.

Fernández, Wilson. 1986. *El Gran Culpable: La Responsabilidad de Los EE.UU. en el Proceso Militar Uruguayo*. Montevideo: Ediciones Atenea.
Fernández Huidobro, Eleutorio. 1973. *La Tregua Armada*. Montevideo: Tae Editorial.
———. 1989. *Actas Tupamaras*. Montevideo: Tae Editorial.
———. 1999. *Historia de los Tupamaros*. Montevideo: Banda Oriental.

Gilio, María Esther. 1971. *La Guerrilla Tupamara*. Montevideo: Biblioteca de Marcha.
Gillespie, Charles. 1991. *Negotiating Democracy: Politicians and Generals in Uruguay*. New York: Cambridge University Press.
González, Luis Eduardo. 1993. *Estructuras Políticas y Democracia en Uruguay*. Montevideo: Fundación de Cultura Universitaria.

Heinz, Wolfgang S., and Hugo Frühling. 1999. *Determinants of Gross Human Rights: Violations by State and State-sponsored Actors in Brazil, Uruguay, Chile, and Argentina, 1960–1990*, vol. 59, *International Studies in Human Rights*. Cambridge, MA: M. Nijhoff.

Junta de Comandantes en Jefe. 1976. *Las Fuerzas Armadas al Pueblo Oriental la Subversión*. Montevideo: Junta de Comandantes en Jefe.

Kohl, James, and John Litt. 1974. *Urban Guerrilla Warfare in Latin America*. Cambridge: Massachusetts Institute of Technology Press.

Langguth, A. J. 1978. *Hidden Terrors* [online]. New York: Pantheon Books [cited 25 November 2002]. Available from http://www.thirdworldtraveler.com/Torture/Hidden_Terrors.html.
Leuer, Joseph. 2000. "The Hot Wars in Latin America: The Panama Years (1961–1984)" [online]. In *Adelante: U.S. Army School of the Americas*, final ed., 15 December, 13. Washington, DC: Department of Defense [cited 25 November 2002]. Available from http://carlisle-www.army.mil/usamhi/usarsa/ADELANTE/ADELANTE%20-%20FINAL%20ISSUE/HotWars.pdf.

Martorell, Francisco. 1999. *Operación Cóndor, el Vuelo de la Muerte: La Coordinación Represiva en el Cono Sur*. Santiago de Chile: Lom Ediciones.

Perelli, Carina. 1993. "From Counterrevolutionary Warfare to Political Awakening: The Uruguayan and Argentine Armed Forces in the 1970s." *Armed Forces and Society* 20 (Fall): 25–49.

Porzecanski, Arturo C. 1973. *Uruguay's Tupamaros: The Urban Guerrilla*. New York: Praeger.

Rial, Juan. 1986. *Las Fuerzas Armadas: Soldados-Políticos Garantes de la Democracia?* Montevideo: CIESU Centro de Informaciones y Estudios del Uruguay.

Servicio Paz y Justicia (SERPAJ). 1992. *Uruguay Nunca Más: Human Rights Violations, 1972–1985*. Philadelphia: Temple University Press.

Trinquier, Roger. 1964. *Modern Warfare: A French View of Counterinsurgency*. New York: Praeger.

United States Agency for International Development. n.d. *U.S. Overseas Loans, Grants and Authorizations July 1, 1945–September 30, 2000* [online]. Washington, DC: Office of Planning and Budgeting, Bureau for Program Policy and Coordination, Agency for International Development [cited 25 November 2002]. Available from http://qesdb.cdie.org/gbk/index.html.

U.S. Army School of the Americas (SOA) data. Available from http://carlisle-www.army.mil/usamhi/usarsa/center.htm.

U.S. Central Intelligence Agency. 1963. *KUBARK Counterintelligence Interrogation* [online]. Washington, DC: U.S. Central Intelligence Agency, 7 [updated July 1963; cited 25 November 2002]. Available from http://www.parascope.com/articles/0397/kubark06.htm.

U.S. Department of Defense. n.d. "SOA Students and Instructors from Uruguay 1949–1996" [online]. Washington, DC: Department of Defense [cited 25 November 2002]. Available from http://www.derechos.org/soa/uy4996.html.

U.S. Embassy, Buenos Aires. 1971, 27 August. *Subject: Uruguayan Situation* [online]. Washington, DC: Department of State [updated 27 August 1971; cited 25 November 2002], 1–2. Available from http://www.gwu.edu/~ nsarchiv/NSAEBB/NSAEBB71/doc4.pdf.

U.S. Embassy, Montevideo. 1971. *Preliminary Analysis and Strategy Paper-Uruguay*, 25 August (cable)[online]. Washington, DC: Department of State, 25 August, 17 [updated 25 August 1971; cited 25 November 2002]. Available from http://www.gwu.edu/~ nsarchiv/NSAEBB/NSAEBB71/doc2.pdf.

U.S. State Department. 1978. *Subject: Second Meeting with Chief of Staff re Letelier Case* [online]. Cable from U.S. Ambassador Robert White (Paraguay) to the Secretary of State, Cyrus Vance. Washington, DC: Department of State, 20 October [updated 6 March 2001; cited 25 November 2002]. Available from http://www.gwu.edu/~nsarchiv/news/20010306/.

Weinstein, Martin. 1988. *Uruguay: Democracy at the Crossroads.* Boulder: Westview Press.

Weschler, Lawrence. 1998. *A Miracle, a Universe: Settling Accounts with Torturers.* Chicago: The University of Chicago Press.

Wilkie, James, ed. 1977. *Statistical Abstract of Latin America.* Latin American Center Publications University of California, Vol. 18. Los Angeles: University of California, Los Angeles.

Zabalza, Jorge. 1995. *El Tejazo y Otras Insurrecciones.* Montevideo: Editorial Tae.

CHAPTER 12

Producing and Exporting State Terror
The Case of Argentina

ARIEL C. ARMONY

Introduction

How are we to explain the use of state terror as a counterinsurgency tool? What are the main factors that account for an authoritarian regime's decision to kill its own citizens? Is state terror only endogenous to a given nation, or can it travel from one country to another? This chapter argues, first, that state terror is a result of a variety of internal factors and external influences—which interact in complex ways—and second, that the know-how associated with state terror can be circulated as a particular type of commodity, thus exported and deployed in different settings. As this chapter shows, the United States—a central actor in the export of know-how for state terror in the 1960s and 1970s—was not the only actor in the Americas playing this role. Indeed, Argentina is an interesting case of a Latin American country that produced and exported state terror expertise, which allowed this nation to assume an important role in the hemispheric struggle against "communism" during the latter part of the Cold War. Argentina played this role initially as an independent actor and then as a proxy for the United States.

The first part of the chapter proposes a model to explain the production of state terror. It illustrates this model with the case of Argentina's dirty war that lasted from the mid-1970s to the early 1980s. Ostensibly launched against subversion—a concept defined by its very unpredictability and measurelessness—the dirty war was waged against enemies who were perceived to range from locally armed guerrillas to the international human rights organizations that denounced the military's abuses. The armed forces, who ruled the country through a military junta from 1976 until 1983, claimed to act on behalf of "the highest interests of the nation" and to be preventing both "the dissolution of Argentine society" and "the disappearance of [the] Fatherland as a state" (Loveman and Davies, 1989, 200, 203).[1] This process tolerated no opposition.

The second part of the chapter discusses some aspects of Argentina's extraterritorial activities and its collaboration with the United States in the promotion of counterrevolution in Central America. The dirty war in Argentina, which resulted in the disappearance of thousands of citizens and left profound scars in the social fabric, served as a prototype for military ventures beyond the country's borders. The perpetrators of the dirty war in Argentina transferred their repressive model to Bolivia and Central America, asserting counterinsurgency as a form of mass murder, torture, and terror. In July 1980, the Argentine military became involved in a major, and violent, extraterritorial operation: the coup d'état in Bolivia led by army commander General Luis García Meza. In the late 1970s and early 1980s, Argentina provided counterinsurgency training and military assistance to El Salvador, Guatemala, and Honduras, and played a crucial role in the organization of exiled Nicaraguan national guardsmen into an anti-Sandinista force.

Argentina's extraterritorial operations in Central America in the early 1980s made tangible the convergence of conceptions of national security held by the Argentine military dictatorship and those of the administration of U.S. President Ronald Reagan. Indeed, the U.S.-Argentine cooperation in Central America was not an incidental concurrence on security issues but the corollary of a coinciding paradigm that viewed popular unrest as the product of an international communist scheme. Paradoxically, Argentine veterans of the dirty war (who had committed atrocious violations of human rights in the name of Western and Christian civilization) became an eventual surrogate force for the U.S. promotion of "democratic" politics in Central America.

A Model to Explain Repression

Accounting for the decision of rulers to kill their own citizens and to instill fear in their societies poses difficult questions, which, in my view, can only be answered from a multidimensional and multilevel perspective. State terror—"a premeditated, patterned, and instrumental form of government violence" (Pion-Berlin and Lopez, 1991, 63)—cannot be explained as the product of perverted military officers, an all-encompassing anticommunist ideology, or a U.S.-sponsored scheme. Indeed, it is necessary to adopt an analytical approach that allows us to understand how interactions at various

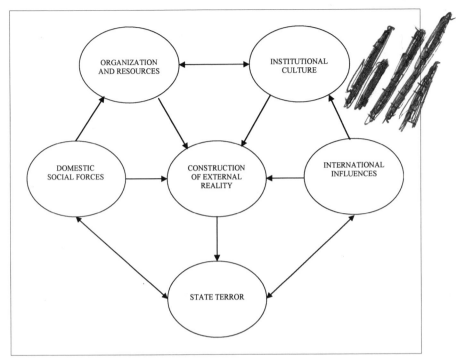

FIGURE 12.1 State terror: a model indicating main linkages.

levels yielded specific state responses to perceived threats to national security. Figure 12.1 presents a model to explain how the interaction between institutional trends, contextual factors (both domestic and international), and "the *interconnection* of perceptions of external reality" accounted for state terror outcomes.[2]

Organization and Resources

A first variable in the model entails the organization and resources of the security forces.[3] In my analysis, I will focus on the military, although the police and other agencies (such as the civilian intelligence services) may be relevant players, as well. Organization refers primarily to the structure of the security forces. Questions about the level of centralization of the security apparatus and the chain of command are relevant to understand this variable. The type and quantity of resources available to the security forces also define this institutional component. For instance, it is important to take into account the military's capacity to mobilize personnel, its technological capabilities, and its know-how in relation to counterinsurgency work.

This capacity is illustrated by the level of training acquired by the military in the implementation of interrogation techniques and whether torture is perceived as an acceptable form of interrogation. Channels of access to these resources, in addition, play a role in shaping this variable. In this respect, it is necessary to distinguish between cases in which sources of domestic expertise are strong from those in which the import of repressive technology is paramount for the counterinsurgency effort. In general, we find that long-term patterns of brutality may be made more systematic and "effective" (although no less ruthless) when the security forces undergo a process of "professionalization" because of foreign influences. This was the case in Guatemala, where various external actors (the United States, Argentina, Israel) played a critical role in training and equipping the Guatemalan security forces.

The study of state terror demands particular attention to the intelligence capabilities of the security forces. Intelligence services play a fundamental role in state-sponsored repression because of their expertise in information gathering, psychological warfare, and interrogation. In the case of Argentina, the growth (over several years) of an intelligence machinery aimed at controlling the political opposition, as well as its increasing autonomy within the state, served as an important organizational platform for the dirty war. Under the authoritarian regime during the late 1970s and early 1980s, intelligence services became an autonomous core within the authoritarian state, acquiring immense power.

Because of the post–World War II shift toward a concern with internal security throughout Latin America, the Argentine military had acquired the resources—both technologies and expertise—to engage in nonconventional conflicts. Personnel underwent specialized training in torture techniques; methods and instruments routinely used to torment prisoners were imported and adapted locally. Indeed, by the time of the dirty war, torture was already a routine practice used to control and shatter political adversaries (Salimovich, Lira, and Weinstein, 1992, 78). Torture was considered legitimate in the context of war.

The United States contributed to this process of the naturalization of torture, in part, through the influence of U.S. advisors, who provided training to Argentines in the 1960s while presenting torture techniques as an "acceptable" device in the counterinsurgency war.[4] This legitimation resulted from two notions: first, that the information needed in the circumstances of war was of "sufficient importance to justify the torture" and, second, that a certain degree of randomness in the use of torture was a necessity in a conflict in which the threat was another state operating through local proxies. In brief, for the Argentine military, torture was justified as "the morally preferable response to threats to state security" (Avelar, 2001, 257; Tindale, 1996).

During the dirty war of the 1970s, the military command established two parallel structures, one official and one secret, that conducted repressive operations throughout the nation. Argentina was divided into zones in order to facilitate the implementation of counterinsurgency actions. The secret state was run by "the intelligence services of all the branches of the armed forces, under the authority of the commanders in chief, the commanders of zone and subzone, and the chiefs of the different areas" (Mittelbach, 1986, 9). In fact, the clandestine apparatus of repression was under the operational command of the army with direct support from the navy and the air force.

The intelligence apparatus emerged as an omniscient center of power within the national security state—with its own procedures and responsible to no one but itself. As declassified documents from the U.S. State Department have confirmed, the military intelligence services played a central role in the repression campaign within and beyond national borders. They exercised major influence upon the government's political agenda. As a memorandum from the U.S. embassy in Buenos Aires noted in 1980, "the policy-making levels of the GOA [Government of Argentina] are prisoners and victims of intelligence services here, particularly the Army's 601 Battalion" (U.S. Embassy, Buenos Aires, 1980b). The officers and civilians associated with the area of intelligence had considerably more power than officers assigned to regular combat units.

Army Intelligence Battalion 601, a key counterintelligence unit responsible for a substantial portion of the disappearances, had a central position in the repressive apparatus and in intelligence gathering. It possessed unparalleled power capabilities, both formal and, especially, informal, to centralize and carry out secret intelligence operations. During the dirty war, all military intelligence units were directed to maintain a permanent exchange of information with this battalion and to route to it all unidentified military equipment and documentation captured from the guerrillas by the security forces (Viola, 1975, 10; U.S. Embassy, Buenos Aires, 1979, 7). By the time the intensity of the antisubversive war in Argentina decreased, the intelligence apparatus had become a full-scale autonomous force of professional agents with the capacity to engage in extraterritorial operations. Battalion 601, in particular, had the manpower and expertise to lead counterrevolutionary operations beyond Argentina's borders.

Institutional Culture

A second variable refers to the military's institutional culture. Predominant doctrines of "internal security" (which are intimately linked to specific conceptions of the state and the nation) are crucial components of this culture. In addition, the military's long-standing patterns of disregard for constitutional constraints and the legal system are relevant to the creation of a specific institutional culture. In general, dominant doctrines provide a blueprint for national strategies, as in the case of the so-called National Security Doctrine in the Southern Cone of Latin America. As Figure 12.1 illustrates, there is a reciprocal connection between the security forces' institutional culture and their organization and resources. A noncohesive institutional culture, for instance, limits the capacity of the armed forces to maintain a centralized command in the counterinsurgency campaign. The Argentine and Chilean cases differ in this respect. The fragmentation of power in the Argentine case had a significant impact on the nature of the counterinsurgency war, especially due to the largely autonomous power of the various branches of the intelligence apparatus. In turn, command structures, institutional autonomy, and distribution of resources within the different branches of the armed forces may have a significant impact on the institution's cultural patterns. In the Argentine case, this influence was illustrated by a pattern of corruption within the armed forces, which was intensified during the dirty war.

The major body of ideas behind the Argentine state terror was the National Security Doctrine (N S D). This doctrine resulted from the military's own interpretation of a set of concepts about national security, Cold War politics, and counterinsurgency warfare. The N S D placed "national security above personal security, the needs of the state before individual rights, and the judgment of a governing elite over the rule of law" (Crahan, 1982, 101). In Argentina, the N S D was the result of a complex, extended process that combined a variety of sources, including German geopolitical thought, the canonical precepts of the Roman Catholic Church, and, principally, French counterrevolutionary doctrine and U.S. Cold War security policies (Crahan, 1982, 121–22, no. 8; Buchanan, 1996, 6–7).

The doctrine of national security emphasized the international dimension of the revolutionary war. Local conflicts were interpreted as an effect of Soviet strategic actions in the framework of an East–West confrontation. This defense doctrine reduced communism "to the condition of internal aggression at the service of a foreign power" and directed the armed forces to create a new societal model that would eliminate any interference with the agenda defined by the armed forces (the so-called national objectives) (Herrera, 1979, 8–9). The concept of a global balance of power played a significant role in the Argentine military's worldview. In the domain of global strategy, every achievement of the Soviet Union was seen as a triumph for communism, and every progress of Marxism in the world political arena was perceived as another step toward the final victory of the Kremlin. According to this worldview, the intensity of the East–West conflict forced developing countries to avoid a neutral, or "third," position in order to preserve their national independence in face of Soviet-sponsored expansionism (Villegas, 1963, 122, 124, 192).

The Argentine military asserted that geographical borders should not be an obstacle to the defense of the Western system. Under the aggression of the Communist International, the concept of national frontiers was subordinate to an ideological dimension. If the Marxist foe applied a global strategy that disregarded the notion of conventional borders, then the Western bloc's reply, as well, could not be launched from independent national positions (Hodges, 1991, 128–29; Verbitsky, 1984, 21; Duhalde, 1983, 81). The Argentine army defined the main threat to national security as an "indirect maneuver" of international communism. In the Cold War's theater of operations, the enemy's strategy was to promote insurgent movements in the Third World with the objective of winning over the population.

The principle of ideological frontiers defined a new kind of security cooperation throughout the hemisphere. Conventional multilateral assistance against external aggression—as established by the Inter-American Treaty of Reciprocal Assistance (Tratado Interamericano de Asistencia Recíproca, TIAR; also known as the Rio Pact), which was put into effect in December 1948—was viewed as insufficient to counteract the new type of conflict. Accordingly, hemispheric security cooperation in the 1970s evolved into a coordinated counterinsurgency program based on a model of unconventional, clandestine military operations (Duhalde, 1983, 114–15, 125; "Argentina

Redraws the Ideological Map," 1980, 5). The problem of internal security, thus, became a central concern for the state, which was compelled to fight insurgency in all areas, particularly in the ideological realm.[5]

International Influences

As several of the chapters in this volume argue, international factors are fundamental to an understanding of the production of state terror. France and the United States, in particular, influenced Argentina's approach to counterinsurgency. Even though Argentine officers were trained at the U.S. Army School of the Americas (SOA) in the Panama Canal Zone and U.S. advisors trained the Argentines in counterinsurgency, interviews with Argentine military officers and an analysis of military journals reveal that the French had a critical impact in shaping the Argentine version of the National Security Doctrine.

The French school of thought that was developed during the wars in Indochina (1945–1954) and Algeria (1954–1962) emphasized an ideological, global approach to the phenomenon of insurgency. It is important to note that the Algerian war marked a fundamental change in the use of torture as a counterinsurgency tool. The use of torture by French troops was defended as a legitimate military device within the limits of the law (Tindale, 1996). The main argument given was that military necessity demanded the use of torture as a form of interrogation (Tindale citing Peters, 1985, 177). As noted, Argentine military officers repeatedly justified the use of torture to extract information as a necessity in the counterrevolutionary war (a criterion that was also shaped by U.S. training in the 1960s).

In the 1950s, the French counterrevolutionary doctrine became an important subject of study in Argentina's war school. The dissemination of the *doctrine de guerre révolutionnaire* in key Argentine army circles rapidly increased with the arrival in 1957 of a French military mission to Buenos Aires and the publication of several articles by French authors in Argentine military journals. Anticommunism and psychological warfare were two themes that had a strong impact on the military's conception of the antisubversion war. By the end of the 1950s, the army had organized the first courses and military exercises in counterrevolutionary warfare. Even though the role of the French doctrine in military training faded a few years later, its principles and ideas continued to influence the upcoming army cohort.[6]

The French ideological and military doctrine of unconventional warfare was updated and reshaped with the addition of lessons drawn from U.S. counterinsurgency techniques used in the Vietnam War. U.S. influence served as a rationale for military involvement in internal security and development (these concepts were viewed as dependent on one another) and stressed the need for a collective defense of the Western Hemisphere against communist expansionism. Argentina added its own sources of expertise in the repression of political dissidents, shaping the "new professionalism" of the armed forces. This professionalism of internal security gave the armed forces a clear objective and, in their view, a preeminent role in the nation. Their central mission was transformed from external defense to internal protection against communist infiltration.[7] The armed forces' new professionalism emphasized the need for direct military involvement in politics and domestic intelligence, the use of unconventional methods to increase effectiveness in the antisubversive war, and the adoption of a new hypothesis of conflict based on the concept of ideological frontiers (McSherry, 1997).

As was the case with members of other Latin American armies, a number of Argentine officers were trained at the School of the Americas, where the Argentines also excelled as counterinsurgency instructors. The U.S. training facility in the Panama Canal Zone's Fort Gulick was a hub for the development of transnational military links during the 1960s and 1970s. Main actors in the establishment of national security states throughout Latin America received some training at the SOA, including General Leopoldo F. Galtieri (Argentina), General Augusto Pinochet (Chile), General Hugo Banzer Suárez (Bolivia), General Policarpo Paz García (Honduras), General Manuel Antonio Callejas y Callejas (Guatemala), General Manuel Antonio Noriega (Panama), and Major Roberto D'Aubuisson (El Salvador). In addition, four of the five officers accused of organizing the infamous Battalion 3–16 in Honduras received counterinsurgency training at the SOA, as did nineteen of the twenty-seven Salvadoran army officers implicated in the brutal murder of six Jesuit priests in November 1989 (Goobar, 1993).

In fact, the School of the Americas played a critical role in establishing continent-wide anticommunist networks among Latin American officers, trained there in intelligence techniques—including torture (Fernández, 1983; Goobar, 1993). This training institute also facilitated the creation of personal connections among important actors in the national security states throughout the hemisphere. These actors played a decisive role in developing counterrevolutionary alliances, mainly because of intense personal loyalties resulting from socialization and recruitment. However, the United States was not the only country providing such an opportunity for the establishment of connections among officers. For instance, Central American officers who had trained in Argentine military academies (Colegio Militar and Escuela Superior de Guerra) in the early 1960s played significant roles in the organization of the paramilitary opposition to the Sandinista regime two decades later.[8]

The preceding discussion has highlighted some of the international influences within military culture that served as foundations for the establishment of state terror networks. It is also important, however, to take note of how broader contextual factors influenced perceptions of the armed forces. Among them were nonmilitary perceptions of their mission and their own members' sense of how society viewed their role. This is a complex problem, but it may be illustrated in part through a brief reference to the role of networks of state and nonstate actors in shaping the international context under which the Argentine armed forces launched their dirty war. On the one hand, international groups such as Amnesty International documented and denounced human rights violations in Argentina. The Carter administration and the governments of Italy, France, and Sweden also exerted pressure on the military regime in response to human rights abuses. The connections between domestic human rights groups and foreign organizations and governments, moreover, evolved into "transnational advocacy networks" that pressured the authoritarian regime to improve its human rights record (Keck and Sikkink, 1998, 103–10).

On the other hand, international actors and transnational networks, several of which would later play important roles in supporting Argentina's extraterritorial activities, emerged to support the Argentine military's actions. Among these were the World Anti-Communist League (WACL) and its Latin American chapter, Confederación Anticomunista Latinoamericana (Latin American Anti-Communist Confederation, CAL); right-wing religious organizations, such as the Reverend Sun Myung Moon's Unification Church and its political arm, the Confederation of Associations for the Unity of the Societies of America (CAUSA); and political parties, such as Guatemala's Movimiento de Liberación Nacional (National Liberation Movement, MLN) and El Salvador's Alianza Republicana Nacionalista (Nationalist Republican Alliance, ARENA).

Domestic Social Forces

At the domestic level, the context for the actions of the security agencies was determined in part by the impact of public opinion, the activities of groups and movements within civil society, and the actions of guerrilla organizations. In this regard, as they exercised an effect on the security forces' construction of the external reality, the country's social forces—both supporting and opposing the military regime—were integral to the production of state terror. The actual and perceived power of the guerrillas, the role of those groups in civil society that opposed the authoritarian regime (imposing some degree of constraint over the deployment of repression), and the role of groups that supported the regime (contributing to the creation of its legitimacy) are important factors to include in the analysis of state-sponsored repression.

Beginning in 1975, the Argentine armed forces launched a vast counterinsurgency effort against the guerrilla organizations—in particular, the Montoneros and the Ejército Revolucionario del Pueblo (People's Revolutionary Army, ERP)—and against labor unions, peasant leagues, student organizations, and many other groups within civil society that were perceived to be part of the "subversive" apparatus. The focus of the repressive campaign was on the guerrillas and their support networks, as defined by military intelligence. The Montoneros, who identified themselves as Peronist, emerged in the years 1968–1970. The Montonero leadership was drawn largely from right-wing Catholic Church activists. In fact, the organization combined Catholic right-wing nationalism with guerrilla warfare. Upon choosing armed struggle as a means to contest political power, the group focused mainly on selective kidnappings and spectacular military actions (Gillespie, 1982). For its part, the ERP was the armed offshoot of the Partido Revolucionario de los Trabajadores (Revolutionary Workers' Party, PRT). Initially a Trotskyist group, the ERP followed the model of the Cuban revolution and the example of guerrilla leader Ernesto "Che" Guevara. Both guerrilla groups developed a tight organizational apparatus and wide support networks among various social groups.

By the mid-1970s, the PRT-ERP had a strong presence across the country.[9] This advance represented a rapid growth in only a few years, considering that the PRT had only been created in 1965 and the ERP in 1970. Indeed, the armed branch of the organization doubled its membership in 1970–1971 and gained increasing popular support through small-scale, propaganda-style guerrilla actions. Between 1973—when Argentina elected a civilian government after years of authoritarianism—and 1975, the guerrilla organization experienced even more dramatic growth. By 1975, the armed organization boasted between five and six thousand militants drawn from working-class neighborhoods, factories, and universities. A study on the P R T- E R P described the level of societal insertion of the organization in 1975:

> [T]he P R T- E R P had cells in more than four hundred of the most important factories in Greater Buenos Aires; it had established a presence in Tucumán, Jujuy and Santiago del Estero; it was one of the major forces among the industrial workers in Córdoba; it had successfully organized cells and organizations among metal and meat-packaging workers in Rosario and workers in the oil sector in the Patagonia. In addition, it had succeeded in organizing groups with an active role in the student movement, among land leasers (*arrendatarios*) in the cotton-producing sector in Chaco, and among judicial employees and teachers in Formosa. Finally, it had established its presence in many cities and towns in the provinces. (Pozzi, 2001, 24; author's translation)

A strong propaganda apparatus supplemented this level of popular insertion. The organization's legal and clandestine publications reached wide audiences. However, in spite of this increase in membership and influence, the organization's climax in 1975 was followed by a rapid downfall in about a year. The sudden collapse was primarily a result of the group's dramatic growth (which bolstered its ranks with inexperienced militants), several political mistakes, and the ruthless and effective counterinsurgency campaign carried out by the armed forces. By mid-1976, this Marxist guerrilla organization had been completely subdued.

After their defeat, Argentine guerrillas reemerged in other countries—either as political exiles or as combatants. For instance, in the late 1970s a dissident group of approximately fifteen members of the E R P in exile joined the Sandinista forces in the final offensive against the dictatorship of Anastasio Somoza. This handful of E R P veterans asserted that armed struggle remained the major strategy to promote revolution, and because Argentina did not offer the appropriate conditions for that quest, they decided to become involved in the Nicaraguan struggle.[10] Following the overthrow of Somoza, these guerrillas remained in Nicaragua as part of the Sandinista security

apparatus. In late 1979, the Montoneros launched a "strategic counteroffensive" in Argentina and, as a result, the security forces killed more than a hundred exiled Montoneros (who had been sent back by the leadership to Argentina). By December of that year, the Montonero guerrilla counteroffensive
against the Argentine military regime had been definitively crushed (Andersen, 1993, 287).

Construction of Reality

As Figure 12.1 makes clear, the "construction of the external reality" plays a
central role in the configuration of repressive outcomes. This variable refers
to the institution's perception of its own role and of the surrounding reality
(della Porta and Reiter, 1998, 22–23, 26). It mediates as a "filter" between institutional and contextual factors, on the one hand, and repressive outcomes,
on the other. The input from domestic and international sources is turned
into "knowledge," which, as noted, results from a multidimensional interconnection of perceptions about reality and not merely from "isolated images" (della Porta and Reiter, 1998, 23).

Of particular importance in the case of Latin America was the military's
perception of the power capacities of "subversion," which included, in their
view, a range from left-wing insurgencies to popular movements and human
rights groups. Knowledge about the military and nonmilitary power of the
guerrilla organizations was central in shaping the armed forces' reaction to
the "subversive" threat. The nonconventional nature of this challenge made
the assessment of the guerrillas' power a difficult task, especially because the
military considered this a war for the "hearts and minds" of the population.
Furthermore, the assumption that popular unrest was a result of a communist scheme—promoted by the Soviet Union via the Cuban proxy—that was
aimed at deepening local sources of discontent played a central role in shaping the perception that guided the military's decision to employ state terror
as a device to destroy the "communist assault" on Latin America.

The guerrilla threat was seen as a complex offensive in both the military
and the ideological arenas. The objective of this offensive was, in the military's view, the destruction of the Argentine state as such. It is worthwhile to
examine how the military, and specifically the army intelligence command
(called Jefatura II), construed the subversive threat. Army intelligence documents expose a map of the "Marxist subversive war" from the viewpoint of
the military. From their beginning in the early 1960s (with the first attempt

to start a guerrilla *foco* in northern Argentina), the "subversive-terrorist" groups (in military terminology) were perceived as having evolved into complex clandestine organizations. They "compris[ed] a *political apparatus* of leadership, propaganda and indoctrination, and an *armed apparatus* responsible for specific terrorist actions including the formation of an 'irregular army'" (Poder Ejecutivo Nacional, 1980, 5–6).

Military intelligence paid particular attention to transnational links among insurgent organizations. Reports stressed the importance of the Junta Coordinadora Revolucionaria (Revolutionary Coordinating Junta, JCR), an umbrella organization created "to continue the Marxist subversive awakening of the 1960s, instilling new stimulus and goals in it" (Comando General del Ejército, EMGE, 1975, 7). The core of the JCR consisted of guerrilla organizations from Argentina, Chile, Uruguay, and Bolivia (Bureau of Intelligence and Research, 1976, 3). This structure, according to the military's reports, served for the exchange of cadres and intelligence, as well as for mutual political and financial support. One military report said that, following its initial strategic objective of creating a unified Latin American revolutionary vanguard, the JCR established contacts with insurgent organizations from Brazil, Paraguay, Peru, Venezuela, Colombia, Mexico, Guatemala, Nicaragua, El Salvador, and the Dominican Republic (Comando General del Ejército, EMGE, 1975, 7–9). In the late 1970s, military intelligence sources maintained that leftist guerrilla organizations in Central and South America were integrated into a unified structure commanded by the Soviet Union, Cuba, and the Sandinista government in Nicaragua (U.S. Congress, 1987, 37–38, 81–81, 106–108).

The military's construction of the threat thus conveyed a notion of subversion seen as

> any concealed or open, insidious or violent action that attempts to change or destroy a people's moral criteria and way of life, for the purpose of seizing power or imposing from a position of power a new way of life based on a different ordering of human values.[11]

The "subversive threat," therefore, demanded a type of response broad enough to destroy the guerrillas' military capacity, dismantle their support network in society, and discipline the population. If national security and the state's survival were at stake—according to the "knowledge" constructed by the armed forces—then they viewed it necessary to implant terror in society as a means of eliminating a potential opposition to the regime's national project and to paralyze the capacity of the popular sectors for mobilization.

State Terror

State-sponsored repression is thus the result of a dynamic interaction among institutional factors (both cultural and organizational), social forces in the domestic arena, international influences, and the body of knowledge developed by the armed forces (della Porta and Reiter, 1998, 10–27). These establishing conditions translate into specific forms of state terror, which change through time as they adjust to the variables described earlier. In addition, as I will explain in the next section, the technological and ideological dimensions of state terror are transferable to other contexts. That is, repressive technology may be exported to other countries and the state terror apparatus (or sectors of it) may be put to work in other settings. For example, the Argentines disseminated their repressive knowledge to Central America with an emphasis on the implementation of procedures for kidnapping political dissidents, the establishment of secret detention centers, the use of torture to extract information from prisoners, and the execution and clandestine disposal of prisoners when they were no longer useful. In addition, the Argentines transferred an ideological framework to their Central American counterparts, contributing to the internationalization of national conflicts by stressing, for example, the role of the Soviet Union, Cuba, and Sandinista Nicaragua in the promotion of revolution across Latin America.

If the confrontation with the Marxist enemy was a boundless war, the military maintained that the response to internal subversion had to involve a comprehensive political, economic, psychosocial, and military strategy (Crahan, 1982, 104). "Subversion is not a problem that requires only military intervention," said the junta's leader, General Jorge Rafael Videla, in April 1976. "It is a global phenomenon demanding a global strategy covering all areas: politics, economics, culture, and the military" (quoted in Hodges, 1991, 124 [citing La Nación, 14 April 1976]). The Argentine armed forces, particularly the security community, mastered the logic of repression and extermination. This expertise ranged from sophisticated torture techniques to the so-called "naval solution"—the practice of throwing drugged or already dead captives from aircraft over the Atlantic Ocean (Verbitsky, 1995a, 1995b; Centro de Estudios Legales y Sociales, 1981, 15). The implementation of a systematic program of "disappearances" after the coup was a key component of a strategy aimed to inhibit the insurgents' ability to mobilize mass support by creating fear among the population.

Once the guerrilla movements had been defeated in Argentina, state-sponsored terrorism continued as a mechanism for social control of the population via manifold restrictions on personal and collective freedoms (Corradi, 1982–1983, 70). These restrictions encompassed a variety of realms—from the academic to the associational and cultural arenas. From the viewpoint of the armed forces, the military victory over "subversion" required an analogous triumph in the political realm (Viola, 1977). This idea was firmly grounded in the military's construction of the notion of subversion, which demanded, as explained, much more than a military reaction to armed insurrection. The objective was to "re-create" the true identity of the nation—as it was defined by the armed forces themselves.

Exporting State Terror

After defeating the local forces of the Left, the Argentine military turned its attention to the external "conspiracy" it saw as threatening the Western world. The military leaders sought to unite Southern Cone countries into a security pact, with the objective of crushing the Marxist forces. They intended, as well, to oppose U.S. President Jimmy Carter's "alienated" foreign policy toward Latin America—that is, the newly established U.S. foreign policy program substantially based on the promotion of human rights. In this period, the military intelligence services of Southern Cone countries organized a clandestine infrastructure (dubbed Operation Condor) for the persecution of political enemies (see McSherry, this volume).

In the 1970s, Chile's Dirección de Inteligencia Nacional (Directorate of National Intelligence, D I N A), in conjunction with the intelligence services of Argentina, Brazil, Uruguay, and Bolivia, organized the transnational Condor network with the aim of coordinating efforts to hunt down exiled political dissidents and to exchange intelligence information. Under Condor, dissidents were kidnapped by local security forces and transferred to secret detention centers in their original homeland. Some of them were refugees but legal residents, some were under the custody of the United Nations High Commissioner for Refugees (McSherry, 1999, 144–74; Comisión Nacional Sobre la Desaparición de Personas, 1986, 255). This transnational repressive network was responsible for numerous operations (including kidnapping, torture, and assassination) against political dissidents in Latin America, the United States, and Europe (Scott and Marshall, 1991, 42; Paoletti, 1987, 419–38). Argentine teams tracked down exiled dissidents in Brazil, Uruguay, Paraguay, Bolivia, Peru, Venezuela, Mexico, Spain, Italy, Switzerland, and Belgium.[12]

As explained, the doctrine of ideological frontiers, for which national boundaries were irrelevant in the confrontation against communism, served the Argentine military as a rationale for meddling in regional conflicts throughout Latin America. For the armed forces, if Argentina had been only a battleground in a global confrontation against communism, escalating turmoil in Central America could be seen as the continuation of the same conflict. As had been the case of Argentina in the early 1970s, Nicaragua, El Salvador, and Guatemala were perceived as targets of an indirect Soviet attack. The Argentine military intelligence ruled out the possibility of a renewed guerrilla offensive against the Argentine regime out of Nicaragua (based on a certitude that neither Montoneros nor the ERP had the capacity to resume military action). Still, some military analysts argued that a Sandinista Nicaragua could serve the exiled Argentine guerrillas as a platform for intelligence operations in South America. Perceived political instability in Bolivia was also a matter of concern for the Argentine authoritarian regime. Accordingly, the recourse to military actions beyond national borders was viewed within some influential army circles as a final, essential phase of the internal war against subversion.[13]

Bolivia

In July 1980, the Argentine military became involved in the coup d'état in Bolivia led by army commander General Luis García Meza. García Meza requested military assistance to oust Lidia Gueiler Tejada, the civilian president designated by the Bolivian Legislative Assembly, and the Argentine army and navy actively participated. Precise planning and brutal execution characterized the coup (Selser, 1982), and Argentine involvement was a key step in the process of Argentine military expansion throughout the subcontinent. According to General Videla, the Argentine armed forces helped to overthrow the interim president, Gueiler—in spite of the Carter administration's decided opposition to the interruption of the democratic process in Bolivia—to prevent the emergence of "a Cuba in South America" (Videla quoted in Joselovsky, 1984, 63). "It was part of the cold war game," said a high-ranking navy officer. "We had to do the dirty job in Bolivia."[14]

In addition to East–West considerations, traditional tensions in the Southern Cone region—particularly, Argentina's rivalry with Brazil—and the importance of buffer states such as Bolivia for the regional balance of power, played significant roles in the Argentines' decision to support García Meza's coup. However, geopolitical logic was not the only reason for the cooperation with the Bolivian military. Powerful groups within the Argentine armed forces were closely linked to transnational illegal networks, mainly drug trafficking, and their participation in the coup—known as the cocaine coup—yielded huge economic benefits. García Meza's partner was drug baron Roberto Suárez Levy, considered one of the world's prime cocaine traffickers in the 1980s. Money supplied by Suárez Levy helped pay for Argentina's involvement in the coup. In turn, those funds supported Argentine military activities in El Salvador. Argentine army general Carlos Guillermo Suárez Mason, a partner of major cocaine traffickers—including García Meza and his minister of the interior, Colonel Luis Arce Gómez—led a powerful network within the Argentine military and paramilitary apparatus that successfully combined anticommunist operations with drug trafficking and other illegal transactions (U.S. Congress, 1987, 154).

One of the irregular paramilitary units most heavily involved in the ruthless repression that followed the July coup was the Servicio Especial de Seguridad (Special Security Service, s e s), a branch of Bolivia's Departamento de Investigación Nacional (National Directorate of Investigation, d i n). "The s e s was reportedly established under the supervision of Argentine advisers, including former officers from the notorious Navy Mechanics School [Escuela de Mecánica de la Armada, e s m a]" (Americas Watch, 1992, 3). The s e s carried out what was considered the most serious human rights crime committed under the García Meza regime: the assassination of eight members of the Movimiento de Izquierda Revolucionaria (Leftist Revolutionary Movement, m i r) in January 1981. Paramilitary agents working under s e s auspices were also responsible for other killings and the brutal torture of political and labor union leaders. Allegedly, Argentine navy advisers used these victims to teach the Bolivians how to keep a prisoner alive while inflicting maximum pain (Americas Watch, 1993, 2, 4, 7–8; Levine, 1993, 58).

Central America

Extending its reach beyond its immediate neighbors, the Argentine anticommunist crusade also entailed a close collaboration with the various security agencies of the Central American nations. Among other activities, Argentine advisors trained Central American officers in the use of psychological procedures for interrogation and torture techniques. The Argentines wanted to reproduce the countersubversive method employed in their country's dirty war—the destruction of opposition organizations by paramilitary operations, working from the periphery (noncombatants) inward to the organizational core (the leadership). Argentine military personnel also worked with government-sanctioned death squads—as in the cases of Guatemala and El Salvador. In Honduras, the Argentines trained Battalion 3–16, a clandestine paramilitary unit responsible for the disappearance and extrajudicial execution of hundreds of Honduran civilians in the 1980s (affidavit of José Barrera Martínez, cited in Human Rights Watch/Americas, 1994, 189). Argentine advisors also trained the very first anti-Sandinista "Contra" organization—the Legión 15 de Septiembre—which included some of the most ruthless representatives of the Contra ethos.

The Argentine military placed intelligence operatives in the United States to coordinate the transfer of funds and arms to Central America. This special intelligence unit, the Extraterritorial Task Force, had been created as an extension of Army Intelligence Battalion 601. Allegedly, the nature and extent of the task force activities in the United States—arms trafficking, illegal financial transactions, and money laundering—were made possible because of the connivance of the U.S. Central Intelligence Agency (CIA). The Argentine intelligence unit handled covert funds in several countries, including the United States and Switzerland. The funds were usually transferred to Central America through Panama (U.S. Congress, 1987, 18–19, 56).

The CIA supported a hemispheric network of right-wing government officials and independent players united under a mandate of anticommunism. One of the most prominent actors of that network was a former CIA deputy director, Lieutenant General (retired) Vernon Walters. In 1980, Walters traveled to Argentina to discuss with high-ranking officers the details for a plan to organize a counterrevolutionary army in Central America. These early efforts were critical for the rapid implementation of a U.S.-sponsored anti-Sandinista program under Argentine supervision (Chamorro, 1987, 5–6).

The election of Ronald Reagan to the U.S. presidency was a turning point for U.S.-Argentine relations. Reagan had strongly criticized Carter's policy toward Argentina and praised the Argentine military for the annihilation of the Marxist threat. Based on the broad coincidence of their ideologies and perceived national security interests—largely defined by intense anticommunism—the administrations of the United States and Argentina swiftly moved into a relationship of mutual understanding and cooperation. This ideological concurrence led to a new model of partnership in which Argentina assumed the role of U.S. surrogate in Central America.

The operations by proxy responded to a number of constraints that made direct U.S. involvement impossible. The most important of those limitations were: (1) the CIA's restricted capacity for covert action at the time, (2) the CIA's vulnerability to congressional scrutiny, and, most importantly, (3) Congress's dislike for any kind of action that could invoke the "ghosts" of Vietnam (that is, a progressive U.S. intervention that would force the United States to become directly involved in a war in Central America) (Ranelagh, 1986, 674, 680–81; Arnson, 1993, 64–65, 74). The CIA's decision to prop up an exile Nicaraguan army trained by a third country provided an effective solution to those problems. The CIA left the day-to-day military management of the operation to the Argentine advisors. Aid to the Nicaraguan Contras was concealed in assistance monies for Argentina. Given the ample prerogatives acquired by CIA Director William Casey, it was possible for the CIA to set up the covert program in Central America without major interference from Congress.

In fact, soon after his appointment as the director of the CIA, Casey learned that Argentine advisors were training an anti-Sandinista force. He immediately understood that the Argentine military could help the Reagan administration to implement its containment policy in Central America. The United States could easily buy into an existing Argentine program. "Bill [Casey] was absolutely delighted," the CIA deputy director, Admiral Bobby Ray Inman, said later. "He knew that the Argentines' hope was to unseat the Sandinistas. And that was farther than the U.S. Congress was ready to let us go" (quoted in Persico, 1990, 273).

Casey instructed the CIA station chief in Buenos Aires to advance a proposal to the army commander in chief, General Galtieri, indicating U.S. interest in the Argentine military program in Central America. The United States was willing to finance the operation, relieving the Argentines of that difficulty in being the leading force behind the anti-Sandinista rebels. Galtieri was captivated by the U.S. offer. A leader of the hard-line faction within the military institution, he viewed an alliance with the United States in Central America as an avenue to reestablishing friendly relations with the leader of the West. Presumably, such an improvement in U.S.-Argentine relations could help to advance Galtieri's personal political project at a time of heightened tensions within the military (Persico, 1990, 272–73; Falcoff, 1989, 47).

In February 1981, President Reagan sent Walters, the retired general, on a Latin American tour with the mission of gathering support for U.S. policy toward Central America. As recalled by a former Contra leader, "Walters himself arranged for all the bands [of exile national guardsmen] to be incorporated within the 15th of September Legion, and for the military government of Argentina to send several army officers to serve as advisers and trainers" (International Court of Justice, 1985, 4–5). A main objective of Walters's trip was to explore the possibilities for military cooperation in Central America between the United States and the armed forces of Argentina, Honduras, and Guatemala.

Later that year, General Galtieri met with Reagan's top foreign policy advisers in Washington, D.C. From the U.S. perspective, Galtieri appeared as the "most cooperative" of the generals regarding the potential for a full-fledged Argentine involvement in Central America. Galtieri ratified an agreement by which the Argentine army would receive U.S. funds and intelligence to help them cut off alleged Cuban-Nicaraguan assistance to the guerrilla movements in El Salvador and Guatemala (Cardoso, Kirschbaum, and van der Kooy, 1983, 29–30). In addition, the Argentine navy sent patrol boats to police the Gulf of Fonseca, supposedly a main route in the Nicaraguan arms pipeline to the Salvadoran guerrillas.[15]

Key sectors in the Argentine military perceived the interest of the CIA in the Argentine operations as an endorsement of the counterinsurgency methodology implemented in the 1970s. "It is possible that the U.S. military and intelligence services saw that what they could not achieve in Central America had been accomplished by the Argentine, Chilean, and Uruguayan Armed Forces in their own countries . . . using a successful counterinsurgency model, which was later questioned and discarded as a result of the debate on the disappeared ones," said an Argentine navy officer. "The United States was losing the war in Central America. It was a war that the Americans could not win by themselves. Had they remained alone, there would have been another Vietnam."[16]

Upon learning about the collaboration with Argentina, some members of the U.S. Congress voiced concern about the CIA's capacity to control the operation. The Argentine counterinsurgency experts and the former members of Somoza's national guard were known for their unorthodox and brutal methods of repression. Responding to these complaints, the White House assured the members of the intelligence committees that the U.S.-backed operation would be firmly controlled, emphasizing that the United States would not tolerate human rights violations. However, as some legislators observed, it was difficult to understand how the CIA could bolster democracy in Nicaragua helped by the Argentine military regime, at that time a "symbol of right-wing dictatorial rule," and the remnants of Somoza's national guard, infamous for their ruthlessness and corruption (Woodward, 1987, 172, 176, 187–88).[17]

Conclusion

Understanding the production of state terror is important not only as a means to improve our conceptualization of this phenomenon but also as a method to account for variations across nations. For example, an exclusive focus on international influences cannot account for the different approaches to counterinsurgency implemented by countries throughout Latin America (see, for instance, Ryan on Uruguay, this volume). Although focused on a single case, this chapter has shown how various domestic and international factors shaped the Argentine program of state terror and how the combination of objective threats and the military's own perception of the nature of the threat shaped the strategy adopted by the military regime to fight "subversion."

The attempt of the Argentine military to destroy insurgency in all areas, particularly in the ideological realm (attacking intellectuals, labor organizers, progressive members of the Catholic Church, and others deemed subversive) was influenced by the same kinds of interactions. An example is the Guatemalan military's objective to "destroy the culture, identity, and communal structures of the indigenous population" in that country (Jonas and Walker, 2000, 10). Each case, however, was marked by variables specific to its setting. In brief, the examination of why the state kills and terrorizes its citizens demands that we view specific cases from a broad analytical perspective.

In turn, the Argentine military's involvement in the wars in Central America during the Reagan years shows how the expertise in repression perfected by the Argentine armed forces during the dirty war was transferred to other countries as part of a broad anticommunist crusade in the hemisphere. Additionally, these cases also raise important questions about the professed goal of the United States to promote democracy in Central America during the 1980s. In support of the CIA's covert action program in that region, the United States began using veterans of Argentina's dirty war to fight a regime perceived as a threat to U.S. values and liberal democracy. As was explained above, Argentine military and paramilitary personnel involved in the Contra operation served in Army Intelligence Battalion 601 and other security agencies that had played a major role in the regime's program of state-sponsored terror. Argentine operatives working in Central America also came from the Argentine Anti-Communist Alliance (Triple-A) and other ultranationalist terrorist organizations (González Janzen, 1986). Many of these "experts" had tortured and killed prisoners in the clandestine internment camps of Argentina's dirty war. Moreover, they continued to promote state terror abroad as a tool to annihilate opposition forces and subdue the population at large. The implications of the U.S. decision to engage in cooperation with the Argentine "dirty warriors"—specially, the impact that this alliance had in terms of human rights violations in Central America—is a matter that awaits a public and open debate in the North as well as in the South.

NOTES

1. Quotes from speeches by two generals: the first from Videla, the second from Galtieri.

2. This model draws from della Porta and Reiter (1998, especially 9–10, 23).

3. The following discussion draws from Armony (1997).

4. Author's interview with José Luis D'Andrea Mohr, in Buenos Aires, August 14, 1991.

5. Author's interview with Colonel Miguel Angel Li Puma, in Buenos Aires, August 18, 1993.

6. Author's interviews in Buenos Aires with the following retired army officers: General José Teófilo Goyret, August 5, 1993; General Ernesto Víctor López Meyer, August 4, 1993; and Colonel Horacio P. Ballester, July 28, 1993.

7. On the transformation of the military's role in the region, see Stepan (1973, 47–68) and McCann (1979, 507, 520).

8. Two prominent cases were Lieutenant Colonel Emilio Echaverry Mejía of the Nicaraguan National Guard and Honduran General Gustavo Alvarez Martínez.

9. The account of the P RT- E R P is based on Pozzi (2001, especially 21–25).

10. Author's July 30, 1993 interview, in Buenos Aires with Luis Bruschtein.

11. Generals Roberto Viola and L. A. Jaúregui, press conference, April 1977, quoted in Hodges (1991, 181).

12. On these extraterritorial operations conducted by paramilitary groups, see Verbitsky (1984, 65–74); Gasparini (1986, 75); Duhalde (1983, 113–14); see also U.S. declassified documents from the U.S. Embassy, Buenos Aires (1980a, 1980c).

13. Author's interview with General Miguel Angel Mallea Gil, in Buenos Aires, August 18, 1993.

14. Author's interview with Admiral Alberto R. Varela, in Buenos Aires, August 17, 1993.

15. Author's interview with Captain Carlos H. Raimondi, in Buenos Aires, August 4, 1993.

16. Raimondi interview (1993).

17. The cooperation between Argentina and the United States in the anti-Sandinista program ended with the Malvinas/Falklands conflict, beginning in spring 1982 (Armony 1997, 69–71).

BIBLIOGRAPHY

Americas Watch. 1992. *Almost Nine Years and Still No Verdict in the "Trial of Responsibilities."* New York: Americas Watch,.
———. 1993. *The Trial of Responsibilities: The García Meza Tejada Trial.* New York: Americas Watch.
Andersen, Martin Edwin. 1993. *Dossier Secreto: Argentina's Desaparecidos and the Myth of the "Dirty War."* Boulder: Westview Press.
"Argentina Redraws the Ideological Map of South America." 1980. *Latin America Weekly Report*, 19 September, sec. WR-80–37, p. 5.
Armony, Ariel C. 1997. *Argentina, the United States, and the Anti-communist Crusade in Central America, 1977–1984.* Athens: Ohio University Press.
Arnson, Cynthia J. 1993. *Crossroads: Congress, the President, and Central America 1976–1993*, 2nd ed. University Park: Pennsylvania State University Press.
Avelar, Idelbar. 2001. "Five Theses on Torture." *Journal of Latin American Cultural Studies* 10 (3): 253–71.

Buchanan, Paul G. 1996. "U.S. Defense Policy for the Western Hemisphere: New Wine in Old Bottles, Old Wine in New Bottles, or Something Completely Different?" *Journal of Interamerican Studies and World Affairs* 38 (1): 1–31.
Bureau of Intelligence and Research. 1976. "South America: Southern Cone Security Practices." Report. Washington, DC: U.S. Department of State, 19 July.

Cardoso, Oscar, Ricardo Kirschbaum, and Eduardo van der Kooy. 1983. *Malvinas, la Trama Secreta.* Buenos Aires: Sudamericana-Planeta.

Centro de Estudios Legales y Sociales (CELS). 1981. "The Doctrine of Global Parallelism." Manuscript. Buenos Aires: Centro de Estudios Legales y Sociales (CELS).

Chamorro, Edgar. 1987. *Packaging the Contras: A Case of CIA Disinformation*. New York: Institute for Media Analysis.

Comando General del Ejército, EMGE. 1975. "Summary of the Origins, Evolution, and Doctrine of the PRT-ERP and JCR." Annex I to secret directive no. 404/75, Col. Carlos Alberto Martínez. Buenos Aires: Cdo. J. Ej. (EMGE-Jef. II), army intelligence vice chief, October 28, p. 7.

Comisión Nacional sobre la Desaparición de Personas (CONADEP). 1986. *Nunca Más: The Report of the Argentine National Commission on the Disappeared*. New York: Farrar, Straus and Giroux.

Corradi, Juan E. 1982–1983. "The Mode of Destruction: Terror in Argentina." *Telos* 54: 61–76.

Crahan, Margaret E. 1982. "National Security Ideology and Human Rights." Pp. 100–127 in *Human Rights and Basic Needs in the Americas*, ed. Margaret E. Crahan. Washington, DC: Georgetown University Press.

della Porta, Donatella, and Herbet Reiter. 1998. "Introduction: The Policing of Protest in Western Democracies." Pp. 1–32 in *Policing Protest: The Control of Mass Demonstrations in Western Democracies*, ed. Donatella della Porta and Herbet Reiter. Minneapolis: University of Minnesota Press.

Duhalde, Eduardo Luis. 1983. *El Estado Terrorista Argentino*. Barcelona: Argos Vergara.

Falcoff, Mark. 1989. *A Tale of Two Policies: U.S. Relations with the Argentine Junta, 1976–1983*. Philadelphia: Foreign Policy Research Institute.

Fernández, Rodolfo Peregrino. 1983. Affidavit before the Comisión Argentina de Derechos Humanos (CADHU). Madrid, Spain, 26 April.

Gasparini, Juan. 1986. *La Pista Suiza*. Buenos Aires: Legasa.

Gillespie, Richard. 1982. *Soldiers of Perón: Argentina's Montoneros*. Oxford: Clarendon Press.

González Janzen, Ignacio. 1986. *La Triple-A*. Buenos Aires: Contrapunto.

Goobar, Walter. 1993. "Escuela de Dictadores." *Página 12* (8 August).

Herrera, Genaro Arriagada. 1979. "Ideology and Politics in the South American Military (Argentina, Brazil, Chile, and Uruguay)." Paper presented at the Woodrow Wilson International Center for Scholars, Washington, DC, 21 March.

Hodges, Donald C. 1991. *Argentina's "Dirty War": An Intellectual Biography*. Austin: University of Texas Press.

Human Rights Watch/Americas. 1994. *Honduras: The Facts Speak for Themselves*. New York: Human Rights Watch/Americas.

International Court of Justice. 1985. "Case Concerning Military and Paramilitary Activities in and against Nicaragua." Washington, DC: International Court of Justice, Edgar Chamorro affidavit in author's files, 5 September.

Jonas, Susanne, and Thomas W. Walker. 2000. "Guatemala: Intervention, Repression, Revolt, and Negotiated Transition." Pp. 3–23 in *Repression, Resistance, and Democratic Transition in Central America*, ed. Thomas W. Walker and Ariel C. Armony. Wilmington, DE: Scholarly Resources.
Joselovsky, Sergio. 1984. "El Ejército del 'Proceso' y su Intervención en Centroamérica." *Humor* (Buenos Aires), circa fall 1984. Author's copy.

Keck, Margaret E., and Kathryn Sikkink. 1998. *Activists beyond Borders: Advocacy Networks in International Politics*. Ithaca: Cornell University Press.

Levine, Michael. 1993. *The Big White Lie: The CIA and the Cocaine/Crack Epidemic*. New York: Thunder's Mouth Press.
Loveman, Brian, and Thomas M. Davies, ed. 1989. *The Politics of Antipolitics: The Military in Latin America*, 2nd ed. Lincoln: University of Nebraska Press.

McCann, Frank. 1979. "Origins of the 'New Professionalism' of the Brazilian Military." *Journal of Interamerican Studies and World Affairs* 21 (4): 505–22.
McSherry, J. Patrice. 1997. *Incomplete Transition: Military Power and Democracy in Argentina*. New York: St. Martin's Press.
———. 1999. "Operation Condor: Clandestine Inter-American System." *Social Justice* 26 (4): 144–74.
Mittelbach, Federico. 1986. *Informe sobre Desaparecedores*. Buenos Aires: La Urraca.

Paoletti, Alipio. 1987. *Como los Nazis, como en Vietnam*. Buenos Aires: Contrapunto.
Persico, Joseph E. 1990. *Casey: From the OSS to the CIA*. New York: Viking.
Peters, Edward. 1985. *Torture*. Oxford: Blackwell.
Pion-Berlin, David, and George A. Lopez. 1991. "Of Victims and Executioners: Argentine State Terror, 1975–1979." *International Studies Quarterly* 35: 63–86.
Poder Ejecutivo Nacional. 1980. *Terrorism in Argentina*. Buenos Aires: Poder Ejecutivo Nacional, 7 January.
Pozzi, Pablo A. 2001. *El PRT-ERP: La Guerrilla Marxista*. Buenos Aires: EUDEBA.

Ranelagh, John. 1986. *The Agency: The Rise and Decline of the CIA*. New York: Simon and Schuster.

Salimovich, Sofia, Elizabeth Lira, and Eugenia Weinstein. 1992. "Victims of Fear: The Social Psychology of Repression." Pp. 72–89 in *Fear at the Edge: State Terror and Resistance in Latin America*, ed. Juan E. Corradi, Patricia Weiss Fagen, and Manuel A. Garretón. Berkeley: University of California Press.

Scott, Peter Dale, and Jonathan Marshall. 1991. *Cocaine Politics: Drugs, Armies and the CIA in Central America.* Berkeley: University of California Press.

Selser, Gregorio. 1982. *Bolivia: El Cuartelazo de los Cocadólares.* Mexico City: Mex-Sur.

Stepan, Alfred. 1973. "The New Professionalism of Internal Warfare and Military Role Expansion." Pp. 47–68 in *Authoritarian Brazil: Origins, Policies and Future,* ed. Alfred Stepan. New Haven: Yale University Press.

Tindale, Christopher. 1996. "The Logic of Torture: A Critical Examination." *Social Theory and Practice* 22 (3): 349–74.

U.S. Congress. 1987. *Testimony of Leandro Sánchez Reisse before the Subcommittee on Terrorism, Narcotics, and International Operations of the Senate Committee on Foreign Relations.* Washington, DC: Government Printing Office, 23 July.

U.S. Embassy, Buenos Aires. 1979. "Nuts and Bolts of the Government's Repression of Terrorism-Subversion." Memorandum of conversation. Washington, DC: Department of State, 7 August.

———. 1980a. "Conversation with Argentine Intelligence Source." James J. Blystone, 7 April 1980. Washington, DC: Department of State, U.S. Embassy, Buenos Aires.

———. 1980b. "Hypothesis: The GOA as Prisoner of Army Intelligence." Towsend B. Friedman Memorandum, 18 August 1980. Washington, DC: U.S. Embassy, Buenos Aires.

———. 1980c. Towsend B. Friedman Memorandum, 21 August 1980. Washington, DC: U.S. Embassy, Buenos Aires.

Verbitsky, Horacio. 1984. *La Última Batalla de la Tercera Guerra Mundial.* Buenos Aires: Legasa.

———. 1995a. "La Solución Final." *Página 12* (3 March).

———. 1995b. *El Vuelo.* Buenos Aires: Planeta.

Villegas, Osiris G. 1963. *Guerra Revolucionaria Comunista.* Buenos Aires: Pleamar.

Viola, Gen. Roberto Eduardo. 1975. "War against Subversion." Annex I (Intelligence) to the secret directive of the Army General Commander no. 404/75. Buenos Aires: Comando General del Ejército, EMGE, Jefatura II Inteligencia, October 28.

———. 1977. "Continuation of the Offensive against Subversion During the Period 1977/78." Annex I to secret directive no. 504/77. Buenos Aires: Comando General del Ejército, EMGE, Jefatura II Inteligencia, April 20, pp. 1–15.

Woodward, Bob. 1987. *Veil: The Secret Wars of the CIA, 1981–1987.* New York: Simon and Schuster.

PART FOUR

◆

CONCLUSION

CHAPTER 13

New Responses to State Terror

CECILIA MENJÍVAR AND NÉSTOR RODRÍGUEZ

Crimes against humanity are characterized by being visible, major, and systematic acts of aggression performed with the aim of terrorizing, paralyzing, and subduing through fear (Rojas, 1999). These actions include particularly severe crimes, such as extrajudicial executions, disappearances, and torture conducted in a deliberate and widespread pattern (Méndez and Mariezcurrena, 1999). When crimes against humanity are committed with the objective to destroy or debilitate an ethnic, religious, national, or other community, they constitute genocide, for instance, as, it is argued, occurred in Guatemala in the 1980s. Such crimes call for a response from the international community. In the case of Latin America, the responses of the international community have included prosecutions before international tribunals and the exercise of extraterritorial civil and criminal jurisdiction by domestic courts. The result has included the prosecution of military officials outside the countries where their crimes were committed.[1]

The Role of the International Community in Seeking Justice: Truth Commissions

When authoritarian regimes in Latin America (military and civilian) were replaced, many of the new democratic governments that followed them created truth commissions to document the systematic nature of the state terror that had transpired. In 1983, President Raúl Alfonsín of Argentina created the Comisión Nacional Sobre la Desaparición de Personas, which produced a report on 9,000 disappearances during the 1976–1983 period of military rule. The report was released under the title, *Nunca Más: Informe de la Comisión Nacional sobre la Desaparición de Personas.* In 1982, President Hernán Siles Suazo of Bolivia issued a decree establishing the Comisión Nacional de Desaparecidos to investigate the disappearance of citizens during the period from 1967 to 1982. This commission documented 155 cases of disappearances, but it dissolved before issuing a final report. In February 1990, President Patricio Aylwin of Chile established the Comisión Nacional de la Verdad y Reconciliación, which released a report on human rights violations, reparations, and on the victims themselves. In September 1996, President Abdala Bucaran of Ecuador established a truth and justice commission to investigate 176 cases of human rights abuses in that country over the previous seventeen years. Similarly, Peru created several truth commissions to investigate different crimes and massacres that had occurred in the preceding twenty years, and a new commission was created in 2001 that is set to investigate more than 10,000 disappearances and 25,000 deaths during the violent decades.

The truth commission of Peru, unlike others, was the first to include public hearings, following the South African model used to investigate crimes committed under apartheid. Through the truth commission, Peruvians have a chance to speak openly about what they saw and experienced. Uruguay set up a commission in 2000 to investigate the fate of the disappeared during the military regime in power from 1973 to 1985. In El Salvador, the Comisión de la Verdad, created as part of the Peace Accords of 1992, issued a report titled, *De la Locura a la Esperanza: La Guerra de 12 años en El Salvador.* In Guatemala, the Commission for Historical Clarification produced a report titled *Memoria del Silencio.* Brazil's *Nunca Mais* report also documents human rights violations during the dictatorship. Additionally, in Panama in 2001, President Mireya Moscoso established a truth commission to investigate human rights violations during the military dictatorships of Generals Omar Torrijos and Manuel Noriega between 1968 and 1989.

In addition to these truth commissions (several of which were set up as part of peace accords monitored by the United Nations), there were parallel ones as well conducted by nongovernmental organizations and/or church groups. For instance, in Guatemala the participants in the Catholic Church project Proyecto Interdiocesano de Recuperación de la Memoria Histórica (REMHI) issued their own report, *Guatemala: Nunca Más,* and in Paraguay, the Catholic Church issued the report *Paraguay: Nunca Más* in 1990, and church and lay workers in rural areas issued the report, *Ko'āga Roñe'eta (Ahora*

Hablaremos): Testimonio Campesino de la Represión en Misiones, 1976–1978 (CEPAG, 1990).

Official truth commissions have in common the goal to tell the truth about what happened during the authoritarian regimes in their countries. This has proven to be a difficult task. Often the commissions have provided important coverage of only a few cases, chosen to represent a particular pattern of violence, and thus have left out many other political crimes. For instance, the truth commission in El Salvador presented excellent information about some massacres, as well as the disappearances and kidnappings of prominent individuals, but it did not cover the structure of death squads, which, as Méndez and Mariezcurrena (1999) observe, was a widespread phenomenon that affected this country in particular.

In addition, these truth commissions have had to work in societies where finding the truth about political crimes is a complex and risky endeavor, where denial and corruption are impenetrable, and where people are fearful of the consequences of speaking up. For example, in 1984, Paraguay's Comité de Iglesias para Ayudas de Emergencia (Churches' Committee for Emergency Assistance, CIPAE) began to document systematically the human rights abuses committed in that country. General Stroessner was still in power and, thus, it was extremely difficult for people to contribute information because they feared for their lives. Even when authoritarian leaders are no longer in power, it is still difficult for truth commissions to do their work, because many of the old formal and informal structures are still in place.

Nonetheless, truth commissions in Latin America have undoubtedly played a key role in recording the collective memory of people for the historical record. With the possible exception of Peru, the massive documentation they have collected points overwhelmingly to the military as responsible for human rights violations in the region. However, these commissions have been faulted for focusing too much on documenting atrocities and not enough on seeking justice. Rojas (1999), for instance, points out that the report by Chile's truth commission included a list of victims, but the facing page, where the names of perpetrators should have been listed, was left blank. Horrible crimes and atrocities were detailed, and although they might have been attributed to the military, no names, actors, or faces were associated with them. The commission effectively conducted an administrative task that had no legal consequences (Rojas, 1999). Human rights organizations and scholars have argued that it is incorrect to assume that judicial proceedings against abusers of human rights are vindictive (Méndez and Mariezcurrena, 1999). Truth commissions' reconciliatory efforts without juridical recourse have led many to believe that impunity for crimes is the hallmark of postauthoritarian regimes in Latin America.

Impunity has been institutionalized mainly through manipulations of legal systems, such as the application of amnesty laws, executive decrees, and pardons, through military court decisions, and through other contorted legal maneuvers that leave existing power relations intact. For instance, Guatemalan politicians passed a decree that freed from prosecution all officers and other state personnel for crimes committed between 1982 and 1986, one of the worst periods of political violence in that country. Argentina, El Salvador, Honduras, Uruguay, and Peru have enacted amnesty laws just in time to prevent convictions of notorious military officers. Many former members of the armed forces who committed heinous human rights abuses not only have been pardoned, but they also have been permitted to continue in their positions. Some even have been promoted or given new political posts.

This trend is also true of U.S. officials who were heavily involved in political work in Latin America. Elliot Abrams, for instance, who misled Congress concerning his knowledge of and involvement in the illegal supply of arms to the Nicaraguan Contras, was selected by President George W. Bush to be the National Security Council's senior director of the Office of Democracy, Human Rights, and International Operations. President George H. W. Bush issued a presidential pardon on Christmas night 1992, just before the end of his term, to prevent Abrams from being sent to prison for his violations of the law.

Another example is John D. Negroponte, who served in the U.S. embassy in Vietnam in the 1960s and was U.S. ambassador to Honduras in the 1980s, during the creation of both the Nicaraguan Contras and the Honduran security organizations that eliminated dozens of critics of the regime. Negroponte became the U.S. ambassador to the United Nations and has, at this writing, taken office as the U.S. ambassador to Iraq. Negroponte's appointment to the United Nations caused great concern among human rights activists. Negroponte is widely seen as being soft on human rights abuses and as having a background of working with militaries that have been accused of committing horrendous political crimes and human rights abuses.

A third example is Otto Juan Reich. During the Reagan administration, Reich served in Latin America–related governmental posts. He was selected by President George W. Bush in 2001 to serve as assistant secretary of state for Western Hemisphere affairs and in 2003 to serve as a special envoy to

Latin America. In the 1980s, Reich was a strong, active supporter of the Reagan administration's controversial Central American policies. A 1987 report by the U.S. comptroller general found that the State Department office for public diplomacy directed by Reich had conducted propaganda activities in violation of Congressional restrictions.

Impunity has had many consequences for Latin American societies. Some persons who have been determined responsible for atrocities have entered politics and have been elected to serve in political offices. A direct result of this personal metamorphosis is that former militaries can easily transfer their know-how and clandestine networks to civilian governments. For example, some observers believe that well-organized kidnapping rings (including some linked to drug-trafficking), which operate under the veil of "common" crime in Latin America, are but one consequence of the continuing work of former military officers. By most accounts, Guatemala's human rights record has continued to deteriorate even after the peace accords were signed. Civilian responses to rising crime and vigilante-style assassinations, such as occur in Guatemala, may in some cases be a smoke screen for politically motivated crimes. Ironically, the apparent lack of "public order and security" and rising levels of crime in countries such as El Salvador and Guatemala may serve to justify a return of military rule and an "iron fist" type of government (Molina Mejía, 1999).

Scholars and government officials in Latin America have argued that prosecuting the guilty for human rights crimes in the 1970s and 1980s would be too difficult to attempt and, consequently, the best course for the countries to move forward is to forget the political crimes of the past. This view has enabled some militaries (and their supporters) to remain powerful and beyond the rule of law. As McSherry and Molina Mejía (1999, 4) observe, "impunity was considered the price of a successful transition." Impunity, thus, leaves without justice the millions of Latin Americans who suffered vicious human rights abuses at the hands of their own states. According to Méndez and Mariezcurrena (1999), amnesties to militaries for their crimes against humanity also constitute a breach of international law.

An awareness of human rights has increased with the growth of democracy movements after the end of the cold war. According to McSherry and Molina Mejía (1999, 6), human rights and global human rights networks are playing a key role, "democratizing a world system previously dominated by states." In Latin America, these groups have worked on tribunals of several militaries and they have helped establish the Permanent People's Tribunal on

Impunity for Crimes against Humanity in Latin America, created in Santa Fé de Bogotá, Colombia, in 1989.

Efforts by truth commissions, local and international groups, and religious workers to record the atrocities and bring to justice the perpetrators sometimes have been met with violence. Some individuals have been disappeared or killed by "unknown groups" after testifying or complaining about human rights abuses. In Honduras, members of the Human Rights Commission have been assassinated after providing information that could be damaging to those who are still in power. In Guatemala, Monsignor Juan Gerardi, who led the Archbishop's Office for Human Rights, was murdered days after delivering the REMHI commission's seventeen-volume report, *Guatemala: Nunca Más*, which exposed the state's role in carrying out systematic, widespread human rights violations. In the case of Myrna Mack Chang, the Guatemalan anthropologist who was brutally murdered in 1990 after writing about human rights abuses, all the lawyers who worked against the accused militaries have had to leave the country. In contrast to others in the region, the peace accords in Guatemala specifically addressed the issue of impunity (Molina Mejía, 1999), but none of the politically linked crimes that have been tried since the peace accords were signed have had a fully satisfactory solution.[2]

International Protection

Important efforts have been made to overcome impunity and to move toward accountability for the atrocities committed in Latin America during the violent 1970s and 1980s. The Inter-American Court of Human Rights (IACHR) and the International Criminal Court (ICC) have sought to implement and oversee international human rights work in the region. In contrast to other international legal bodies that only consider cases brought by state parties, these courts can investigate allegations of crimes brought by the victims themselves or by nongovernmental organizations. The Inter-American Court of Human Rights has focused on charges against states, whereas the International Criminal Court has focused on charges against individuals and the identification of those responsible for atrocities.

The Inter-American Court of Human Rights is not a juridical body but a consultative one. It is charged with "protecting human rights as set forth in any international treaty applicable to the American States" (Simmons, 2003) and generating recommendations and sanctions to states that violate their citizens' human rights. The court has deliberated on human rights cases that have resulted from state terror, as well as from other sources, such as economic or social policies that infringe on the rights of citizens. These cases have concerned such matters as disappearances and murders during the Venezuelan riots protesting the debt crisis in 1989, the kidnapping and murder of several individuals in Honduras, the killings of members of the Saramaca tribe in Suriname, the political rights of the indigenous Awas Tigni community in Nicaragua, and censorship in Peru and Chile (Simmons, 2003).

The court asks states to investigate cases and to find and prosecute those who are determined to be culpable, and it proposes reparations to victims. When a state does not comply, the court refers the case to the Organization of American States, which then decides what measures to take.[3] The court can consider cases outside the country where they occurred but only in countries that are members and have ratified the court (Zavala, 2002). When the court considered the case of Myrna Mack, Guatemala's foreign minister sent a letter to the president of the court recognizing that "Guatemala accepts unconditionally its responsibility in the Mack Chang case." This marked the first time that a foreign minister took such a position in responding to a demand made by the court to a state in this type of human rights case.[4]

The International Criminal Court has jurisdiction over the most serious crimes for which an individual, or individuals, are responsible. These crimes include genocide, crimes against humanity, and war crimes. Moreover, "a head of state or a former head of state cannot claim immunity in relation to proceedings before the ICC" (Duffy, 1999, 121). Understandably, some states opposed the establishment of this court, most notably those criticized by international bodies for their human rights records. However, the United States has been its most vociferous opponent and has sought to prevent the possibility that U.S. citizens could be prosecuted by the court (Duffy, 1999).

International legal bodies have ruled on cases where a state has brought another state to court. For instance, in 1986 the Nicaraguan government filed a case against the United States with the International Court of Justice to protest U.S. backing of insurgency activities against Nicaragua. The court ruled on behalf of Nicaragua that by training, arming, equipping, financing, and supplying the Contra forces and otherwise encouraging, supporting, and directly participating in operations against Nicaragua, the United States had acted in breach of its obligation under customary international law not to intervene in the affairs of another state. The court also rejected the justification of self-defense that the United States maintained to defend its activities against

Nicaragua. The court ordered the United States to make reparations to Nicaragua for all injuries resulting from the military and paramilitary operations it supported.[5] To this day, the United States has ignored the verdict.

International bodies alone do not represent a solution for establishing accountability and seeking reparations, but they are important steps in an overall effort to establish a system of international justice.

Other International Tribunals

When former military officers have been tried in their home countries, sometimes the verdicts have been less than satisfactory. In Guatemala, for instance, only one of the three military men implicated in the assassination of Myrna Mack was condemned. On different occasions, the families of the six Jesuit priests and their two workers assassinated in El Salvador in 1989 have taken to trial high-ranking officers for the crimes without success. Some trials conducted outside of the countries where the crimes were perpetrated, however, have produced different results.

A French court in 1991 sentenced an Argentine colonel in absentia for the murder of two French nuns during the dirty war in Argentina. In another noted case, Spanish judge Baltasar Garzón issued an arrest warrant in order to extradite former Chilean dictator Augusto Pinochet from Britain to Spain. Also worth mentioning are the cases of "the Generals," the Salvadoran militaries first tried and acquitted in Florida in 2001 for the kidnapping and murder of four U.S. religious workers in El Salvador in 1980. They later were tried successfully in a case brought by the Center for Justice and Accountability on behalf of three Salvadorans who were tortured by security forces during El Salvador's civil war in the early 1980s. President Ronald Reagan had awarded one of the generals the U.S. Legion of Merit medal, which is bestowed to recognize exceptionally meritorious performance of service to the United States. In 1993, General Colin Powell presented the same award to the other defendant. The Salvadoran generals were rewarded by the U.S. government for exceptional leadership in the very armed forces named in the Salvadoran truth commission report as responsible for more than 85 percent of wartime atrocities, and which resulted in the deaths of more than 75,000 persons and thousands of disappeared.

The trials of human rights violators outside their countries indicate a growing acceptance of the principle of "universal jurisdiction." This legal concept provides that certain crimes—specifically, torture, genocide, crimes against humanity, and war crimes—are so egregious that perpetrators can be tried in any nation's courts, no matter where the abuses took place or where the alleged offenders currently live. This concept has its roots in the Nuremberg trials of 1945–1947 and in the creation of two ad hoc international criminal tribunals for the prosecution of human rights violations in the former Yugoslavia in 1993 and in Rwanda in 1994. The arrest of Augusto Pinochet in Britain in 1998 breathed new life into the concept. Awareness of "universal jurisdiction" is gaining momentum and it is being used in an increasing number of cases.

In the United States, the principle is firmly established and rests on even earlier statutory enactments. The Alien Tort Claims Act of 1789 provided that aliens might avail themselves of U.S. courts to seek redress for violations of international law, for war crimes, genocide, and other crimes, but only in tort. In 1980, the United States Court of Appeals for the Seventh Circuit in New York held a Paraguayan torturer liable in tort to the relatives of the man he tortured and killed in Paraguay.[6] According to Amnesty International, hundreds of human rights abusers currently reside in the United States, where many of their victims also live. Thus, it is likely that more cases against human rights abuses will be brought to U.S. courts in the future.

Coming Full Circle?

The fact that former Latin American militaries and state officials, as well as thousands of victims, are currently living in the United States is neither surprising nor a coincidence. As some scholars have noted, the emergence of a regular migration flow into a strong state requires the penetration of the institutions of that state into those of the weaker one (Portes and Böröcz, 1989). In the case of the United States and Latin America, U.S. foreign policy and military training and intervention helped structure such linkages. Thus, it is not surprising that, except for Mexico, the largest flows of Latin American migration to the United States originate in countries that experienced the largest or longest U.S. intervention (for example, Guatemala, El Salvador, the Dominican Republic and, more recently, Colombia). The same U.S. foreign policy and doctrine of regional security that sought to "secure" the hemisphere helped fuel the state terror that many sought to flee.

Once in the United States, most of the thousands of victims of state terror in Latin America have not been welcomed. In general, there seems to be a relationship between a country's foreign relations and the granting of political asylum (Menjívar, 2000). Indeed, the United States has a record of granting asylum mainly to groups that serve its national security interests.

Thus, United States–Latin America foreign relations shaped the kind of reception that Latin Americans received upon their arrival in the United States.

The logic for rejecting most Latin Americans' claims for asylum was, implicitly, that these people could not be fleeing en masse from countries where governments were actively supported by the United States (Menjívar, 2000, 81). In addition, granting asylum to those who fled conditions created with U.S. backing would have contradicted U.S. foreign policy. For instance, only between two to four percent of the persons fleeing El Salvador and Guatemala were granted asylum during the period of heightened political violence in those countries. The point is made even more clearly in the case of Chile. During the socialist government of President Salvador Allende Gossens (in office 1970–1973), the United States quickly granted asylum to Chileans who left their country claiming political persecution. However, after General Augusto Pinochet took power through a U.S.-backed coup d'état, most Chileans seeking asylum in the United States were denied such protection.

Prospects for U.S.-Latin American Interstate Relations
What are the prospects for U.S.-Latin America interstate relations for the twenty-first century? Knowledge of the prominent role the United States has played in the creation of state terror in the region has led to several developments. President Clinton, for instance, during a visit to Guatemala in 1999, admitted that the United States provided support for widespread repression in Guatemala's thirty-six-year reign of military and paramilitary terror. He apologized for his country's wrongdoings in that country. The current ambassador to Guatemala, John Hamilton, has expressed his concern for the death threats to human rights advocates and for the deteriorating human rights situation in that country, and he has promised to oversee a better compliance with the peace accords and respect for fundamental human rights.[7]

The United States also has been in the process of declassifying key documents that link its officials and institutions to the reign of terror in Latin America in the 1970s and 1980s. For example, newly declassified documents demonstrate that U.S. officials helped to set up "safe houses" in the presidential palace, for use by Guatemalan security force agents and their U.S. counterparts. There is now documentary evidence that the Central Intelligence Agency maintained close ties to the Guatemalan army in the 1980s, even putting on its payroll high-ranking Guatemalan military officers involved in brutal human rights violations, and that U.S. officials were aware that the Guatemalan army and its paramilitary allies were massacring thousands of Mayan villagers. These documents have become public and are available through the website of the National Security Archive.

It seems that some of the structures that led to the terror reported in this volume are still in place. When President George W. Bush and Congress authorized military aid to Colombia in 2003, they expanded the range of activities that it could be used for. Instead of using it solely to aid in the fight against the traffic of narcotics, it can now be used to fight subversive groups as well.

Thus, to seek justice for the atrocities committed in Latin America during the reign of terror, it would be helpful if the United States would be more forthcoming about its involvement by acknowledging, as President Clinton did in Guatemala, the U.S. national security doctrines that assisted and coordinated such campaigns. The United States does not bear sole responsibility for every act of state terror in Latin America, as the authors in this collection make clear. Yet, it is important to acknowledge that the U.S.–Latin American interstate regime played a key role in setting up and operating campaigns of terror to eliminate perceived "subversives." Perhaps acknowledging this link more clearly in truth commissions, tribunals, and the like would lead to lasting structures that would be truly conducive to peace and justice in the region.

NOTES

1. Although several countries have done so, others have refused to take cases. For instance, a Spanish judge refused to initiate a case brought by Nobel Prize winner Rigoberta Menchú Tum against former Guatemalan president General Efraín Ríos Montt (current president of the Guatemalan congress) and seven other generals. The Spanish magistrate argued that the crimes of which the militaries were being accused were essentially "war crimes" and since the armed conflict had already ended in Guatemala he could not initiate a trial. The Spanish court suggested that the Guatemalans should first seek justice in the courts of their own country and then, once those resources had been exhausted, other courts would consider taking up the case.

2. Some of Guatemala's cases taken to court have been unprecedented. For instance, the case of the 1995 Xamán massacre marked the first time in the country's history that an indigenous community had demanded the army be put on trial (Molina Mejía, 1999).

3. For instance, when Peru threatened to withdraw from the court's jurisdiction because of an adverse ruling, the Organization of American States condemned Peru's threat, and Peru withdrew its renunciation request.

4. www.derechos.org/nizkor/guatemala/doc/myrna28.html.

5. www.icj-cij.org/icjwww/idecisions/isummaries.

6. The authors are grateful to Sandra Coliver for information concerning universal jurisdiction.

7. http://www.c.net.gt/ceg/diario/2003/ene2003/dimpo110.html#1.

BIBLIOGRAPHY

CEPAG. 1990. *Ko'ãga Roñe'eta (Ahora Hablaremos): Testimonio Campesino de la Represión en Misiones (1976–1978)*. Asunción: Centro De Estudios Paraguayos "Antonio Guasch."

Duffy, Helen. 1999. "Toward Eradicating Impunity: The Establishment of an International Criminal Court." *Social Justice* 26 (4): 115–24.

McSherry, J. Patrice, and Raúl Molina Mejía. 1999. "Introduction to *Shadows of State Terrorism: Impunity in Latin America.*" *Social Justice* 26 (4): 1–12.

Méndez, Juan E., and Javier Mariezcurrena. 1999. "Accountability for Past Human Rights Violations: Contributions of the Inter-American Organs for Protection." *Social Justice* 26 (4): 84–106.

Menjívar, Cecilia. 2000. *Fragmented Ties: Salvadoran Immigrant Networks in America.* Berkeley: University of California Press.

Molina Mejía, Raúl. 1999. "The Struggle against Impunity in Guatemala." *Social Justice* 26 (4): 55–83.

Portes, Alejandro, and József Böröcz. 1989. "Contemporary Immigration: Theoretical Perspectives on its Determinants and Modes of Incorporation." *International Migration Review*, 23 (3): 606–30.

Rojas, Paz B. 1999. "Impunity and the Inner History of Life." *Social Justice* 26 (4): 13–30.

Simmons, William Paul. 2003. "Establishing the Legitimacy of a Human Rights Court: Lessons from the Inter-American Court of Human Rights." Paper presented at the Rocky Mountain Council for Latin American Studies Annual Meeting, Tempe, AZ, February.

Zavala, Claudia. 2002. "Hablan, Pero no Hay Voluntad Real." San Salvador: Vértice, Diario de Hoy [on-line; cited 22 September 2002]. Available from www.elsalvador.com/vertice/2002/09/22/entrevista.html.

About the Contributors

Ariel C. Armony is assistant professor of government at Colby College. He has written on U.S.-Latin American relations, civil society, and democratization. His most recent publication is *The Dubious Link: Civic Engagement and Democratization* (Stanford: Stanford University Press, 2004).

Abderrahman Beggar holds a doctorate in Hispanic studies from the University of Paris–Sorbonne and has an additional degree from the Center for Diplomatic and Strategic Studies (Paris). His research and publications concern media discourse and political transitions in Latin America. He is the author of *La Transition au Nicaragua vue de Paris et Madrid dans la presse quotidienne* (Paris: Editions de L'Harmattan, 2001).

John C. Dugas is associate professor and chair of the Department of Political Science at Kalamazoo College. His research and publications focus on issues of political reform, human rights, and democratization in Colombia.

Richard Grossman is a visiting lecturer in history at Northeastern Illinois University. He currently is working on a book about Augusto C. Sandino and Sandinista resistance to the U.S. occupation of Nicaragua.

Joan Kruckewitt received her B.A. from the University of California, Berkeley, and her M.A. in Latin American studies from Stanford University. She spent the 1980s in Nicaragua working as a correspondent for various U.S. media, including ABC Radio News. She is the author of *The Death of Ben Linder: The Story of a Northamerican in Sandinista Nicaragua* (New York: Seven Stories Press, 1999).

Pat Lauderdale received his Ph.D. from Stanford University and currently is professor of justice and social inquiry and adjunct professor of law at Arizona State University. He is the author of the new edition of *A Political Analysis of Deviance* (Willowdale, Ont.: de Sitter Publications, 2003) and currently is completing another volume on Costa Rica from a global perspective.

Aldo A. Lauria-Santiago is associate professor of history and director of Latin American and Latino studies at the College of the Holy Cross. He recently authored *An Agrarian Republic: Commercial Agriculture and the Politics of Peasant Communities in El Salvador* and coedited *Landscapes of Struggle: Politics, Society, and Community in El Salvador*, both published by the University of Pittsburgh Press. He is finishing a book with Jeffrey Gould on the 1932 revolt and massacre in El Salvador.

J. Patrice McSherry, associate professor of political science and director of the Latin American & Caribbean Studies Program at Long Island University, has authored many works on Condor and on Latin American militaries. She unearthed the White and Blystone memoranda discussed in her chapter.

Cecilia Menjívar is associate professor of sociology at Arizona State University. Her publications include the monograph *Fragmented Ties: Salvadoran Immigrant Networks in America* (Berkeley: University of California Press, 2000) and the edited volume *Through the Eyes of Women: Gender, Social Networks, Family and Structural Change in Latin America and the Caribbean* (Willowdale, Ont.: de Sitter Publications, 2003).

Kristin Norget is professor of anthropology at McGill University. Her current research includes an investigation of the relation between religion and social movements in Mexico. Her forthcoming publications include the book *Days of Death, Days of Life: Death and its Ritualization in Oaxacan Popular Culture*.

Annamarie Oliverio, president of the Social Research Institute of Arizona and adjunct professor of justice at Arizona State University, is the author of *The State of Terror* (Albany: SUNY Press, 1998) and a number of related articles on the production of hegemony and terrorism. She has recently completed a comparative Fulbright research project on violence, the state, and international politics.

Néstor Rodríguez is chair of the Department of Sociology and co-director of the Center for Immigration Research at the University of Houston. His research areas include immigration, political sociology, and world systems. He is the 2004–2006 Joseph S. Werlin Scholar of Latin American/Hispanic Studies at the University of Houston.

Jeffrey J. Ryan is associate professor of political science and Latin American studies at the University of Arkansas. His research focuses on democratization, political violence, and neoliberal reforms. He has published in a number of journals, including *Comparative Politics, Public Administration Review,* and *Derecho y Cultura.*

M. Gabriela Torres currently holds a postdoctoral fellowship with the Social Sciences and Humanities Research Council of Canada. Her research and writing focuses on the links between political violence, state development, and gender.

Index